DATE DUE		

Macanché Island, El Petén, Guatemala:
Excavations, Pottery, and Artifacts

Macanché Island, El Petén, Guatemala:

Excavations, Pottery, and Artifacts

P R U D E N C E   M.   R I C E

University Presses of Florida
University of Florida Press / Gainesville

UNIVERSITY PRESSES OF FLORIDA is the central agency for scholarly publishing of the State of Florida's university system, producing books selected for publication by the faculty editorial committees of Florida's nine public universities: Florida A&M University (Tallahassee), Florida Atlantic University (Boca Raton), Florida International University (Miami), Florida State University (Tallahassee), University of Central Florida (Orlando), University of Florida (Gainesville), University of North Florida (Jacksonville), University of South Florida (Tampa), University of West Florida (Pensacola).

ORDERS for books published by all member presses of University Presses of Florida should be addressed to University Presses of Florida, 15 NW 15th Street, Gainesville, FL 32603.
Printed in the U.S.A. on acid-free paper.∞

Library of Congress Cataloging in Publication Data

Rice, Prudence M.
  Macanché Island, El Petén, Guatemala: excavations, pottery, and artifacts.

  1. Macanché Island Site (Guatemala)
2. Mayas—Antiquities.   3. Excavations (Archaeology)—Guatemala.   4. Indians of Central America—Guatemala—Antiquities.   5. Guatemala—Antiquities.   I. Title.
F1435.1.M22R52 1987 972.81'2 87−2040
ISBN 0−8130−0838−7

Dedicated to
William R. Bullard, Jr.,
a pioneer
in the study of
the Petén Postclassic

Contents

Figures ix
Tables xi
Plates xii
Color Plates xiii
Preface xv

PART I. **Introduction**

CHAPTER 1. Cultural and Methodological
Background 1
  Cultural Context: The Lowland Maya
    Civilization 1
  Study of the Macanché Data 2

CHAPTER 2. Geographical Setting,
Excavations, and Settlement History 6
  Lake Macanché 6
  Macanché Island 12
  Macanché Island Occupational
    Summary 33
  Bullard's Other Excavations and
    Collections 44
  Conclusions 47

PART II. **Terminal Classic and Postclassic
Pottery Type Descriptions**

  SECTION A. **Terminal Classic Pottery of
  the Romero Ceramic Complex** 55

CHAPTER 3. The Terminal Classic
Romero Ceramic Complex at Macanché
Island 55
  Sphere Identification 56
  Technological Characteristics 58
  Summary 59

CHAPTER 4. Type-Variety Descriptions of
the Pottery of the Romero Ceramic
Complex 63
  Tinaja Ceramic Group 63
  Harina Ceramic Group 71
  Achote Ceramic Group 74
  Payaso Ceramic Group 76
  Cambio Ceramic Group 77
  Danta Ceramic Group 82
  Daylight Ceramic Group 83
  Altar Orange Ceramic Group 84
  Ceramic Group Unspecified 85
  Non-Romero Complex Sherds 86
  Miscellaneous Preclassic and Early
    Classic Pottery Sherds 89

  SECTION B. **Postclassic Pottery of the
  Aura, Dos Lagos, and Ayer Ceramic
  Complexes** 90

CHAPTER 5. Postclassic Pottery of the
Aura and Dos Lagos Complexes and
Protohistoric Pottery of the Ayer Ceramic
Complex at Macanché Island 90
  The Early Postclassic Aura Ceramic
    Complex 91
  The Late Postclassic Dos Lagos Ceramic
    Complex 95
  A Provisional Protohistoric Ayer Ceramic
    Complex 102

CHAPTER 6. Pastes and Slips of the
Paxcamán and Trapeche Ceramic
Groups 104
  Paste Characteristics 105
  Trace Elemental Composition 109

Slip Characteristics   112
Summary   116

CHAPTER 7. Type-Variety Descriptions o
the Pottery of the Aura, Dos Lagos, and
Ayer Ceramic Complexes   118
   Paxcamán Ceramic Group   118
   Trapeche Ceramic Group   139
   Gray Group Unspecified   155
   Topoxté Ceramic Group   157
   Augustine Ceramic Group   165
   Slateware Group Unspecified   167
   Fine Paste Ware Ceramic Groups   168
   Tachís Ceramic Group   170
   Pozo Ceramic Group   170
   Chilo Ceramic Group   179
   Patojo Ceramic Group   184
   Ídolos Ceramic Group   195
   Unslipped Group Unspecified   197
   Unidentified Specials   198

**PART III. Ceramic and Nonceramic
Artifacts from Macanché Island**

CHAPTER 8. Ceramic Artifacts   201
   Miniature Vessels   201
   Figurines   202
   Mold Fragment   203
   Pestles   203
   Notched Sherds and Pellets   204
   Miscellaneous Worked Sherds   208

CHAPTER 9. Chipped Stone
Artifacts   210
   Chert   210
   Obsidian   219

CHAPTER 10. Ground Stone Tools   221
   Manos and Metates   221
   Bark Beaters   226
   Spindle Whorls   228
   Stone Bead   229

CHAPTER 11. Miscellaneous
Materials   230
   Worked Bone   230
   Shell   230
   Miscellaneous Faunal Remains   230
   Human Remains   231
   Other   231

PART IV. Summary and Conclusions

CHAPTER 12. Macanché Island and the
Petén Postclassic   235

Appendixes
   1. Sherd Type Frequencies by Lot   241
   2. Directory of Ceramic Typological
      Units at Macanché Island   252
References   255
Index   261

FIGURES

1. The Central Petén lakes region, Guatemala. 7
2. The basin of Lake Macanché. 10
3. Sequence of named ceramic complexes of Proyecto Lacustre (CPHEP) in the Central Petén lakes region. 11
4. Map of Bullard's excavations on the mound on Macanché Island 15
5. Key to conventions used in excavation profile illustrations. 16
6. Profile of the west wall of Bullard's Operation IA. 18
7. Profile of the northern wall of Bullard's Operation IB. 20
8. Profile of Bullard's Operation IC. 20
9. Profile of the eastern wall of Bullard's Operation ID. 22
10. Profile of the northern wall of Bullard's Operation IE. 23
11. Profile of the eastern wall of Bullard's Operation IF. 24
12. Profile of Bullard's Operation IG. 24
13. Profile of the northern wall of Bullard's Operation IH. 26
14. Contour map of Macanché Island, showing CPHEP test pit locations. 28
15. Profile of the excavations in CPHEP test pit 2. 29
16. Profile of the southwest wall of CPHEP test pit 3. 30
17. Plan of the northwestern corner of the structure foundation wall in CPHEP test pit 3. 31
18. Profile of the excavation in CPHEP test pit 4. 33
19. Profiles of the southeast walls of CPHEP test pits 5A (a) and 5B (b). 34

20. Profile of the east wall of CPHEP test pit 6. 35
21. Approximate spatial positioning of Bullard's test pits with relation to CPHEP excavations and to structure foundations on top of the mound. 36
22. Idealized reconstruction of the sequence of mound construction activities on Macanché Island. 38
23. Tentative reconstruction of the aboriginal platform and structures on Macanché Island. 39
24. Map of a "small ceremonial center," traced from Bullard's original sketch. 45
25. Location of Bullard's excavations into Mound 6 at the "small center" on the Lake Macanché mainland. 46
26. Bullard's test pit 1 at the base of the large mound at Ixlú to the west of Lake Salpetén. 48
27. A stone "idol." 49
28. A pottery "mask." 50
29. A "jar" or vase. 51
30. Key to conventions used in slipped pottery illustrations. 65
31. Tinaja Red. 66
32. Subín Red, Cameron Incised, Chaquiste Impressed, and Pantano Impressed. 68
33. Harina Cream and Largo Red-on-cream. 73
34. Achote Black. 75
35. Cambio Unslipped. 78
36. Encanto Striated, Jato Black-on-gray, Daylight Orange, miscellaneous unidentified specials, and Late Classic polychromes. 81

37. Polychrome dish. 87
38. Late Classic polychrome vessels and decorative motifs. 88
39. Ward's clustering solution using CLUSTAN program for Paxcamán and Trapeche sherds. 111
40. Paxcamán Red. 120
41. Paxcamán Red. 121
42. Ixpop Polychrome. 124
43. Ixpop Polychrome. 125
44. Ixpop Polychrome. 126
45. Sacá Polychrome, and Macanché Red-on-paste (cream). 132
46. Picú Incised and Chamán Modeled. 136
47. Trapeche Pink. 142
48. Trapeche Pink. 143
49. Trapeche Pink. 144
50. Mul Polychrome and Picté Red-on-paste (cream). 148
51. Xuluc Incised. 151
52. Xuluc Incised and Chuntuci Composite. 152
53. Group Unspecified Gray. 156
54. Topoxté Red and Chompoxté Red-on-cream. 158
55. Miscellaneous Postclassic types. 166

56. Pozo Unslipped. 174
57. Pozo Unslipped. 175
58. La Justa Composite. 177
59. Chilo Unslipped. 182
60. Gotas Composite. 184
61. Patojo Modeled. 188
62. Patojo Modeled. 189
63. Patojo Modeled. 190
64. Patojo Modeled. 191
65. Mumúl Composite. 193
66. Ídolos Modeled. 196
67. Miniature vessels. 202
68. Moldmade figurine. 203
69. Fragment of mold for making Postclassic censer faces. 204
70. Pestles. 205
71. Frequency distribution of ceramic line sinkers. 207
72. Projectile points. 214
73. Chipped chert tools. 216
74. Chipped chert tools. 217
75. Manos. 222
76. Metate fragments. 225
77. Stone spindle whorls. 228
78. Bone tools. 231

TABLES

1. Phase assignments of lots from Bullard's excavations at Macanché Island.   37
2. Chronometric dates pertaining to the Terminal Classic and Postclassic occupation on Macanché Island.   40
3. Frequency of ceramic units of the Terminal Classic Romero Complex at Macanché Island.   60
4. Ceramic units of the Postclassic and Terminal Classic contexts investigated by Bullard.   92
5. Ceramic units of the Early Postclassic Aura Complex at Macanché Island.   94
6. Ceramic units of the Late Postclassic Dos Lagos Complex at Macanché Island.   96
7. Comparison of slipped, unslipped, censer, and other categories of pottery in Early and Late Postclassic lots at Macanché Island.   97
8. Comparison of ceramic group frequencies and percentages in upper and lower levels of the Late Postclassic midden at Macanché Island.   97
9. Comparison of ceramic group frequencies and percentages in Late Postclassic midden lots from mound summit and mound slopes at Macanché Island.   99
10. Ceramic units of the provisional Protohistoric Ayer Complex at Macanché Island.   103
11. Mean concentrations (ppm) of 19 elements in 44 samples of sherds and clays from Petén.   108
12. Descriptive characteristics of Paxcamán and Trapeche group sherds used in neutron activation and cluster analyses (figure 39).   110
13. Correlation of paste and slip colors in Late Postclassic Paxcamán and Trapeche group pottery from CPHEP 1979 excavations at Macanché Island.   113
14. Comparative measurements on notched sherd sinkers in the Maya Lowlands.   208
15. Distribution of chipped stone artifacts in Bullard's excavation units on Macanché Island.   213
16. Distribution of mano and metate fragments in Bullard's excavations at Macanché Island.   223
17. Distribution of faunal remains in Bullard's excavations at Macanché Island.   231
18. Faunal remains from Bullard's excavations on Macanché Island.   232

PLATES

I. Aerial view of Lake Macanché.   8
II. View of Macanché Island.   13
III. The mound on the northwest corner of Macanché Island.   14
IV. Bullard's Operation IA.   19
V. Bullard's Operations IE and IF.   23
VI. Bullard's Operation IH.   25
VII. CPHEP test pit 3.   32
VIII. Ixpop Polychrome sherds.   127
IX. Ixpop Polychrome restricted orifice bowl.   128
X. Mul Polychrome tripod dish.   147
XI. Chompoxté Red-on-cream sherds.   162
XII. Chilo Unslipped olla.   181

XIII. Patojo Modeled censer fragments and adornos.   186
XIV. Ceramic figurine and Patojo Modeled censer heads.   187
XV. Ídolos Modeled censer fragments and adornos.   194
XVI. Notched sherds and pellets.   206
XVII. Chert caches.   211
XVIII. Chipped arrow points.   212
XIX. Chipped lance or spear points.   215
XX. Bifacial tools.   218
XXI. Manos and fragments.   223
XXII. Metate fragments.   224
XXIII. Metate fragments.   226
XXIV. Bark beater.   227

COLOR PLATES

1. Photomicrographs of thin sections of
   Petén Postclassic pottery.   *facing page 110*
   1a. Ixpop Polychrome tripod dish.
   1b. Paxcamán Red tripod dish.
   1c. Chompoxté Red-on-cream tripod
        dish.
   1d. Trapeche Pink: Tramite Variety
        tripod dish.
   1e. Paste colors of Petén Postclassic
        pottery.

2. Slip color variability of the Paxcamán,
   Trapeche, and Topoxté ceramic groups.
   facing page 111
   2a. Slips of Paxcamán ceramic group.
   2b. Slips of Trapeche ceramic group.
   2c. Slips of Topoxté ceramic group.

PREFACE

THE Postclassic period has long been neglected in the Maya Lowlands. In the past six years or so this has changed, and a number of conferences, articles, and books have recently treated this subject. Although the Postclassic archaeology of the northern Lowlands—perhaps because of its well-preserved architecture and heavy colonial occupation—has commanded a great deal of attention, in the Central and Southern Lowlands the Postclassic period has been a poor stepchild, overshadowed by the brighter star of the Classic period.

The Lake Macanché basin is a small but nonetheless important satellite in the universe of the Lowland Maya Postclassic. Archaeological investigation of Postclassic occupation in this locale, begun on Macanché Island by William R. Bullard, Jr., in 1968 and supplemented eleven years later by the Central Petén Historical Ecology Project (CPHEP), has provided valuable new data on the nature of the Classic-to-Postclassic transition in the central Petén and the sequence of culture history during the Postclassic period.

I first became acquainted with Bullard's Macanché project in 1974, after I had just completed, with Don Rice, a program of archaeological surveys in the basins of central Petén Lakes Yaxhá and Sacnab. That project included excavations at the Postclassic island site of Topoxté, where Bullard had worked in 1960. Gordon R. Willey and Bullard's widow, Mary R. Bullard, expressed an interest in giving us access to the Macanché material in order to complete Bullard's initial analyses,

feeling that our recent experience with the Petén Postclassic would be an advantage in providing a broad assessment of the significance of the collection.

We were gratified by their proposal, but expressed the reservation that the analysis would be enhanced by a delay until study of the Topoxté materials was more advanced. In addition, we were hoping to extend our historical ecology project research design from Yaxhá-Sacnab to other lakes in central Petén—including the Lake Macanché basin—in order to provide supplementary materials to aid us in our descriptions and interpretations. Late in 1978, we were awarded a National Science Foundation research grant to undertake a three-year project of survey, mapping, and excavations at four lake basins in the central Petén. CPHEP test-pitting operations at Macanché Island began in early June of 1979.

Preparation of this report on Bullard's excavations at Macanché Island has taken an unconscionably long time, but I am convinced that had this material been described and written up several years earlier, the report would have not done justice to his data. The delays—during which CPHEP excavations and analyses were undertaken at other Petén lakes, and the work of other projects focused on the Postclassic in a variety of Lowland areas was published—permitted the establishment of an essential historical context without which the Macanché artifacts could not have adequately been interpreted.

I am very grateful to Mary (Mrs. William

R.) Bullard and to Gordon R. Willey for generously allowing me the opportunity to study this important collection, which has played such a significant role in my own comprehension of the Petén Postclassic. Their patience and forbearance throughout the last ten years, when they must have been convinced that this material would never be written up, is acknowledged with gratitude and not a little shame.

I must also thank Antonio Ortiz and his family—especially Aura, Tony, and Rufino—for their unfailing hospitality and kindness in allowing CPHEP personnel to work on Macanché Island and elsewhere on their land in the Lake Macanché basin in 1979.

The CPHEP excavations at Macanché in 1979 were made possible by a grant from the National Science Foundation, BNS78-13736. Permission for surveys and excavations was granted by Lic. Francis Polo Sifontes, then director of the Instituto de Antropología e Historia of Guatemala. The able assistance of David Batcho in mapping and test pit supervision on the island is gratefully acknowledged, together with the contributions of Mark Brenner, who persevered in the field despite incipient hepatitis. Since his recovery, Mark has continued to be of assistance in providing me with interpretations of the ecological and limnological data from the lakes area.

At the Florida State Museum, Jerald T. Milanich and William R. Maples graciously provided storage and analysis space for the Macanché collection through all these long years; they are to be applauded for suppressing their skepticism for the ten years during which I assured them that I *was* working on the material. Jill Loucks painstakingly stippled figures 28, 61–64, 66, and 68; Joan Ling aided in parts of the ceramic analyses; above all, Mimi Saffer provided continuous support and assistance in the technological studies. Genevieve Roessler and John Lanza of the Department of Nuclear Engineering at the University of Florida performed the neutron activation analyses reported in chapter 6. Mary Pohl of Florida State University identified Bullard's faunal material (see chapter 11 and table 18). Frank Blanchard of the Department of Geology, University of Florida, assisted with the photo micrographs (color plate 1a–d). I would like to thank Muriel Kirkpatrick and Arlen Chase, who very kindly shared with me their ideas and comparative collections relevant to the Petén Postclassic, and Grant Jones, for access to the Postclassic pottery from Negroman-Tipú, in Belize. The assistance of D. D. Bean and Sons, Inc., in Jaffrey, New Hampshire, is gratefully acknowledged; Mr. Delcie D. Bean graciously provided laboratory space to Bullard for his early analyses of the Macanché material in 1968–69, before he moved to the Florida State Museum in Gainesville.

Finally, I want to express my sincerest gratitude to Mary R. Bullard and Lyman G. Bullard, whose generous donation in memory of William R. Bullard, Jr., facilitated publication of the Macanché data.

PART I

Introduction

CHAPTER 1

Cultural and Methodological Background

THIS report is a description and interpretation of archaeological excavations and artifacts dating primarily to the Postclassic
period of Maya prehistory. The Postclassic is
the third and last of the major subdivisions
of Lowland Maya prehistory, preceded by the
Preclassic and spectacular Classic periods;
in the central and southern Maya Lowlands
of Petén (Guatemala) and Belize, it has until
recently been considerably overshadowed by
the developments of these earlier eras.

Cultural Context: The Lowland Maya Civilization

The long Preclassic period, customarily
dated by archaeologists between ca. 2000
B.C. and A.D. 250/300, witnessed the movement of farmers into the lowland tropical
forest environment of Belize, Petén, and Yucatán. During these two millennia, Maya
populations expanded to fill almost every
niche in this low, karstic terrain, and their
sizable civic-ceremonial centers began to exhibit many of the characteristic traits of the
later Classic civilization: organization of
mounds around plazas, vaulted architecture,
stucco mask embellishments, and so on.

The Classic period, beginning around A.D.
250/300 and ending roughly around A.D.
900/950, is most distinctively represented by
the large political and religious centers in the
southern part of the lowlands, especially
northern Petén. These centers are known by
a variety of traits: towering temples and
sprawling "palaces"; sumptuous tombs containing exotic items ranging from exquisite
polychrome pottery and jade to stingray

spines; and sculptured stelae proclaiming
the heroic exploits of local dynasties, pre-
cisely dated by the Maya's esoteric means of
reckoning time, known as the Long Count of
days. All these traits testify to the presence
of a powerful and demanding elite class
among the Lowland Maya. Indeed, most of
the archaeological work that has been done
in the lowlands has been directed toward
understanding the elites, which occupied
the large architectural centers in the Classic
period, in order to unravel their dynastic his-
tories and calendric observations, trace their
construction enterprises, and determine
how they governed a large populace of farmers and craftsmen.

Beginning about A.D. 800 or perhaps a few
years earlier, southern Lowland Maya society began to experience a series of stresses
that led to what has been known as the "collapse" of the Classic Maya. The nature of
these stresses has been debated in great de-
tail (Culbert 1973a). Probably a conflation of
social and environmental factors operating
in slightly different ways in different areas
within the lowlands precipitated the centers'
decline. Earliest harbingers of trouble appeared on the western peripheries of the central and southern lowlands, where new pottery styles and sculptural motifs signaled
"Mexican" intruders; elsewhere, within
only decades, other disruptions seem to have
been felt. By A.D. 900 or shortly thereafter,
the stelae with Long Count dates were no
longer being erected, polychrome pottery
was no longer produced, construction activity at the large centers declined, and the

centers themselves were abandoned. Traditional reconstructions of this catastrophe suggest that the demographic collapse was so severe that the entire central and southern lowlands were effectively depopulated.

The northern lowlands, by contrast, did not experience such a social and demographic "collapse" but rather effloresced during these same centuries. Whether developed by indigenous Maya or stimulated by Mexican contacts, an ornate and distinctive architectural style characterized the northwestern Yucatán Peninsula in the Puuc area and at Chichén Itzá. The latter site, long identified with widespread population intrusions into the lowlands of non-Maya groups variously termed "Mexican," "Putún," "Chontal," "Itzá," or—in the case of Chichén Itzá particularly—"Toltec," flourished until approximately A.D. 1100.

Following the fall of Chichén Itzá, the dominant site in the northern lowlands was Mayapán, a shoddy and miniaturized architectural imitation of Chichén Itzá, which headed a confederated "league" of city-states in the northern part of the peninsula until the mid-fifteenth century. According to chronicles and legends, in a Katun 8 Ahau in the Maya calendar (corresponding to a date of A.D. 1458, or perhaps 1201, in the Gregorian calendar), Mayapán collapsed and its Itzá populations fled southward, finally settling around a large lake. This lake is generally considered to be Lake Petén-Itzá, in the modern Department of El Petén, Guatemala.

This outline of Maya prehistory establishes two models that prevailed in most of the early studies of the Postclassic period in Petén: demographic collapse and legendary in-migration. That is, whether tacitly or explicitly, it was generally accepted that the Petén area had been abandoned since the Classic "collapse" and was not repopulated until the late fifteenth-century immigration of Itzá refugees from Mayapán. These late Itzá groups represented the core of subsequent lake-based populations noted by Hernán Cortés and his army in the early sixteenth century as they crossed through Petén on their way from Acalán, on the Gulf coast of Mexico, to Honduras. Within the framework of these models, evidence for Classic-to-Postclassic population continuity in the southern lowlands was neither expected nor sought.

The artifacts from Macanché Island, however, suggest a different sequence of events. The island has provided evidence of population continuity from the Late Classic period through the collapse and into the Postclassic period, suggesting that although the large administrative centers of the southern lowlands may have been abandoned, life continued with less disruption in rural regions. In addition, the excavations provide a stratigraphic and artifactual foundation for phasing the subdivisions of the Postclassic era, thereby resolving many questions surrounding the chronology of events in Petén following the Classic period.

Study of the Macanché Data

Most of the artifacts reported in this study were recovered from the small island in Lake Macanché, in the Department of El Petén, Guatemala, by the late William R. Bullard, Jr. Bullard spent approximately three weeks in Petén in the last half of March and the early part of April 1968 conducting excavations on Macanché Island. During this same period, he also mapped a "small ceremonial center on the shore" of Lake Macanché and excavated two test pits into one structure there. In addition, he visited the site of Ixlú, on the neck of land separating Lake Salpetén (west of Lake Macanché) from Lake Petén-Itzá, and placed two test pits into the principal mound at that site.

Bullard shipped most of the artifactual materials from his excavations to the United States and soon began their classification and description. In 1969, he accepted a position as chair of the Social Sciences Department of the Florida State Museum in Gainesville, and the Macanché artifact collection accompanied him to this new location.

Bullard continued to work on the material, corresponding with James Gifford at Temple University concerning possible relationships of the Macanché material to collections from Barton Ramie in Belize and completing preliminary type descriptions and illustrations. He incorporated some of his ideas concerning the significance of the Macanché materials into his summary paper on the Petén Postclassic (Bullard 1973) prepared for the School of American Research Advanced Seminar on the Lowland Maya Collapse, held in Santa Fe, New Mexico, in October 1970. Bullard died in 1972 before analysis and publication of the Macanché material could be completed.

My own studies of the Macanché material began in 1975–76 when I moved to Gainesville, where the Macanché collection was still curated at the Florida State Museum. In 1979, fieldwork finally began for our newly funded project, Proyecto Lacustre, which is part of a broader interdisciplinary program of archaeological and ecological investigations, the Central Petén Historical Ecology Project (CPHEP), that focused on the lakes in central Petén. Three weeks of test excavations at Macanché Island began in June. The specific purpose of the Macanché excavation was to provide clarification and supplementation of the stratigraphic associations of ceramic and other artifactual materials in the Bullard collection.

As frequently happens in such matters, the additional information from CPHEP investigations at Macanché Island raised as many questions as it answered. The focus of CPHEP is regional, and it was of inestimable value in studying the Macanché Island collection to have data from the Macanché mainland as well as from other Postclassic sites in the area. The abundance of data, however, from two projects on Macanché Island, from CPHEP excavations on the Macanché mainland, and from CPHEP operations elsewhere in the lakes region (plus Bullard's own testing at the mainland site and at Ixlú) made it difficult to establish the topical and geographic limits of the present report.

Report Preparation

I finally decided to confine this report principally to a description and interpretation of the materials from Bullard's excavations on Macanché Island. This decision was reached in part for reasons of time but also because the initial invitation by Mrs. Bullard was to study and report on Bullard's collection, which we sought to supplement by our own excavations. Data from CPHEP excavations are brought into the discussion where appropriate to clarify and supplement the original Bullard findings. The report is in three parts.

In the first part I describe Lake Macanché, its settlement history (as revealed by CPHEP surveys), and the excavations that were carried out at the island. Because a major contribution of the Macanché Island work by both Bullard and CPHEP was to illuminate Postclassic period chronology, the stratigraphy of the island is the focus of discussion, and most of the interpretation in this section is based on the CPHEP-controlled test-pitting operations in the 1979 field season.

The second (and much larger) part of this report consists of pottery type descriptions, divided into five chapters: chapters 3 and 4 present the Terminal Classic pottery of the Romero complex, chapters 5, 6, and 7 present the Postclassic pottery of the Aura and Dos Lagos complexes and the provisional Protohistoric pottery of the Ayer complex. The data reported here are almost exclusively from Bullard's excavations; for example, the type frequencies given are those from his excavations. The material from CPHEP test pitting is included from time to time to augment the data on forms, dimensions, decorative motifs, and so forth but is not included in counts of types and varieties. Similarly, the very tiny amount of material from Bullard's excavations on the "small center" in the Lake Macanché basin, from Ixlú, and from Punta Nimá is included where appropriate in the type descriptions but does not constitute a separate section. A listing of the pottery types and other artifacts catalogued in each of Bullard's lots is presented in appendix 1. Appendix 2 is an alphabetical directory of the ceramic wares, groups, types, and varieties of the material in Bullard's collection from Macanché Island and related areas.

The third part of the report is devoted primarily to nonceramic artifacts from Bullard's excavations. This part is necessarily brief because Bullard did not save such materials from his excavations; his counts, measurements, and sketches, together with comparative data from the other lakes where appropriate, constitute the basis for the descriptions.

The first part of the report, describing the excavations and attempting a reconstruction of the history of the island's occupation, necessitates a few caveats. The maps and drawings accompanying it represent a "best fit" between Bullard's data and the observations of Proyecto Lacustre personnel in 1979. Bullard's work at the island involved sketch mapping the island contours and laying out test pits with reference to compass indications. Lacking a transit, he did not establish a site datum for his map or for tying together the various strata in his excavations. Similarly, because many of his pits were not excavated to sterile subsoil, a "lower datum" cannot be determined either.

The CPHEP mapping and excavation activities were carried out with transit measurements, the site datum being established at 11.3 m above the 1979 lake level, and all pits were excavated to sterile soil. Although this established a basis for stratigraphic interpretations internal to our own work, it still did not permit precise correlation with Bullard's excavations because it was not possible to map the horizontal locations of his pits with any certainty. Furthermore, when the CPHEP map was compared with Bullard's map, it was discovered that there was a difference of approximately 7° in magnetic north.

The maps and figures discussed in chapter 2 represent an effort to combine the data from the two projects. Despite the lack of immediate vertical comparability between the two sets of excavations, horizontal relations could be determined in part by reference to visible permanent features noted both by Bullard and by Proyecto Lacustre. One of these is the line of stones on the upper west surface of the mound; another was provided by the inadvertent intersection of one of the CPHEP test pits with a corner of one of Bullard's excavations. The result is a tentative restoration drawing of platform construction as it may have appeared at the end of Postclassic/Protohistoric occupation on the island.

The Ceramic Analysis

Because the artifacts included in Bullard's collection were exclusively ceramic (chipped and ground stone, bone, and so forth were counted, drawn, and photographed by Bullard but not saved), a word about the methods employed in this analysis is in order. At the time of Bullard's death, he had completed preliminary type descriptions only for the Paxcamán ceramic group together with one paragraph of notes on the Topoxté ceramic group. In addition, a number of illustrations and photographs had been prepared.

Bullard had included in the "Paxcamán" category all slipped sherds exhibiting snail inclusions in the paste, regardless of their slip color. He was intrigued, however, by the significant differences in slip color within this group and offered some hypotheses as to their cause (see chapter 6, "Pastes and Slips of the Paxcamán and Trapeche Ceramic Groups"). He did not, however, separate the cream-colored slips into a separate ceramic unit, and I continued to maintain this comprehensive categorization in my initial studies (e.g., P. Rice 1980). In the intervening years, a new Trapeche ceramic group with cream-to-pink slips on light gray snail-inclusion paste was described (A. Chase 1979). I have since reclassified almost all of the original "Paxcamán" ceramics into these two classificatory units in accordance with this new typological category.

My early studies placed emphasis on some of the technological characteristics of the Postclassic pottery in order to try to place the slip and paste variability into a framework that could be interpreted in terms of production and function as well as chronology and materials.

One step involved thin-sectioning of five sherds of Paxcamán and Trapeche group pottery. A second avenue of investigation was neutron activation analysis (NAA) of a small number of sherds from Macanché Island together with some Petén clays (P. Rice 1978). The five thin-sectioned sherds were also included in the NAA study. Finally, the relationship of paste and slip colors to the conditions of the original firing and the depositional environment was explored in two ways. One was to refire small fragments of Paxcamán and Trapeche group sherds in an oxidizing atmosphere in an electric kiln to note changes with increasing temperature of refiring. A second investigation involved

soaking some sherd fragments in solutions of varying acidity and alkalinity and noting changes in slip color. Details of the specific procedures and results of these analyses are reported in chapter 6.

These examinations involved only a small number of sherds in the Bullard collection. A larger sample was studied by the more standard procedure of breaking off small fragments of the sherd and looking at the fresh cross section under a binocular microscope (magnification 10 to 50×). Color measurements were taken with a Munsell color chart; in all cases these were made indoors under fluorescent lighting. Sherd profiles were drawn full size and inked at approximately 50 percent reduction. Counts of sherds in the type descriptions are given as totals before cross-mending. Where this step is clearly misleading, i.e., in situations where a large number of sherds can be fitted together into a partially restorable vessel or are merely suspected to represent a much smaller number of vessels, it is so indicated in the "Vessel Forms and Dimensions" section of the type descriptions.

CHAPTER 2

Geographical Setting, Excavations, and Settlement History

Lake Macanché

Macanché Island is a small, low island in the northeast corner of Lake Macanché, one of a chain of lakes extending east-west across the central portion of the Department of El Petén, Guatemala. Formed by the filling in of depressions along a system of geological faults in Petén's karst plateau, the lakes are closed basins that receive stream inflow but lack external drainage. Like the other bodies of water in the chain—Lakes Yaxhá and Sacnab lying some 24 km to the northeast, and Lakes Salpetén, Petén-Itzá, Quexil, Peténxil, Sacpuy, and Perdida to the west (fig. 1)—Lake Macanché's surrounding topography is marked by a steep scarp on its northern and western shores. The lake itself lies at an elevation of approximately 150 m above mean sea level, with the northern shore climbing sharply to an elevation of over 200 m above mean sea level. Although the southern and eastern shores have more gradual inclines, the lake appears to be sunk in a deep basin. Indeed, Lake Macanché is the deepest body of water in the central Petén lake chain, with a maximum depth (in 1979) of nearly 60 m; at the same time it is one of the smallest lakes, having a shoreline of only 7 km. Two *juleques* (natural, small, deep sinkholes) lie off the northeastern corner of the lake, and a small stream runs south of them into Lake Macanché.

All the central Petén lakes exhibit variability in their water chemistry and in the agricultural characteristics of the surrounding soils. Lake Macanché's waters are high in magnesium sulfate (chemically comparable to Epsom salts), for example, while neigh-boring Lake Salpetén is saline and undrinkable because of excessive calcium sulfate. These differences are consequences of varying topography and the composition of the underlying limestone, which is mixed with dolomite (a calcium-magnesium carbonate) or interspersed with gypsum (hydrated calcium sulfate) in the specific case of Lake Salpetén (Deevey, Brenner, and Binford 1983). Such variability in the potability of the water supply might be presumed to have influenced to some degree the nature of both prehistoric and modern settlement within the basins.

Lake Macanché is the only lake besides Lake Petén-Itzá to have on its shores a large modern community (population 1,251 in 1977; N. Schwartz, personal communication). Unlike Lake Petén-Itzá's, however, this comparatively recent settlement has developed within the last thirty years. As a consequence of this large and growing modern settlement, most of the land surrounding the lake has long ago been cleared for housing, milpa, or cattle ranching, and little of the original high tropical forest remains in the basin. Contributing to the steady movement of modern settlers into the pueblo of Macanché is the ease of movement and communication with other areas: the road from Flores, the *cabecera* or administrative center of Petén, which heads eastward to the Belize border, bisects the Macanché community at the lake's southwest corner (plate i).

The modern town of Macanché is merely the endpoint of a long history of occupation of the Lake Macanché basin revealed by ar-

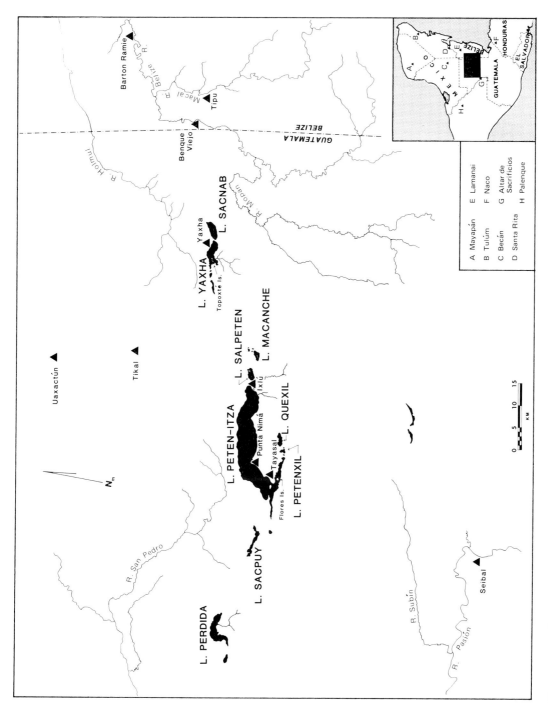

FIGURE 1. The Central Petén lakes region, Guatemala.

PLATE I. Aerial view of Lake Macanché, looking to the east, showing the modern community of Macanché (fore-ground), the Flores-Melchor road (right), and Macanché Island (upper left). Photo 1983, by D. S. Rice.

chaeological surveys in the area. In spring 1968, William R. Bullard, Jr., conducted excavations on Macanché Island. He was initially attracted to the lakes area of Petén because of its potential for contributing to an understanding of the Postclassic period, given the known propensity of the sixteenth-century Itzá Maya to settle on islands in the Petén lakes. His work at Macanché provided much of the basis for his chronological reconstruction of the "Central Petén Postclassic Tradition" (Bullard 1973). In addition to his excavations on the island in Lake Macanché in 1968, Bullard also mapped and test-pitted a "small ceremonial center" on the shore of the lake.

Bullard's 1968 project established the background for later survey, mapping, and excavations by Proyecto Lacustre personnel in 1979–81 at Lake Macanché (D. Rice and P. Rice 1980, 1982, 1984, n.d.). Three transects, 2 km long and 500 m wide, were placed at an angle of 135° and 315° from north on the northern (one transect) and southern (two transects) shores of the lake (fig. 2), and these were surveyed for settlement remains. Of the 246 structures mapped in the basin, a sample was test-excavated and the periods of construction and occupation were determined by the pottery recovered in the excavations. This program revealed a long sequence of settlement of the Macanché basin in the Preclassic, Classic, and Postclassic periods, with sizable occupations during all intervals except the Early Classic, when there was apparently a sharp reduction of population. The sequence of named ceramic complexes identified for Proyecto Lacustre operations in the Petén lakes region is given in figure 3.

In addition to the transect surveys on the mainland, CPHEP personnel mapped a small ceremonial center on the southeast shore of the lake. This site, named Cerro Ortiz after Antonio Ortiz, owner of the land on which the site was located and of the island in the lake, was a very early civic-ceremonial locus in the lakes area (Rice and Rice n.d.). Test pits in three plaza locations of the site yielded

deep Middle Preclassic through Late Preclassic construction fill (nearly 5 m deep in one pit). No excavations were conducted into actual structures at Cerro Ortiz, but sherds recovered from the many looters' trenches into mounds at the site indicated the same periods of construction. There is a remote possibility that this site was the "small center" sketch mapped and tested by Bullard in 1968, but it is unlikely. Although Cerro Ortiz is a sizable center, easily visible from the Flores-Melchor road and thus an enticement for investigation, the total lack of correspondence between Bullard's map and the CPHEP map of Cerro Ortiz suggests that Bullard was at a different area, probably on the north shore of the lake.

Bullard's major contribution in documenting the Postclassic settlement on Macanché Island was later amplified by the CPHEP excavations on the island as well as around the mainland. CPHEP surveys and excavations revealed considerable Postclassic settlement on the mainland (D. Rice 1986; D. Rice and P. Rice 1984; P. Rice and D. Rice 1979, 1985), including Postclassic construction within a defensive walled site, Muralla de Leon, at the northeast corner of the lake (D. Rice and P. Rice 1981). The work also suggested that in the Macanché area, Postclassic settlement may have continued into the Historic period (Jones, Rice, and Rice 1981).

Indications of very late occupation of the Macanché basin—Protohistoric period—come from ethnohistorical documents rather than artifacts, however. These accounts (Villagutierre 1933; Pagden 1971) provide the names of numerous Itzá settlements known to the Spanish soldiers and priests in the sixteenth and seventeenth centuries, and these place-names seem to have survived to modern times. Of particular interest are the names of lakes and communities around the lakes, including "Maconché," "Zacpetén," "Eckixil," and "Seipuy." Maconché and Zacpetén are settlements within a larger polity known as Yalain or Alain, said to be located to the east of the main Itzá settlement situated around what is now called Lake Petén-

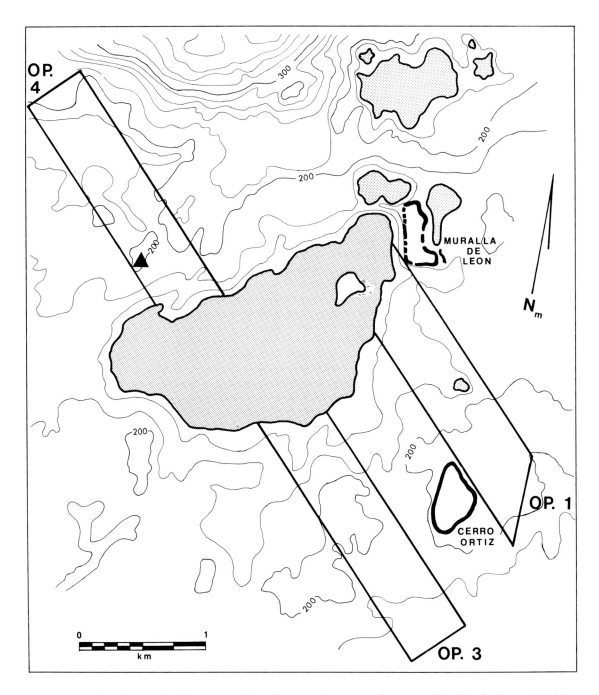

FIGURE 2. The basin of Lake Macanché, showing location of Macanché Island, three CPHEP survey transects (Operations 1, 3, and 4), the defensive walled site of Muralla de León (Operation 2), and the small Preclassic center named Cerro Ortiz. The solid triangle on Operation 4 indicates the probable location of Bullard's "small center" on the mainland.

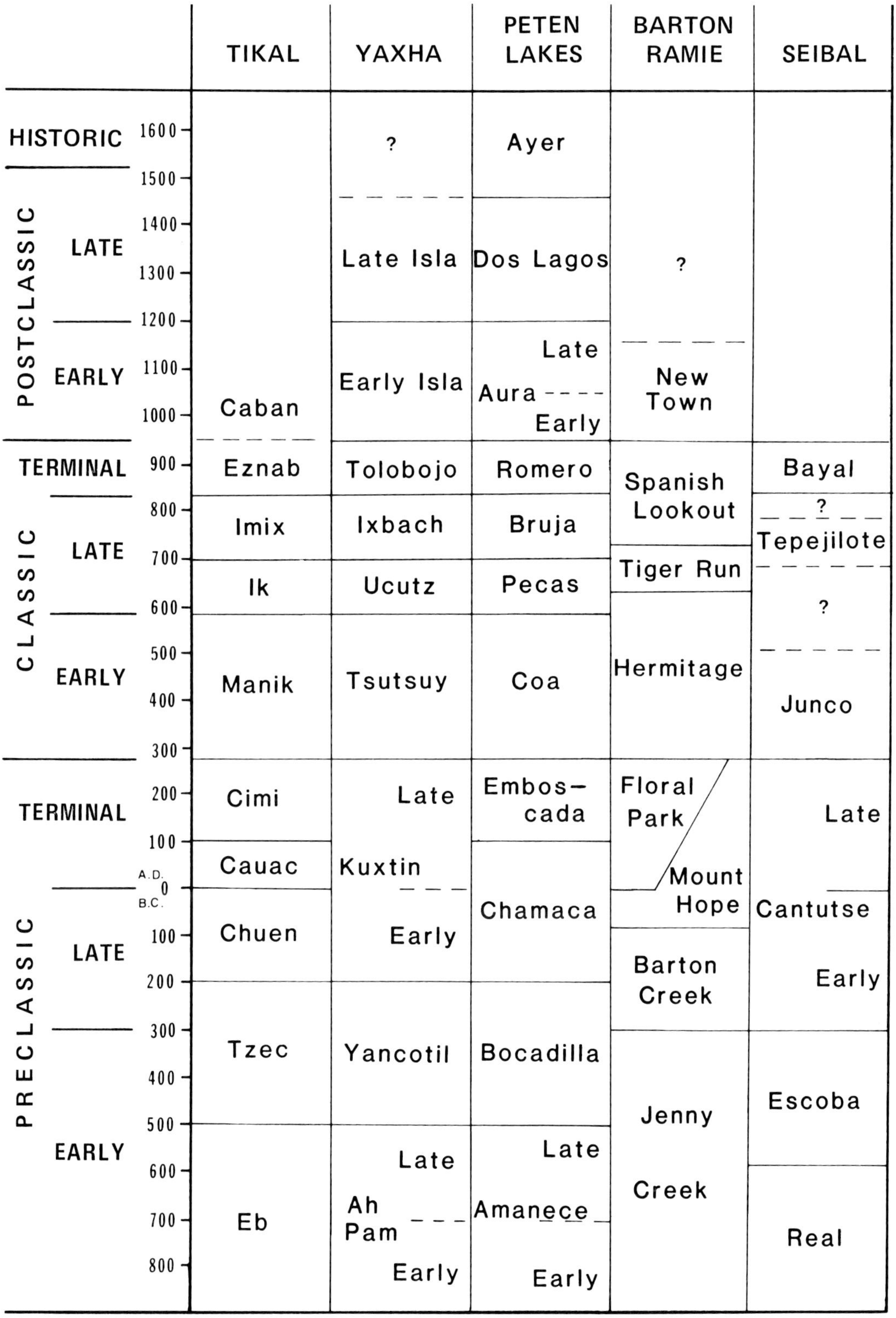

		TIKAL	YAXHA	PETEN LAKES	BARTON RAMIE	SEIBAL
HISTORIC	1600		?	Ayer		
	1500					
POSTCLASSIC — **LATE**	1400		Late Isla	Dos Lagos	?	
	1300					
	1200					
POSTCLASSIC — **EARLY**	1100	Caban	Early Isla	Late / Aura / Early	New Town	
	1000					
CLASSIC — **TERMINAL**	900	Eznab	Tolobojo	Romero	Spanish Lookout	Bayal
	800	Imix	Ixbach	Bruja		? / Tepejilote
CLASSIC — **LATE**	700	Ik	Ucutz	Pecas	Tiger Run	
	600					?
	500	Manik	Tsutsuy	Coa	Hermitage	Junco
CLASSIC — **EARLY**	400					
	300					
PRECLASSIC — **TERMINAL**	200	Cimi	Late	Emboscada	Floral Park	Late
	100	Cauac	Kuxtin			
	A.D. 0 B.C.	Chuen	Early	Chamaca	Mount Hope	Cantutse
PRECLASSIC — **LATE**	100				Barton Creek	
	200	Tzec	Yancotil	Bocadilla		Early
	300				Jenny Creek	
	400					Escoba
	500	Eb	Late / Ah Pam / Early	Late / Amanece / Early		Real
PRECLASSIC — **EARLY**	600					
	700					
	800					

FIGURE 3. Sequence of named ceramic complexes of Proyecto Lacustre (CPHEP) in the Central Petén lakes region.

Itzá. Verification of Postclassic construction around Lakes Macanché and Salpetén by CPHEP in 1979–80 has led to the hypothesis that these two lakes may constitute the core of the ethnohistorically known province of Yalain. Occupation of the Lake Macanché basin may thus have lasted well into the sixteenth or seventeenth century, or even later.

Macanché Island

Macanché Island (plate II) is roughly triangular in shape, with its sharpest apex pointing south-southwest. The eastern apex, which drops off gradually into shallow marsh, is closest to the mainland. In the summer of 1979, the island measured approximately 212 m northeast-southwest and 145 m northwest-southeast. The rise in lake levels in all the Petén lakes beginning late in 1979 has changed the island's contours as they are visible from the Flores-Melchor road, but its dimensions have not been remeasured.

Situated on the highest portion of the island at the northeastern end is a low mound of aboriginal construction; its base is approximately 8 m above the 1979 lake level and its summit 11.3 m above it. The mound is a quadrilateral structure measuring approximately 55 m on its long (northwest-southeast) axis; it is roughly 3.0 m high and 41 m wide on its northwestern end and 2.0 m in height and 28 m in width on the southeastern end. A few lines of stone on the surface suggest that at least two aboriginal structures originally sat atop the platform.

There has been some modern construction activity on the summit of the mound: erection of the frame for a house and a smaller kitchen structure roughly 10 m to the southeast, and planting of coconut palms, hibiscus, and other ornamental plants (plate III). This activity has created some disturbance to the platform, as evidenced by piles of stones and open holes on the mound that were noted in 1979. At the time of Bullard's excavations, and in 1979 as well, the damage appeared to be most severe on the upper surface, con-

founding recognition of superstructure outlines but not destroying the constructional or stratigraphic integrity of the mound as a whole. Some sherds were recovered from these digging activities and were saved by the Ortiz family; Bullard combined them with his own surface collection of the island (catalogued as Lot 4).

Bullard Excavations, 1968

William R. Bullard, Jr., conducted excavations on Macanché Island in late March and early April 1968. His objective was "to find a Postclassic site which would link the archaeological data of Topoxté [where he worked in 1960] with that from Lake Petén, and would allow the development of a chronological framework for the Postclassic period in Petén" (W. R. B., letter to Carlos Samayoa Chinchilla, director, Instituto de Antropologia e Historia, Guatemala, 8 November 1967). He made eight test pits or trenches on the island (fig. 4) and referred to them as "operations" with an alphabetic designation. Seven of these operations were placed around the periphery of the mound or on its northwestern summit, sampling an overall surface area of the mound that was about 28 m by 32 m in extent. The eighth operation (Operation IC) was placed some distance to the southeast of this area, 9 m beyond the modern "kitchen structure."

Bullard's Operation IA (fig. 6; see key, fig. 5) was a 2.7-by-5.5-m test pit, with the long axis oriented 17° west of north, on the southwest slope of the mound. The material from the north end of the excavation southward for a distance of 3.25 m was described by Bullard in his field notes as large (up to 0.5 m) loose rock "platform fill [that] appears roughly layered with large and small stones." At 3.25 m south of the northern limits of the pit, he noted what may have been the facing of the platform upon which later structures were built. Unfortunately, the large quantities of cultural material from this operation were divided into horizontal rather than vertical provenience units (lots 5, 7, and 10),

PLATE II. View of Macanché Island from the lake, looking northeast. Photo 1968, by W. R. Bullard.

PLATE III. The mound on the northwest corner of Macanché Island, showing modern structures on the summit. The view is to the northeast. Photo 1974, by D. S. Rice.

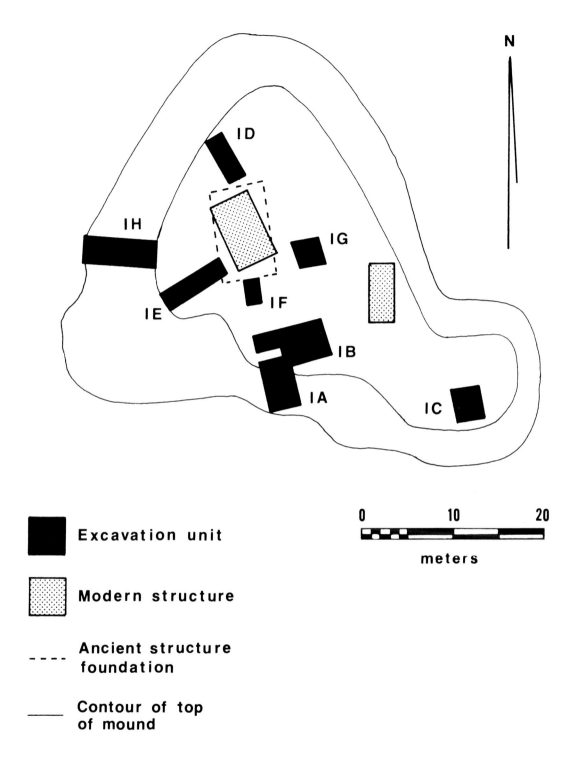

N

Excavation unit

Modern structure

Ancient structure
foundation

Contour of top
of mound

0   10   20

meters

FIGURE 4. Map of Bullard's excavations on the mound on Macanché Island, drawn from his
    original sketches.

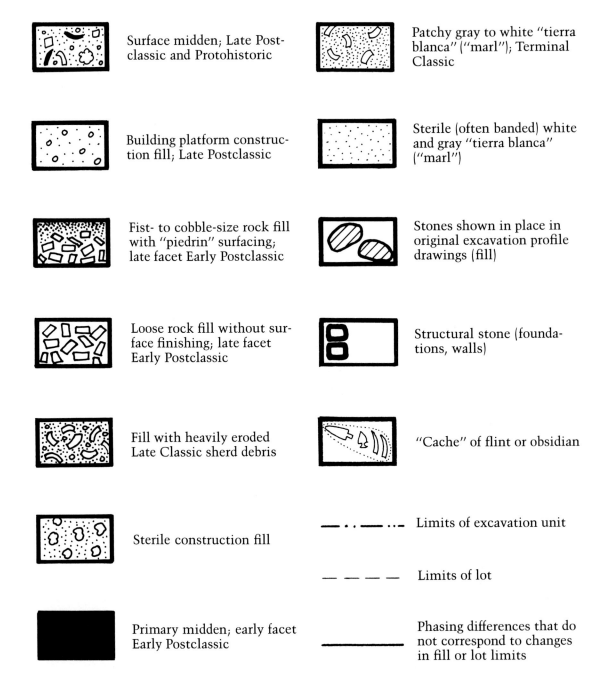

Surface midden; Late Post-classic and Protohistoric

Patchy gray to white "tierra blanca" ("marl"); Terminal Classic

Building platform construction fill; Late Postclassic

Sterile (often banded) white and gray "tierra blanca" ("marl")

Fist- to cobble-size rock fill with "piedrin" surfacing; late facet Early Postclassic

Stones shown in place in original excavation profile drawings (fill)

Loose rock fill without surface finishing; late facet Early Postclassic

Structural stone (foundations, walls)

Fill with heavily eroded Late Classic sherd debris

"Cache" of flint or obsidian

Sterile construction fill

Limits of excavation unit

Limits of lot

Primary midden; early facet Early Postclassic

Phasing differences that do not correspond to changes in fill or lot limits

FIGURE 5. Key to conventions used in excavation profile illustrations, figures 6–13, 15–16, 18–20, and 26.

and this stratigraphic mixing made the material relatively useless for dating the construction.

As revealed in Operation IA, the platform had been built over a stratum of white "marl" (technically a calcareous clay) mixed with small stones, which was sampled by Bullard's excavations (plate IV). Sherds were abundant in the upper portion of this 20–25-cm-thick layer (lots 6 and 11), but lower levels were sterile. Below the white marl-stone layer was a light gray banded marl, containing very little stone and few sherds (Lot 12).

Operation IB (fig. 7) was a trench with a panhandle extension located immediately north (upslope) of Operation IA. The extension is 1.85 m north of IA and pushes into the center of a low, 40-cm-high circular rise (ca. 4.5 m in diameter) just north of IA and west of the main part of IB. The main portion of IB is a 4.0-by-5.0-m excavation northeast of IA. The upper 30 cm of excavation over the entire pit yielded rather small quantities of sherds and other artifacts (lots 8 and 9). At 30 cm, the matrix changed to core material composed of large loose rock with little soil or plaster binder. Midway along the northern excavation limits at this level a semicircle approximately 75 cm in diameter and 30 cm deep appears in Bullard's profile drawing; it may be a pit of some sort, but there is no information as to its contents. The eastern half of the test pit was excavated below this surface level (Lot 16). An incomplete and rough "retaining wall" (probably a core face; Loten and Pendergast 1984:7) ran north-south in the eastern end of the excavation, set on an irregular base of stone core about 50 cm below surface. One to two courses of stone appear to be preserved, with the stones ranging in size up to 40 by 30 by 20 cm. Around and below this wall to a depth of 1.5 m below surface was a matrix of loose rock core. It appears, on the basis of Bullard's description and the proximity of operations IA and IB, to be a continuation of the core visible in IA.

Operation IC (fig. 8) was a pit 3.6 by 3.2 m, its northwest corner approximately 14 m

southeast of the southeast corner of Operation IB. The upper 40 cm appeared to be a mixture of humus and rock, with artifact quantities diminishing with depth (lots 13 and 14). At 50 cm below surface, construction core was encountered, consisting of large rocks (up to 50 by 30 cm) with little soil or binder, and excavations terminated at the top of this stratum. No walls, facings, or other features were noted in this operation.

Operation ID (fig. 9) was a narrow rectangular excavation, 5.2 by 2.0 m in size, with its long axis oriented approximately 30° west of north. The trench was on the north side of the mound on a sloping surface, its southern end approximately 17 m north of the northern limits of Operation IB. The upper 15 to 20 cm yielded comparatively few sherds in a matrix of humus and topsoil (Lot 15). An additional 30–35 cm were excavated through rock debris in the central third of the trench, down to a level of large rock core (Lot 23), at which point excavations were terminated.

Operation IE (fig. 10) was a 7.3-by-2.0-m trench, oriented roughly 30° south of west, on the relatively level western upper surface of the mound. The east end of the pit overlapped a row of stones, approximately 25 by 35 cm in size, that formed the foundation for a structure on top of the mound (Lot 17). The bottom of these stones was about 30 cm below surface. At 2.5 m west of this wall, another line of stones, 75 cm wide and with upper edges 15 cm below surface, appeared in the pit. Consisting of parallel aligned courses of stone set on edge, with rubble coring between them, this line lay parallel to the wall foundation stones and formed the western facing of the building platform upon which the upper structure sat (plate va). The western half of the pit (west of the second and lower wall line) was excavated to a depth of 60–70 cm below surface (Lot 21); the matrix consisted of gray soil and stones. A "cache" of 78 chert flakes was located 50 cm west of the second wall at a depth of 50 cm below surface. In the eastern part of the pit, excavations penetrated the core of the building platform, which Bullard described as

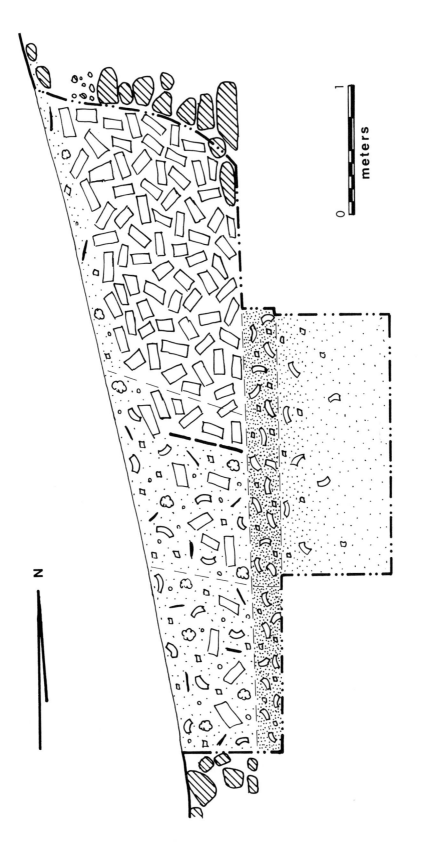

FIGURE 6. Profile of the west wall of Bullard's Operation IA. See key in figure 5.

PLATE IV. Bullard's Operation IA, showing excavation through platform construction fill into the underlying white "marl" or tierra blanca. Compare with PLATE VI.

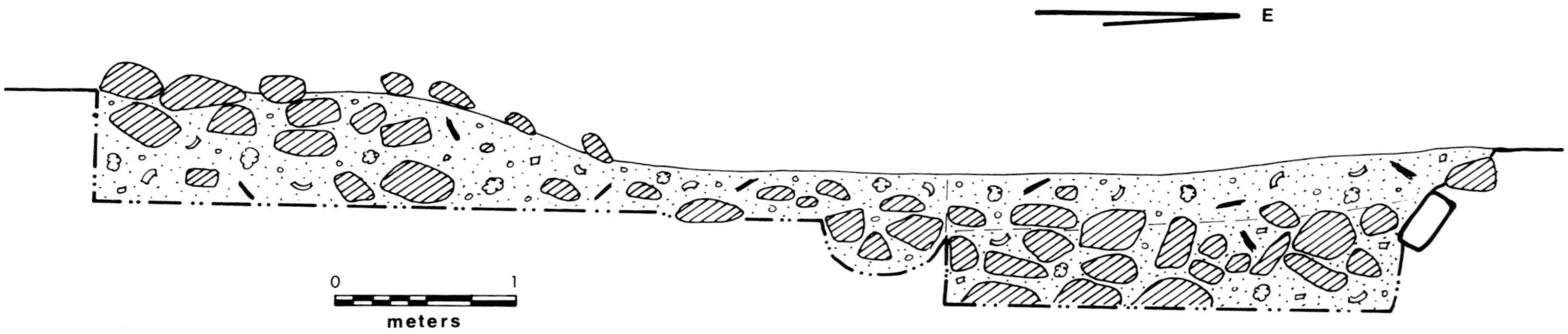

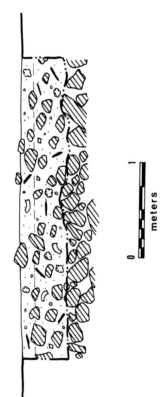

E

FIGURE 7. Profile of the northern wall of Bullard's Operation IB. See key in figure 5.

FIGURE 8. Profile of Bullard's Operation IC. No directional data were provided in his notes. See key in figure 5.

tight fill consisting of small stones and hard-packed soil. There was an apparent change in consistency of the core at about 80 cm below surface, but sherd yields were low and he did not separate lots above and below this change (Lot 39). The large loose fill noted in Operations IA, IB, and ID was not encountered in IE.

Operation IF (fig. 11) was a small rectangular trench, 1.5 by 3.0 m, the long axis oriented roughly 9° west of north. The north end of the pit abuts a line of stones that represents the southern portion of the same foundation wall noted in the eastern edge of Operation IE (plate vb). Bullard (field notes, 21 March 1968) described the wall as consisting of "two courses. Base stones, set vertically on irregular rock fill, are about 25 cm wide by 35 tall, and about 20 cm deep. Chinking stone used." Excavations (lots 18 and 22) were terminated at 35 cm below surface, where a fairly regular layer of rock core was encountered. No intact flooring or plaster was found to confirm this as a prepared floor, although the existence of a level surface suggests that it probably represents the upper surface of the building platform noted in Operation IE, upon which the structure rested. It was not penetrated by excavation.

Operation IG (fig. 12) was a square pit, 3 by 3 m in size, north of Operation IB and east of Operations IE and IF. At 45 cm below surface (lots 19 and 20) a regular surface was encountered, although again without visible plaster paving or finishing. Below it there was approximately 60 cm of gray core composed of "fist-sized stones, rather evenly selected for size," plus some larger rocks up to 40 cm in size (Lot 26). Grading down from this was loose core composed of larger stones (Lot 32). The excavations closed at a depth of 2.3 m below surface as a result of wall cave-ins and lack of cultural materials.

Operation IH (fig. 13) was a large 3-by-8-m trench on the western slope of the platform, its long axis oriented 4° north of west. At the eastern end of the pit in the upper 20 cm of the excavation (primarily Lot 24) was a cache of over 550 chert chips, 11 small points, and

3 obsidian blades. It will be remembered that Operation IE, location of another lithic cache, was also on the western side of the mound (see chapter 9 for description of these artifacts). At the western end of IH, between the surface and a white marly deposit (encountered 20 cm below surface at the westernmost limits of the trench), a large concentration of sherds was found, many of which appeared to be primary breakage (Lot 25). Six Postclassic slipped tripod dishes from this concentration were reconstructible, together with four other partially reconstructible vessels, and large quantities of unslipped *olla* fragments. A small, 1-m extension of the pit was opened to the south to recover more of this material (Lot 35).

Besides this midden, two earlier cultural strata were encountered in Operation IH. One was loose core with little soil, possibly comparable to core noted in Operations IA and IB (not penetrated in the latter). This material was present in the eastern half of Operation IH, approximately 40 to 100 cm below surface in depth, depending on the surface slope. A suggestion of a slumped "retaining wall" or facing marking the westward extension of the loose rock core was noted 5.5 m from the east wall of the pit, separating the core or masonry (lots 31, 33, 34, 36, and 37) from collapse debris in the western part of the pit (lots 27 and 28).

The second cultural stratum noted in Operation IH was a 1-m thick deposit of "white marl below platform fill. Contains small pebbles, small bits of charcoal and occasional stones." This white marl was excavated in a smaller pit, 1.4 by 3.3 m, in the center floor of the original unit of IH (plate vi). Large quantities of sherds and other artifacts were recovered from this level; many of the sherds appeared to be primary breakage (lots 40 and 41). The quantity of artifacts diminished in the lower 50 cm of the marl layer (Lot 42), and below the marl the soil was sterile with some apparently natural banding.

A mixture of these two deposits was noted in one area. In the northern 1.6 m of the pit,

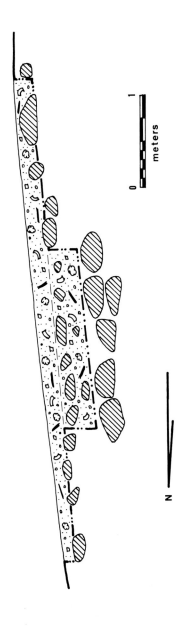

FIGURE 9. Profile of the eastern wall of Bullard's Operation ID. See key in figure 5.

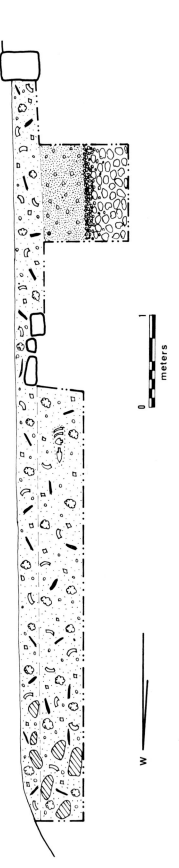

FIGURE 10. Profile of the northern wall of Bullard's Operation IE. See key in figure 5.

A

B

PLATE V. Bullard's Operations IE and IF. **a**, Operation IE, showing the line of foundation stone of the structure on the mound summit. **b**, Operation IF, showing the line of foundation stones marking the low platform upon which the upper structure was built (foreground).

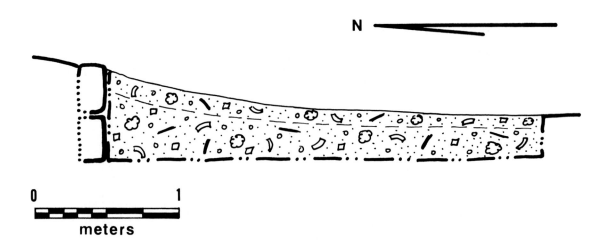

FIGURE 11. Profile of the eastern wall of Bullard's Operation IF. See key in figure 5.

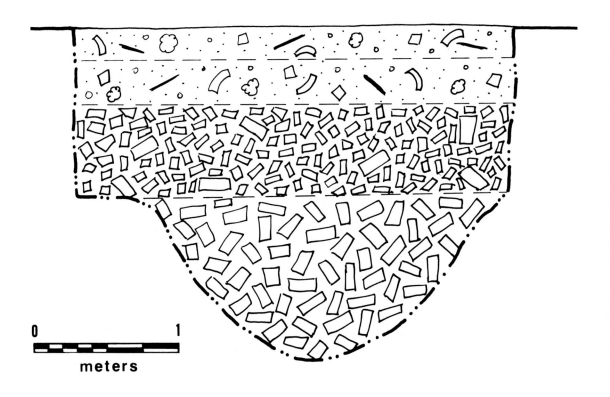

FIGURE 12. Profile of Bullard's Operation IG. No directional data were provided in his notes. See key in figure 5.

PLATE VI. Bullard's Operation IH, showing excavation through platform construction fill into the underlying white "marl" or tierra blanca. Compare with PLATE IV.

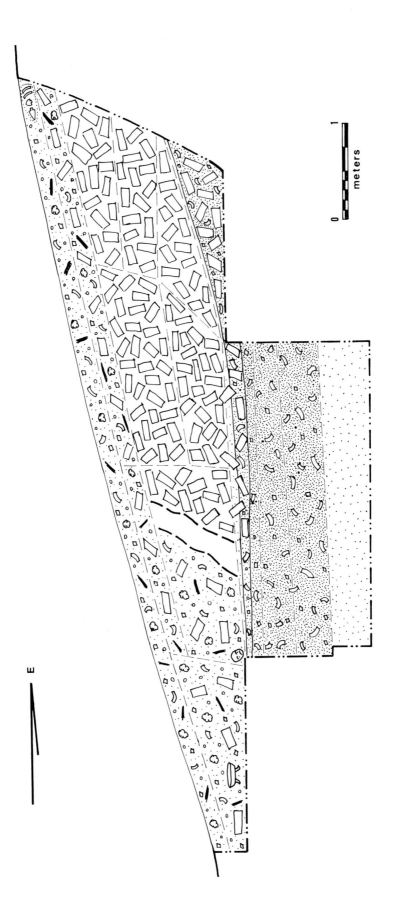

FIGURE 13. Profile of the northern wall of Bullard's Operation IH. See key in figure 5.

from approximately 1.5 to 1.75 m below sur-face (Lot 38), Bullard found a "distinct de-posit of rocks mixed with white marl. Prob-ably the edge of Late Classic house ruin. Heavy sherd concentration."

CPHEP Excavations, 1979

Additional excavations on Macanché Island were undertaken in June 1979 as part of the Proyecto Lacustre archaeological investiga-tions under the CPHEP research umbrella. The purpose was to supplement the strati-graphic and ceramic data of Bullard's earlier excavations. The site was contour mapped and eight test pits were excavated (fig. 14), one at the southern apex of the island, two at the base of the mound on the west-southwest side, three at the slope of the mound on the south side, and two on top of the mound. All excavations continued until sterile subsoils were reached.

Test pit 1, a 2-by-2-m pit at the southern apex of the island, and pit 2 (fig. 15), west-southwest of the mound, displayed similar stratigraphy, although pit 1 was virtually sterile. A dark brown-gray surface layer 20 cm thick, which yielded sherds and shells of *Pomacea* (a large, round, freshwater mol-lusk), overlay a soft, white powdery stratum which we called *tierra blanca* (apparently equivalent to the stratum Bullard termed "marl"). The upper 25 cm of this tierra blanca is generally streaky gray, giving way to white sterile material beneath it. Sherd quantities decreased with depth, and the deposit was sterile below 45 cm. At 120 cm below sur-face, dark gray clayey marl was encountered under the softer white material in pit 2.

Pit 3 (fig. 16) was a 3-by-3-m pit on the summit of the mound at its northwestern end. The pit was placed over a line of surface stones marking the corner of a structure foundation wall (plate VII), the same struc-ture identified by Bullard in his Operations IE and IF. In pit 3, the wall consisted of paral-lel lines, ca. 25 cm apart, of dressed and undressed limestone blocks (fig. 17). The stones measured up to 20 by 25 by 40 cm in size, their bases apparently set on a building platform whose surface was approximately

40 cm below the ground surface. Interior to the structure, the core was light gray-brown with some large collapse stones; a level of apparent *piedrin* surfacing (small pebbles in a powdery gray matrix) was found at approxi-mately 40 cm below the surface (70 cm be-low datum). Dark midden lay to the exterior of the foundation, and at the level of the base of the wall stones (i.e., on the surface of the building platform at 40 cm below the sur-face) were a number of large censer sherds. These represented at least two vessels and appeared to be primary breakage.

Below this structure, 20 cm of small stone ballast was encountered, then larger rocks (ca. 20 cm diameter) within dirt matrix. This core material continued, with some layering evident, to a depth of 120 cm below the sur-face (1.5 m below datum), forming a sub-structure approximately 80 cm in height. At 1.1 to 1.2 m below surface, several concen-trations of burned earth and stone were noted, but they could not be clearly isolated as distinct constructional features. These, together with large concentrations of sherds and other artifacts, including obsidian blades, bone tools, pieces of marine shell, and metate fragments, suggest that this level may have been an ancient mound surface. Beneath 1.7 m below surface, the core changed to large rock in little matrix, with declining yields of artifacts (sherds were ex-tremely eroded and consisted of Late Classic forms). Sterile core was encountered at 2.3 m, and sterile tierra blanca was reached at 3 m below surface (or 3.3 m below datum).

Pit 4 (fig. 18) was a 2-by-3-m excavation unit oriented east-west at the base of the west-northwest slope of the mound, 5.5 m below the mound summit. The upper 20–30 cm consisted of heavy midden—the same deposit sampled by Bullard's Operation IH— with large quantities of bone, shell, and sherds present in black, loamy soil. Material from the northwest quadrant of the pit was 1/4-in. screened, and flotation samples were taken from each level. At 30 cm below the surface (5.8 m below datum), the pit could be divided into two areas. In the western half, the midden continued, appearing somewhat

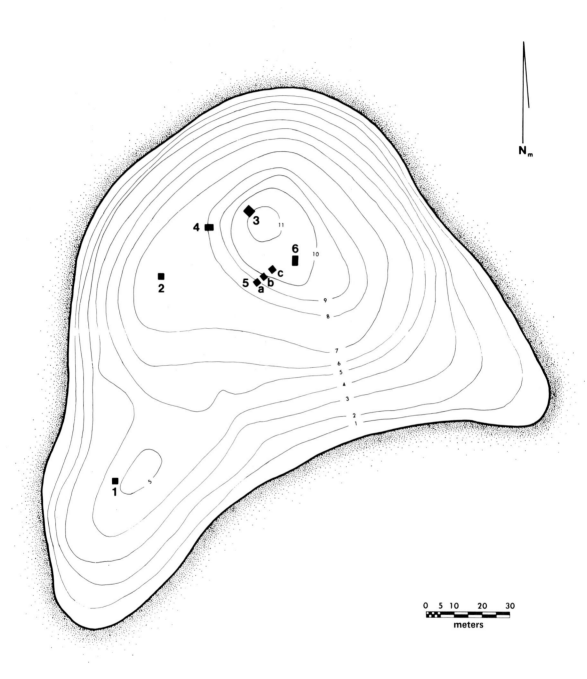

FIGURE 14. Contour map of Macanché Island, showing CPHEP test pit locations. Contours in meters above the 1979 lake level. After original map by D. Batcho.

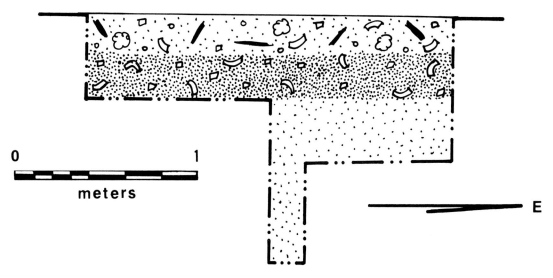

0

1

meters

E

FIGURE 15. Section of the excavations in CPHEP test pit 2, drawn on the east-west
centerline. See key in figure 5.

darker in color. In the eastern half, a thin, light gray, ashy layer overlay a level 10 cm thick of tierra blanca, which appeared as a capping layer. Below this white capping in the entire pit was more dark midden ca. 5–8 cm thick, overlying a leached gray zone, which in turn overlay sterile tierra blanca. Sherd yields were considerably reduced in the gray zone below the midden.

Pits 5A, 5B (fig. 19a, b), and 5C were each 2 by 1.5 m in size and were spaced 3 m apart along a line oriented 235° from north at the center of the southern slope of the mound. This slope seemed to have a tiered or ter-raced face, and it was hoped that the test ex-cavations would reveal whether it was actual construction. Pits 5A and 5B exhibited stra-tigraphy much like pit 2, with 30–50 cm of black midden material overlying tierra blanca; sherds were present in the upper 15–20 cm of the tierra blanca, but below 70 cm the pit was sterile. Neither pit had any quantity of stone suggestive of actual platform or terrace construction core, nor were platform or core faces recovered. Pit 5C intersected the southeastern corner of Bull-ard's Operation IA and was largely mixed backfill.

Pit 6 (fig. 20) was a 2-by-3-m pit oriented

north-south in the interior of a rectangular space marked by three lines of stone. The stones demarcate the foundation platform for a structure on the south-central portion of the mound, which is 70 cm lower than the northwestern end. The upper 1.3 m (down to 2.0 m below datum) excavated in pit 6 con-sisted of surface midden material overlying rock core mixed with gray soil. Although the test pit location was in the interior of the structure as marked by the stone lines, no clear surfacing or flooring was evident to suggest the surface of a platform upon which the building was placed. Only changes in the size of rock and in artifacts occurring at ca. 80 cm below surface (1.5 m below datum) indicated that two separate episodes of core deposition may have been involved. Below the platform core, 20 cm of what appeared to be an earlier ballast or surfacing layer created a roughly level area above a thin, sloping black midden. This midden in turn overlay tierra blanca (at 2.2 m below datum) which, as in pits 2, 4, 5A, and 5B, was grayish and charcoal-stained in the upper 20 cm. As in these other pits, the upper portion of the tierra blanca in pit 6 yielded sherds but was sterile below 20 cm of thickness.

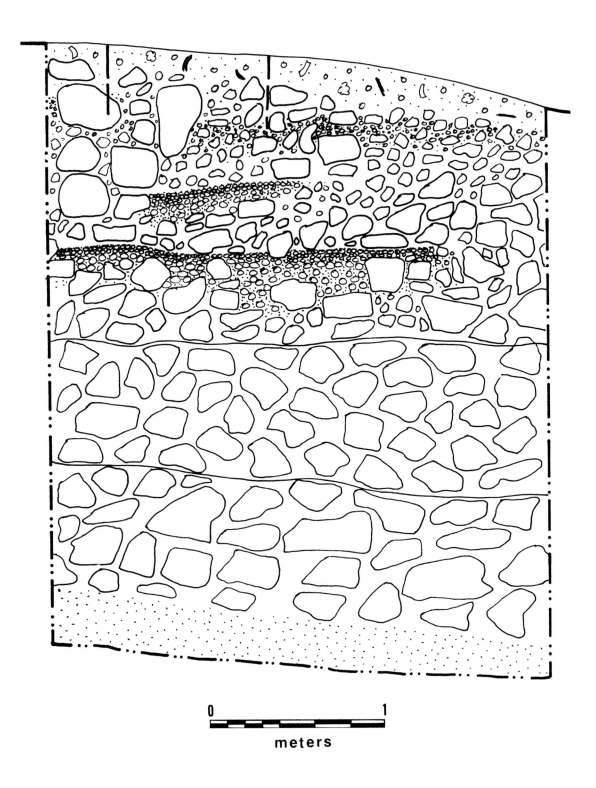

0   1

meters

FIGURE 16. Profile of the southwest wall of CPHEP test pit 3. Vertical lines in upper 40 cm denote area where the excavation cut the structure foundation wall at an angle. Large collapse stones lie inside the structure. See key in figure 5.

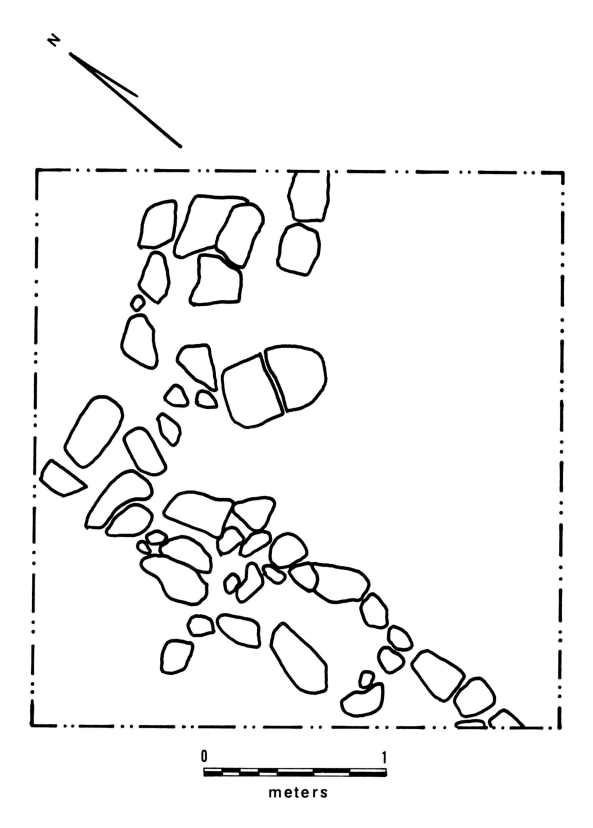

N

0   1

meters

FIGURE 17. Plan of the northwestern corner of the structure foundation wall in CPHEP test pit 3, at a depth of 20 cm below surface.

PLATE VII. CPHEP test pit 3, showing construction stones of the northwest corner of the structure on the top of the mound, the same structure represented in PLATE V-a. The view is to the southeast.

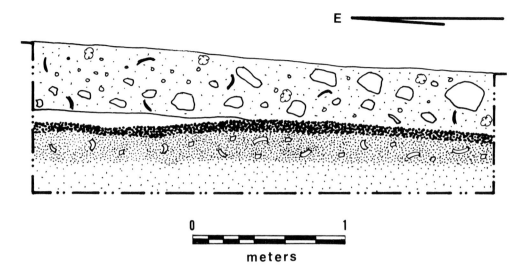

FIGURE 18. Section of the excavation in CPHEP test pit 4, taken on the east-west centerline. See key in figure 5.

Macanché Island Occupation Summary

As best can be reconstructed from the information provided by the test pits excavated on Macanché Island, the island appears to have been first occupied in the Late or Terminal Classic period. Preclassic and Early Classic sherds are extremely rare in the excavated material, and even characteristic Tepeu 1 forms and slips are scarce. Most of the Late Classic pottery is late Late Classic, or Tepeu 2, to judge by forms, although the extreme erosion of many sherds suggests a break between some kind of Late Classic utilization of the island and the heavier occupation of the Terminal Classic period. The artifacts from construction and midden lots indicate that the habitation of the island was primarily a Postclassic period phenomenon.

Although the island has suffered modern disturbance, and there is little architectural trace of the structure or structures that may have been built upon the mound, the available evidence suggests that the use of Macanché Island was probably principally residential. The relatively large variety of censers, however, would indicate some ceremonial activity as well.

The following discussion summarizes the occupational history of the mound on the island as reconstructed from Bullard's excavations, supplemented for purposes of stratigraphic interpretation by data from the CPHEP test pits (see figs. 21 and 22). This habitational activity involved a series of low platform constructions, which are depicted in a tentative restoration drawing in figure 23. Table 1 presents the phase assignments of Bullard's excavated lots on the island; tabulations of sherds in these lots are provided in appendix 1.

Terminal Classic Period

Prior to aboriginal Maya use, the island probably had a maximum height of about 8 m above the 1979 lake level, the highest point being its northern section. Maya activities seem to have focused on this portion of the island, beginning with construction of a low mound at an unknown date. Pit 3, in the area of what is now the highest point of the island, revealed an early platform approximately 70 cm high constructed over tierra

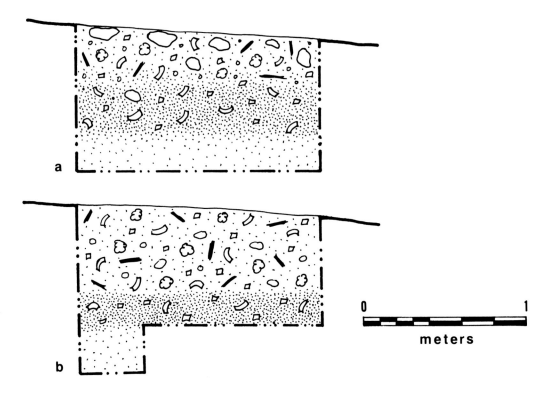

FIGURE 19. Profiles of the southeast walls of CPHEP test pits 5A (a) and 5B (b). See key in figure 5.

blanca; the fill consisted of large rock, and was devoid of sherd material by which to date it. The fact that no cultural debris was incorporated into the fill suggests that it represents the first formal occupation of the island. By inference, this early construction is probably Late Classic in date. Only about 0.3 percent of the more than 15,000 sherds recovered from Bullard's excavations on the island were clearly Preclassic or Early Classic types, suggesting that the island was virtually ignored by the Maya prior to the Late Classic period.

Sometime later, there seems to have been considerable modification and leveling of the white-to-gray, often banded, natural "marly" substrate of the island. The picture is one of fairly extensive clearing, sweeping up whatever debris remained from the earlier use of the island, and perhaps leveling the tierra blanca, then using this material to build up the northern end of the island. The early

platform was not removed in this clearing of the island's surface debris, and it formed the core of later building construction, which began in the Terminal Classic period.

At some point, the platform was remodeled and raised 1.1 m in height. This effort probably involved tearing up any surfacing remaining on the earlier structure, because there is no break in core consistency. The same (or a similar) construction episode—core containing Late Classic sherds overlying sterile core—was sampled by the lower portion of Bullard's Operation IG (Lot 32), which was not excavated to a natural sterile stratum. A radiocarbon sample of wood taken from 150 cm below surface in CPHEP pit 3 (table 2) yielded a date of 1180 ± 65 years b.p. (UM-1890); the corrected date (Ralph, Michael, and Han 1973) is A.D. 830–850 ± 75, with a 1-sigma range of A.D. 745–915. It should be remembered that this date refers to the core material, however,

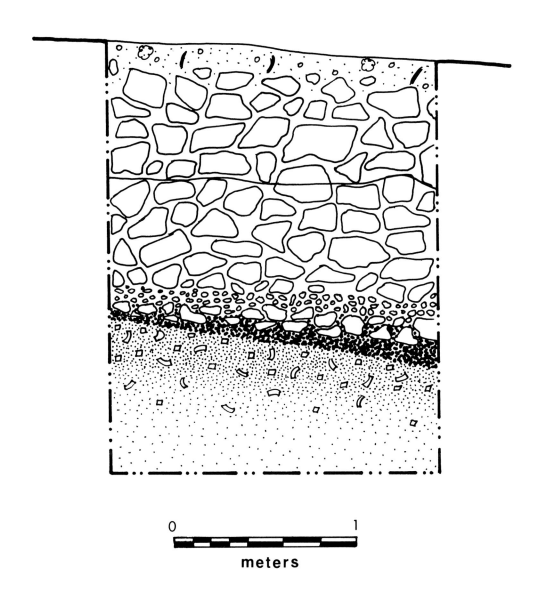

N

0   1

meters

FIGURE 20. Profile of the east wall of CPHEP test pit 6. See key in figure 5.

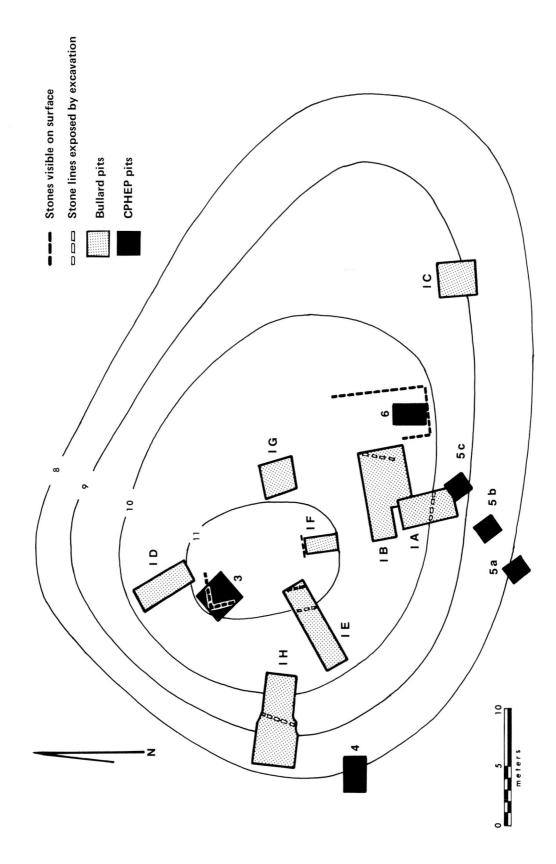

FIGURE 21. Approximate spatial positioning of Bullard's test pits (see figure 4) with relation to CPHEP excavations, and to foundations of structures on top of the mound.

Table 1

Phase Assignments of Lots from Bullard's Excavations at Macanché Island

Terminal Classic Romero Phase: marl and Classic platform construction core

Oper. A	Lots 6, 11, 12	Marl
B	Lot 32	Late Classic core
C	Lots 38, 40, 41, 42	Marl; lot 42 is Late Classic

Early Postclassic Aura Phase: platform construction core

Oper. E	Lot 39	Stratigraphically mixed
G	Lot 26	Early facet; loose rock core
H	Lots 31, 33, 34, 36, 37	Late facet; loose rock core

Late Postclassic Dos Lagos Phase: platform core

| Oper. A | Lot 10 | Mixed core and collapse debris |
| B | Lot 16 | Collapse debris (mixed) |

Late Postclassic Dos Lagos Phase: midden

Oper. A	Lots 5 and 7	Midden and collapse debris, mixed
C	Lot 14	
D	Lot 23	
E	Lot 21	
F	Lot 22	
G	Lot 20	
H	Lots 25, 27, 28, 30, 35	Lots 25, 30, and 35 are mixed with collapse debris

Protohistoric Ayer Phase: surface midden

Oper. B	Lots 8 and 9	
C	Lot 13	
D	Lot 15	
E	Lot 17	
F	Lot 18	
G	Lot 19	
H	Lot 24	

rather than to the date of the actual constructional activity.

The refurbishing effort incorporated sherds into the core, sherds that had been exposed to weathering for some time, because they had very heavily eroded surfaces and little or no slip remaining. Forms suggest primarily typical Late and Terminal Classic jars, dishes, and large incurved-rim bowls characteristic of Tinaja Red and Subín Red. These sherds may have been part of the detritus left over the mound by the builders of the earlier structure and then accumulated for the later construction core in the clearing operations suggested above. An obsidian blade, ID 42 (see table 2; also P. Rice n.d. a)

from 100–120 cm below surface in pit 3, a stratum containing eroded sherds, was hydration dated to A.D. 878 ± 33 years (A.D. 845–911).

The clearing and leveling of surface debris and "marl" at this time seems to have been a major undertaking. Over most of the island, particularly at the edges of the present platform's extent, sterile white tierra blanca is overlaid by a layer approximately 20–25 cm thick of mixed, organically stained or leached tierra blanca; it is white or light gray and mottled and contains sherds, shells, and charcoal flecks. In Operation IH, this white or gray sherd-bearing material was as much as 1 m thick over sterile banded "marl," sug-

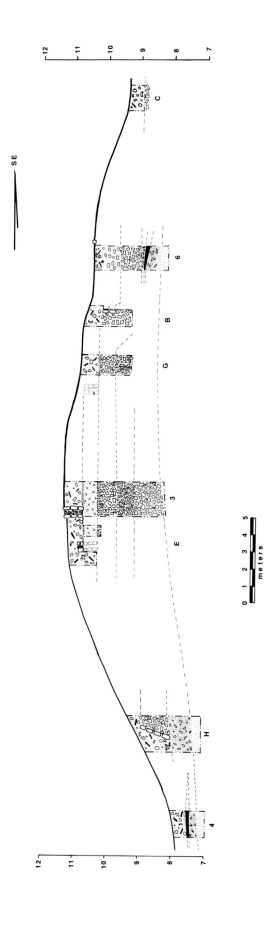

FIGURE 22. Idealized reconstruction of the sequence of mound construction activities on Macanché Island, as suggested by a schematic profile taken on a northwest-southeast line through the mound. This reconstruction combines data from excavation units 4, IH, IE, 3, IG, IB, 6, and IC (moving from west to east). Elevations are in meters above the 1979 lake level.

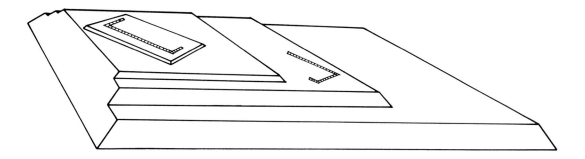

FIGURE 23. Tentative reconstruction of the aboriginal platform and structures on Macanché Island.

gesting considerable modification. In Operation IA, only 10–15 cm thickness was noted. Similar grayish white, patchy or mottled tierra blanca containing sherds and cultural material was also noted in Proyecto Lacustre pits 2, 4, 5A, 5B, and 6. In 5A and 5B this mixed tierra blanca and rubbish constituted one or more of the apparent low terraces on the southwest face of the mound. The clearing and mounding of mixed tierra blanca and debris as evident in excavations around what is the periphery of the present-day mound may represent early efforts to build up the entire northern area to the level of the original Late Classic mound, because in a few locations midden debris overlies the tierra blanca. An obsidian from tierra blanca in pit 5A was hydration dated, yielding a date of A.D. 826 ± 39 years, or A.D. 787–865 (table 2; P. Rice n.d. a).

The ceramic material from the white and mottled tierra blanca is the basis for defining the Terminal Classic Romero complex at Macanché (Bullard 1973 : 227), which I have identified as a peripheral member of the Eznab ceramic sphere (see chapter 3). The principal ceramic units in this complex are the Tinaja group (including types Tinaja Red, Subín Red, and Chaquiste Impressed) and the Cambio (unslipped) group.

In addition to these well-known Classic types, several very distinctive new classes of pottery appeared consistently in the early levels of Bullard's and CPHEP excavations, and these have been given group, type, or variety designations: the Harina group, a cream-slipped group with some vessels having red-painted polychrome decoration; Payaso Orange-brown type, a very hard, thin-walled, fire-clouded type associated with jar forms; and Coarse Gray Variety of Cambio Unslipped. With regard to these new ceramic units, it is curious that CPHEP excavations into Terminal Classic structures on the Macanché mainland revealed striking differences between the ceramic material there and that on the mainland (see below). No censer fragments were recovered in Terminal Classic deposits on the island. Nonceramic artifactual material from Terminal Classic levels on the island included numerous lithics (including obsidian), bone awls, stone spindle whorls, and a conch shell trumpet (the latter from CPHEP pit 6).

All told, the Terminal Classic period is represented at Macanché Island by three deposits or areas of activity. One is the 1-m-thick deposit of tierra blanca (leveling for platform extensions?) built up in the area of Operation IH. Although partially recon-

Table 2

Chronometric Dates Pertaining to the Terminal Classic and Postclassic Occupation on Macanché Island (see P. Rice n.d. a)

Phase	Pit	Lot	Date (A.D.)	Remarks
Terminal Classic	5A	22	826 ± 39	Tierra blanca; obsidian hydration date
	3	42	878 ± 33	Eroded sherds; obsidian hydration date
	3		830/850 ± 75	Eroded sherds; corrected[a] radiocarbon date (UM-1890)
Early Postclassic	5A	20	1056 ± 21	
	6	71B	1357 ± 31	Tierra blanca; erroneous phasing? obsidian hydration date
	3	32	1040 ± 56	Obsidian hydration date
	3	38	1083 ± 30	Obsidian hydration date
	6		915 ± 100	Base of core; corrected[a] radiocarbon date (UM-1891)
Late Postclassic	6	63	1307 ± 19	Top of mound; obsidian hydration date
	4	12	1362 ± 22	Midden; obsidian hydration date
	4	13	1307 ± 19	Midden; obsidian hydration date
Protohistoric	4	10	1301 ± 27	Obsidian hydration date; blade re-use?
	5B	57A	1436 ± 19	Obsidian hydration date

a. Corrected with reference to Ralph, Michael, and Han (1973).

structible vessels indicate primary breakage for some of this material, the tierra blanca had no organic staining and very little bone was present, so it does not appear to represent primary midden deposition. A second locus of Terminal Classic activity is the grayish, mottled tierra blanca in pits IA, 2, 4, 5A, 5B, and 6. The presence of partially reconstructible vessels in Operation IA again hints at primary breakage for this material, and the gray color suggests some organic midden accumulation; but the relative lack of bone in both Bullard's and CPHEP excavations does not enhance this interpretation. A third probable locus is the construction or modification of the platform at the lower levels of pit 3 and Operation IG.

Early Postclassic Period

The next episode of occupation and cultural deposition was uncovered in pits 4 and 6, which had a thin but dense black midden layer overlying gray, mottled tierra blanca. This material may represent the occupational debris of the group that carried out

the clearing and accumulation of the mixed tierra blanca and rubbish or the remains left by a later group of users of the platform. This organic midden also may be responsible for the gray staining in the underlying tierra blanca in pits 4 and 6.

The midden material has been used in the tentative identification of an early facet of the Early Postclassic occupation of the island. Defined as the early facet of the Aura Early Postclassic ceramic complex, the ceramic material in the midden included three types or wares noted in the Terminal Classic Romero complex (Payaso Orange-brown, Coarse Gray Variety of Cambio Unslipped, and an unnamed, hard, unslipped ash paste), plus four groups characteristic of the Postclassic period in Petén—Paxcamán, Trapeche, Augustine, and Pozo. Notched sherd net sinkers were recovered from the midden exposure in pit 6, and one was recovered from Operation IH. In pit 4, part of the midden was covered with a capping layer of white tierra blanca near the base of the mound structure.

The succeeding phase of activity on the island involved the construction of a large platform, 80 cm in height, of loose fist- to cobble-sized stone core over the earlier platform. No surfaces of either the earlier construction or this later platform were clearly visible, so that the height and extent of the platform were difficult to ascertain. At approximately 1.2 cm below the surface (1.5 m below datum), areas of burned rock and heavy artifact concentrations may be the remains of previous use of the earlier platform that was sealed over by the new construction. In some places in pit 3, the upper surface appeared to be indicated by a layer of piedrin overlying the large rock core, at a level 40 cm below surface (70 cm below datum). Some layering of large rocks and small pebbles may indicate phases of construction or remodeling, but there were no changes in artifact content. The character of the core between the two structures is virtually continuous, except for several burned areas and possible rock alignments (structures?) at 120 cm below the surface (1.5 m below datum). The same platform surface was exposed but not penetrated by Bullard's Operation IF on the south side of the structure, where he suggested that the level was a surfacing or a floor.

The identical platform construction episode was encountered in pit 6, as indicated by similar fist- to cobble-sized rock core and late Early Postclassic sherds. In pit 6, the levels of changes in core and artifact content show parallels to those in pit 3, suggesting a platform 80 cm high built above one 50 cm in height (1.5 m below datum). In pit 6, however, they do not register late Early Postclassic over Terminal Classic periods of building. Instead, the upper 80 cm (from 1.5 to 0.7 m below datum) is late Early Postclassic (and includes small amounts of Topoxté group sherds). The lower 50 cm is also late facet Early Postclassic but lacks sherds of the Topoxté group. In addition, the piedrin surfacing noted in pit 3 was missing from the upper part of the platform in pit 6; this may be a consequence of the fact that this upper surface is at ground level (0.7 m below datum) and was not surmounted by additional construction as appeared in pit 3. A radiocarbon sample (table 2) from the base of the lower portion of Early Postclassic platform core in pit 6 (UM-1891) yielded a date of 1105 ± 90 years b.p.; the corrected date (Ralph, Michael, and Han 1973) is A.D. 915 ± 100, with a 1-sigma range of A.D. 800/820–1005. Again, core material rather than constructional activity per se is being dated.

Similar variations in platform core are probably sampled in Bullard's Operation IE. In this pit he noted a change in core consistency at 80 cm below surface which may correspond to the core changes noted in pits 3 and 6. He did not separate the artifactual material from above and below this change, however (Lot 39). The relationship of these levels to the loose core in Operation IB, west of a core face or "retaining wall" as well as *beneath* the face to a depth of 1.5 m, cannot be determined. In the absence of an absolute datum for Bullard's excavations, and because Operation IB was not excavated to sterile subsoil, it is difficult to establish securely the levels of this wall base or surface, but the top of the wall stones lay 30 cm below the present ground surface.

Besides Operation IB, Bullard's excavations in Operations IA and IH also encountered "large, loose rock fill" with little soil binder, which is probably comparable to the late Early Postclassic platform core of the Proyecto Lacustre excavations. In these two pits, unlike Operation IB, excavations were carried through the core, and it was found that this loose rock core overlay "marl" or tierra blanca. The building activity represented by this deposit represents an effort of some magnitude, probably involving several tiers of construction. The three "retaining walls" or faces associated with this core in Bullard's excavations appear to be situated at different absolute levels; in Operations IA and IH, the wall rested upon tierra blanca, although apparently at different absolute levels, IA being higher. In IB, the highest of the three faces held back one core segment while resting upon another one (the core of the platform associated with the intermediate level wall or face in IA?). Operation IC, sampling the lowest portion of the mound at its southeastern corner, encountered large, loose rock core at 50 cm below surface, but it was not penetrated by excavation, so it cannot be determined if this was also an extension of this same constructional activity.

Ceramic material from this (these) platform(s) has been grouped into a late facet of the Early Postclassic Aura ceramic complex. Included are sherds of the Paxcamán, Trapeche, and Pozo ceramic groups, plus a few sherds of Augustine Red. The Terminal Classic types from the preceding early facet Aura complex no longer consistently appeared in the assemblage. Topoxté group sherds are occasionally recovered from this core material in small quantities and are not considered intrusive.

It should be noted that temporal faceting distinctions between midden and platform construction were made on the basis of CPHEP excavations. Bullard's Lot 26 from construction core in Operation IG may tentatively be assigned to the early facet, while his Operation IH excavations into platform construction (lots 31, 33, 34, 36, and 37) suggest by their negligible quantities of Terminal Classic types that they represent a late facet episode. Three obsidian blades from Early Postclassic levels in CPHEP excavations have been hydration dated (table 2; P. Rice n.d. a): two dates from pit 3 are A.D. 1083 ± 30 (A.D. 1053–1113) and A.D. 1040 ± 56 (A.D. 984–1096); one from pit 5A is A.D. 1056 ± 21 (A.D. 1035–1077).

Late Postclassic and Protohistoric Periods

The final phase of occupation of the island dates to the Late Postclassic period, with probable continuation through the sixteenth century. The Dos Lagos Late Postclassic ceramic complex is characterized by the presence of Paxcamán, Trapeche, and Topoxté slipped groups, by Pozo and Chilo unslipped groups, and by a variety of effigy and non-

effigy censer materials. Three separate construction or occupation activities are identifiable as dating from the Late Postclassic habitation of the island.

As seen in pit 3, a structure was built over the northwestern portion of the preceding platform (late facet Early Postclassic), and only its stone foundation lines are now visible. These foundations consisted of two lines of stones separated by approximately 25 cm of rubble coring; in the Proyecto Lacustre excavations only one course of stones was clearly visible, whereas two courses were noted in Bullard's Operations IE and IF. The use of double lines of foundation stones is characteristic of Postclassic structures throughout Petén (P. Rice and D. Rice 1985; D. Rice 1986), and, as measured by Bullard, the foundation stones outlined a rectangular structure approximately 9.5 by 6 m, oriented north-south. This structure at Macanché Island probably had stone walls for the lower 50–60 cm or so; these were surmounted by upper walls and a roof made of perishable material such as pole and thatch. Compared with structures of the Classic period, Postclassic structures such as this one have very little collapse debris on them.

A second area of Late Postclassic construction may have been located on the central portion of the mound. Late Postclassic construction debris and surface midden overlay the lower late facet Early Postclassic platform in this area but were not clearly separated from it by change in core characteristics or surfacing. A structure was erected in the area of pit 6, as indicated by a single line of foundation stones that made two right angles, marking an outline roughly 4 m in width and in length greater than 10 m. These foundation stones did not appear to have been set on any visibly surfaced platform core. It is not known how many courses of stone existed.

That the Late Postclassic occupation of Macanché Island was of long duration, sizable, and intense is suggested by the presence of 20–50 cm of rich black midden over the entire mound area of the northern portion of the island. The midden was particularly heavy on the higher western portion of the mound and on the adjacent slopes to the south (Operation IA) and west (Operation IH). Recovered from this deposit were substantial quantities of Late Postclassic pottery, plus a variety of ceramic and nonceramic artifacts, shell (chiefly *Pomacea* and *Pachychilus* sp.), and animal bone (principally deer, turtle, tepescuintle, armadillo, and boar [see chapter 11], as well as a variety of small birds). This midden was the major deposit sampled by Bullard's excavations, which in many cases did not penetrate any construction core, and by all CPHEP test pits. Late Postclassic pottery from the midden includes Paxcamán, Trapeche, and Topoxté slipped groups and Pozo and Chilo unslipped groups, plus a variety of vase and effigy censer forms. Three obsidian hydration dates from this midden material in pit 4 vary between A.D. 1301 and 1367 (or A.D. 1287–1383, using the standard deviations; see table 2; also P. Rice n.d. a). One obsidian date from pit 6 is A.D. 1307 ± 19, and one from pit 5B is A.D. 1436 ± 19 (A.D. 1417–1455).

The western side of the structure, the building platform, and the mound as a whole seem to have been primary areas for household activity, possibly ritual activity, and refuse disposal. Quantities of censer sherds were found in pit 3, exterior to the structure walls at the northwest corner of the building, and in Operation IH, on the western mound slope. Two possible "caches," or deposits of large amounts of chert chipping debris and chert and obsidian tools, were noted by Bullard in his excavations of this midden deposit in Operations ID and IH, west of the structure platform near the mound summit. In two areas at the base of the mound platform overlying tierra blanca—in Operations IA and IB to the south, and at the far end of Operation IH to the west—Bullard recovered deposits of sherds that suggested primary breakage. In Operation IH, at least ten vessels could be fully or partially restored from this area, including a censer, three unslipped

jars, a neckless jar, and six small polychrome tripod dishes. In IA and IB, reconstructible vessels included two Paxcamán dishes and four unslipped jars. Other artifactual material found throughout the late midden includes spindle whorls, mano and metate fragments (of limestone, granite, and vesicular basalt), net sinkers, and small quantities of such items as beads, bark beaters, chipped stone "axe" fragments, and chert and obsidian points, blades, and flakes.

Sherds of the Chilo ceramic group occurred in significant quantities primarily in the upper 20–30 cm of the midden deposit on the island, and partially reconstructible Chilo vessels and censers were recovered from midden in Operations IH, ID, and IB. The occurrence of these rather crudely made, poorly finished types in the upper portion of the midden on the island suggests a basis for formulation of a provisional Protohistoric Ayer ceramic complex. This complex includes Chilo as a principal identifying member, together with the continuation of Paxcamán, Topoxté, and Pozo material. The similarities of Chilo Unslipped to pottery made in the Petén lakes area up to the mid-twentieth century provide further support for this possibility (Reina and Hill 1978 : 143).

The number and status of individuals residing on the island during its various phases of construction and occupation cannot be determined with any certainty but probably involved no more than a few families. The mound itself is small, its surface area perhaps as little as 1000–1400 sq m, and only two structures are clearly visible on the mound surface today, enclosing an interior area of slightly less than 100 sq m of living space.

Comparison of the island construction and artifactual materials with those of some of the other Postclassic units around the lake basin, together with the fact that this settlement was on an island, suggests that the occupation may have been by individuals or families of comparatively high socioeconomic or sociopolitical standing, at least late in the sequence. The lakes area of Petén may have been a zone to which elites of the Classic centers repaired during the difficult transition period of the "collapse"; this is suggested by the presence of late stelae in these lacustrine (and riverine) areas. The easily defended islands and lakes of Petén continued to be religious and administrative centers throughout the Postclassic period, as is known by the abundance of censers and architectural complexes in these locations (D. Rice 1986). The differences between island and mainland pottery, particularly evident during the Terminal Classic period, may reflect differences in social status but could equally pertain to differing ethnic affiliations or exterior ties (see chapter 3). The test-pitting operations of neither Bullard nor CPHEP were of the sort to permit rigorous investigation of questions concerning function and status of the Macanché Island settlement.

Bullard's Other Excavations and Collections

Macanché Mainland

Besides his excavations on Macanché Island in 1968, Bullard also briefly worked at a small "ceremonial center" on the lakeshore. His notes are not clear about its location, and his map (fig. 24) shows little correspondence with structures at the other known center in the basin, Cerro Ortiz, on the southeastern shore. Similarities between his sketch map and a structure group on the north shore of the lake, in CPHEP transect 4, suggest that it might be the area where he worked. In addition to this group, he mentions a "nearby hilltop group with plain altar," but no altars were noted in CPHEP transects on the shore in 1979.

Bullard mapped and numbered seven structures at this "center," noting that the highest mounds, 1, 3, and 5, were approximately 3 m in height. Mound 5 "may have been vaulted, judging by shape of mound." His excavations were into Mound 6, a 30-m-long platform roughly 70 cm high in the northern part of the plaza at this "center," its long axis running east-west (fig. 25). On the northwestern corner of the top of the platform was a 30-cm-high wall or bench running halfway along the back edge of the mound and across most of the western edge. This "bench-type" structure is typical of Postclassic constructions in the lakes area (D. Rice 1986).

Test pit A, a 1.8-by-1.5-m excavation unit, was sunk into the upper center of the platform. The upper 30 cm contained most of the sherds of the pit; from 30 to 70 cm below surface the excavations encountered fill of large and small rocks and soil. No floors were identified. Test pit B was a 2-m sq pit "along south base wall. Possibly struck edge of stairs which are in poor condition. Base wall was large upright stones" (W. R. B., field notes, 19 March 1968). The last comment calls attention to another constructional characteristic of Petén Postclassic architecture, vertical stone placement. At 30 cm below surface in pit B, a plaster plaza floor was encountered; excavations proceeded only 10 cm below that floor. Only 68 selected sherds were saved from these excavations, out of a total of 187 from pit A and 97 from pit B; these were combined as Lot 29. The sherds were primarily Terminal Classic in date, although the presence of four Paxcamán sherds and one Chilo sherd supports the idea that this structure represents a Postclassic construction.

Ixlú

In 1968, Bullard also visited the site of Ixlú, a small center lying at the western end of Lake Salpetén. As originally mapped by Blom in 1924 (Morley 1937–38: plate 210a), the site was shown to have twenty structures and two stelae with late Cycle Ten dates. Specifically, these stelae dated 10.1.0.0.0 (A.D. 859) and 10.2.10.0.0 (A.D. 879), making them among the latest in Petén, and both bore Tikal emblem glyphs. The presence of these stelae is significant in terms of understanding the nature of the Classic-to-Postclassic transition in Petén. One important point is that the location of these and other Cycle Ten stelae in Petén underscores the role of

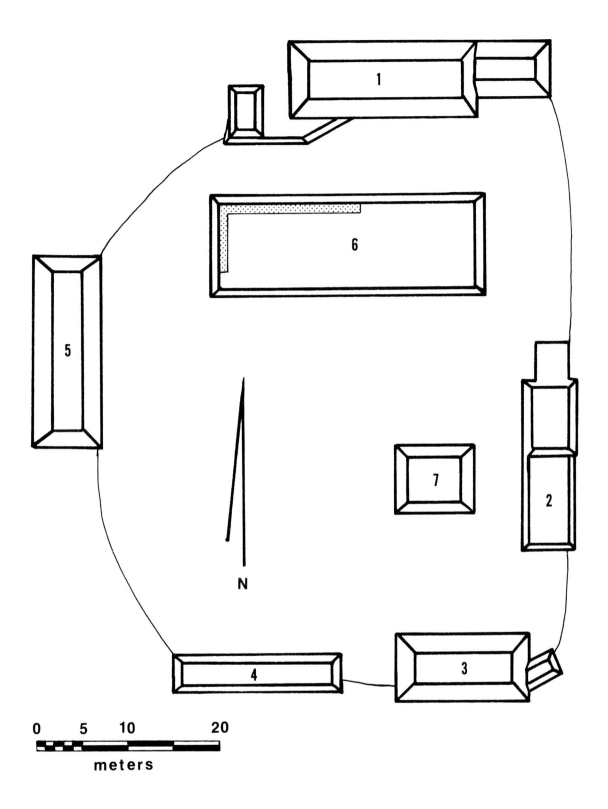

FIGURE 24. Map of a "small ceremonial center," traced from Bullard's original sketch. The location of this center is unspecified, but it is believed to be on the northern shore of the lake, in or near CPHEP Operation 4 (see figure 2).

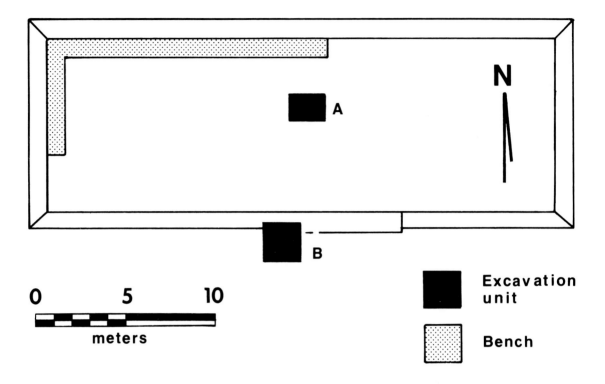

FIGURE 25. Location of Bullard's excavations into Mound 6 at the "small center" on the Lake Macanché mainland (figure 24).

lacustrine and riverine areas, peripheral to the main architectural centers of Classic civilization, as nodes of social and demographic continuity through the centers' collapse. In addition, the stelae demonstrate the presence in these areas of elite groups who were still able to commission the sculpture and erection of these monuments. The occurrence of the Tikal emblem glyph is of particular interest as a sign of political networks, paralleled by the peripheral affiliation of the Romero Terminal Classic ceramic complex with the Tikal-focused Eznab Tepeu 3 ceramic sphere.

When Ixlú was remapped by Proyecto Lacustre personnel in 1981, a total of 50 structures was revealed. Eleven had surface manifestations suggesting the typical Postclassic architectural forms noted elsewhere in the lakes area, such as at Zacpetén, Macanché, and Topoxté (see map, D. Rice 1986). No excavations were undertaken by Proyecto Lacustre to confirm the apparent Postclassic dating of these structures at Ixlú.

In 1968, Bullard placed two test pits into the principal mound at the site, a large pyramidal structure with a lower tier or apron, situated at the eastern end of the site. This structure was the location of four monuments at the time of Morley's visit, two stelae on the lower tier of the mound and two plain altars at its base. Bullard noted one sculptured stela on the lower tier in his 1968 map.

Bullard's test pit 2 was placed at the rear (east) end of the structure's lower tier approximately at the center of its north-south axis. The pit, 1.5 by 1.0 m in size, was excavated to a depth of 70 cm. A probable floor was encountered 50 cm below surface, but it was not well preserved. The artifacts recovered from the pit were few, small, and weathered and were not saved. Bullard's notes illustrate an unslipped bolstered jar rim that looks like rims of the Pozo group (Postclassic), but without the actual specimen it is difficult to say more about it.

Test pit 1 was a 2-m-sq pit into the plaza adjacent to the base of the mound, south of the altars (fig. 26). A "retaining wall," core face, or step was encountered in the eastern half of the pit, and Floor 1, the plaza floor, turned up to it. This floor, approximately 55 cm below surface, was unbroken and in excellent condition. A second floor lay 20 cm below Floor 2 but was found only in the north half of the pit and seemed to turn down. Floor 3 was encountered at a depth of 1 m below surface, and excavations terminated without penetrating this surface.

The pottery from the excavation of pit 1 was labeled lots 43–46. Lot 43, the uppermost, contains Chilo Unslipped but no Topoxté group material (its occurrence is rare in the Lake Petén-Itzá vicinity) and is assigned a Late Postclassic date. No Postclassic sherds were identified in the remaining lots, which included material from just above Floor 1, as well as below it to the level of Floor 3. Within these lower lots were large, well-preserved sherds of Late Classic polychromes, including lateral ridge plates and barrel-shaped vessels of orange, cream, and buff polychromes.

Miscellaneous

Small amounts of Postclassic artifacts were amassed by Bullard elsewhere in central Petén and were included in his collection at the Florida State Museum and/or referenced in his notes. A small number of sherds (n = 106) were collected from "mounds at sand pits" at Punta Nimá, on the north shore of the Tayasal Peninsula in Lake Petén-Itzá. Eight additional sherds, said to come from Punta Nimá and San Miguel, were purchased at the San Miguel market. These materials, comprising Bullard's lots 1, 2, and 3, were

useful for extending the range of forms and decorations in some of the Postclassic types, especially Augustine and Chilo, and a few are illustrated in this report.

The lower half of a stone "idol" (fig. 27), found by the caretaker for Antonio Ortiz' hotel, was said to come from the "water near point of Tayasal peninsula(?)." A small pottery "mask" (fig. 28) and effigy tripod foot, said to come from San Francisco, Petén (Lot 48), were purchased at Santa Elena. Finally, a "jar" or drum-like vessel (fig. 29) was in the possession of a citizen of Macanché village, who found it in a cave approximately 2 km southwest of the town. It is made of what Bullard termed in his notes "Macanché Red ware" (presumably equivalent to the red-slipped snail-inclusion paste Paxcamán group, for he notes that the paste had shell inclusions). The vessel had blue paint on the interior of the base. Inside it were a "trumpet foot" and "8 little pebbles . . . 3 of which appear to be quartz crystals." The vessel was sketched but not photographed.

Conclusions

Postclassic material culture in Petén, in terms of slipped and unslipped ceramics, censers, architecture, and lithics, is very distinctive. Despite this ease of recognition, however, a major problem in treating the Petén Postclassic has been to achieve a satisfactory chronology and stratigraphy. The artifacts from Bullard's 1968 project at Macanché, supplemented by the excavations and analyses of CPHEP, have largely resolved many of the difficulties.

Macanché Island was first occupied in the Late Classic period, and use of the island continued during the Terminal Classic "collapse" and throughout the entire Postclassic period. Table 2 presents the available dates, from radiocarbon and obsidian hydration analyses, for the occupation and construction episodes on Macanché Island.

No Colonial or European artifacts have been found in clear association with any known Postclassic pottery types at Macanché or elsewhere in central Petén (cf. Chase

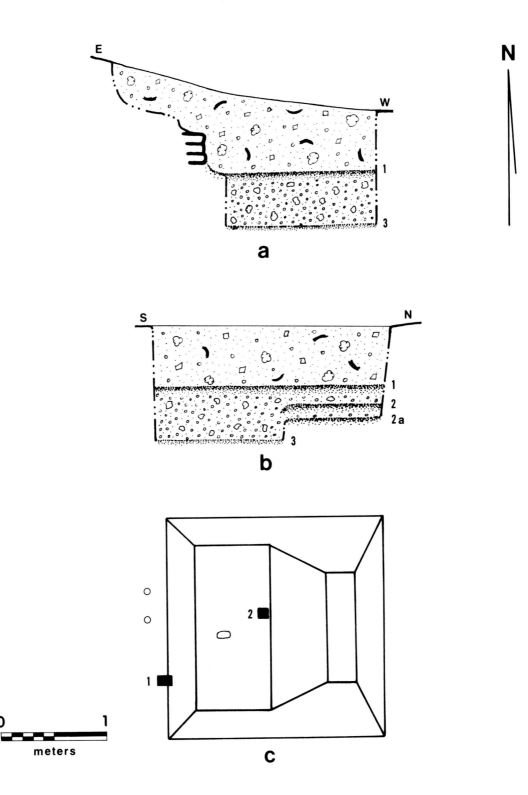

FIGURE 26. Bullard's test pit 1 at the base of the large mound at Ixlú, situated to the west of Lake Salpetén. Numbers denote floors. **a**, South profile showing step or retaining wall to east. **b**, West profile. **c**, Mound and position of tests (numbered solid squares) and monuments (circles), not to scale. See key in figure 5.

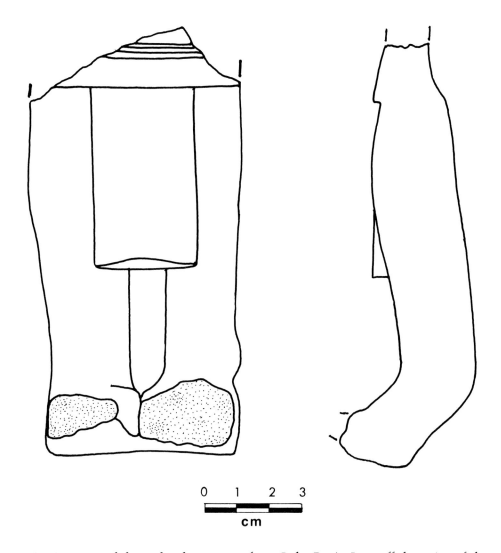

0   1   2   3
cm

FIGURE 27. A stone "idol" said to have come from Lake Petén-Itza, off the point of the
          Tayasal peninsula, Lot 47. Front and side views. Traced from Bullard's notes.

1983:779 for mention of a single majolica sherd at Tayasal). The late mission site of Negroman-Tipú in western Belize is the closest location of recovery of European olive jars and majolica sherds in association with Paxcamán, Topoxté, and Pozo ceramic groups (P. Rice 1985a). Because of the lack of European artifacts at Petén sites, it is nearly impossible to determine whether any Postclassic sites in the lakes area investigated by CPHEP may have experienced direct contact with Spanish visitors. Thus far, there is nothing in the artifactual evidence to suggest that sporadic Spanish intrusions had any impact on ceramic production in Petén in general or in the central Maya lowlands as a whole. Indeed, the relative poverty of the Yucatán Peninsula as a Colonial Spanish enclave (Farriss 1984:30–39), in contrast to areas such as central Mexico, leads to the conclusion that the Spaniards invested little in transforming the local economy or productive enterprises, such as pottery making.

The lack of European artifacts or modi-

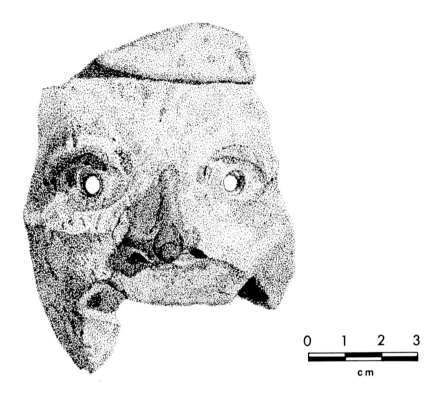

FIGURE 28. A pottery "mask" said to be from San Francisco, Petén, Lot 48. Drawing by Jill
Loucks.

fications of native wares along European lines at Postclassic Petén sites has made it difficult to establish an ending date for the Postclassic/Protohistoric periods in Petén. The latest obsidian hydration date obtained for the lakes area comes from the heavy Postclassic settlement on the Zacpetén peninsula in Lake Salpetén, where an obsidian artifact was dated A.D. 1532 ± 26 years, or A.D. 1506–1558 (P. Rice n.d. a).

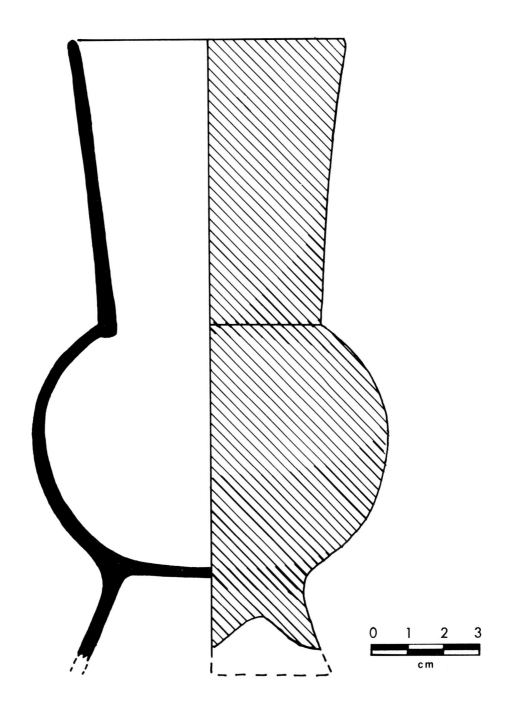

FIGURE 29. A "jar" or vase found in a cave south of Macanché village, described by Bullard as "Macanché Red ware." Traced from Bullard's notes.

PART II

Terminal Classic and Postclassic Pottery Type Descriptions

CHAPTER 3

The Terminal Classic Romero Ceramic Complex at Macanché Island

TERMINAL Classic pottery from Macanché Island and the Romero complex itself were first named and described by Bullard (1973: 227–28). The complex is described here on the basis of over 3,000 sherds from eight lots (lots 6, 11, and 12 from Operation IA, Lot 32 from IG, and lots 38 [mixed], 40 [mixed], 41, and 42 from IH) excavated by Bullard. In addition, over 1,100 sherds of identifiable Late Classic or Terminal Classic types were counted in the material from Postclassic core and midden in Bullard's excavations; most of these Terminal Classic sherds were from Early Postclassic contexts.

Of the sherds in Bullard's Terminal Classic lots, 26.2 percent are slipped types, 20.7 percent are ash paste sherds that may have originally been slipped, and 45.6 percent are unslipped (another 3.5 percent are unidentifiable as to type; 3.6 percent are Postclassic intrusions; and 0.4 percent are Preclassic or Late Classic types). It is useful to compare the Macanché frequencies with those at Tikal, where Culbert (1973b:81) noted that the Eznab complex consisted of 26 percent Tinaja (red-slipped) group, less than 5 percent Achote group (black-slipped), and 15 percent Encanto Striated. At Macanché Island, the comparable figures (excluding uni-

dentifiable and Preclassic types) are 12.9 percent for Tinaja, 5.8 percent for Achote, and 5.7 percent for Encanto. The frequency of the Tinaja group at Macanché Island would be increased, of course, if some or all of the ash paste sherds were presumed to represent that group.

Many of the Terminal Classic sherds recovered from Bullard's excavations into these contexts are large and can be fitted together into partially reconstructible vessels. Of particular interest are partially reconstructible Tinaja Red jars, large Subín Red incurved-rim bowls, Cambio Unslipped: Coarse Gray Variety jars, and small Largo (Harina group) Red-on-cream bowls, which were found in lots 6 and 11 in Operation IA, and in Lot 41 in Operation IH. The presence of these materials in the white and grayish marl or tierra blanca deposits on the island suggests primary breakage. This does not appear to have been midden accumulation, judging from the relative lack of bone and organic discoloration.

Despite the apparent primary deposition, there is a strong possibility of mixing in some of these Romero lots. Of the more than 3,000 sherds from Bullard's Terminal Classic lots, 111 (3.6 percent) are Postclassic types.

The interpretive problems occur primarily with lots 38 and 40, which account for 84 of the 111 Postclassic sherds. These units are not sealed from later overlying material: Lot 40 is a "marl" level underlying later midden; Lot 38 is a deposit of marl and rock described as "mixed" in Bullard's notes, which underlies platform construction. Given the lack of a seal between these levels to preserve the integrity of the earlier material, and considering the nature of the activity involved in accumulating the later deposits, it is not difficult to understand how mixing between earlier and later strata in these and other lots could occur.

The problem for interpretation of these mixed materials lies in dating the beginnings of manufacture and use of two Postclassic pottery categories, the Augustine ceramic group (see Bullard 1973:227; P. Rice 1979:75) and the Daylight ceramic group. Two diagnostic Augustine vessel supports (the only ones found at the island) were recovered from lots 11 and 38, but no Augustine sherd dated to the Terminal Classic period was represented in CPHEP lots from Macanché Island. Their presence in the lots from Bullard's excavations is regarded as intrusive. Sixteen sherds tentatively identified as Darknight Variety of Daylight Orange type and representing two or three dishes were recovered from lots 6 and 11 in Operation IA. The identification of this material as belonging to the Daylight group is uncertain, and its presence in the Terminal Classic is problematical. Besides these sherds, only two other sherds of the group were recovered on the island, and those were in mixed Lot 10. No Daylight group sherds were identified in CPHEP excavations.

The presence of eight grater bowl sherds in these lots is also problematical. Although this vessel form per se is known in the greater Petén area prior to the Postclassic period (at Seibal in Tinaja Red and Achote Black [Sabloff 1975:180–181, 185], and in the Dolorido and Tinaja groups at Becan in the early facet Xcocom complex [Ball 1977:88, 90]), the ones in the Romero complex at Macanché represent the Trapeche and Paxcamán ceramic groups of the Postclassic period. Among the graters were four fragments of a single yellowish brown ash paste Paxcamán group (Picú Incised: Thub Variety) bowl (see chapter 6, "Pastes and Slips of the Paxcamán and Trapeche Ceramic Groups") from Lot 41, a lot that contained numerous reconstructible Terminal Classic vessels and appears to represent primary deposition.

Sphere Identification

Bullard (1973:228) had initially pointed to ties of the Macanché Terminal Classic ceramic materials—particularly on the basis of forms—to the Boca Terminal Classic ceramic sphere of the Pasión area of Petén. On other criteria, however, the materials can be used to argue equally for membership in the Eznab ceramic sphere of the central Petén. The Tinaja group is particularly interesting in this regard, because both the Eznab and Boca spheres share an emphasis on the types in this group and at Macanché the Tinaja group vessels share traits of both spheres.

With respect to ties to the Boca sphere, the Tinaja group at Macanché includes significant quantities of Subín Red bowls (14.1 percent) which are associated with the Pasión area. In addition, the Tinaja Red jars at Macanché have indented bases, a characteristic noted previously only in the Pasión region. Finally, a relatively small number of sherds within Tinaja Red have carbonate pastes, yet another trait tying the Romero complex to Boca, because calcite pastes have not been commonly observed in this type elsewhere in the central part of Petén. Arguing against strong affiliation of Romero with Boca, however, is the fact that most of the Tinaja group sherds at Macanché are tempered with volcanic ash, as are those within the Eznab sphere.

With respect to types and groups other than Tinaja, the evidence is more strongly in support of Eznab sphere identification. For example, the Romero complex at Macanché includes negligible amounts (one sherd) of Fine Orange wares; finewares were a significant diagnostic component of Pasión Terminal Classic assemblages, however. (Fine Orange was present in highly variable but always very small quantities in the other central Petén lake basins surveyed by CPHEP.) Also, CPHEP excavations in the lakes area did not yield Lombriz Orange Polychrome, which is found in the Pasión region (although it should be noted that Macanché Island is almost entirely lacking in polychrome pottery of any sort in the Terminal Classic period).

The occurrence of striated pottery at Macanché is equivocal with respect to answering questions of sphere affiliation. Encanto Striated is present in relatively small amounts at Macanché Island, but its occurrence there is considerably greater than elsewhere in the lakes region. Because striated jars were a significant component of Late Classic assemblages in the Pasión region, their presence in the Romero complex may be an additional, though weak, bit of evidence favoring ties to the Boca sphere.

I decided to include the Romero complex as a peripheral member of the Eznab sphere rather than within the Boca sphere. This affiliation is based primarily on the dominance of volcanic ash tempering in the Tinaja group (as well as in other eroded sherds that may be part of that group) and on the absence of significant quantities of fine paste wares in Romero. It is acknowledged, however, that this lack may simply be a function of Macanché's "rural" status, Fine Orange being more typically associated with large stela-bearing centers. (The presence of the Tikal emblem glyph on Cycle Ten stelae at Ixlú, however, may be another line of argument for stronger Eznab rather than Boca [Pasión] affiliations.) In addition, cream-slipped and red-on-cream decorations (Harina group) in the Romero complex at Macanché also support closer ties to central or northeastern Petén polychrome traditions.

There is doubtless some significance to be attached to the fact that the major ties of the Romero complex to the Pasión area exist almost exclusively in the forms and pastes of ceramic types in a single slipped group, the Tinaja group. The vessels of interest are the jars and large bowls probably used in serving or food-preparation tasks. Besides these, the only other comparison worth noting is the slight emphasis on striation in utility jars. Whatever the nature of any putative relationship with the Pasión area that is indicated by these ceramic ties, it does not appear to be based on the introduction or trade of "elite" or "exotic" pottery, given the general lack of Fine Orange. Rather, it is based on shared modes within otherwise standard and widespread utilitarian or functional categories.

One of the puzzling aspects of the Terminal Classic period pottery in the Lake Macanché basin as a whole is that there appear to be differences between the material on the mainland and that recovered from the island. The Terminal Classic assemblage recovered from the CPHEP excavations on the mainland shows closer affinities to Eznab Terminal Classic pottery from throughout the lake basins, while pottery from the island is somewhat different. Mainland materials include Jato Black-on-gray type, a distinctive firing variant (Canjil) in the Tinaja group (see below), and greater quantities of the typical pastes and forms associated with Late and Terminal Classic polychromes and monochromes. The pottery from the island, on the other hand, is distinctive both typologically and technologically. Technological variations in paste and firing have in some cases been accorded classificatory recognition (for example, a group of very coarse, thick, poorly finished unslipped sherds is designated as "Coarse Gray Variety" of Cambio Unslipped).

The differences between mainland and island pottery assemblages may be related to ethnicity, status, trade, function, or temporal factors, or some combination of these. It was suggested earlier (chapter 2) that the island may have been occupied by groups of relatively high socioeconomic status later in the Postclassic period, but it is difficult to determine if this might also have been the case in the Terminal Classic period. On neither the island nor the mainland is there clearly identifiable elite pottery, such as Fine Orange or polychromes, to demonstrate political, economic, or social affiliations with either the Pasión or Tikal (or other) areas. The Terminal Classic period in Petén is still poorly understood at both centers and rural areas alike, but it seems to have been a time of transition politically and demographically. In this atmosphere, there are likely to have been ephemeral sociopolitical alliances, settlement shifts, and microregional variations in material culture that will remain murky and opaque in the archaeologist's eye for some time to come.

No clear Terminal Classic phasing or sphere affiliation could be claimed for the material in the ceramic collections Bullard obtained from Ixlú and Punta Nimá. The distinctive ceramic groups, types, and varieties occurring in the Romero phase at Macanché Island—Harina, Payaso, Coarse Gray Cambio—were not recovered at these areas. At Ixlú, Lot 44 was immediately above, and lots 45 and 46 were within, platform core in front of the main pyramid; the pottery from this excavation suggests a Late Classic (Tepeu 2) date of construction of the plaza. These levels, together with the surface Lot 43 containing Postclassic sherds, also yielded quantities of Late Classic polychromes, but none of the typical Terminal Classic diagnostics widely noted elsewhere in the lakes district, such as the Canjil paste or firing variant (see below) or Jato Black-on-gray, was identified. A thick, heavy, fire-clouded Tinaja Red jar with an indented base was included in the collection from Punta Nimá, however.

Vessel forms represented by the polychromes from Ixlú and Punta Nimá were primarily tripod plates (many with lateral ridge) and barrel-shaped jars, although hemispherical bowls and a cylinder were also included. The types represented by these materials are tentatively suggested to be those of the Saxché and Palmar ceramic groups, including probably Palmar (?) Orange Polychrome, Paixban (?) Buff Polychrome, and Zacatel (?) Cream Polychrome. These vessels do not, strictly speaking, belong to the types or periods relevant to understanding the Macanché Island collection, but because they were recovered as part of Bullard's 1968 project they are described here.

Technological Characteristics

In general, the technological characteristics of Terminal Classic Romero complex pottery suggest a rather poor or careless level of manufacturing control that is particularly related to firing procedures (cf. Culbert 1973b:82). Most of the pastes on the island are gray—in fact they look like minor variations on a single carbonate-tempered gray paste—which suggests incomplete oxidation (in firing) of an organic-rich clay. Although there is some resemblance to later wares of the Paxcamán and Trapeche groups (see below), these Terminal Classic materials lack the distinctive fragments of snail shell that are characteristic of the Postclassic ceramic groups. Fire-clouding is common in the surface coloration of many of the types (e.g., Payaso Orange-brown), a trait that is also common in early facet Early Postclassic Paxcamán and Trapeche group pottery (see P. Rice 1980:79); it too implies poor firing control. The slips of many of the groups (e.g., Harina, Achote, and some of the Tinaja material, especially that with gray paste) are thin and streaky; surface finishing in slipped wares (especially gray paste sherds of the Tinaja group) is poor, exhibiting drag marks and scraping facets. Breaks along coil fractures are common, particularly in the large Subín Red incurved-rim bowls.

On the other side of the coin, much of the Terminal Classic Romero complex pottery (including gray pastes) is thin-walled and very hard. Usually it is the ash-tempered pastes that are harder and have a "ring" when tapped (cf. Culbert 1973b:81). An example of this phenomenon is what I have named the

"Canjil" paste or firing variant of the Tinaja group. The Canjil firing variant is an unusual and easily recognizable bright pinkish orange color; the vessels are moderately thick, hard, ash-tempered, and apparently relatively well fired. Canjil paste occurs in tiny but regular amounts in characteristic Tinaja forms in late deposits in all lake basins. It is worthwhile to note, however, that at Macanché Island, although they are associated with Terminal Classic forms, the Canjil sherds are found stratigraphically in Postclassic deposits rather than in Terminal Classic contexts. In any case, the existence of this and other hard ash pastes in the Terminal Classic period suggests achievement of a certain kind of technical superiority, above and beyond mere accidental "overfiring."

The significance of the technological variability in Terminal Classic pottery from Macanché Island is difficult to assess. In part it may simply reflect the much greater quantity of material excavated from the two projects undertaken on the island compared to that from the few locations of Terminal Classic occupation sampled by CPHEP excavations on the mainland. What may be significant, though, is that some of these characteristics—e.g., gray pastes, fire-clouding—are also common in the succeeding early facet Early Postclassic Aura complex. Whether this is indicative of production by relatively unskilled potters, the use of new slip and clay resources, the use of new fuels, or some combination of all these changes is indeterminate at present.

Many of the traits described above, however, such as poor firing control and streaky slips, suggest "transitional" or developmental links between Terminal Classic and Postclassic ceramics, both typologically and technologically. These traits are particularly evident in the Harina (cream) ceramic group, which may be a predecessor to the Trapeche (pink) group, and in gray pastes (not given formal varietal status) within the Tinaja group. In turn, this latter category suggests, by virtue of paste and slip characteristics (fire-clouded and generally dark red in color),

a relationship to the Postclassic Paxcamán red-slipped group.

Summary

Overall, the Terminal Classic Romero ceramic complex material from Macanché Island (table 3) is characterized principally by the presence of the Tinaja (red) group and its constituent types, represented by jars and large bowls with incurving rims, in addition to the following:

(1) A body of cream-slipped sherds, including a red-on-cream decorated type, designated as the Harina group. This group seems to be part of the general Petén Late Classic "gloss ware" tradition in decoration and forms, which are primarily small hemispherical or slightly restricted orifice bowls.

(2) Small quantities of Encanto Striated. Only one sherd of a distinctive "herringbone" pattern of striation was noted.

(3) A thick, coarse, crudely finished unslipped ware. Probably a local late variant of Cambio Unslipped, it has been given a varietal designation as Coarse Gray Variety within that type.

(4) Small quantities of Achote Black. The slip varies from strong glossy black to streaky, creamy or almost pearly gray, with a dull or matte finish. Vessels include large open bowls or basins with a rounded lip, and narrow-neck jars.

(5) A tan, hard ash paste used for slipped, polished, very thin-walled vessels. Classified as Payaso Orange-brown type, these sherds exhibit heavily fire-clouded surface colors ranging from yellow-orange to brown (often greenish) and gray-black. Large sherds suggest jars; one sherd has an indented base, but no rims were found.

(6) A similar tan, hard, volcanic ash paste commonly occurring in jars and large bowls. Jars had indented bases and were apparently unslipped and unpolished but had very smooth, well-finished surfaces. This material has not been given a type designation; some of it may be eroded, weathered examples of Tinaja Red.

(7) The apparent absence of polychromes.

Table 3

Frequency of Ceramic Units of the Terminal Classic Romero Complex at Macanché Island

| | Frequency | | | | |
| | Macanché Island | | | | |
	Terminal Classic	Post-classic	Other	Total	Percent of Group
Petén Gloss Ware					
Tinaja Ceramic Group					
Tinaja Red: Variety Unspecified	315	216	64	595	83.1
Subín Red: Variety Unspecified	57	39	5	101	14.1
Cameron Incised: Variety Unspecified		12		12	1.7
Chaquiste Impressed: Variety Unspecified		2	3	5	0.7
Pantano Impressed: Pantano Variety		1	2	3	0.4
Total Tinaja Group	372	270	74	716	100.0
Achote Ceramic Group					
Achote Black: Variety Unspecified	167	8	7	182	100.0
Harina Ceramic Group					
Harina Cream: Harina Variety	126	73		199	86.9
Largo Red-on-cream: Largo Variety	27	3		30	13.1
Total Harina Group	153	76		229	100.0
Payaso Ceramic Group					
Payaso Orange-brown: Payaso Variety	105	1		106	100.0
Danta Ceramic Group					
Jato Black-on-gray: Variety Unspecified	1			1	100.0
San Pablo Gloss Ware					
Daylight Ceramic Group					
Daylight Orange: Darknight Variety (?)	14	2		16	100.0
Fine Orange Paste Ware					
Altar Ceramic Group					
Altar Orange: Variety Unspecified	1			1	100.0
Uaxactún Unslipped Ware					
Cambio Ceramic Group					
Cambio Unslipped: Variety Unspecified	255	51	9	315	20.0
Cambio Unslipped: Coarse Gray Variety	999	12		1,011	64.2
Encanto Striated: Variety Unspecified	164	72	13	249	15.8
Total Cambio Group	1,418	135	22	1,575	100.0

These may have been present at Macanché Island but are not identifiable because of the erosion of sherd surfaces (particularly those Late Classic sherds from early platform construction levels).

(8) The apparent absence of censers. Although hourglass censers with appliquéd spikes and/or fillets are common in Terminal Classic assemblages elsewhere in Petén, they do not occur in the Romero complex.

In summary, Terminal Classic materials from Macanché reflect a characteristic noted in the lakes area in general (P. Rice 1986), on the Tayasal peninsula (A. Chase 1979: 94–95), and at Tikal (Culbert 1973b: 81–82), and that trait is variability. There seems to be a considerable degree of variability on a regional scale, with differences in occurrence of types and modes from site to site; within sites, variability is also evident in technical skills employed in slipping, painting, and firing the pottery. It may be this inconsistency of quality that led Gifford to comment that the late material from Barton Ramie was composed of "a rag-tag of crudely fashioned unslipped odds and ends very difficult to classify" (Willey et al. 1965:384).

The "rural" Macanché area is distinguished by the near total absence of Terminal Classic markers associated with elites and large centers elsewhere in Petén, although these are present in somewhat greater quantities at some of the other lakes. Most notably missing from the island and mainland is trade pottery (Plumbate, Slatewares, Modeled-carved, and Fine Orange in general) and polychromes (especially particular motifs such as the "dress shirt" or feather motif). All of these would provide evidence of ties not only to large centers within Petén but also to spheres of contact beyond (e.g., Cehpech- or Sotuta-related influences from Yucatán). Despite the absence of these exotic or elite items, much of the pottery that is associated with the Romero complex at Macanché Island is thin-walled and hard-fired and, except for the erosion of vessel surfaces, appears to be technically well made.

I have suggested elsewhere (P. Rice 1986) that the archaeological data from Macanché Island and the lakes area in general argue for continuity of habitation from the Late Classic period through the Terminal Classic and into the Postclassic. The settlement data in the lake basins support this point (D. Rice 1986), as do the obsidian hydration and radiocarbon dates presented in table 2. Another line of evidence is presented by the pottery (cf. Willey 1973:101), in which the gray carbonate pastes and fire-clouded surfaces of some of the Terminal Classic material, particularly the Tinaja and Harina groups, argue for technological continuity into the Postclassic period.

It is tempting to speculate from this Terminal Classic ceramic assemblage that the ash-tempered vessels, especially those of the Tinaja group and the unnamed ash paste, may have been brought into the basin from other producing locations. (These areas may have been situated near the large centers, which were still able to import quantities of volcanic ash in the Terminal Classic period.)

The gray carbonate pastes, on the other hand, may represent local manufactures: potters used locally available lacustrine clays that are high in organic matter and marly and encountered some difficulties in achieving proper firing. Increasing experience and familiarity with these clays led to modifications in processing, firing, and surface finishing which eventually culminated in widespread use of the characteristic gray-to-light-brown snail-inclusion carbonate paste for manufacture of Postclassic pottery in the lakes area (see chapter 6, "Pastes and Slips of the Paxcamán and Trapeche Ceramic Groups").

Bullard remarked on the regional ceramic variability and discontinuous distribution of "Period I" pottery of the Central Petén Postclassic Tradition, evidenced at the two sites where he had worked, Topoxté and Macanché. He felt that "perhaps Yaxhá and Macanché were held by Terminal Classic groups antagonistic to the makers of the new pottery" (Bullard 1973:230). The larger body of information now available on Terminal Classic settlement distributions in the lakes area reveals that the situation is a good deal more complex than it appeared to be in 1973. The nature of Terminal Classic activities is likely to be very different at Yaxhá/Topoxté than at Macanché, in part because of the presence of the large Yaxhá center on the north shore of the lake. These considerations notwithstanding, the variability in ceramic styles at Petén Terminal Classic sites, and the differential access to exotic wares at these locations, suggests that if there was not a situation of outright antagonism, there were at least different spheres of interaction and participation in exchange. Judging from the differences between Macanché Island and the mainland, these may have existed on a microscale.

Macanché Island seems to be unusual in receiving apparent influences from the Pasión area that are evident in red-slipped wares at the two areas. This is unusual in the broader context of the central Petén lakes, for at Tayasal there was a lack of ceramic similarity with the south and ties were to the north instead (Chase and Chase 1983: 106). Furthermore, the occurrence on an island of these nonlocal elements, together with traits indicating technological continuities with the Postclassic period, suggests that the island served as a defensible location or a refuge during what might have been a difficult transitional period, culminating in a nearly exclusive focus on island settlement in the following centuries.

CHAPTER 4

Type-Variety Descriptions of the Pottery of the Romero Ceramic Complex

Tinaja Ceramic Group

The Tinaja ceramic group constitutes 12.5 percent of the Terminal Classic sherds in Terminal Classic deposits excavated by Bullard at Macanché Island. It is represented primarily by two types in both Bullard's and CPHEP lots, Tinaja Red and Subín Red. In his initial comments on the occurrence of the Tinaja group at Macanché, Bullard (1973: 228) also mentioned the presence of Cameron Incised and Pantano Impressed, but these are very rare at the site and were recovered from Postclassic rather than Terminal Classic lots (as was the Canjil firing variant). Similarly, only two sherds of Chaquiste Impressed type were noted in Bullard's excavations, and one of these was in a Postclassic lot. I have not given varietal designations to most of this material, and even the type identifications are tentative, being based on paste and form alone in many cases, as the slip has generally eroded off (see Sabloff 1975: 161, 168).

Except for jars, the forms within this group—particularly the large incurved-rim bowls of Subín Red, Chaquiste Impressed, and Cameron Incised types—at Macanché Island are very similar to material recovered elsewhere in Petén during the Late and Terminal Classic periods. In slip and paste characteristics, however, some of this material is distinctive, different from that at other lakes in Petén, and especially different from that at Yaxhá. To what extent these differences may be due to postdepositional alteration, I cannot say.

Few sherds have their slips preserved. On some of these the slip is the dark red, sometimes fire-clouded, low-luster slip commonly seen elsewhere in the lakes area. It is generally associated with hard, well-fired, thin-walled, gritty, ash-tempered pastes that are usually light brown in color but sometimes are light gray. On other sherds the slip is an orange or brownish red and sometimes has a streaky, faded appearance; these slips are typically associated with slightly darker (more reddish brown) and thicker ash pastes.

The greatest variability is evident in the pastes associated with the Tinaja group pottery at Macanché Island. Much of the material, especially the large bowls, is of a hard ("clinky"), gritty, volcanic-ash-tempered paste, usually light gray to tan in color. A small percentage of the sherds appears to have been made of the same dark-gray, thin-walled, carbonate-tempered paste used in making Harina (cream) group pottery, a paste that I feel may be an antecedent to that used for the later Trapeche and Paxcamán groups of the Postclassic period. Finally, a very small number of Tinaja group sherds were of a distinctive bright pinkish orange, very hard, ash-tempered paste; this is apparently a firing variant of the standard light gray ash paste, because both colors are sometimes seen on the same sherd. This firing variant, which I have named Canjil paste, is an easily recognizable marker for Terminal Classic (or later) material at all the lakes surveyed by CPHEP, although nowhere does it occur in significant quantities.

To these comments on paste in the Tinaja

group at Macanché should be added the observation that in general there seems to be a great deal of slip and paste variability in this group throughout Petén, especially in the Terminal Classic period. Culbert has named two paste variants, the standard Tinaja paste and Taman paste (the latter being used also in manufacture ´of Sahcabá Modeled-carved pottery); both of these are volcanic-ash-tempered and are recognizable by hardness and "ring" when tapped. At Yaxhá, at least four pastes were noted: one is equivalent to Culbert's buff-colored Taman, one is Canjil, one is the light gray-to-brown ash paste described above (Culbert's Tinaja paste?), and the last is very similar to the cream-colored paste used in later manufacture of Postclassic Topoxté group pottery.

At Seibal, on the other hand, the paste of Tinaja Red is calcite- or "sand"-tempered (Sabloff 1975:158), and although forms are identical with those described elsewhere, no mention is made of the distinctive hardness noted in specimens of the central Petén ash-tempered paste variants. Ejército Red, however, another red-slipped type dating to the Late Classic (Pasión complex) and Terminal Classic (Boca complex) phases at Altar de Sacrificios, was distinguished by its hardness and "ring" when tapped (R. Adams 1971:23–24).

The presence of these paste variations argues for the existence of competing production units of Tinaja group pottery and for distribution primarily within the region dominated by a large center. While many of the paste variants appear to be highly localized (e.g., a cream-colored paste at Yaxhá), others are traded in minor (Canjil) to significant (the Tinaja paste) quantities within a region. There is not a sufficient amount of information available on the occurrence of these pastes in Petén to assess their implications for Late and Terminal Classic commodity distribution, however.

Name. **Tinaja Red: Variety Unspecified.**
Frequency: 595 sherds, of which 531 were from Bullard's excavations at Macanché Is-

land (of these, 315 were from Terminal Classic deposits and 216 from Postclassic lots); also 17 sherds from the mainland "center," 44 from Ixlú, and 3 from Punta Nimá. Tinaja Red constitutes 83.1 percent of the Tinaja ceramic group in Bullard's collections.

Ware: Petén Gloss ware.
Complex: Romero ceramic complex.
Established: The Tinaja type and group were established by Smith and Gifford (1966; R. E. Smith 1955) at Uaxactún.
Principal identifying modes: Tinaja Red type is identified by red slips on a variety of vessel forms, principally jars.
Paste and firing: The paste of the Tinaja group as a whole is highly variable, as noted, although at Macanché Island and elsewhere there appear to be two gross paste categories represented. One is a thin-walled, dark gray carbonate paste similar to that used in the Harina group. This is in turn similar to that used in the later Postclassic Paxcamán and Trapeche groups.

The other paste variant, occurring far more commonly, is a hard ("clinky"), volcanic-ash-tempered paste, usually light brown (7.5YR 6/6 to 10YR 7/4) but occasionally gray (7.5YR 4–5/0) in color. The paste is dense and compact, though not particularly fine textured; sparse inclusions of white and light tan pumice/ash particles range up to 2 mm in size. Gold mica particles are occasionally visible. The slip has eroded off many of the ash paste specimens, but evidence of fire-clouded slips, plus pronounced variations in paste color from the vessel exterior to interior when seen in cross section, suggest poor control of firing.

Nine ash-tempered sherds exhibited an unusually high temperature or well oxidized firing (Canjil firing variant), having light red ("pink") colors of 10YR 5–6/8, rarely 7.5YR 6/4. These sherds were all recovered from mixed material in Postclassic lots on the island rather than in Terminal Classic contexts.

Surface treatment and decoration: Surfaces are generally very well smoothed on the interior and exterior prior to application

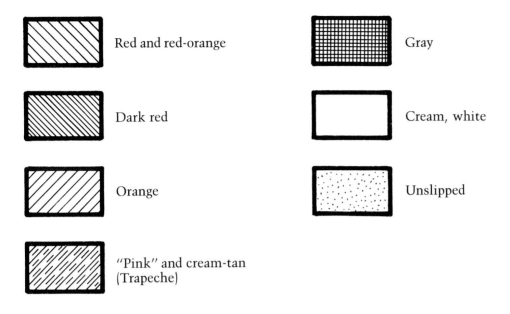

FIGURE 30. Key to conventions used in slipped pottery illustrations.

of the slip. Sherds of the gray carbonate paste variant are an exception to this, often being poorly smoothed with scraping or burnishing facets and drag marks visible on the surface. The red slips vary in color and quality and in general are very eroded, so that much of the variability may be due to postdepositional alteration. Colors are often fire-clouded. Well-preserved samples (rare) are red (10YR 5/6–8 to 2.5YR 4/6–8), but firing effects and erosion cause colors to vary around 2.5YR 3–5/4 as well. The slip is often finely crazed where fire-clouding is severe. Small but diagnostic amounts of Terminal Classic Tinaja Red material at Macanché, Ixlú, and the lakes in general have a distinctly orange-brown slip, varying to 5YR 5/8, which typically occurs on deeper brown ash-tempered pastes.

Forms and dimensions: The Macanché Island Tinaja Red sherds exhibit a reduced form repertoire compared to that at other sites in Petén, such as Tikal or Yaxhá. No small plates or bowls were found, the majority of sherds suggesting medium-sized jars. The bodies of these jars are rather squat and globular, rather than elongate as at Altar de Sacrificios (R. E. W. Adams 1973: fig. 15), and the bases are indented. Slips on the rims and bases were eroded off, but by paste and form (comparison with materials from other sites) the sherds are presumed to be of Tinaja Red type. Most rims indicate jars with medium outflaring necks and thinned, unelaborated lips; the mouth diameter of one specimen appears to be about 14 cm, while the average interior neck diameter is 8 cm. Other jar necks have wider mouths, higher necks, and flat, squared-off rims; mouth diameters (two vessels) are 21 cm. Wall thickness varies. Gray carbonate paste sherds are generally thin-walled (ca. 4 mm); the larger numbers of ash paste sherds are both more variable and greater in thickness, varying from 5 to 9 mm, most falling between 6 and 7 mm. Two rim sherds were from restricted orifice bowls; one small bowl with an incised lip was recovered from Punta Nimá.

Illustration: figure 31.

Intrasite references: Tinaja Red was found in all Terminal Classic deposits on the island, as well as in Postclassic deposits. Three

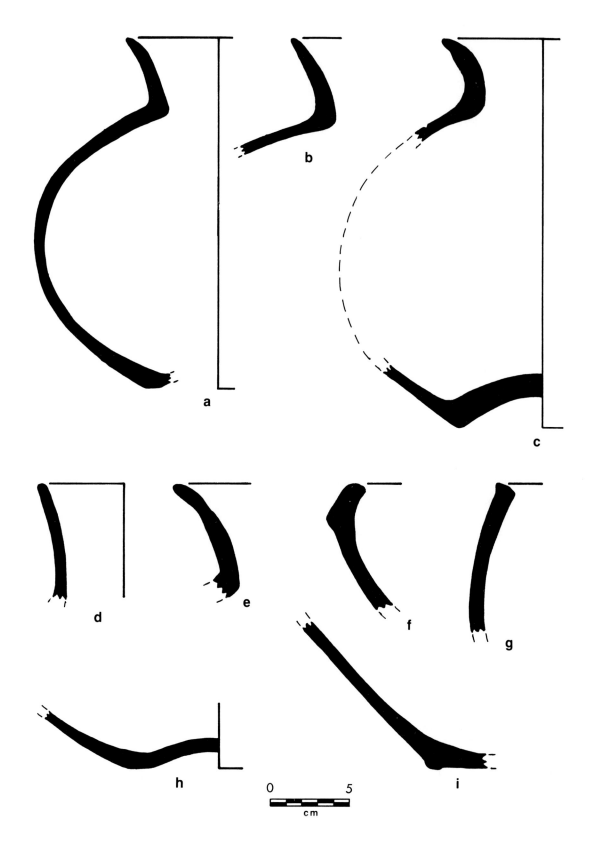

FIGURE 31. Tinaja Red: Varieties Unspecified.

partially reconstructible vessels—two jars and one bowl—were among the materials exhibiting primary breakage in Operation IH.

Intersite references: Tinaja Red is the standard red monochrome type of the Late and Terminal Classic periods throughout Petén, appearing at Uaxactún (R. Smith 1955), Tikal (Culbert 1973b), Seibal (Sabloff 1975), Altar de Sacrificios (R. E. W. Adams 1971), and Yaxhá (personal observation). Tinaja vessels were also represented in Bullard's collections from Punta Nimá, including a large, thick, heavy, fire-clouded jar with indented base. At most of the Petén sites, a number of different varieties have been named on the basis of paste variations. Only at Altar de Sacrificios is there a specific reference to a jar with an indented base in the Boca complex (R. E. W. Adams 1971: fig. 58b). It is difficult to determine whether this basal form existed elsewhere because for the most part jar bases are not illustrated. Rare indented base sherds and one sherd of Canjil paste have been noted at Negroman-Tipú in western Belize (personal observation).

Name: **Subín Red: Variety Unspecified.**
Frequency: 101 sherds, of which 96 were from Bullard's excavations on Macanché Island (57 of these were from Terminal Classic lots and 39 from Postclassic lots); also 5 sherds from Ixlú and Punta Nimá. Subín Red constitutes 14.1 percent of the sherds of the Tinaja ceramic group in Bullard's collections.
Ware: Petén Gloss ware.
Complex: Romero ceramic complex.
Established: Subín Red was established as a type in the Subín ceramic group by R. E. W. Adams (1971: 22–23) on the basis of material recovered from Altar de Sacrificios; at Seibal the red-slipped bowls of Subín were identified as a type within the Tinaja ceramic group (Sabloff 1975: 163).
Principal identifying modes: Subín Red type consists of large bowls with incurved sides, thickened rim, and a ridge just below the rim on the exterior of the bowl.
Paste and firing: Sherds presumed (given their lack of slip preservation) to be Subín

Red are entirely of hard volcanic-ash-tempered paste (see "Paste and firing" of Tinaja Red type, and comments on the Tinaja group in general). Postdepositional alteration has given surfaces an almost uniform light beige-gray color as a result of the white marl or tierra blanca in which they were found, but fresh breaks reveal greater variation in paste color from brown to gray. Dark coring is fairly common.

Surface treatment and decoration: Judging from sherds of this type at other sites, interior surfaces had been covered with a red slip. At Macanché, however, the slips are almost completely eroded; on a few sherds, traces of slip remain, and on these fire-clouding has often resulted in a gray color. Sabloff suggested (1975:161) that many Subín bowls at Seibal may originally have been unslipped and that the slip was "fugitive." Approximately 1 to 2 cm below the thickened or bolstered lip on the vessel exterior is a narrow appliquéd fillet that is usually triangular in cross section, but sometimes the apex is slightly rounded or flattened. The area of the vessel from the lip to just below this fillet is very well smoothed; it often appears that a finger was stroked around the circumference of the bowl above and below this fillet. Below that, the vessel surfaces were often less carefully smoothed and retain faint scrape marks. Vessel exteriors apparently were not slipped below the fillet.

An interesting observation can be made concerning the manufacture of these vessels. Many of the rim sherds broke approximately 8.5 to 10 cm below the lip of the bowl. This line of breakage is relatively straight and parallel to the rim and sometimes occurs at the approximate line of greatest vessel diameter. The fracture pattern suggests that the bowls may have been made in two separate parts—a lower half formed first, then a coil of clay added to it in order to build the upper half. The joining edge of the lower part may have often been too thin or too dry to allow proper bonding with the upper portion, hence the breakage pattern.

Forms and dimensions: Vessels are large

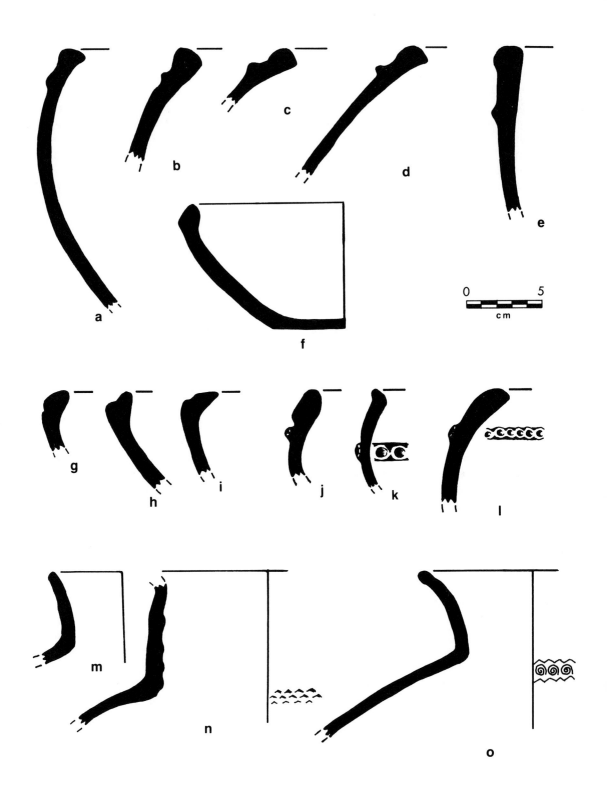

FIGURE 32. **a–f**, Subín Red: Variety Unspecified. **g–i**, Cameron Incised: Variety Unspecified.
j–l, Chaquiste Impressed: Variety Unspecified; **k, l**, decoration on exterior.
m–o, Pantano Impressed: Pantano Variety; **n, o**, decoration on exterior. Note
"rilling" on interior of **n** (see text).

bowls with restricted orifices and incurving rims. The lip of the examples from Macanché tends to be slightly "squared" or flattened rather than pointed (compare, for example, with Chaquiste Impressed). Small numbers of rims suggest more open, hemispherical bowls rather than the common closed shape. Walls of Subín bowls are generally thicker than those of the Tinaja jars, varying between 7 and 10 mm at the approximate midpoint of the side of the vessel. Mouth diameters vary from 32 to 36 cm (nine measurements). Bases may be either flat or annular, but because these large bowls occur in Tinaja, Cameron, Subín, and Chaquiste types, it is difficult to determine which type the three base sherds represent.

Illustrations: figure 32a–f.

Intrasite references: Subín Red was recovered from Bullard's excavations in the white and gray marly or tierra blanca deposits of the Terminal Classic, and the type continues to occur in later mixed construction and midden material of the Early and Late Postclassic periods. At least one partially reconstructible vessel was recovered from adjacent lots 6 and 11 in Operation IA.

Intersite references: Subín Red is found principally in the Pasión area; it was not identified as a separate type or variety at Uaxactún. The vessel form, however, is a common one in the Late and Terminal Classic periods throughout Petén. Because of the abundance of this form, it would be desirable to be able to determine some temporally significant variations in primary or secondary form details (e.g., wall angle or lip shape), but this was not possible at Seibal (Sabloff 1975:162). At Altar de Sacrificios, where Subín was identified as a distinct ceramic group rather than a type within the Tinaja group (Sabloff 1975:163), R. E. W. Adams was able to distinguish three chronologically significant varieties (1971:22–23).

Name: **Cameron Incised: Variety Unspecified.**

Frequency: 12 sherds from Bullard's excavations at Macanché Island, all from Post-

classic lots. Cameron Incised sherds constitute 1.7 percent of the Tinaja ceramic group in Bullard's collection.

Ware: Petén Gloss ware.

Complex: Romero (and early facet Aura?) ceramic complex.

Established: Cameron Incised type was defined by Smith and Gifford (1966; R. E. Smith 1955) in the Uaxactún ceramic collections.

Principal identifying modes: Cameron Incised is a red-slipped type distinguished by one or more incised lines, which may be very broad and shallow or narrow and pronounced and which encircle incurved-rim bowls and plates.

Paste and firing: See general comments on the Tinaja group. Two of the sherds from Macanché Island are the Canjil firing variant.

Surface treatment and decoration: Vessels may or may not have had a red slip applied to the vessel interiors (see Subín Red). On the Macanché examples, a shallow groove or incised line appears on the lip or just below a small bolster on incurving side bowls. Sometimes the groove is so faint that it appears as if the potter simply ran a finger along the join of the bolster to the wall to accentuate it. On one sherd the line is a pronounced incision below a sharply incurved rim.

Forms and dimensions: Macanché Island lacks the range of bowl and plate forms of Cameron Incised that are found widely and in some quantities elsewhere in Petén. Instead, the emphasis is on large bowls with gently incurving sides; the mouth diameters on two of these vessels are 32 and 38 cm. One vessel is a broad open basin with a rather sharply incurved rim; the sherd is too small to obtain an estimate of mouth diameter.

Illustrations: figure 32g–i.

Intrasite references: Twelve sherds of Cameron Incised bowls were recovered from Bullard's excavations, all from Postclassic lots, representing both Early Postclassic construction fill and Late Postclassic midden. This context raises the possibility that this type or bowl form, as well as the Canjil firing variant, was a very late or transitional manufacture in the area at the close of the Classic period and in the early facet of the Early Postclassic Aura complex.

Intersite references: Cameron Incised is a widely occurring member of the Tinaja group at other sites in Petén and occurs in both the Eznab ceramic sphere complexes of Tikal, Uaxactún, and Yaxhá and in the Boca ceramic sphere complexes in the Pasión area. At Seibal, Cameron Incised is associated with a grater bowl form in the Bayal complex, which is an apparent imitation of a form found in Fine Orange paste ware pottery (Sabloff 1975:180–81). Elsewhere in the lakes area, especially at Yaxhá, Cameron Incised occurred in tripod plates with an incised and notched basal flange, but this plate form is missing from Macanché Island, as well as from Ixlú and Punta Nimá.

Name: **Chaquiste Impressed: Variety Unspecified.**
Frequency: 5 sherds, of which 2 were from Bullard's excavations on Macanché Island, 1 from the mainland "center," and 2 from Punta Nimá. Chaquiste Impressed sherds represent 0.7 percent of the sherds of the Tinaja ceramic group in Bullard's collections.
Ware: Petén Gloss ware.
Complex: Romero ceramic complex.
Established: Chaquiste Impressed was defined by R. E. W. Adams (1971:47) in the collection from Altar de Sacrificios.
Principal identifying modes: Chaquiste Impressed vessels are large bowls with incurved rims and an impressed fillet applied below the rim on the exterior.
Paste and firing: See Subín Red.
Surface treatment and decoration: See Subín Red. At Macanché the slips are eroded off (one sherd is extremely weathered) as in Subín Red, and as Sabloff noted (1975:68) some or all of the vessels may have originally been unslipped. The appliquéd fillet on these two sherds has been impressed with a finger; one sherd has round, overlapping, distinct impressions, while the other has more widely spaced, faint impressions.
Forms and dimensions: Only one of the

two sherds from Macanché Island is a rim; the mouth diameter is 24 cm. A larger bowl from Punta Nimá has a diameter of 32 cm.
Illustrations: figure 32j–l.
Intrasite references: Only two sherds of Chaquiste Impressed were recovered from Bullard's excavations; these came from the lower levels of construction fill containing Terminal Classic and Early Postclassic sherds in his Operation 1G.
Intersite references: Like Subín Red, Chaquiste Impressed–type vessels comprise a very common bowl form associated with the Late and Terminal Classic periods all over Petén. This particular type is identified strictly in the Pasión area, although analogous impressed fillet-decorated bowls are known from surface finds at Uaxactún (e.g., R. E. Smith 1955: fig. 48a9, 11–12, 15–18). Two varieties of the type were identified at both Altar de Sacrificios (R. E. W. Adams 1971) and Seibal (Sabloff 1975); at Macanché, as at Seibal, most of the sherds were left "variety unspecified," because they did not have stamped decoration.

Name: **Pantano Impressed: Pantano Variety.**
Frequency: 3 sherds, of which 1 was from Early Postclassic fill at Macanché Island and 2 from the Punta Nimá collection. Pantano Impressed sherds constitute 0.4 percent of the Tinaja ceramic group in Bullard's collections.
Ware: Petén Gloss ware.
Complex: Romero ceramic complex.
Established: Pantano Variety of Pantano Impressed was identified by Smith and Gifford (1966; Smith 1955) on the basis of the Uaxactún collections.
Principal identifying modes: Pantano Impressed: Pantano Variety vessels are red-slipped jars with impressed decoration occurring on the upper shoulder of the jar, just below the join with the neck.
Paste and firing: See Tinaja Red and Subín Red.
Surface treatment and decoration: As with the other members of the Tinaja group

in the area, surfaces are often eroded, but vessels are covered with a red slip. One jar from Punta Nimá has a well-preserved brownish red slip which covers the entire exterior of the jar and the interior neck to just below the angle to the body. Post-slip impressed decoration consists of a row of spirals or whorls set between a border of triangles; the band is 1.3 cm in width. The second example from Punta Nimá is a jar with a bulging neck, its lip having broken off and the slip having completely eroded. The impressed decoration is a band, approximately 1.1 cm wide, of three lines of impressed triangles. The interior neck of this vessel is unusual for it has parallel circumferential ridges ("rilling") similar to those found typically on wheel-made pottery. This similarity raises the possibility that potters used some sort of rapidly rotating *kabal-* or *molde*like apparatus in finishing the necks of vessels, and perhaps in other steps of manufacture also (R.H. Thompson 1958; Foster 1959).

Forms and dimensions: The complete jar rim from Punta Nimá had a mouth diameter of 15 cm (interior neck 8.5); the missing lip on the other specimen precluded measurement of the mouth diameter, but the interior neck diameter was approximately 14 cm. The jars appear to be smaller than the Tinaja jars from Macanché Island.

Illustrations: figure 32m–o.

Intrasite references: Only one sherd of this type was recovered from Bullard's and CPHEP excavations, and that was in Early Postclassic fill.

Intersite references: Like Chaquiste Impressed bowls, Pantano Impressed jars have a wide temporal and geographical spread in Petén during the Late and Terminal Classic periods. They appear to be particularly common or elaborated in the Pasión area, where a stamped variety has also been found at Altar de Sacrificios and at Seibal. The decoration on the examples from Punta Nimá, particularly the rows of triangles, falls well within the range of motifs known from Seibal (see Sabloff 1975: fig. 314).

Harina Ceramic Group

Name: **Harina Cream: Harina Variety.**

Frequency: 199 sherds from Bullard's excavations on Macanché Island, of which 126 were from Terminal Classic deposits and 73 were from Postclassic lots. Harina Cream sherds constitute 86.9 percent of the sherds of the Harina ceramic group; the Harina group represents 5.3 percent of the sherds from Terminal Classic lots at Macanché Island.

Ware: Petén Gloss ware.

Complex: Romero ceramic complex; also early facet Aura complex in CPHEP excavations.

Established: Present work.

Principal identifying modes: Harina Cream is identified by a cream slip that is often thin and streaky and sometimes exhibits fire-clouding on vessel forms including bowls and jars.

Paste and firing: Paste is dark gray to gray-brown, generally fairly dense, with tiny white inclusions, ranging up to rare examples of 1.0 mm in size. Small manganese nodules are sparse to common. Some sherds are ash-tempered; they have a gritty feel, and mica is visible on the surfaces. Other sherds look like they might have had ash added to the clay, but in very small quantities, and at 50× magnification it is not always clearly identifiable. The ash-tempered paste appeared to be the same gray to gray-brown paste as the majority of the specimens, differentiated only by the addition of variable amounts of ash. The paste is otherwise very similar to that of the Postclassic Trapeche and Paxcamán ceramic groups, except that it lacked snail shells.

Surface treatment and decoration: Vessels were covered with a cream (10YR 8/1–2 to 2.5YR 8/2) slip that was apparently originally well polished but now is often severely eroded. The luster varies from moderate to matte. In some places the slip was streakily or unevenly applied and looks semitranslucent, as the gray paste is visible underneath. The interiors of some small vessels are fire-clouded gray. About 20 percent of the sherds, principally those of carbonate pastes, are heavily fire-clouded, with blotchy colors ranging between pink and gray.

Forms and dimensions: The predominant vessel form is a small round-sided bowl. Sometimes bowls have slightly restricted orifices; two have outflaring sides. Mouth diameters of bowls range from 12 to 20 cm; dishes with outflaring sides have diameters of 26 and 32 cm. Vessel walls are variable in thickness but are generally thin, ranging between 3 and 7 mm. The bases of the bowls are flat, and some are excised on the exterior. Additional vessel forms include two sherds of jars with short outflaring neck; mouth diameters are 12 and 13 cm. One small bulbous foot was identified, but the form of the actual vessel was indeterminate.

Illustrations: figure 33a–j.

Intrasite references: Harina Cream was recovered from buried midden layers and tierra blanca levels dating to the Terminal Classic, and in early facet Early Postclassic excavations by CPHEP. Three partially reconstructible vessels were recovered from primary breakage and accumulated debris sampled in Bullard's Lot 41.

The characteristically gray paste and streaky cream-to-fire-clouded-gray slip made it very difficult to be totally confident about the consistency of sorting and separating Harina Cream sherds from those of Achote Black and later Trapeche Pink categories. Vessel forms and the general thinness of the walls of Harina Cream provided the best diagnostic criteria, but a great deal of ambiguity remained. There appears to be considerable technological overlap or transition in these categories.

Intersite references: Harina Cream was not found in Terminal Classic deposits in any of the other Petén lake basins surveyed by CPHEP, at the Macanché mainland "center" excavation conducted by Bullard, or at Ixlú or Punta Nimá.

Monochrome cream-slipped types have no immediate links to Late Classic or Terminal Classic ceramic groups in Petén, although

neither the small bowl forms nor the flaring neck jar of Harina Cream are atypical of Late Classic vessels in monochrome and polychrome types. Some technological characteristics of Harina Cream—uneven firing, blotchy colors, gray carbonate paste—suggest strong ties to the later Trapeche group in the Early Postclassic (see the preceding comments on the Tinaja group, and chapter 6, "Pastes and Slips of the Paxcamán and Trapeche Ceramic Groups").

Outside central Petén, some distant relationships can perhaps be seen with Ticul Thin Slate in the Xcocom Terminal Classic/Early Postclassic complex at Becan (Ball 1977:38, fig. 14). At Seibal an "unnamed cream slip" hemispherical bowl, characterized by varied color and firing, was found in Bayal Burial 26 along with two Tinaja group vessels (Sabloff 1975:221–22), and this vessel may provide another link between the Romero complex and the Boca sphere. At Barton Ramie, Yaha Creek Cream is a monochrome-slipped, calcite-paste type used in the manufacture of jars, and it appears primarily in the Late Classic Spanish Lookout complex (Gifford 1976:272–273). A cream incised sherd was noted there in the New Town Postclassic complex (Sharer and Chase 1976:311).

Name: **Largo Red-on-cream: Largo Variety.**
Frequency: 30 sherds from Bullard's work on Macanché Island. Sherds of Largo Red-on-cream type comprised 13.1 percent of the sherds of the Harina ceramic group.
Ware: Petén Gloss ware.
Complex: Romero ceramic complex.
Established: Present work.
Principal identifying modes: Largo Red-on-cream type is identified by thin, orangey red painted decoration on cream slips. Vessel forms include small bowls or cups and rare plates.
Paste and firing: See Harina Cream.
Surface treatment and decoration: For slip characteristics, see Harina Cream. Painted decoration appears as a faint reddish orange coloring, often considerably glossier than

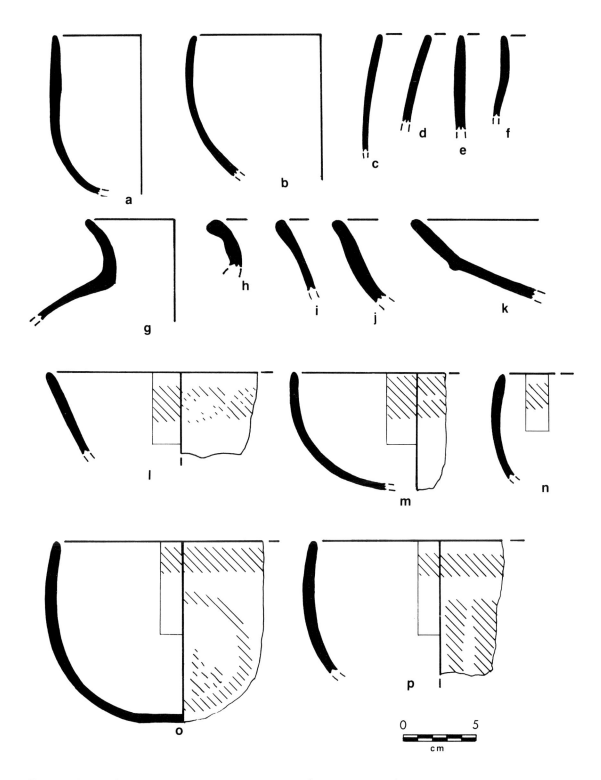

FIGURE 33. **a–j**, Harina Cream: Harina Variety. **k–p**, Largo Red-on-cream: Largo Variety.

the slip, occurring as single or double broad bands (1.5 to 2.5 cm) below the lip on both interior and exterior. One vessel has a 2.5-cm-wide band of glyphs or pseudoglyphs. Vertical stripes appear on one vessel. Yet another motif is a medallion with a quatrefoil in the center. In all examples the paint is eroded and weathered and barely visible on the surfaces.

Forms and dimensions: See Harina Cream. Vessel forms are generally small, hemispherical, simple silhouette bowls, sometimes with very slightly restricted orifices. Vessel diameters range from 17 to 20 cm. Plate or dish forms are less common; one has a lateral ridge, while another has an outflaring rim and an exterior ridge. The diameter of the latter plate is 32 cm. Plates typically have somewhat thicker walls than do bowls.

Illustrations: figure 33k–p.

Intrasite references: The red-on-cream type occurs in considerably reduced frequency and in more restricted locations on Macanché Island than did Harina Cream. It is also less common in CPHEP Early Postclassic lots: no sherds were recovered from Bullard's Postclassic lots, although three sherds came from his surface collections on the island. Two partially reconstructible vessels were recovered from Lot 41 in Operation IH.

Intersite references: Cream polychrome decoration (red-on-cream, black-and-red-on-cream) is common in the Late and Terminal Classic periods in the lowlands. In Petén, types include Naranjal Red-on-cream, Joyac Cream Polychrome, and Zacatel Cream Polychrome (see R. E. Smith 1955; Smith and Gifford 1966). An unnamed Red-on-cream type occurred at Seibal in the Bayal phase but shows little relationship to the Macanché specimens (Sabloff 1975:224, fig. 433). At Becan, although numerous red-on-cream types were common in the Bejuco (early Late Classic) complex, in the Late Classic/Early Postclassic transition (Chintok and Xcocom complexes) the principal types appear to be Sayán Red-on-cream, Droga Red-on-cream, and Dolorido Cream Polychrome (Ball 1977:

62–64, 81). Sayán Red-on-cream is described in the Chintok complex as having a "low-luster, thin, flaky slip irregularly colored and clouded due to poor firing control" (Ball 1977:134), which resembles the same general level of technological competence seen in the Harina group overall. At Tancah, a Sayán vessel was found in a burial; it is described as "an excellent marker for the last gasp of the Classic period" (Miller 1985:35).

The red-on-cream sherds from Macanché may represent relationships—direct or indirect—with any of the above-mentioned types. Pottery like this Largo Red-on-cream type in the Harina group was not found in any quantities in Terminal Classic deposits around any of the other lakes investigated by CPHEP or at Ixlú, although Late Classic cream polychrome decorated sherds were recovered there. Ties of this type to the later consistent appearance of red-on-"cream" painted decoration in the Postclassic period (small amounts in the Trapeche group, as well as the more abundant Chompoxté Red-on-cream type in the Topoxté [red-slipped] group) may be indicated by this Macanché material. It is also of interest to note the style of painting the quatrefoil in the medallion on one of these Largo Red-on-cream bowls (a similar style is seen on an Orange Polychrome sherd from Punta Nimá as well; fig. 36i). The "petals" of the "flower" are executed with double lines, a broad volute with a finer line in its interior curve. This style of painting plumelike elements is common in Postclassic pottery.

Achote Ceramic Group

Name: **Achote Black: Variety Unspecified.**

Frequency: 182 sherds, of which 175 were from Bullard's excavations on Macanché Island (167 sherds from Terminal Classic contexts) and 7 from other locations investigated by Bullard. Sherds of the Achote group (Achote Black type) comprised 5.8 percent of the sherds from Terminal Classic lots excavated by Bullard on Macanché Island.

Ware: Petén Gloss ware.

Complex: Romero ceramic complex.

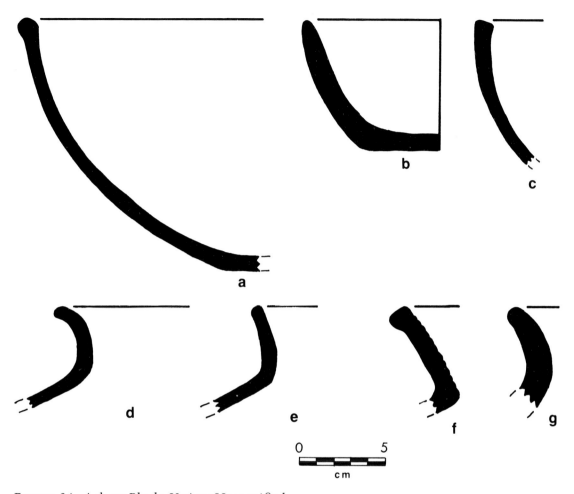

FIGURE 34. Achote Black: Variety Unspecified.

Established: The Achote ceramic group was established by Smith and Gifford (1966; R. E. Smith 1955) at Uaxactún.

Principal identifying modes: Achote Black is characterized by a thin slip varying from black to creamy gray, applied to jars and large open bowls or basins.

Paste and firing: Achote Black pottery has a heavy, dark gray carbonate paste. Because of its color and lack of oxidation, other particles in the paste are often not visible to the naked eye, but scattered light-colored particles, probably small fragments of carbonate material, are frequently evident in sizes up to approximately 1.5 mm.

Surface treatment and decoration: The black slip is neither of good quality nor well fired, being generally thin, streaky, and matte to low-luster. The color varies from creamy or milky gray (7.5YR 7/0 to 10YR 8/2) to very dark gray (2.5YR 4/0) and black and is often blotchy with fire-clouds. Thicker slips occasionally show flaky erosion. Some sherds with relatively glossier slips (usually also with thinner walls) may be earlier Classic black-slipped types. Large bowls are generally partially slipped on the exterior (e.g., for 6–8 cm below the lip), and in this area the surfaces and the slip itself are unpolished, still showing fine, faint striations of the fingers or other smoothing procedure. The interiors of bowls are often lighter or more cream-colored than are the exteriors.

Forms and dimensions: Achote Black,

like Terminal Classic red monochrome slipped types, occurs primarily as jars and large open bowls. Few jar rims are available; direct rims seem to be most common, with occasional bolsters, and necks are moderately short and straight. Some of the necks have shallow circumferential striations on the interior, as though from smoothing or scraping. The three jar mouth diameters measured ranged between 16 and 26 cm. One black-slipped indented base was noted. Bowls are principally large, open, round-sided hemispherical bowls or basins, sometimes with a thickened rounded lip; one had a slightly incurved rim and interior thickening. Two bowls had diameters of 36 and 37 cm; one had a flat base. A smaller bowl had a diameter of 16 cm. Walls of most of the Achote Black specimens, whether bowls or jars, are relatively thick, ranging from 0.6 to 1.2 cm.

Illustration: figure 34.

Intrasite references: Achote Black appeared in small quantities in CPHEP excavations on the island; the Terminal Classic sherds from Bullard's excavations were recovered primarily in Operations IA and IH. In the "marl" or tierra blanca underlying mound construction in IH, a large, partially reconstructible Achote bowl was recovered from a deposit containing sherds apparently representing primary breakage.

Intersite references: Achote Black specimens from elsewhere in the lakes region are sparse in occurrence. In general, Achote Black is more common in Terminal Classic deposits from the Lake Salpetén basin than from other basins in CPHEP surveys, including Lake Macanché. At other sites in the lowlands, blackwares seem to have had more importance than they did in the lakes area as a whole, with incised and gouged-incised types being recovered in the group (e.g., at Becan [Ball 1977:135] and Seibal [Sabloff 1975:181]). At Seibal, however, the forms of Achote Black were similar to the large bowls from Macanché, and the slip was described as "thin and 'washlike'" with a low luster (Sabloff 1975:181). Achote Black at Uaxactún seems to show a very different range of

forms (R. E. Smith 1955; Smith and Gifford 1966), except for one illustration of a bowl (R. E. Smith 1955: fig. 50a16).

Payaso Ceramic Group

Name: **Payaso Orange-brown: Payaso Variety.**

Frequency: 106 sherds from Bullard's excavations on Macanché Island, of which 105 were from Terminal Classic contexts. Sherds of the Payaso ceramic group (Payaso Orange-brown type) comprised 3.6 percent of the Terminal Classic assemblage on Macanché Island in Bullard's lots.

Ware: Petén Gloss ware (?).

Ceramic complex: Romero ceramic complex; also early facet Aura complex in CPHEP excavations.

Established: Present work.

Principal identifying modes: Payaso Orange-brown is a very hard, thin-walled, ash-tempered ware that usually exhibits a wide range of surface colors as a consequence of variations in the firing atmosphere. Forms appear to be solely jars.

Paste and firing: The paste is volcanic-ash-tempered and very hard but varies considerably in color, from brown (10YR 6/5) to dark gray. Much of the dark gray paste looks like that used for Harina group, especially those sherds that had some ash added to them. Most sherds appeared to be relatively well fired (except for the fire-clouding) and were hard and "clinky."

Surface treatment and decoration: Surfaces were burnished somewhat carelessly: on many sherds facets are visible, and near the base of a jar sherd some areas were entirely missed. Many of the sherds appeared to have been slipped, but the putative slip is very thinly applied and difficult to see even at 50× magnification. In some cases this slip seems to have been lightly polished; in others it was left matte.

Surface colors are highly variable, even on a single sherd, and in many examples the colors are blotchy or streaky. Colors range from gray (2.5YR 5/0), often greenish gray (2.5YR 4–5/2), to dark brown (5YR 4/2), yellowish brown (10YR 6/6) to orange (5YR 6/6). Gray and dark brown surfaces usually exhibit very fine crazing.

Forms and dimensions: No rims have been found in this type. The large size and gentle curvature of the sherds suggests that vessels of this type were jars; one has an indented base. Walls are thin, ranging from 3 to 5 mm in thickness.

Illustrations: None.

Intrasite references: Payaso Orange-brown occurred in slightly less than half of the Terminal Classic/early facet Early Postclassic lots excavated at Macanché Island.

Intersite references: The typological connections of this distinctive pottery—antecedent, contemporaneous, or sequential—are unknown. The type was not encountered at any of the other lake basins in the central Petén excavated by CPHEP or in the other ceramic collections obtained by Bullard. At Macanché Island, the paste—ashy, thin, hard, tan in color—is similar to much of the Tepeu 3 pottery on the island, but the slip is unusual. There may be some vague affinities of the slip to Traino Brown: Lodo Variety at Becan, which Ball describes (1977:29) as having a "yellowish" hue; however, he notes an absence of jar forms. Jars are present in the Traino Variety (Ball 1977:26), but these have flat rather than indented bases.

The closest relationship may be to an unnamed "Special: Orange and Brown" at Barton Ramie in the New Town phase (Sharer and Chase 1976:312), which had a polished but streaky and mottled slip that varied in color from orange to greenish brown. The vessel form was a jar but, unlike the Macanché specimens, its walls were quite thick.

Cambio Ceramic Group

Name: **Cambio Unslipped: Variety Unspecified.**

Frequency: 315 sherds, of which 255 were from Terminal Classic deposits excavated by Bullard on Macanché Island (51 sherds were from Postclassic lots) and 9 large rims were present in Bullard's collection from Punta Nimá. Sherds of Cambio Unslipped: Variety Unspecified comprised 8.8 percent of the sherds from Terminal Classic lots at Macanché Island; they constituted 20 percent of the sherds of the Cambio ceramic group in Bullard's collections.

Ware: Uaxactún Unslipped ware.

Complex: Romero ceramic complex.

Established: Cambio Unslipped was identified and described on the basis of the Uaxactún materials (R. E. Smith 1955; Smith and Gifford 1966).

Principal identifying modes: Cambio Unslipped is the principal unslipped type of the Late Classic period, identified by unslipped and unpolished gray to tan surfaces and paste. Vessel forms are principally large jars with outcurved necks and generally some form of lip bolster.

Paste and firing: Paste is variable in texture and color. In general at Macanché Island, it is coarse to moderately coarse with calcite inclusions. Paste colors are usually light, ranging from light gray to light tan. Fire-clouding is not common.

Surface treatment and decoration: The quality of the surface treatment is variable, with surfaces being moderately well to poorly smoothed. Most sherds show some degree of pockmarking, leaching, and drag marks. The necks of vessels are better smoothed than is the body. No decoration has been noted, except for pinching or impressing the rim of four sherds into a "piecrust lip."

Forms and dimensions: Unslipped vessels appear to be primarily large jars, with medium to wide mouths; rim sherds indicate high and outflaring necks with everted lip. Mouth diameters vary from 28 to 32 cm; interior neck diameters average 16 cm. Some sherds had direct rims, others had small rounded or triangular lip bolsters, and three had an extended and thinned lip bolster that could almost be termed a labial flange. Four sherds, all from Postclassic lots at Macanché Island, had a "piecrust lip."

Illustrations: figure 35a–d.

Intrasite references: Cambio Unslipped occurred in varying amounts in virtually all

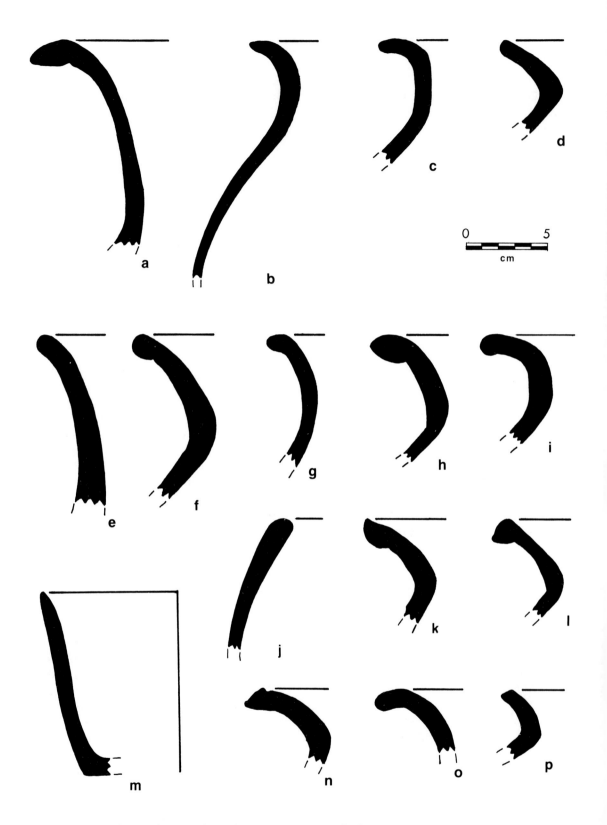

FIGURE 35. **a–d**, Cambio Unslipped: Variety Unspecified. **e–p**, Cambio Unslipped: Coarse Gray Variety.

excavations on the island but principally in the construction fill sampled by Bullard's Operation IG. It is likely that quantities of sherds of this type also occurred in Post-classic lots, but only rim sherds were identified and counted separately as "miscellaneous Classic" for those lots. Body sherds were generally unrecognizable by type and were included as "miscellaneous unidentified."

Intersite references: Cambio Unslipped, as the principal unslipped type in the Late Classic in the central Lowlands, encompasses a great deal of variability in paste and form. Following Sabloff's suggestion (1975: 154) that Cambio Unslipped type be the residual category of the Cambio group leaves room for even greater variability, and it would be most desirable to arrive at some breakdowns having temporal significance. One possibility is rim and lip form. At Seibal, thickened and folded rims may be late (Sabloff 1975:154); at Benque Viejo, J.E.S. Thompson indicates (1940: figs. 42, 43) that everted and "piecrust" lips were common on late (BV IV) unslipped jars.

This distinctive "piecrust lip" was not noted in Terminal Classic deposits at Macanché Island (the only four examples being from Postclassic lots) and occurred only rarely at most of the lakes surveyed by CPHEP. It was, however, abundant in Late and Terminal Classic materials from Yaxhá, serving as an immediate diagnostic of late occupation. This same extreme rim eversion and "flange"-like bolster does not seem to be characteristic of the Barton Ramie late jars (except see Gifford 1976: figs. 180g, 181m), which also generally have shorter necks.

Another possibility for temporal discrimination is on the basis of paste. A distinctive thick, coarse gray paste was identified at Macanché Island in Terminal Classic deposits but has not been found elsewhere in the lakes region (see "Intersite references, Coarse Gray Variety," below). At the other lakes, and on the Macanché mainland itself, another paste variant characterized as a thick, dark, reddish brown paste, with scraping marks on the surfaces, was regularly as-

sociated with Terminal Classic deposits. This paste variant was not found on the island, however.

Name: **Cambio Unslipped: Coarse Gray Variety.**

Frequency: 1,011 sherds from Bullard's excavations on Macanché Island, of which 999 were recovered from Terminal Classic lots. The Coarse Gray Variety of Cambio Unslipped comprised 34.6 percent of the sherds from Terminal Classic lots excavated by Bullard at Macanché Island; it represents 64.2 percent of the Cambio ceramic group in Bullard's collection.

Ware: Uaxactún Unslipped ware.

Complex: Romero ceramic complex; also early facet Aura complex in CPHEP excavations.

Established: The Coarse Gray Variety of Cambio Unslipped is being created on the basis of the Macanché collections; the type itself was established by Smith and Gifford (1966; R. E. Smith 1955) at Uaxactún.

Principal identifying modes: This variety may be distinguished on the basis of a coarse, thick, dark gray, unslipped paste and poorly finished surfaces.

Paste and firing: Coarse Gray Variety has a coarse paste with light gray-brown to white (often crystalline) calcite inclusions, ranging from very tiny (ca. 0.2 mm) up to 5 mm in diameter. Inclusions visible to the unaided eye include abundant particles in the range of 1–3 mm; larger ones are common. Paste is uniformly dark gray; surface colors are usually lighter, probably through postdepositional alteration resulting from the white "marl" or tierra blanca burial matrix.

Surface treatment and decoration: Exterior surfaces of body sherds vary from moderately well smoothed to extremely poorly finished; most appear not to have had any smoothing at all. Exteriors are pockmarked, frequently have drag marks from large temper particles being dragged in scraping, and sometimes show broad (ca. 3 cm), shallow facets from scraping. Only the neck and rim portions of the vessel exteriors are well finished, a qualitative difference between neck and body that is much more pronounced on Coarse Gray Variety jars than on those of Variety Unspecified. Jar interiors, on the other hand, are very smooth but show no signs of scraping; perhaps these vessels were made over a mold.

Forms and dimensions: Forms are generally large jars with moderately high (4 to 10 cm), outflaring necks. Rim treatments exhibit a great deal of diversity and show many of the same variations seen in "Variety Unspecified" jars: rounded and direct, everted, sometimes folded, or with a slight bolster or triangular flange. One unusually well made sherd is similar to Postclassic Pozo Unslipped short straight jar rims. Mouth diameters range from 18 to 40 cm, with an average for nine specimens of 28 cm; interior neck diameters are slightly greater than those of Variety Unspecified, averaging 19 cm. Wall thickness varies from 6 to 13 mm; most are in the range of 8–9 mm. One large sherd represents about half of a vessel with a "flowerpot" shape; its height is 11 cm and diameter ca. 18 cm. Another vessel is a large restricted orifice basin with a mouth diameter of 40 cm. One sherd indicates that some vessels (perhaps basins or bowls?) may have had annular bases.

Illustrations: figure 35e–p.

Intrasite references: The Coarse Gray Variety of Cambio Unslipped occurred principally in nonconstructional deposits on Macanché Island, especially in tierra blanca. This variety did not appear, for example, in the lower levels of construction fill in CPHEP pit 3, and this fill had other characteristic Terminal Classic types either missing (e.g., Payaso Orange-brown) or present in negligible amounts (Harina Cream). Well over three-quarters of the total number of Coarse Gray Variety sherds from Macanché Island occurred in tierra blanca in Bullard's Operations IA (with many large jar rims in Lot 11) and IH. This variety is present in the Terminal Classic and the early facet of Early Postclassic at Macanché and is the predominant unslipped category.

Intersite references: Coarse Gray Variety may be one of the few subdivisions of Cambio Unslipped to have chronological significance (see Sabloff 1975:154 for a review of some of the problems), but its usefulness is diminished by the fact that thus far its distribution is restricted to Macanché Island. At Barton Ramie a black paste variant of Cayo Unslipped: Cayo Variety was noted (Gifford 1976:278–79), which may have some relationship to Coarse Gray Variety of Cambio Unslipped. No Coarse Gray Variety sherds were recovered from the mainland "center" or from Ixlú or Punta Nimá.

Name: **Encanto Striated: Variety Unspecified.**

Frequency: 249 sherds, of which 236 were from Bullard's excavations on Macanché Island (164 were from Terminal Classic lots) and 13 sherds from other areas investigated by Bullard. Sherds of Encanto Striated type comprise 5.7 percent of the Terminal Classic assemblage on Macanché Island; they represent 15.8 percent of the sherds of the Cambio ceramic group in Bullard's collections.

Ware: Uaxactún Unslipped ware.

Complex: Romero ceramic complex; also early facet Aura (?).

Established: The Encanto type was established by Smith and Gifford (1966; R. E. Smith 1955) at Uaxactún.

Principal identifying modes: Relatively coarse unslipped paste with exterior surfaces covered with fine regularly spaced striations.

Paste and firing: Encanto Striated has a coarse gray to grayish brown paste, with white calcite inclusions. The paste is very similar to that of Cambio Unslipped: Coarse Gray Variety, but it is not as coarse in texture and does not have the common large inclusions (3–5 mm) as does Coarse Gray. Surfaces of Encanto Striated are frequently lighter gray or gray-brown than the paste. Some fire-clouding is evident. A large rim and shoulder sherd from Punta Nimá had a reddish brown paste.

Surface treatment and decoration: Surfaces are covered with generally widely sepa-

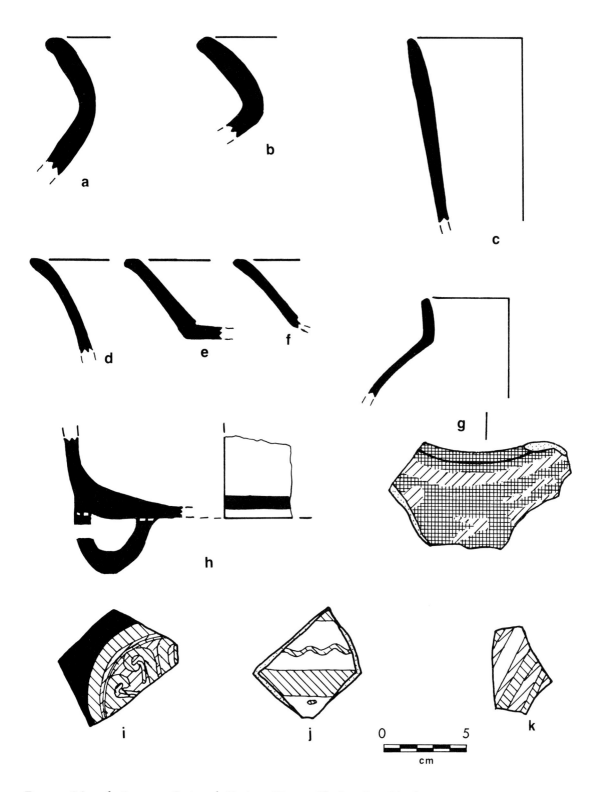

FIGURE 36. **a**, **b**, Encanto Striated: Variety Unspecified. **c**, Jato Black-on-gray: Variety Unspecified. **d–f**, Daylight Orange: Darknight Variety. **g**, **h**, Miscellaneous unidentified specials. **i–k**, Late Classic polychromes. **i**, decoration on exterior; **j**, **k**, decoration on interior.

rated (2–4 mm), clear, fine striations. Overlapping occurs on approximately half the sherds. Only two rims are present, both from Punta Nimá: on one the striations are horizontal, on the other at a slight angle from vertical. One sherd from CPHEP excavations on the island has herringbone-patterned striations.

Forms and dimensions: Most sherds appear to be from jars, but no rims or bases were found on the island. (Rims, of course, could have been included with Coarse Gray Variety of Cambio Unslipped, because on the two available Encanto jar rim and shoulder sherds the striations were not present on the neck.) Thickness of the sherds varies from 5 to 8 mm, with most between 6 and 7 mm. The orifice diameter of one of the rim sherds from Punta Nimá was 21 cm.

Illustrations: figure 36a, b.

Intrasite references: Striated sherds formed a small but consistent portion of the Terminal Classic unslipped utilitarian sherd assemblage at Macanché Island. Most of the CPHEP sherds came from construction fill in pit 3, which lacked Coarse Gray Variety of Cambio Unslipped and had other significant typological departures from the Terminal Classic norm. Large numbers of striated sherds were also recovered in Bullard's Lot 38 in Operation IH. Because of similarities of paste between Encanto Striated and Coarse Gray Variety of Cambio Unslipped, it is possible that the poor surface finishing on the latter represents careless efforts to smooth striated surfaces. Striated pottery was rare on the mainland.

Intersite references: Striation as a surface-finishing technique was never as common in the lakes area of Petén at any time during the prehistoric sequence as it was elsewhere in the northern region or the Pasión area. At Tikal, Encanto Striated comprised 15 percent of the Eznab ceramic assemblage (Culbert 1973b: 81); at Seibal the occurrence was even higher at 20 percent (Sabloff 1975: 155) compared to 5.5 percent at Macanché. In the Terminal Classic period, it is more common on the island than anywhere else in the lakes area, which may be an additional bit of supporting evidence for Bullard's links of the Romero complex with the Boca sphere in the Pasión region. Two large striated rim sherds were in Bullard's collection from Punta Nimá (one of which was an unusual reddish paste); nine sherds were recovered in excavations at Ixlú and two came from the mainland "center."

I am inclined to follow Sabloff's suggestion (1975: 154) that Encanto Striated should be included in the Cambio ceramic group, with Cambio Unslipped as the residual type of the group, because of the difficulty of using the same surface criteria to type rim sherds and body sherds. For the Macanché striated sherds, the varietal designation was left unspecified in this type. Because the striations are fine, the material probably is most closely related to the Encanto Variety at Altar de Sacrificios (R. E. W. Adams 1971); the Pisote Variety at that site has heavy striations in a herringbone pattern. Similarly, at Becan, Yokat Striated has a herringbone pattern and its occurrence is described as "abundant" (Ball 1977: 15–16).

Danta Ceramic Group

Name: **Jato Black-on-gray: Variety Unspecified.**

Frequency: 1 sherd from Bullard's excavations on Macanché Island.

Ware: Petén Gloss ware.

Complex: Romero ceramic complex.

Established: Jato Black-on-gray was established as part of the Danta ceramic group at Uaxactún by Smith and Gifford (1966; R. E. Smith 1955).

Principal identifying modes: Jato Black-on-gray may be identified by black paint, most frequently as encircling bands, on the lip and/or base of gray-slipped and polished vessels. Forms are usually cylinders and tripod plates.

Paste and firing: The one sherd from Bullard's excavations at the island was hard-fired with a dense, volcanic-ash-tempered paste that was light gray-brown in color.

Surface treatment and decoration: The

slip and paint on the sherd from the island were nearly completely eroded off, but a faint black band appeared on the lip, extending 3 mm on the exterior and 1 cm on the interior.

Forms and dimensions: The one sherd from Bullard's excavations was a "flowerpot" shape, with a diameter of 14 cm and a height of greater than 11 cm.

Illustration: figure 36c.

Intrasite references: Jato Black-on-gray occurred in small amounts in only two pits on the island: one sherd came from Bullard's Operation IH in tierra blanca, while 11 were recovered from CPHEP pit 5A, in the gray mottled zone above tierra blanca.

Intersite references: Jato Black-on-gray seems to be a reliable indicator of Terminal Classic activity in the central lakes area (though it is not at all notable to the northeast, at Yaxhá-Sacnab), and is associated with burials in many cases (P. Rice 1986). A. Chase (1983) reports Jato from a burial on the Tayasal peninsula, as well. The placement of this type in the Danta group on the basis of the Uaxactún collection may be questioned, because in the lakes there are a variety of incised and fluted composite types. It is anticipated that one or more new type or variety names and/or a new group designation will arise out of final classification of the CPHEP materials.

Daylight Ceramic Group

Name: **Daylight Orange: Darknight Variety (?).**

Frequency: 16 sherds from Bullard's excavations at Macanché Island, 14 of which were from Terminal Classic contexts. Sherds of the Daylight ceramic group (Daylight Orange: Darknight Variety) constitute 0.47 percent of the Terminal Classic assemblage in Bullard's excavations at Macanché Island.

Ware: San Pablo Gloss ware.

Complex: Romero complex (?).

Established: The type and variety names were established by Gifford (Willey et al. 1965) at Barton Ramie; the ware designation is by A. Chase (1983).

Principal identifying modes: Darknight Variety of Daylight Orange consists of dishes with an orange slip that is marked by patterns of blackened, fire-clouded areas.

Paste and firing: The paste is a gray carbonate paste that is moderately hard and thick. Firing, while not fully oxidizing, was apparently well controlled in order to produce the decoration of dark and light areas.

Surface treatment and decoration: Darknight Variety has a moderately hard slip which at Macanché lacks the waxiness noted at Barton Ramie. In luster and in the character of the blemishes from rootlet marking, the sherds of this type are closely akin to Classic period gloss wares. The color of the slip is a dull orange (5.5YR 6/6) that is browner in areas of fire-clouding, while in eroded portions it is slightly yellowish. The decoration consists of irregular dark gray to black fire-clouded splotchy areas covering large portions of the vessel interiors and exteriors.

Forms and dimensions: Vessel forms include dishes with outflaring or gently outcurving sides and apparently flat bases; one has a flattened lip. Diameters of two specimens are 22 and 26 cm; wall thickness varies from 5 to 8 mm. One sherd with higher walls and a smaller mouth diameter (16 cm) may be a jar. A distinctive feature of the dishes is a groove on the interior at the join of wall to base.

Illustrations: figure 36d–f.

Intrasite references: Darknight Variety of Daylight Orange was found in Terminal Classic lots 6 and 11 in Bullard's Operation IA, and in lot 10 (mixed). I am not at all confident of the correct classification of these sherds into the Daylight group, for although they exhibit the characteristic fire-clouding of the Darknight Variety, some of the attributes of slip and form suggest closer ties to Classic gloss wares. In any case, their presence in the Terminal Classic lots is regarded as probably intrusive.

Intersite references: Darknight Variety was defined at Barton Ramie, which seems to be the principal site of its occurrence.

This variety was not identified at Tayasal, although one sherd of Daylight Variety of Daylight Orange was found there. The variety is attributed to the early facet of the Early Postclassic New Town phase at Barton Ramie. Daylight Orange is said to be a derivative of the Taak ceramic group in northern Belize (D. Chase 1984).

Altar Orange Ceramic Group

Name: **Altar Orange (?).**
Frequency: 1 sherd from Terminal Classic deposits in Bullard's excavations on Macanché Island.
Ware: Fine Orange Paste ware.
Complex: Romero ceramic complex.
Established: The Altar ceramic group was established by R. E. W. Adams (1971:27) on the basis of material from Altar de Sacrificios.
Principal identifying modes: Altar Orange may be identified on the basis of extremely fine orange paste lacking inclusions, which is found in characteristic bowl and vase forms.
Paste and firing: The sherd from Bullard's excavations on the island has a very fine textured orange (7.5YR 6.5/4) paste that appears to have no inclusions in it. The presence of a distinct gray core indicates incomplete oxidation of organic matter as a consequence of the very fine, dense paste.
Surface treatment and decoration: The surfaces are very well smoothed, but if any slip or paint appeared, it has long since eroded away.
Forms and dimensions: The sherd suggests a bowl with a "bead lip," but is so small that rim orientation cannot be established. The walls are relatively thick for Orange ware at 7 mm.
Illustrations: None.
Intrasite references: Fine Orange pottery at Macanché Island was variable but generally sparse in occurrence, being found in Postclassic deposits as well (see chapter 7, below). Five sherds from Terminal Classic midden CPHEP pit 6 were of Islas Gouged-incised, a type named in the material at

Seibal (Sabloff 1975:198–199, 204), and represented a "pear-shaped" or pyriform vase.
Intersite references: The Altar ceramic group is widespread throughout the northern and western Maya Lowlands in the Terminal Classic/Early Postclassic periods (see R. E. W. Adams 1971:27; Sabloff 1975; Ball 1977; R. E. Smith 1955), although it is absent or lacking in parts of central Petén (A. Chase 1979; G. Cowgill 1963) and Belize (Gifford 1976). The technological and compositional aspects of production and distribution of Fine Paste wares is summarized by Rands, Bishop, and Sabloff (1982).

Ceramic Group Unspecified

Name: **Unnamed hard ash paste.**
Frequency: 1334 sherds, of which 1305 were from Bullard's excavations on Macanché Island (644 were from Terminal Classic lots and 661 were from his excavations in Postclassic contexts); also 29 sherds were from Ixlú. Ash paste sherds comprised 22.3 percent of the sherds from Terminal Classic lots excavated by Bullard.
Ware: Unspecified.
Complex: Romero ceramic complex, and early facet Aura ceramic complex.
Principal identifying modes: These sherds are distinguished by being hard-fired, and having volcanic ash temper. No slip is apparent on the surfaces at present.
Paste and firing: Sherds are of a brown or tan gritty paste with volcanic ash used as temper. Flecks of mica are often visible on the surfaces. The sherds appear to have been relatively well fired, being quite hard, with a "ring" when tapped, and lack significant dark coring or fire-clouding.
Surface treatment and decoration: The surfaces of these sherds are well smoothed; if they were originally slipped, little to no trace remains. Twenty-seven sherds from Lot 11 in Operation IA have a thin cream wash-like coating on their surface that may be a postdepositional coating (from the "marl" or tierra blanca, as was present on Coarse Gray Variety of Cambio Unslipped) or a thin "self-slip" applied by gently rubbing the wet sur-

face of the vessel with a hand or some other object. Other sherds, if slipped, could have been part of the Tinaja group (red-slipped) or perhaps polychromes, because of general similarities of paste between this collection and known pastes in those types. Thinner or more eroded sherds may relate to the Payaso group.

Forms and dimensions: The size and curvature of the sherds suggest that they come primarily from jars and large bowls. One basal sherd had an excised base. Thickness is moderate, ranging between approximately 6 and 9 mm; 133 sherds were thinner, with thicknesses of 4.5 to 6 mm.

Illustrations: None.

Intrasite references: Sherds of this paste were recovered from virtually all test pits into Macanché Island. CPHEP pit 3 lacked this material in its lower levels containing other Late and Terminal Classic sherds, as did Bullard's Operation IG.

Intersite references: At Ixlú, this ash paste was present only in the mixed Postclassic surface debris overlying the plaza floor (Lot 43). The absence of this paste in the early levels of platform fill on the island and at Ixlú suggests that it may be specifically associated with the Terminal rather than the Late Classic period in the lakes region. Similar pastes seem consistently to comprise a small percentage of Late and Terminal Classic monochrome-slipped wares in north-central Petén, but are less common at Pasión sites. The absence of a slip on these sherds may be a function of erosion, but could also very likely be intentional, calling to mind Sabloff's comments (1975:161) concerning the lack of slips, or the possibility of "fugitive" slipping on Subín Red at Seibal.

Name: **Unidentified Special.**
Frequency: 2 sherds from Terminal Classic contexts on Macanché Island.
Ware: Petén Gloss ware.
Complex: Romero ceramic complex (?).
Description: These sherds have a glossy slip in mottled gray (10YR 5/1), with what is apparently resist decoration in a variable

brownish orange (colors range within 7.5–10YR 5–6/6–8). One sherd is the rim of a short-necked jar, having a neck height of 2.2 cm and a mouth diameter of 10 cm, and thin walls. The paste is fine textured and gray, with carbonate rather than volcanic ash inclusions. The only published reference to anything comparable to this sherd is a "Special: Orange and Brown" vessel at Barton Ramie (Sharer and Chase 1976:312), or a resist orange type in the Augustine ceramic group (Chase and Chase 1983:105).

Illustration: figure 36g.

Name: **Unidentified Special.**
Frequency: One sherd.
Ware: Petén Gloss ware.
Complex: Romero ceramic complex.
Description: The sherd is from a relatively straight-sided vessel which would have had four (?) rounded supports. The carbonate paste is heavy and thick (7 mm). Surfaces are cream-gray in color (ca. 10YR 7/2), with a faded and fire-clouded, but apparently black, band encircling the lower wall just above the basal angle. The diameter of the vessel at the base is 18 cm. There may be some relationship of this vessel to cream polychrome types or to Jato Black-on-gray. Another point of comparison is with an "unusual type" associated with the Tepeu 3 complex at Uaxactún (R. E. Smith 1955: fig. 75b2).

Illustration: figure 36h.

Non-Romero Complex Sherds
Miscellaneous Late Classic Polychromes

Name: **Miscellaneous Late Classic polychromes, probably of the Saxché and Palmar ceramic groups.**
Frequency: 106 sherds, only 6 of which were from Macanché Island (and 4 of those were from Postclassic lots); remainder from Ixlú (66 sherds) and Punta Nimá (34 sherds).
Ware: Petén Gloss ware.
Complex: Imix (Tepeu 2) ceramic complex.

Established: The Saxché and Palmar groups were established at Uaxactún by Smith and Gifford (1966).

Paste and firing: Vessels are primarily made of a well-fired, reddish brown, ash-tempered paste.

Surface treatment and decoration: Vessel surfaces are generally very eroded, and with slips and painted decoration largely missing. Remnant traces on some sherds, combined with characteristic forms, provided the basis for their classification as probable poly-chromes, but were insufficient for identification of specific types. In many cases a background slip color could only be guessed; the ambiguous category "Buff Polychrome" was frequently employed on those occasions when the typical cream-to-"buff" (10YR 7/3) underslip on Late Classic polychromes acted as a background color by reserve or negative painting.

At Ixlú, 16 sherds were classed as Orange Polychrome, 13 as "Buff" Polychrome, 12 as Cream Polychrome, and 25 were unidentifiable. At Punta Nimá, two sherds were Buff Polychrome, two were Cream Polychrome, two were Orange Polychrome, and the remainder (28) were, because of erosion, tentatively classed as "Buff or Orange Polychrome."

Because of erosion, the polychrome decorative motifs themselves are difficult to identify. One Cream Polychrome plate from Ixlú has a band of glyphs painted in black on the "cream" underslip. A flat body sherd, probably the interior of a Naranjal Red-on-cream plate, has red bands and a squiggly line painted on a cream background. A partially reconstructible Orange Polychrome dish from immediately under the plaza floor at Ixlú has alternating circumferential bands on the exterior of black and red (on a "buff" background?); the interior is slipped orange.

At Punta Nimá, a barrel-shaped vessel and a hemispherical bowl both have vertical red stripes on a "buff" or orange background. An Orange Polychrome body sherd has a quatre-foil medallion painted in red on an orange ground; the surrounding area was black. A cylinder body sherd has diagonal broad red and orange stripes on a cream or "buff" background.

The best preserved polychrome sherd is one in the lot of material Bullard purchased at San Miguel: a small flare-sided dish with an indented base (fig. 37). The exterior decoration suggests a close resemblance to "Codex Style" vessels of Petén. The vessel exterior was covered with a creamy "buff"-colored (9YR 6.5/3) primary slip, and over this a decorative band is bounded by parallel encircling black lines with a red glossy lip stripe at the top. The decorative band features a creature similar to the earth monster or the so-called Resurrection deity illustrated by Robicsek and Hales (1981: tables 23F and 24C), although the characteristic elongate maxilla cannot be securely identified on the sherd because of breakage. The eye of the creature has a curl in it; the body terminates with an element that may represent either plumes or the "waterlily" motif characteristic of this "Resurrection complex" on Codex vessels. The background of the vessel is covered with glossy red paint, so that the creature's body is painted on the primary slip almost in a resist or negative technique. This San Miguel vessel is similar to the work of one individual painter of the Codex Style called the "Calligraphic Painter," who often painted the monster heads on bowls with a black background; vessels by this artist also often had "a peculiar flesh-colored or pinkish wash" (Robicsek and Hales 1981:247). The interior of this sherd has a black lip stripe, a broad red band below that, and an orange glossy slip covering the remaining area.

Forms and dimensions: The greatest variety in vessel forms was present in the Punta Nimá collection. These sherds included: 10 plates, typically with lateral ridge (one notched) and ranging in diameter from 30 to 42 cm; 13 barrel-shaped vessels with diameters of 15–18 cm; one cylinder; one hemispherical bowl (diameter 20 cm); and one small flare-sided dish with indented base (diameter 19 cm, height 5.1 cm). Vessels from

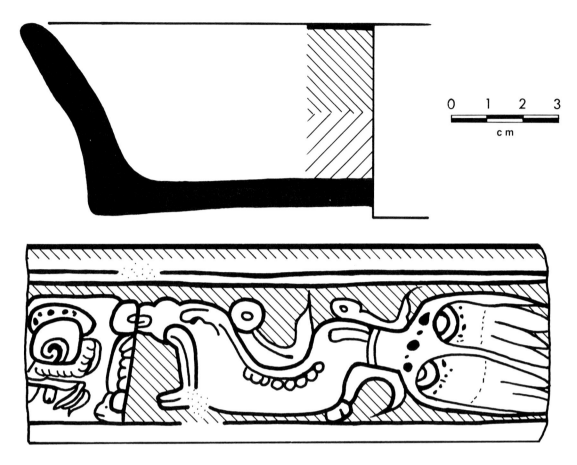

FIGURE 37. Polychrome dish with exterior decoration resembling the earth monster–
"resurrection god" motif seen on Codex Style vessels of Petén. From collection
Bullard purchased at San Miguel.

Ixlú included two small flare-sided dishes (one, an Orange Polychrome tripod with basal flange, was partially reconstructible; diameter 17 cm, height 6 cm). A plate had a diameter of 45 cm. One polychrome sherd from Macanché Island was a barrel-shaped vessel of bright orange-red paste.

Illustrations: figures 36i–k, 37, and 38.

Intrasite references: At Macanché Island, only four polychrome sherds that suggested the Saxché-Palmar ceramic groups were identified, and these came from Postclassic lots. Other vessel forms typically associated with these Late Classic polychrome ceramic types and groups occurred in various lots (especially in Lot 26, which is Early Postclassic), but were completely eroded and could not be

identified as anything other than "Late Classic." The paucity of these types and forms and their heavily eroded condition suggest that there was little emphasis on use of the island during this period, and that a hiatus of some duration occurred prior to Terminal Classic occupation and construction.

Intersite references: At Ixlú, polychrome sherds occurred both above the plaza floor 1, in which 17 polychrome sherds were mixed with Postclassic debris (Lot 43), and in the lots between that floor and the ones beneath (floors 2 and 3; 49 sherds). Because the sherds were generally in such poor condition of preservation and, at Punta Nimá, recovered from other than primary contexts (see also Chase 1983:1101–1105), it is impossible to

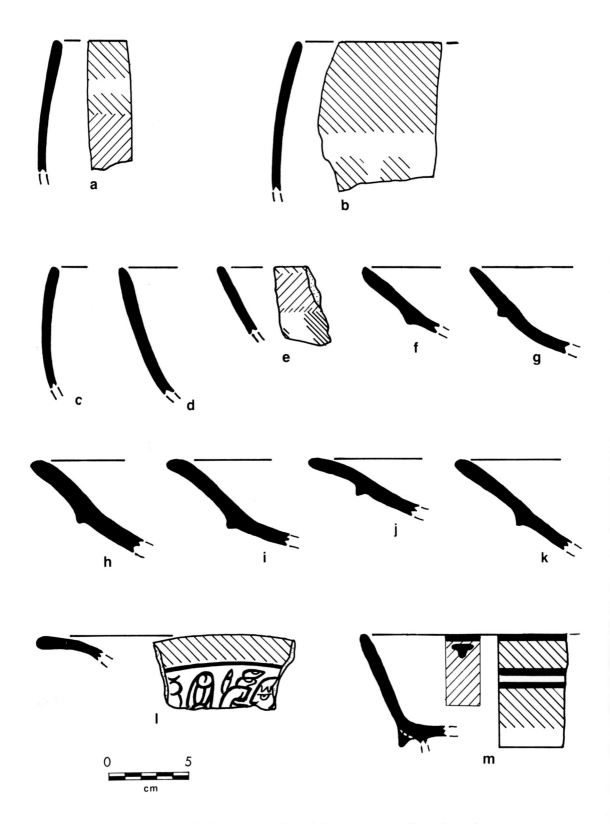

FIGURE 38. Late Classic polychrome vessels and decorative motifs. **a**, **b**, **e**, decoration on exterior; **l**, decoration on interior.

0   5

cm

make any comparative statement on their occurrence or significance. The forms and decorative treatments identified on these sherds are those occurring widely in Petén in the Late Classic.

Miscellaneous Preclassic and Early Classic Pottery Sherds

Bullard's collections from Macanché Island, Ixlú, and Punta Nimá included 41 sherds of Preclassic and Early Classic types and forms. Eight Preclassic/Early Classic sherds were recovered from excavations into Terminal Classic contexts on the island; three came from Postclassic contexts; eight were from the "center" on the Lake Macanché mainland; one was from Punta Nimá; and 21 were from the Ixlú excavations. The sherds include the following types: one Calam Buff (from Ixlú); eight Polvero Black (including one large jar fragment from Punta Nimá); 17 Sierra Red; two Joventud Red; five Flor Cream (including a large labial flange dish sherd); and eight fragments of Balanza black (including five sherds of a scutate lid from Macanché Island).

CHAPTER 5

Postclassic Pottery of the Aura and Dos Lagos Ceramic Complexes and Protohistoric Pottery of the Ayer Ceramic Complex at Macanché Island

THE occupation on Macanché Island was principally Postclassic in date, as indicated by the volume of construction and midden on the island dating to this period. Of the 39 lots excavated or surface collected by Bullard on the island, 31 of them were attributed to Postclassic activity; of the more than 15,000 sherds from those excavations and collections, over 7600 (51 percent) were classifiable Postclassic types (table 4).

Bullard did not assign phase or complex names to the Postclassic materials he recovered, either with reference to Macanché specifically or to Petén in general. Instead, he described a "Central Petén Postclassic Tradition" (1973), subdivided into three periods. The bases for his description and definition of the Petén tradition were not only his excavations on Macanché Island but also his earlier investigations at Topoxté Island (Bullard 1970), and the work of George Cowgill (1963) around Lake Petén-Itzá. The three subdivisions of the Central Petén Postclassic Tradition were founded on the sequential but overlapping appearance of three important pottery groups in the Postclassic: Augustine, then Paxcamán, and finally Topoxté.

It has already been noted (P. Rice 1979:

75–76) that parts of Bullard's 1973 summary article have been misread, resulting in misinterpretation of the Postclassic occupation at Macanché Island. Part of the difficulty concerns the Augustine ceramic group. While the Early Postclassic occurrence of Augustine in Petén seems indisputable, the problem lies in the idea that this is supported stratigraphically at Macanché. Bullard mentioned two examples of diagnostic effigy supports in association with the Terminal Classic Romero complex at Macanché, but indicated that he felt some "suspicion about the validity of the Augustine Ceramic Group as a classificatory entity" because it is highly variable (1973:226, 227). This statement suggests that he may also have experienced difficulty in identifying sherds of this type. In fact, the two effigy sherds mentioned were two of only three sherds in the collection that he had specifically isolated and identified as members of that group.

The Augustine group *is* difficult to identify at Macanché. I have sorted out only fifty-some sherds in Bullard's collection from the island, including those two vessel supports, and all of these sherds were from Postclassic lots. In the CPHEP materials, the small quan-

90

tities of Augustine that were noted occurred only in Postclassic rather than Terminal Classic deposits. Given the problems discussed earlier concerning some of Bullard's Terminal Classic lots at the island (see chapter 3, "The Terminal Classic Romero Complex"), I feel that Augustine can be confidently associated only with the Postclassic there.

One of the accomplishments of the CPHEP excavations on Macanché Island was to establish a more secure stratigraphic and chronological basis for interpreting Postclassic construction and occupational activity on the island. The three ceramic types Bullard used in describing the Petén Postclassic Tradition, Augustine, Paxcamán, and Topoxté, were important in this regard, as were three other ceramic groups, Pozo (P. Rice 1979), Trapeche (A. Chase 1979), and Chilo (described below). In addition, obsidian hydration dates on artifacts from the various levels provided further support for the phasing and sequencing of activity. The "post-Classic" period in the lakes area is described here in terms of three periods and three ceramic complexes: the Aura Early Postclassic complex, the Dos Lagos Late Postclassic complex, and the provisional Ayer Protohistoric complex.

The Early Postclassic Aura Ceramic Complex

The Early Postclassic complex at Macanché Island (table 5) is distinguished by the beginning of use of characteristic Postclassic types and forms, such as Trapeche, Paxcamán, Augustine, and Pozo. Materials of this complex were recovered in both midden and construction core on the island. Excavations by CPHEP provided a basis for determination of early and late facets (P. Rice 1980) of the complex, the early facet being characterized especially by the continuation of ceramic types from the Terminal Classic Romero complex. These types include Payaso Orange-brown, Harina Cream, Coarse Gray Variety of Cambio Unslipped, and the unnamed hard

ash paste; there is some possibility that manufacture of Cameron Incised may also have continued into the early part of the Early Postclassic period.

The pottery from CPHEP excavations used to identify the early facet of the Early Postclassic Aura complex manifested technological continuities with the preceding Terminal Classic period, in addition to these typological ones. Technological continuities were particularly evident in firing, because the early facet sherds of Paxcamán (red-slipped) and Trapeche (cream-pink-slipped) groups exhibited considerable fire-clouding of the surfaces. Continuities also may be seen in the use of a gray carbonate paste for these red-slipped and cream-pink-slipped wares (see chapter 6, below, "Pastes and Slips of the Postclassic Paxcamán and Trapeche Groups").

Because only a few of Bullard's excavations at Macanché Island penetrated construction core to any extent, the Early Postclassic Aura complex is not heavily represented in his collections. The greatest quantity of material comes from lots 31, 33, 34, 36, and 37, which were construction core lots in Operation IH. The general lack of Terminal Classic sherds in these lots suggests that this was late facet Early Postclassic core probably representing the same platform as that sampled by CPHEP pits 3 and 6.

Two other lots are rather ambiguous in terms of their status as Early Postclassic material. Lot 26, in Operation IG, sampled a construction situation very much like that of pit 3—loose rock core overlying Terminal Classic core (Lot 32)—which in turn overlay sterile core, with no clear demarcation between any of the episodes. The sherds in Lot 26 were almost entirely (96.3 percent) Terminal Classic, raising the possibility that the few Postclassic sherds in the lot were merely intrusive. Thus this lot might best be regarded as mixed or simply Early Postclassic in general. A similar ambiguous situation of mixing pertains to Lot 39, from Operation IE on top of the mound. This lot contained

Table 4

Ceramic Units of the Postclassic and Terminal Classic Contexts Investigated by Bullard

	Macanché Island						Non-Mac. Isl.	TOTAL	Percent of Group
	T.Cl.[a]	E.PC.	L.PC.	Proto.	Mix.	Surf.			
Volador Dull-Slipped Ware									
Paxcamán Ceramic Group									
Paxcamán Red: Pax. Var. & Vars. Unspec.	25	49	355	477	300	15	30	1251	78.4
Ixpop Polychrome: Ixpop Variety			105	58	23[b]	4	3	193	12.1
Sacá Polychrome: Sacá Variety		2	12	4				18	1.1
Macanché Red-on-paste: Macanché Variety			1	12	11	1	1	26	1.6
Picú Incised: Picú Variety			2	3	1	1	1	8	0.5
Picú Incised: Thub Variety	5		10	4	1	4		24	1.5
Chamán Modeled: Variety Unspecified			1	1	1			3	0.2
Unidentified Paxcamán Group Polychromes	3		22	33	8	1	4	71	4.5
Total Paxcamán Group	33	51	508	592	345	26	39	1594	99.9
Trapeche Ceramic Group									
Trapeche Pink: Tramite V. and Vars. Unspec.	37	142	151	64	1119	17		1530	79.6
Mul Polychrome: Manax Variety	1	2	12	5	135			155	8.1
Picté Red-on-paste: Picté Variety					6[b]			6	0.3
Xuluc Incised: Ain Variety		1	8	5	19	33	1.7	33	1.7
Xuluc Incised: Tzalam Variety	2	8	5		25			40	2.1
Chuntuci Composite: Variety Unspecified		2						2	0.1
Unidentified Trapeche Group Polychromes		2	17	5	131			155	8.1
Total Trapeche Group	40	157	193	79	1435	17		1921	100.0
Group Unspecified Gray: Types and Vars. Unsp.	9[c]		10	11	31			61	100.0
Clemencia Cream Paste Ware									
Topoxté Ceramic Group									
Topoxté Red: Top. Var. and Vars. Unspec.	1[c]	1	37	209	112	15		375	72.6
Pastel Polychrome: Pastel Variety			1	1				2	0.4
Chompoxté Red-on-cream: Chompoxté Variety			7	4	6	3		20	3.9
Chompoxté Red-on-cream: Akalché Variety			3	6	1			10	1.9
Dulces Incised: Dulces Variety				1				1	0.2

	Macanché Island						Non-Mac. Isl.	TOTAL	Percent of Group
	T.Cl.[a]	E.PC.	L.PC.	Proto.	Mix.	Surf.			
Unidentified Topoxté Group Polychromes			11	57	37	4		109	21.1
Total Topoxté Group	1[c]	1	59	278	156	22		517	100.1
Ídolos Ceramic Group									
Ídolos Modeled: Ídolos Variety		1[c]	9	34	4			48	100.0
Vitzil Orange-Red Ware									
Augustine Ceramic Group									
Augustine Red: Variety Unspecified	3	13	21	12	2		11	62	100.0
Montículo Unslipped Ware									
Pozo Ceramic Group									
Pozo Unslipped: Pozo Variety	20	42	324	445	1935	30	40	2836	99.0
La Justa Composite: La Justa Variety	2[c]	2	3	19	4	1	2	33	1.0
Total Pozo Group	22	44	327	464	1939	31	42	2869	100.0
Uapake Unslipped Ware									
Chilo Ceramic Group									
Chilo Unslipped: Chilo Variety	1[c]	1[c]	31	377	94	4	12	520	94.9
Gotas Composite: Gotas Variety			2	18	5		3	28	5.1
Total Chilo Group	1[c]	1[c]	33	395	99	4	15	548	100.0
Ware Unspecified									
Patojo Ceramic Group									
Patojo Modeled: Patojo Variety			3	2	40		8	53	58.2
Mumúl Composite: Mumúl Variety			1		25		12	38	41.8
Total Patojo Group			4	2	65		20	91	100.0
Group Unspecified Unslipped Hubelna Unslipped: Hubelna Variety			2		1			3	100.0
Other (Fine Orange, Slateware, Tachís)	1		3	5	3		7	19	100.0
Preclassic and Classic[a] *Types*	2997	437	319	210	251	5	199	4418	100.0
Miscellaneous Unidentified sherds	5	591	976	877	399	2	81	2931	100.0
Total sherds	3112	1296	2464	2959	4730	107	414	15,082	

[a] See Table 3 for ceramic units of the Terminal Classic Romero Complex.
[b] Probably represent Early Postclassic material.
[c] Sherds are probably intrusive into these levels.

Table 5

Ceramic Units of the Early Postclassic Aura
Complex at Macanché Island

Volador Dull-Slipped Ware
  Paxcamán Ceramic Group
    Paxcamán Red: Paxcamán Variety
    Ixpop Polychrome: Ixpop Variety
    Sacá Polychrome: Sacá Variety
  Trapeche Ceramic Group
    Trapeche Pink: Tramite Variety
    Mul Polychrome: Manax Variety
    Picté Red-on-paste: Picté Variety
    Xuluc Incised: Ain Variety
    Xuluc Incised: Tzalam Variety
    Chuntuci Composite: Variety Unspecified

Clemencia Cream Paste Ware
  Topoxté Ceramic Group
    Topoxté Red: Topoxté Variety

Vitzil Orange-Red Ware
  Augustine Ceramic Group
    Augustine Red: Variety Unspecified

Slateware
  Group Unspecified
    Unnamed Trickle-on-gray Slate

Fine Orange Paste Ware
  Group Unspecified
    Type and Variety Unspecified

Fine Gray Ware
  Tres Naciones Ceramic Group
    Poité Incised: Variety Unspecified

Montículo Unslipped Ware
  Pozo Ceramic Group
    Pozo Unslipped: Pozo Variety

---

relatively few sherds (100), and is known
from Bullard's notes to have included material from two different categories of core.
The lowest of these may be the late facet
Early Postclassic platform mentioned above.

Thus Bullard's excavations on Macanché
Island included five late facet Early Postclassic lots, and two mixed lots that may be
Early Postclassic in date. The total sherds
from these lots, just under 1300, included
20.7 percent Postclassic types and 79.2 percent Classic and or unidentified material. If
the two mixed lots are removed from consideration, the percentage of Postclassic sherds
in the late facet Early Postclassic platform

alone climbs to 35.3 percent. Among the
Postclassic sherds in all seven lots, the totals
are for slipped types 78.9 percent, unslipped
14.2 percent, censers 1.5 percent, and "other"
5.4 percent.

The principal Postclassic ceramic groups
in the Early Postclassic period at Macanché
Island are the Trapeche group (60.1 percent
of total Early Postclassic type sherds), Paxcamán (18.4 percent), and Pozo (13.8 percent). "Other" categories include one sherd
of "trickle" slateware from Lot 26, and 13
sherds of the Augustine group, of which 12
were in Lot 33 and one was in Lot 26. It
should be remembered, however, that two
vessel supports of the Augustine group (discussed above in chapter 3) were recovered in
Terminal Classic lots 38 and 11. The remainder of the sherds of the Augustine group
were from Late Postclassic lots. In CPHEP
excavations on Macanché Island, Augustine
was associated with the late facet of the
Early Postclassic period, although this was
not the case at Lake Quexil. At Tayasal, Augustine stratigraphically preceded Paxcamán
(Chase and Chase 1983 : 102).

Questions of mixing arise with respect to
the presence of some sherds of types traditionally regarded as Late Postclassic markers
in the relatively intact late facet Early Postclassic platform core of Operation IH. One
Chilo Unslipped sherd is probably intrusive,
but the presence of four censer fragments
and one Topoxté group sherd may be valid associations. Three of the censers are La Justa
Composite, a type of censer with appliqué
spikes or fillets within the Pozo ceramic
group; the other sherd is Ídolos Modeled
(Clemencia Cream Paste ware, associated
with Topoxté group pottery). The three composite censer sherds may be genuine associations of this type with the late facet Early
Postclassic, but the Ídolos sherd raises additional issues.

It is of particular interest that sherds of
the Topoxté ceramic group occur in very
small amounts in the late facet Early Postclassic platform core. The Topoxté group was
traditionally hypothesized to be a product of
the Late Postclassic period (Bullard's "Period

III," beginning after A.D. 1250) largely on the basis of the comment that at Macanché, "Topoxté pottery arrived at the close of the occupation" (Bullard 1973:231). While it is true that this material occurs most abundantly in the upper 40–50 cm on Macanché Island, 12 sherds were recovered from CPHEP excavations into late Early Postclassic platform fill in pits 3 and 6. In addition, one sherd was recovered in Bullard's Lot 26 from Operation IH, and one sherd of Ídolos Modeled came from Lot 31.

Recent reanalysis of the pottery from excavations at Canté Island (P. Rice 1986) and obsidian hydration dates from those excavations (P. Rice n.d. a) have led to the realization that the occupation of the Topoxté islands in Lake Yaxhá had an Early Postclassic (Early Isla) component as well as a late (Late Isla) one. The presence of these Topoxté group sherds in construction fill contexts on Macanché Island also argues against the exclusively late importation of the Topoxté group to Macanché. These few late facet Early Postclassic sherds at Macanché, like the few apparently Early Postclassic Paxcamán sherds at Canté Island (P. Rice 1979, 1986), may indicate a different category of economic relationships that were later altered, when Topoxté moved quantities of its pottery out to Macanché, but acquired no Paxcamán or Trapeche imports in turn.

Three obsidian hydration dates were obtained for Early Postclassic deposits excavated by CPHEP (table 2), and all fell in the eleventh century. If the standard deviations are used as a basis for suggesting beginning and ending dates of this phase, the Early Postclassic period can be dated from approximately A.D. 984 to 1113, which might be rounded off for convenience to roughly A.D. 950 to 1150 or 1200.

The Aura complex at Macanché is probably a member of the New Town sphere which seems, by tacit agreement, now to be used to refer only to Early Postclassic complexes rather than encompassing both Early and Late Postclassic manifestations. Although the New Town sphere was originally defined from materials from the Barton Ramie site,

two of its diagnostics as given by the 1965 Maya ceramic conference, Plumbate and pyriform vases (Willey, Culbert, and Adams 1967), were not even present there. Sharer and Chase (1976:290) consequently redefined the sphere to emphasize the presence of Paxcamán and Augustine groups, and footed dishes. The presence of the Trapeche group at Tayasal and Macanché, and the presence of the Daylight group in both these locations suggests that the sphere identification might be broadened to include these two groups.

The Chilcob Early Postclassic ceramic complex of the Tayasal-Paxcamán zone is related typologically and in spatial proximity to the Aura complex at Macanché. Chilcob is characterized by Augustine, Trapeche, Paxcamán, and Tanché as the primary slipped groups. Tanché, is a red-slipped ash-paste group with "different forms" (Chase and Chase 1983:104) that appears briefly in the late facet of the complex, as the Trapeche group is disappearing from it. Plumbate and Daylight groups (one sherd) are also present in the Chilcob complex, which is a member of the New Town sphere.

The Late Postclassic Dos Lagos Ceramic Complex

The bulk of the material recovered from excavations on Macanché Island, both by Bullard and by CPHEP, pertain to the Late Postclassic period, which I date between approximately A.D. 1200 and 1450. (This interval encompasses to what others have called the "Middle" Postclassic, dated variously A.D. 1200–1300 at Mayapán, A.D. 1140–1350/1400 at Lamanai, and A.D. 1200–1450 at Tayasal.) The Late Postclassic pottery from Macanché can be divided into early and late components, and it is the latter that I feel extend late enough (i.e., ca. sixteenth century or later) to call it "Protohistoric" or "Historic," rather than "Late Postclassic." This issue will be taken up later, and here the entire temporal range will be referred to as Late Postclassic.

Twenty-two of Bullard's lots were phased to the Late Postclassic period; these were principally from the upper 50 cm of humus,

Table 6

Ceramic Units of the Late Postclassic
Dos Lagos Complex at Macanché Island

Volador Dull-Slipped Ware
  Paxcamán Ceramic Group
    Paxcamán Red: Paxcamán Variety
    Ixpop Polychrome: Ixpop Variety
    Picú Incised: Picú Variety
    Picú Incised: Thub Variety
    Macanché Red-on-paste: Macanché Variety
    Chamán Modeled: Variety Unspecified
  Trapeche Ceramic Group
    Trapeche Pink: Tramite Variety
    Mul Polychrome: Manax Variety
    Picté Red-on-paste: Picté Variety
    Xuluc Incised: Ain Variety
    Xuluc Incised: Tzalam Variety
  Group Unspecified Gray: Type and Variety
    Unspecified

Clemencia Cream Paste Ware
  Topoxté Ceramic Group
    Topoxté Red: Topoxté Variety
    Pastel Polychrome: Pastel Variety
    Chompoxté Red-on-cream: Chompoxté
      Variety
    Chompoxté Red-on-cream: Akalché Variety
    Dulces Incised: Dulces Variety
  Ídolos Ceramic Group
    Ídolos Modeled: Ídolos Variety

Vitzil Orange-Red Ware
  Augustine Ceramic Group
    Augustine Red: Variety Unspecified

Fine Orange Paste Ware ?
  Group Unspecified
    Type and Variety Unspecified

Fine Gray Ware ?
  Tres Naciones Ceramic Group
    Poité Incised: Variety Unspecified

Montículo Unslipped Ware
  Pozo Ceramic Group
    Pozo Unslipped: Pozo Variety
    La Justa Composite: La Justa Variety

Uapake Unslipped Ware
  Chilo Ceramic Group
    Chilo Unslipped: Chilo Variety
    Gotas Composite: Gotas Variety

Ware Unspecified
  Patojo Ceramic Group
    Patojo Modeled: Patojo Variety
    Mumúl Composite: Mumúl Variety

midden, and collapse debris on the island. The sherd yield in these lots was generally high, and 10,100 sherds were recovered, of which over 7100 (70.7 percent) were Postclassic types and forms.

The Late Postclassic Dos Lagos complex at Macanché Island (table 6) is characterized in part by three ceramic groups that continued from the Early Postclassic complex: the Paxcamán (red) group; the Trapeche group, the slip color of which changed from cream-pink to tan or orange; and the Pozo (unslipped) group. Although Augustine group sherds continue to be encountered in Late Postclassic deposits, they occur in small numbers and may reflect earlier material churned up in fill or midden.

The Late Postclassic is also distinguished by the presence of three new (or newly conspicuous) group or form categories or both: Topoxté (red) ceramic group, Chilo (unslipped) ceramic group, and a collection of distinctive censers (principally effigies in the Ídolos and Patojo ceramic groups). There is also a small number of sherds (52) from Bullard's excavations with gray slips that have the same forms and decorations as Paxcamán/ Trapeche, but the gray slip is so even in color that it could be intentional rather than a result of fire-clouding. This group has not been named.

Overall in the Dos Lagos complex from Macanché Island, slipped sherds (Topoxté, Paxcamán, Trapeche, and unnamed gray groups) constitute 52.0 percent of the sherds, 44.9 percent are unslipped, 2.4 percent are censers, and 0.6 percent are "other." It is particularly interesting to compare the percentages of slipped and unslipped sherds in Late Postclassic lots with those categories in the Early Postclassic (table 7): it can be seen that slipped sherds decreased significantly in frequency, while there are almost three times as many unslipped sherds in the Late complex as in the Early Postclassic.

Because of the large quantity of Late Postclassic sherds from Bullard's excavations on the island and the variety of contexts and locations sampled by those excavations, it is useful to break down this material to investi-

Table 7

Comparison of Slipped, Unslipped, Censer, and Other Categories of Pottery
in Early and Late Postclassic Lots at Macanché Island

	Slipped		Unslipped		Censer		Other		
	N	%	N	%	N	%	N	%	Total N
Early Postclassic[a]	206	78.9	37	14.2	4	1.5	14	5.4	261
Late Postclassic	3,715	52.0	3,211	45.0	169	2.4	47	0.6	7,142

a. Lots 26, 31, 33, 34, 36, and 37.

gate additional temporal and functional concerns relating to the island's occupation.

Temporal Subdivision

One breakdown of Bullard's material is stratigraphic, and results in three categories of Late Postclassic lots: early, late, and mixed. In some of Bullard's pits, he separated the upper 15–20 cm of surface material from lower levels, which frequently (at least on top of the mound) terminated at the upper surfacing of platform construction characterized by "loose stone fill," roughly 40–50 cm below ground surface. The lots coming from the lower 20–50 cm b.s. of these excavations are, for purposes of discussion, here distinguished as "early" Late Postclas-

sic, and include lots 14 (Operation IC), 20 (IG), 21 (IE), 22 (IF), 23 (ID), and 27 and 28 (IH). The upper 0–20 cm b.s. is called "late" Late Postclassic or Protohistoric, and includes lots 8 and 9 (Operation IB), 13 (IC), 15 (ID), 17 (IE), 18 (IF), 19 (IG), and 24 (IH). The third category of lots are those that are a stratigraphic mixture of both upper and lower levels; these "mixed" lots include lots 5, 7, and 10 from Operation IA (although Lot 10 may sample platform core dating to the late facet Early Postclassic), Lot 16 (Operation IB), and lots 25, 30, and 35 from Operation IH.

The ceramic content of these upper and lower midden lots can be compared (table 8) in order to shed light on possible changes

Table 8

Comparison of Ceramic Group Frequencies and Percentages in Upper and Lower
Levels of the Late Postclassic Midden at Macanché Island

Ceramic group[c]	Lower (Late Postclassic)[a]			Upper (Protohistoric)[b]			Total	
	N	% across	% down	N	% across	% down	N	% down
Paxcamán	508	45.4	43.6	610	54.6	32.3	1,118	36.6
Trapeche	201	71.8	17.3	79	28.2	4.2	280	9.2
Unidentified Gray	10	47.6	0.9	11	52.4	0.6	21	0.7
Topoxté	51	15.5	4.4	278	84.5	14.7	329	10.8
Other	24	58.5	2.1	17	41.5	0.9	41	1.3
Pozo	324	42.1	27.7	445	57.9	23.5	769	25.1
Chilo	31	7.6	2.7	377	92.4	19.9	408	13.4
Censer	16	18.0	1.4	73	82.0	3.9	89	2.9
Total	1,165	38.1		1,890	61.9		3,055	

Note: Mixed lots have been omitted.
a. Lots 14, 20, 21, 22, 23, 27, and 28.

b. Lots 8, 9, 13, 15, 17, 18, 19, and 24.

within the Late Postclassic Dos Lagos complex over its duration. The increase in Chilo Unslipped is evident in the upper or "late" levels, as is the greater frequency of Topoxté group sherds, in comparison with lower or "early" levels of the Late Postclassic midden. There is a significant reduction in the quantity of slipped wares, particularly in the Trapeche group, from lower to upper midden as well, slipped wares (Paxcamán, Trapeche, Topoxté, and unnamed gray groups) accounting for 66.1 percent of the total 1164 Postclassic sherds in the lower midden, versus 51.7 percent of sherds in the upper midden. A decline in frequency of decorated wares beginning in the late facet of the Early Postclassic and continuing through the Late Postclassic has previously been remarked at Macanché Island (P. Rice 1980:80).

Functional Subdivision

A second approach to examining the content of the Late Postclassic midden at Macanché Island is to compare quantitatively and qualitatively the ceramic material from pits located at the summit of the mound (Operations IC, ID, IE, and IF) with those at the lower slope or base of the mound (Operations IA, IB, and IH). This practice can be somewhat deceptive, at least quantitatively, because of the much greater amounts of excavated material from the larger pits at the base of the mound. The fact that these lower slope pits contain considerable quantities of partially reconstructible vessels has already been discussed, although it should be noted that some partially restorable dishes and jars (including slipped, unslipped, and censer categories) were recovered from around the structures on the mound summit as well.

There are, however, differences in the occurrence of various types and forms on the top of the mound as compared to the mound slopes in Bullard's excavations (table 9). The top of the mound is dominated by Paxcamán and Chilo groups, whereas sherds of the Trapeche group occur with greater frequency in the midden deposits at the base or slope of the mound, rather than on the top. Only 53

sherds of the Trapeche group were recovered from Bullard's excavations on the top of the mound, versus 1663 on the slopes. In addition, the assemblage from the lower midden (in both Bullard's excavations and those of CPHEP) tends to have a slightly greater proportion of dishes relative to jars within the slipped wares. The apparent abundance of censers on the mound slopes is skewed by Operation IH: all but three effigy censer sherds come from that excavation unit alone. Slipped groups and types themselves are present in nearly the same quantities in the midden at the base of the mound, constituting 52.0 percent of Postclassic pottery in that deposit, as compared to 51.9 percent of the Postclassic pottery in the midden at the top of the mound.

The seven "mixed" lots yielded quantities of Late Postclassic sherds that exceeded the quantities from the "early" and "late" categories combined; the number of non-Postclassic sherds in these stratigraphically mixed lots was only a fraction of that from the faceted lots, however. It is revealing that a comparison of the percentages of some of the specific ceramic groups in the mixed lots with those of the faceted lots suggests that with respect to certain significant categories (e.g., Topoxté, Trapeche, Chilo, and censers) the mixed lots are quantitatively more similar to those of the early facet of the Late Postclassic than they are to those of the late facet. Because these mixed lots are primarily from Operations IA and IH, which are excavation units located on the lower slopes of the mound, and because they contain significant amounts of sherds indicating primary breakage, it is likely that these lots represent early Late Postclassic midden accumulated by tossing debris off the edge of the mound.

One caveat to this interpretation should be added concerning the large quantities of partially reconstructable censers (especially effigies) in Operation IH. These are distributed in "early facet," "late facet," and mixed lots in this operation, suggesting that the midden in this area is either very mixed, or this side of the mound was specifically asso-

Table 9

Comparison of Ceramic Group Frequencies and Percentages in Late Postclassic[a] Midden
Lots from Mound Summit and Mound Slopes at Macanché Island

| | Top of Mound[b] | | | Mound Slopes | | | | | | Total | |
| | | | | Intact Lots[c] | | | Mixed Lots[d] | | | | |
Ceramic group	N	% across	% down	N	% across	% down	N	% across	% down	N	% down
Paxcamán	401	27.4	37.0	717	49.0	36.4	344	23.5	8.4	1,462	20.5
Trapeche	53	3.1	4.9	227	13.2	11.5	1,436	83.7	35.1	1,716	24.0
Unidentified Gray	11	21.1	1.0	10	19.2	0.5	31	59.6	0.8	52	0.7
Topoxté	98	20.2	9.0	231	47.6	11.7	156	32.1	3.8	485	6.8
Other	10	19.1	0.9	31	63.8	1.6	9	17.0	0.2	50	0.7
Pozo	245	9.0	22.6	523	19.3	26.5	1,935	71.6	47.4	2,703	37.9
Chilo	263	52.2	24.3	145	28.8	7.4	96	19.0	2.3	504	7.1
Censer	3	2.3	0.3	86	50.6	4.4	80	47.1	2.0	169	2.4
Total	1,084	15.2		1,970	27.6		4,087	57.2		7,141	

a. Data from table 8 plus mixed lots.
b. Lots 13, 14, 15, 17, 18, 21, 22, and 23.
c. Lots 8, 9, 19, 20, 24, 27, and 28.
d. Lots 5, 7, 10, 16, 25, 30, and 35.

ciated with patterns of discard of censer material over a considerable period of time. Reconstructible censers were also recovered from the exterior of the structure on top of the mound sampled by CPHEP pit 3, in "early" Late Postclassic contexts at 40 cm below surface.

This midden on the slopes may also have some differentiation with respect to other artifact categories: both chipped and ground stone artifacts were more abundant on the slopes than on the top of the mound (see chapters 9 and 10), and it will be remembered that the large chert "cache" was from Operation IH, on the western slope. Notched sherds, or line or net sinkers (chapter 8), are evenly distributed in summit versus slope contexts, however, and animal bone (chapter 11) probably is not a reliable indicator of functional differences because not all bone may have been recovered and counted.

Vessel Form, Function, and Style

In addition to issues concerning the implications of differences in deposition of censers and slipped versus unslipped vessels in the Late Postclassic midden on the island, there are two other questions that can be raised. These concern the relationship of form and function in some of the vessel categories used in the Dos Lagos complex.

One matter concerns the tripod dishes of the Paxcamán and Trapeche groups, specifically their size. At Macanché, these dishes are very small, with mouth diameters typically ranging between 18 and 24 cm and averaging between 19 and 20 cm. They are also rather shallow, meaning that they can hold only a relatively small amount of food or other contents. These dishes are noticeably smaller than similar vessels of the Augustine and Paxcamán groups at other sites (e.g., Barton Ramie), as well as being only a fraction of the size of earlier Classic dishes and plates. A gradual reduction in size of Paxcamán tripods throughout the Postclassic has been noted at Tayasal-Paxcamán (Chase and Chase 1983:108), but at Macanché the small size is characteristic of the entire period.

Related to this is the fact that despite their small size, it is possible to see a functional link in food serving between these small Postclasssic tripods and the large, flat Classic plates. There are, however, no functional equivalents or replacements in Postclassic assemblages for the large incurved-rim bowls or basins that were so common in Subín Red, Chaquiste Impressed, and Cameron Incised types in the Late and Terminal Classic periods. A possible replacement is a bowl or dish with an outflaring collar, but again the receptacle's volume is considerably smaller than that of the Late Classic precedessors.

The question that arises, then, is whether these reductions in size of preparation and serving vessels reflect changes in kind of food consumed, in patterns of preparing, serving, and consuming foods, in size of the consuming unit, or in some combination of these changes. That the changes are primarily dietary rather than strictly social is suggested by modifications in food production technology in the Postclassic period that are significantly correlated with these smaller plates: these include the appearance of *molcajetes*, or "chile grinding" bowls, net or line sinkers for fishing, and the disappearance of large chipped stone "standard bifaces" from Postclassic lithic assemblages (Aldenderfer 1982, and personal communication). All of these features may be correlated with changed patterns of food production and consumption that relate to alterations in the household economic unit (see Wonderley 1985 for discussion of similar dietary and artifact changes in the Naco and Sula valleys, Honduras).

A second formal/functional issue in the Postclassic ceramic assemblages that warrants attention again concerns comparisons with Classic assemblages. This is that the "jars" of Pozo Unslipped bear little resemblance to their Cambio Unslipped counterparts. The Cambio Unslipped jars had high and comparatively restricted necks over a large globular body; the rim of the jar was usually outflaring and had some elaboration of the lip—a flange, bolster, etc.—of the sort that is often associated with greater ease of fastening a cover securely over the orifice. The neck, while restricted with respect to the body and orifice, is nonetheless sufficiently open to permit insertion of a hand (or perhaps a gourd or pottery ladle) to extract the contents.

The Postclassic Pozo Unslipped vessels, by contrast, are ollas—relatively open, wide-mouthed containers with short necks set nearly vertically over a body that expands little below the neck. Ease of access to the contents is facilitated by the lack of restriction in the neck, but it would have been impossible to fasten a cover securely on many of these vessels. Although no complete specimens are available, judging from the relative size and curvature of the body sherds the volumetric capacity of the Postclassic olla appears to be considerably smaller than that of Classic jars.

The unslipped Classic jars are generally referred to as "storage" or "utility" jars; the elaboration of the lip that facilitates securing the orifice suggests that either long-term storage or prevention of spillage of the contents during transport may have been important functional concerns for the makers and users of these vessels. That they were not primarily used for cooking is suggested by the rarity of sooting on body sherds and the inappropriateness of the neck restriction.

The Pozo Unslipped ollas likewise do not evidence sooting, but the differences in size and secondary form characteristics suggest that these Postclassic vessels served slightly different functions from the unslipped jars of the Classic period. The lack of orifice restriction and security of closure might indicate short-term storage of vessel contents, need for frequent access to them, a lack of frequent need to transport the vessels and their contents, or some combination of these. If these unslipped vessels are, as a class, related to water storage and transport functions, the changed attributes of the Postclassic vessels may relate to the island or peninsular location of Postclassic settlement: with water always close at hand, there is little need for specialized vessels to transport and store it.

Two stylistic categories bear further discussion with respect to the Late Postclassic: the Tachís ceramic group, and the occurrence of reptilian motifs in incised and painted decoration. The Tachís group has been somewhat ambiguous since its earliest definition (G. Cowgill 1963). In Bullard's collections, only a small number of sherds from Punta Nimá seemed to be classifiable in that category, while no sherds from anywhere in the other lakes investigated by CPHEP were likely candidates. The Tachís group may be specifically localized to the Lake Petén-Itzá area.

Reptilian images are a characteristic peculiar to the Late Postclassic in the lakes area investigated by CPHEP. These are the most common—and virtually the only—identifiable motifs in Postclassic pottery of this area, and while they are scarce in general, they are particularly to be found at Macanché Island (see Bullard 1973: fig. 38). This apparent abundance is no doubt at least partially a consequence of the extensive excavations that were undertaken at that island, in comparison to the more restricted CPHEP test-pitting operations at other Postclassic locations. Nonetheless, a few examples were found at Salpetén, and Bullard's collection from Punta Nimá included one specimen.

Three reptilian motifs—"profile" (see figs. 44b and 51), "quasi-split representational" (see fig. 43 and plate IX), and "RE glyph" (see fig. 44a)—have been identified in incised and in painted pottery of the Paxcamán and Trapeche groups, and their occurrence is believed to relate to both pan-Mesoamerican status symbol systems as well as to possible functions in agricultural/renewal ritual (P. Rice 1983a, 1983b, 1985b). The vessels bearing the reptilian motifs occurred both in the late Early Postclassic platform fill on Macanché Island (as sampled by CPHEP pit 3) as well as in the "early" Late Postclassic midden material. They occurred both in excavations on the top of the mound around the structure and in the midden on the slopes and base of the mound, the only differentiation being that representations in the Paxcamán group (Ixpop and Picú) vessels tended to be found at the top of the mound, whereas reptilian motifs were more common in Ain Variety of Xuluc Incised (Trapeche group) at the bottom of the mound. Vessels bearing these motifs did not exhibit any tendency to occur in deposits associated with large quantities of censers.

Some of the reptilian motifs show similarities to earlier Late Classic "Codex Style"

vessels. For example, the "quasi-split representational reptile," in its general layout, is similar to the long-nosed "earth monster" or "Resurrection complex" deities on some Codex vessels (e.g., Robicsek and Hales 1981: tables 23D, 24C), while the "profile" version is similar to rain god serpent heads (Robicsek and Hales 1981: table 16). There are also similarities in the painting technology between these Late Classic and Postclassic styles (see below, also P. Rice 1985c).

Exterior Relationships

The contents of the Dos Lagos ceramic complex bear little similarity to those of the contemporaneous "Middle" Postclassic Cocahmut complex identified and described in the Tayasal-Paxcamán zone of Lake Petén-Itzá (A. Chase 1979; Chase and Chase 1983). Only the Paxcamán ceramic group is shared between the two, and the Cocahmut complex contains a very restricted inventory of types and groups, by comparison to both earlier and later complexes in the zone, and to the contemporaneous Dos Lagos complex in the Macanché area. Two characteristic groups of the Dos Lagos complex are missing in Cocahmut, Trapeche and Topoxté (although the latter appears in small amounts in the succeeding Kauil complex), and censers rarely occur in the hourglass and effigy forms of the Macanché area.

The Dos Lagos ceramic complex at Macanché Island appears, by the presence of Topoxté group pottery, Pozo Unslipped ollas, and effigy censers, to be a member of the Isla ceramic sphere defined for the Topoxté islands (P. Rice 1979: 78–79). Only the Chilo group, which was not identified at Topoxté, stands as an oddity in this complex at Macanché.

Dating the Dos Lagos complex has been difficult to accomplish. Five obsidian hydration dates from Macanché Island (table 2) range from A.D. 1301 to 1436; with their standard deviations added and subtracted, the dates range from A.D. 1274 to 1455. Dates from other lakes in the region suggest a similar time of beginning of the period, but two obsidian dates, one from Lake Quexil and the other from Lake Salpetén (P. Rice n.d. a), push the dating of the Isla ceramic sphere and the Late Postclassic period into the early sixteenth century (see below).

More specific dating problems concerned the temporal relationships among the Topoxté ceramic group, the Chilo group, and the effigy censers. Establishing such relationships was extremely problematical, and two reasons may be suggested for this. One is that obsidian, a useful item for dating, was a rare commodity in the upper levels of the CPHEP excavations into Late Postclassic midden on Macanché Island, hinting at a decline in trade or in the availability of this commodity toward the end of the occupation. The other reason is that most of the CPHEP excavations were placed at the top of the mound, where Chilo was common, rather than at the base of the mound, where effigy censers seem to have been typically discarded. For these reasons, it was difficult to find obsidian (for dating), Chilo, and censers all in association. As a result, none of the obsidian dates from the lakes area can be extended to date the presence of effigy censers; all but one of the dates in table 2 are in association with Chilo, however, and all are in association with Topoxté group pottery. Thus, it seems safe to date the appearance of the Late Postclassic Dos Lagos complex, and the association of two (Topoxté and Chilo) of its three diagnostics, at least as early as the end of the thirteenth century, and perhaps the more commonly used round date of A.D. 1200 is justifiable. Whether effigy censers came to be used at the same time or later cannot be determined at present from the evidence at Macanché.

The Middle Postclassic Cocahmut complex at Tayasal-Paxcamán lacks Topoxté, Chilo, and effigy censers, but includes Paxcamán and the Pozo homolog, Nohpek Unslipped. This complex has been included in the New Town sphere and dated to A.D. 1200–1450 (Chase and Chase 1983:107). The succeeding Kauil complex, which has no sphere identification, contains Topoxté and Chilo groups and is dated A.D. 1450–

1750. No data are presented concerning the stratigraphic (or other specific chronological) relationships of the Kauil complex to the Cocahmut complex, however, in order to justify its very late dating or the identification of the two as separate complexes. Kauil is said to be intrusive into a Cocahmut deposit in one location (A. Chase, personal communication). Considering the appearance of Topoxté and Chilo in "early" Late Postclassic contexts at Macanché (presumably ca. A.D. 1200), it is possible that these types (and the Kauil complex itself) can be dated earlier at Tayasal as well.

A Provisional Protohistoric Ayer Ceramic Complex

The differences in content between "early" and "mixed" compared to "late" components of the Late Postclassic at Macanché Island raised the possibility that the "late" material should be used to define instead a separate Protohistoric and/or Historic complex. The "late" Late Postclassic was identified on the basis of artifacts in the upper 20 cm of midden on the island, and while it demonstrates clear typological continuities with the "early" material, there are significant changes in proportions of the categories (table 8): a decrease in decorated pottery, a decline in the Trapeche group, the absence of the reptile motifs, and the prominence of Chilo. The poorly fashioned pottery of the Chilo group is perhaps the most provocative of the categories, because of the similarities of forms of jars and bowls to vessels made as recently as the twentieth century in San José, on the north shore of Lake Petén-Itzá (Reina and Hill 1978:143).

The dating of this hypothetical Protohistoric phase would begin ca. A.D. 1400–1450 and include most of the fifteenth and sixteenth (and later) centuries. The phase thus encompasses Bullard's Period IV of the "Central Petén Postclassic Tradition." As mentioned above, however, there were difficulties in obtaining chronometric dates for this very late occupation as a result of the comparative rarity of obsidian in the upper levels of the late midden. The latest obsidian date at Macanché Island was A.D. 1436 ± 19, on a blade from pit 5B. Three other obsidian dates from elsewhere in the lakes area (P. Rice n.d. a) that would correspond to this Protohistoric occupation come from Lake Salpetén (A.D. 1532 ± 26), Lake Quexil (A.D. 1509 ± 15), and Canté Island in Lake Yaxhá (A.D. 1471 ± 31).

The presence of these late obsidian dates, taken together with the known human habitation of the lake basins in the sixteenth and seventeenth centuries, strongly suggests that some effort must be made to identify these populations by their material culture. The kinds of sporadic military and missionizing contacts that the Spaniards had with the indigenous peoples of Petén were not of the sort to result in major transformations of the ceramic assemblage, either by adding to it or by substituting new forms or techniques. Unfortunately, such a situation can only result in frustration for archaeologists seeking to define periods of occupation by the typical criteria of changes in ceramic forms, types, and decoration.

The social and economic stresses experienced throughout the Maya area in the sixteenth and seventeenth centuries were felt less directly and intensely in the isolated Petén interior. To the extent that these stresses would have had any impact on the ceramic record at all (see W. Y. Adams 1979), it is likely that the effects would be alterations in the existing complex taking the form of simplification rather than additions to it (see P. Rice 1984c). Clues can be gathered from studies of pottery in other areas of the New World where Spanish contact was far more prolonged and oppressive than that in Petén. Spanish conquest of both the Inca and the Aztec left little impression on local utilitarian pottery, for example, and production of traditional forms and designs continued relatively unchanged. One typical finding of

Table 10
Ceramic Units of the Provisional Protohistoric Ayer Complex at Macanché Island

Volador Dull-Slipped Ware
  Paxcamán Ceramic Group
    Paxcamán Red: Paxcamán Variety
    Picú Incised: Thub Variety
    Macanché Red-on-paste: Macanché Variety
  Trapeche Ceramic Group
    Trapeche Pink: Tramite Variety

Clemencia Cream Paste Ware
  Topoxté Ceramic Group
    Topoxté Red: Topoxté Variety
    Pastel Polychrome: Pastel Variety
    Chompoxté Red-on-cream: Chompoxté Variety
  Ídolos Ceramic Group
    Ídolos Modeled: Ídolos Variety

Montículo Unslipped Ware
  Pozo Ceramic Group
    Pozo Unslipped: Pozo Variety
    La Justa Composite: La Justa Variety

Uapake Unslipped Ware
  Chilo Ceramic Group
    Chilo Unslipped: Chilo Variety
    Gotas Composite: Gotas Variety

these studies is that surface finishing declined (Tschopik 1951; Charlton 1968), an indication of simplification and reduced labor investment in manufacture.

These changes have parallels in the provisional Protohistoric Ayer complex of Petén, as seen in the reduction in slipped and decorated pottery, the decline of the Trapeche group, and the increase in the crudely finished Chilo category. I would therefore define the provisional Ayer Protohistoric complex (table 10) and Ayer sphere as consisting of Paxcamán, Topoxté (early), Pozo, and Chilo groups, and characterized further by a general decline in frequency of decorated pottery versus unslipped categories.

CHAPTER 6

Pastes and Slips of the Paxcamán and Trapeche Ceramic Groups

THE Paxcamán ceramic group is a classificatory entity that is of considerable importance in reconstructions of Petén Postclassic history, having both a broad geographical spread and an impressive temporal persistence. The types of this red-slipped group were first identified as being Postclassic in date at Tikal (Adams and Trik 1961), and then Paxcamán was recognized as the principal slipped group in Postclassic Petén by means of George Cowgill's (1963) work in the area of Lake Petén-Itzá. It is thus not surprising that when Bullard began study of the materials from Macanché Island, he included all sherds of the distinctive "snail inclusion paste" in the Paxcamán group, regardless of the variations in slip color. His preliminary count was 3402 sherds from Macanché Island in the Paxcamán ceramic group.

Since this early work, a new pink-to-cream-slipped Postclassic ceramic group, the Trapeche group, which also features the snail-inclusion paste characteristic of Paxcamán, has been identified in central Petén (A. Chase 1979). Although the geographic and temporal ranges of the Trapeche group have proven to be considerably more restricted than those of Paxcamán, this group exhibits variations in slip and paste that are significant with regard to their correlations with other spatial, temporal, and socioeconomic phenomena of the Petén Postclassic.

At Macanché, the material originally categorized by Bullard as Paxcamán was reclassified into the types of the Paxcamán and Trapeche ceramic groups. In the process of this classification, it was noted that the longevity of these two groups, combined with differing depositional contexts, could be associated with a striking variability within the technological characteristics of the sherds, especially within the Trapeche group. The two ceramic groups share a virtually identical range of forms and decorative treatments within their member types. While the decorative variations—incising, polychrome painting, and so forth—provided a ready basis for classification of the material into types and varieties, the variations in "ware" characteristics were not so tractable. This variability exists as a continuum of color change in pastes, but more dramatically in slips.

As is common in such cases, the continuum proved difficult to divide into discrete classificatory units. The Paxcamán group represents one rather well defined end (red) of the slip color continuum, while the Trapeche group represents a rather amorphous body of material at the other end (cream) and in the middle (pink or orange-tan). Variability in the Trapeche group has a strong temporal component, further compounding the technical and classificatory problems. Nonetheless, the variations in both ceramic groups were potentially significant for contributing to an understanding of questions of production as well as solving problems of Postclassic chronology.

Several different avenues were explored in order to examine variability in the Paxcamán and Trapeche ceramic groups, both decoratively and technologically. Some of these data have been presented elsewhere (P. Rice

1980), but a more complete discussion of variability and its implications for classification and Petén Postclassic history is warranted here.

Paste Characteristics

Paxcamán and Trapeche group sherds at Macanché Island, as well as elsewhere in Petén, are made of a fine-textured, compact paste, generally characterized by the presence of snail shell inclusions. This paste has been called "snail inclusion ware" by George Cowgill (1963) and "light gray paste ware" by Arlen Chase (1979 : 105). Paste variability falls along two axes in the two ceramic groups: (1) within the snail-inclusion paste, there is a range of color from brown to dark gray, with the majority of the sherds being a light brown-gray; and (2) over and above the snail-inclusion paste, there are a small number of "odd" pastes used in the manufacture of characteristic Paxcamán and Trapeche types and forms. Most significant of these are a relatively coarse reddish brown paste and a yellowish ash-tempered paste.

Covariation in the occurrence of different pastes with specific time periods, vessel forms, or decorative categories may be significant in terms of distinguishing temporal and/or geographical variations in these long-lived and widely used groups. Snail-inclusion paste occurs in relatively minor quantities at Barton Ramie (Sharer and Chase 1976), for example, but it seems to be the standard paste for production in Petén. Variations within it may reflect very localized or idiosyncratic production units.

Snail-Inclusion Paste

Inclusions. Snail-inclusion paste is fine-textured, dense, and fairly soft. An unslipped surface rubbed with the fingers has a distinctive smooth, soft, silty feeling that is never the slightest bit gritty. Perhaps the most distinctive feature of this standard paste, however, is the presence of snail shell inclusions. Shell fragments and occasionally whole shells range up to as much as 4 mm in size,

but are typically about 1 to 2 mm. Unlike the Paxcamán "snail inclusion ware" sherds from Lake Petén-Itzá, which Cowgill (1963 : 281) described as having "several shells or large fragments per cubic centimeter," the sherds from Macanché generally had somewhat sparser quantities of shell (color plates 1e2, 1e3). In many sherds the presence of shell was actually questionable, because of either sparseness or tiny size, although the other distinguishing attributes of this paste were clearly present.

The snails in the paste are all freshwater aquatic genera. G. Cowgill reports (1963 : 282) identification of *Cochliopina francesae* in his sherds from around Lake Petén-Itzá. Sherds from Macanché contain shells of *Tropicorbis, Aroapyrgus,* and *Pyrgophorus,* in addition to *Cochliopina sp.* (F. Thompson, personal communication 1978). Cowgill concluded that the clay used for Paxcamán "snail inclusion ware" was probably "obtained with very little cleaning or modification from a clay that naturally contained occasional snail shells and hematite lumps, but very little else above 1/10 mm in diameter" (1963 : 282–283).

The presence of freshwater snails and the otherwise relatively uniform fine-sorting of the particles suggest that this pottery may be made from the lacustrine clays common along the margins of most of the Petén lakes. Cowgill (1963 : 283) reports taking a sample of such a clay from the Candelaria Peninsula, on the western end of Lake Petén-Itzá.

The sediments of several of the central Petén lakes have been analyzed chemically and mineralogically by CPHEP ecologists, and the results of these studies are informative as to the composition of the Macanché pottery. Snail shells are fairly common in the sediments, along with diatoms and the skeletons of other lacustrine animals. It is significant that snails from soil pits excavated on the south side of Lake Salpetén, within 200 m of the 1980 lake shoreline, contained these same genera. The species identified within the upper 40 cm include *Pyrgophorus exi-*

guus, Cochliopina infundibulum, and *Aroapyrgus petenensis* (F. Thompson, personal communication to Mark Brenner).

The clays in the lake sediments are primarily montmorillonites, together with some mixed-layer clay minerals; montmorillonite clays are, in turn, the principal constituents of the soils of forested areas north of and surrounding the lakes (Deevey, Brenner, and Binford 1983; U. Cowgill and Hutchinson 1963a, 1963b), as distinct from the kaolins of the savannas to the south. Calcite (calcium carbonate) is also common as detrital grains in these sediments; dolomite (calcium-magnesium carbonate) and gypsum (hydrated calcium sulfate) occur in small amounts in Lake Salpetén, which is underlain by a gypsum deposit.

Lakes Salpetén and Macanché are of particular interest here because of the salinity of their waters: Lake Salpetén is undrinkable today because of the high calcium sulfate content; Lake Macanché's water is potable, but the high magnesium sulfate (epsom salts) content can have undesirable side effects. The point is the large amounts of sulfur in the waters: the sediments of the lakes have a distinctly sulfurous odor, and the Paxcamán/ Trapeche snail-inclusion paste sherds, especially those that are gray and incompletely fired, often release a sharp odor of sulfur when they are broken. If the sulfur content (in milliequivalents) of the waters of the Petén lakes is compared, Salpetén has 68.9 meq/l^{-1} of SO_4, Macanché has 4.9, Petén-Itzá has 3.2, and Lakes Yaxhá-Sacnab are considerably less than 1.0 meq (M. Brenner, personal communication). Although precise compositional analyses of these clays have not been carried out, the circumstantial evidence of the snails and high sulfur content may argue for manufacture of much of the gray paste Paxcamán/Trapeche pottery in the basin of Lake Salpetén.

Thin sections were made of four sherds of the snail-inclusion paste. The most abundant clastic mineral present in these sections is fine, sometimes polycrystalline, calcite generally less than 0.5 mm in size (color

plate 1a). The calcite is typically dirty with organic matter, and grayish in color (the particles are often black to the naked eye); it is so abundant that the clay paste is best termed marly. Sparse to moderate quantities of quartz (presumably authigenic in the sediments) were also visible, occurring in the same size range as the calcite. Rare rhombohedral grains (dolomite) were noticeable in only one of the sections. Besides the shell fragments, other minerals noted occasionally in the sections are hematite particles, diatoms (or satinspar gypsum?), and rare small dark hexagonal crystals (pyrite?).

Color. Most sherds of snail-inclusion paste from Petén are gray-brown in color. There is actually a range of color within this paste, however, that falls into three areas of concentration along a continuum. Sherd colors range from brown (7.5YR 5/4; color plate 1e1) to light gray-brown (10YR 6/1–2; rarely 5/2; color plate 1e2) to dark gray (10YR 4–5/1; color plate 1e3). The three color groupings noted here were all included in George Cowgill's (1963) color code "A10" for his Paxcamán group specimens, which all seemed to be light gray or brown in color. In typical mixed sherd collections from CPHEP excavations, particularly those in which the sherd surfaces were eroded, the Paxcamán and Trapeche groups' snail-inclusion paste sherds were usually immediately discernible because they exhibit a faintly greenish cast, especially in the gray pastes.

The brown-through-light-to-dark-gray color continuum is clearly one of firing, reflecting the different conditions of time, temperature, and atmosphere in which the vessels were fired. Variations in these conditions in turn led to varying degrees of completeness of oxidation in the finished vessels, relatively better oxidation being indicated by the brown sherds as opposed to the gray ones. The overall impression is one of incomplete oxidation in firing, however, even for the brown sherds. Refiring experiments, in which sherds were heated for a period of about two hours in an electric furnace that reached a maximum temperature of 750° C, caused all sherds to have a similar pinkish brown (varying around 5YR 7/4) paste color. When the refired fragments were broken, the sherds that were originally gray in color generally still retained a heavy gray core. This is a consequence of the high organic content and density of the paste as well as the montmorillonite composition, which favors retention of carbon.

To say that the color variation results from firing conditions does not establish the significance of such conditions, however; the question that remains is why these firing variations occurred? Bullard, in his notes on the Macanché "Paxcamán" group pottery, suggested two possible interpretations. One was that the brown paste red-slipped ("true" Paxcamán) sherds may have been later in time than the dark gray paste cream-slipped (now Trapeche) sherds. He based this hypothesis on the more common occurrence of brown paste/red-slipped sherds in lots from the top of the mound, i.e., what seemed to be the latest residential debris. As discussed in chapter 5 and below, the slip color variants that form the basis for differentiation of the Paxcamán and Trapeche groups do, in fact, occur differentially in the Late Postclassic midden sampled by Bullard's excavations when the top of the mound and the mound slopes are compared. The only clear temporal discrimination that can be made, however, is the decline in frequency of Trapeche in the "late" Late Postclassic/Protohistoric component. Bullard's second observation was that the association of gray pastes and cream-to-pink and tan slip color variants (now Trapeche group; see below) may have been intended as imitations of contemporaneous Yucatecan Slateware vessels (Bullard 1973: 233). Whether this is the case cannot be proven.

A further consideration of the significance of the color variation of Paxcamán and Trapeche snail-inclusion paste is geographic: different paste colors may have different areal distributions. Although paste color variation has not been systematically studied in existing Paxcamán group collections,

preliminary indications are that most sherds from Petén fall into the brown to light gray color range. This is true of Cowgill's (1963) material from the Lake Petén-Itzá region. There is considerable difference in the color distribution of Paxcamán group pottery from Macanché Island itself, however, when Bullard's collection is compared with the material from the 1979 CPHEP excavations. In the Bullard collection, nearly half (52 percent) of the snail-inclusion sherds were dark gray in paste color, whereas the percentage of dark gray paste sherds from the 1979 excavations varied from only 18 percent to 33 percent, depending on the particular phase or facet of the Postclassic.

The depositional context of the paste color variants, their temporal associations, and their covariation with slip color and vessel decoration, form, and dimensions, led to more systematic investigation of their significance. The nature of the examination, and preliminary conclusions, are discussed below in the section on slip color.

"Odd" Pastes

Apart from the common or standard snail-inclusion paste, a number of paste variants exist within the Paxcamán ceramic group in Petén (including adjacent Belize). Although Cowgill's paste descriptions (1963: 89, 275–285) imply a certain uniformity of Paxcamán pastes, his "near" Paxcamán, "near" Ixpop, kinds of identifications suggest recognition of paste, as well as decorative, differences. At Barton Ramie, Paxcamán group sherds exhibited considerable variability in fabric, with four distinct pastes identified. The standard paste at that site was leached, calcite-tempered, and brown in color; a white paste and small quantities of volcanic-ash-tempered paste were also noted. Only about 25 percent of the sherds had snail inclusions.

At Tayasal, gray snail-inclusion paste was used for most types and varieties of the Trapeche ceramic group, where it was first referred to as "Trapeche Light Gray Paste ware" (A. Chase 1979). Chase used paste differences as the basis for creation of a tentative

Table 11

Mean Concentrations (ppm) of 19 Elements in 44 Samples of Sherds and Clays from Petén (see figure 39)

Sample	Sc^{46}	Cr^{51}	Fe^{59}	Co^{60}	Cs^{134}	Ce^{141}	Hf^{181}
Paxcamán/Trapeche Snail Paste (N = 16)	8.40	35.38	23,650	4.57	0.68	28.1	4.07
Paxcamán Yellow Ash Paste (N = 30)	8.69	27.7	29,733	13.7	4.62	80.4	6.45
Petén Clays (N = 6)	21.7	96.3	50,066	11.8	2.4	60.6	14.9
Yaxhá Clays (N = 9)	12.6	93.5	37,488	13.2	3.8	64.3	6.7
Topoxté Ceramic Group (N = 10)	4.2	39.9	13,162	4.7	0.75	17.5	1.8
San José Clay (N = 1)	12.4	75.9	40,800	14.8	2.09	60.1	7.4
Tikal[a]	—	16–60	—	3–10	—	—	.6–2.0
Bajo[b]	16.4	85.2	—	7.84	—	—	—

a. Data from U. Cowgill and Hutchinson 1963a.　　b. Data from U. Cowgill and Hutchinson 1963b.

variety within the Trapeche Pink type: Halal Variety is characterized by a reddish brown calcitic paste lacking snail shell. In the present report on the Macanché pottery, although red-brown non-snail-inclusion pastes were identified in small quantities in the Trapeche and Paxcamán groups, they have not been accorded varietal status, and the Halal Variety has not been formally recognized. This procedural decision was made for several reasons. First, because numerous paste variants were recognized in these groups (as in Tinaja group earlier), it did not seem wise to single out one for formal varietal status; they all would have to be named varieties, an ultimately clumsy procedure. Second, if paste is used as the basis for identifying a variety in one type, it would have to be a variety in another type as well. But what happens, then, if a sherd of the Tan Variety of Xuluc Incised type is of reddish brown (Halal) paste? Is this then a separate variety of Xuluc Incised, or a sub-variety of Tan Variety?

At Macanché, non-snail-inclusion pastes were definitely minority wares in the Paxcamán and Trapeche groups. These pastes included a yellowish ash-tempered paste (color

plate 1b), a coarse gray paste (color plate 1d), and a coarse red-brown paste (possibly equivalent to Chase's Halal Variety). The "white" paste noted at Barton Ramie was not found at Macanché, although a few sherds of a leached brown calcite paste similar to the standard Barton Ramie pastes were identified. The ash-tempered paste at Macanché was particularly interesting: it was very hard, well oxidized, and yellowish brown (10YR 6/4) in color. Besides volcanic ash, there were quartz, feldspar, and mica in the paste (color plate 1b). It is possible that the few sherds of this paste at Macanché are equivalent to Chase's Tanché group, which occurred in the late facet of the Early Postclassic Chilcob ceramic complex at Tayasal (Chase and Chase 1983:104). These sherds may also have some relationship to the ash-tempered Paxcamán sherds at Barton Ramie (see Sharer and Chase 1976:295).

"Odd" pastes comprised less than 10 percent of Bullard's Paxcamán-Trapeche collection at Macanché, but their frequency within the group varies by time period as well as by form and type (P. Rice 1980). They were most common in the early facet of the Early Postclassic, in monochrome-slipped

(Table 11)

Samples of Sherds and Clays from Petén (see figure 39)

Ir^{194}	La^{140}	As^{76}	Sb^{124}	Sm^{153}	Au^{198}	Zr^{95}	Zn^{65}	Tb^{160}	Eu^{153}	Ta^{182}	Rb^{86}
12.98	23.15	6.80	1.02	2.48	.027	197.87	44.35	.364	.297	.442	44.14
5.37	42.5	5.3	.785	4.64	—	52.0	74.6	1.18	.737	.422	77.76
9.9	16.4	6.0	1.9	2.5	.04	44.5	65.2	.88	.581	1.2	—
14.5	36.0	4.4	.716	5.8	.003	121.0	146.5	1.17	.678	.619	—
15.1	41.8	0.7	.3	3.8	.012	—	15.0	.071	.083	.032	29.4
3.37	15.3	4.9	.237	2.46	.158	—	139.0	—	.627	.677	—
—	—	—	—	—	—	62–295	6–43	—	—	—	36–145
—	71.3	—	—	—	—	516.8	—	—	—	—	—

vessels (e.g., the yellowish brown ash paste occurred only in monochromes) as opposed to polychrome painted types, and in tripod dishes as opposed to jars or bowls. Odd pastes probably represent products of distinct production units, distributed locally as well as regionally.

Trace Elemental Composition

Variability in the composition of Postclassic pottery at Macanché in particular and in Petén in general was also investigated by means of a trace elemental analysis of sherds of the Paxcamán, Trapeche, and Topoxté groups, as well as some clays from Petén (P. Rice 1978). Neutron activation analysis of 55 samples was performed at the nuclear reactor on the University of Florida campus in accordance with the following procedures.

Fragments of sherds selected for neutron activation analysis were first heated in an electric furnace for 2½ hours to a temperature of 750° C. Slips and possible surface contamination were removed with a tungsten carbide drill. The clays chosen for analysis were mixed with distilled/deionized water, fired for one hour at 750° C, and then cooled. All samples were ground into a fine

powder in an agate mortar, and then small amounts (0.125–0.500 mg.) were irradiated for seven hours in the University of Florida reactor, operating at a flux of 8.563 x 10¹¹ neutrons/cm²/sec). Samples were analyzed with a Ge(Li) detector at intervals of 5, 15, 30, and 90 days after irradiation.

Table 11 presents the concentrations (in parts per million, or ppm) of 19 elements measured for 44 samples, and averaged among five sample categories. In this table, it can be seen that the two major pottery groups (Paxcamán/Trapeche and Topoxté) are characterized by low rare earth elements (Ce, La, Sm, Tb, and Eu); Topoxté is particularly distinguished by very low concentrations of all elements measured, being high only in Ir (a characteristic of the Yaxhá clays as well). The Paxcamán and Trapeche yellow ash paste sherds are high in rare earth elements (probably a function of the mica and unidentified heavy minerals that accompany volcanic ash) and Rb, but low in Zr.

In comparison to the sherds, the two groups of clays analyzed—those from central Petén and those from the Yaxhá area specifically—are strikingly similar only in high Cr and the absence of Rb. Otherwise, the Pe-

Table 12

Descriptive Characteristics of Paxcamán and Trapeche Group Sherds Used in Neutron Activation and Cluster Analyses (see figure 39)

ID number	Type	Paste[a]	Form	Lot number
CLUSTER I				
1	Paxcamán Red	Brown	Collared bowl	22
2	Trapeche U. Polychrome	Coarse gray		5
3	Sacá Polychrome	Light gray	Jar	19
4	Xuluc Inc.: Ain	Dark gray	Restr. bowl	10
5	Macanché Red-on-cream	Dark gray	Tripod dish	5
6	Patojo Modeled	Coarse gray	Censer	[b]
7	La Justa Comp.	Red	Censer	[b]
8	Macanché Red-on-cream	Light gray	Collared bowl	[b]
9	Ixpop Polychrome	Brown	Tripod dish	21
10	Ixpop Polychrome	Light gray	Restr. bowl	21
11	Paxcamán Red	Light gray	Jar	19
12	Ixpop Polychrome	Light gray	Bowl	20
13	Paxcamán Red	Light gray	Collared bowl	21
14	Mul Polychrome: Manax	Dark gray	Tripod dish	25
15	Macanché Red-on-cream	Light gray	Tripod dish	28
CLUSTER II				
16	Paxcamán Red	Brown	Tripod dish	21
17	Paxcamán Red	Coarse red	Tripod dish	5
18	Xuluc Inc: Tzalam	Dark gray	Grater bowl	40
19	Trapeche Pink	Dark gray	Tripod dish	40
20	Trapeche Pink	Dark gray	Restr. bowl	25
CLUSTER III				
21	Paxcamán Red	Yellow ash	Tripod dish	20
22	Paxcamán Red	Yellow ash	Grater bowl	41
23	Trapeche Pink	Yellow ash	Tripod dish	5

a. All sherds are of variants of the shell-inclusion paste except identification nos. 6, 7, 21, 22, 23.
b. Sherds nos. 6, 7, and 8 are from Topoxté (Canté Island), not Macanché Island.

tén clays have comparatively high concentrations of virtually all elements (especially rare earths), while the Yaxhá clays are high only in Ir, Cr, Zn, and Tb. In interpreting the elemental compositions of the central Petén clays, it should be noted that three of the six clays are principally kaolinite rather than montmorillonite clay minerals, and were recovered from outside the lake basins area proper. It is regrettable that at the time of these analyses, soils and clays from the Salpetén basin were not available.

Table 11 presents additional information on the trace elemental composition of one of the clays averaged in the "Petén clay" group, the San José clay. This sample was acquired from a potter in San José, on the north shore

of Lake Petén-Itzá, in 1972, and according to the potter it was obtained from the stream in Santa Elena, on the south side of the lake. Finally, the comparable data on minor constituents of pottery samples from Tikal (U. Cowgill and Hutchinson 1963a), and of clays from the nearby Bajo de Santa Fe (U. Cowgill and Hutchinson 1963b), are presented in table 11 for comparative purposes.

Cluster analyses were performed on the trace elemental compositions of Postclassic pottery and clays, using Ward's Method clustering algorithm of the CLUSTAN IC (Wishart 1978) program (P. Rice 1978). In the clustering, which involved a search for separate solutions for various combinations of sherds and clays, it was interesting that the only

PLATE 1a–d. Photomicrographs of thin sections of Petén Postclassic pottery, approximately 31× magnification.

1a. Ixpop Polychrome, tripod dish, light gray-brown snail-inclusion paste. Fabric consists of large quantities of fine carbonate mineral grains, with occasional quartz (angular clear particles, top and bottom left). Note the presence of a red slip and white underslip on surface of sherd, distinguished from the sherd paste by their birefringence. (Crossed nicols.) **1b.** Paxcamán Red, tripod dish, yellow ash paste. The paste contains abundant volcanic ash occurring as acicular fragments and occasional pumiceous fragments (e.g., bubbly-looking particle in the center). The light grains to the left are quartz and feldspar; the opaque dark grain to the right is mica. (Plane polarized light.) **1c.** Chompoxté Red-on-cream, tripod dish. Like the pastes of the Paxcamán and Trapeche ceramic groups, Clemencia Cream Paste

of the Topoxté ceramic group is characterized by abundant fine carbonate particles. The red slip on the exterior of the dish overlies a white underslip (compare with 1a), both visible by changes in color and birefringence in thin section. (Crossed nicols.) **1d.** Trapeche Pink: Tramite Variety, tripod dish, coarse gray paste. Paste contains abundant medium to large carbonate grains, occasional quartz grains (upper center), and ferruginous inclusions (opaque grain in left center). Compare difference in grain sizes with 1a. (Crossed nicols.)

1e. Paste colors of Petén Postclassic pottery, shown in freshly broken cross sections. 1, Paxcamán Red, brown snail-inclusion paste. 2, Paxcamán Red, light gray-brown snail-inclusion paste. 3, Trapeche Pink, dark gray snail-inclusion paste. 4, Augustine Red (from Negroman-Tipú). 5, Pastel Polychrome, Clemencia Cream Paste (Topoxté ceramic group). 6, Topoxté Red, Clemencia Cream Paste.

PLATE 2a. Slips of the Paxcamán ceramic group, varying from dark red to pink to orange-red.

PLATE 2b. Slips of the Trapeche ceramic group, varying from cream to pink to tan. Note the rootlet marking on right.

PLATE 2c. Slips of the Topoxté ceramic group, varying from red to red-orange. The light color of the paste is visible where the slip has eroded (e.g., on left), and the fine striations from wiping the wet paste are visible under the thin slip.

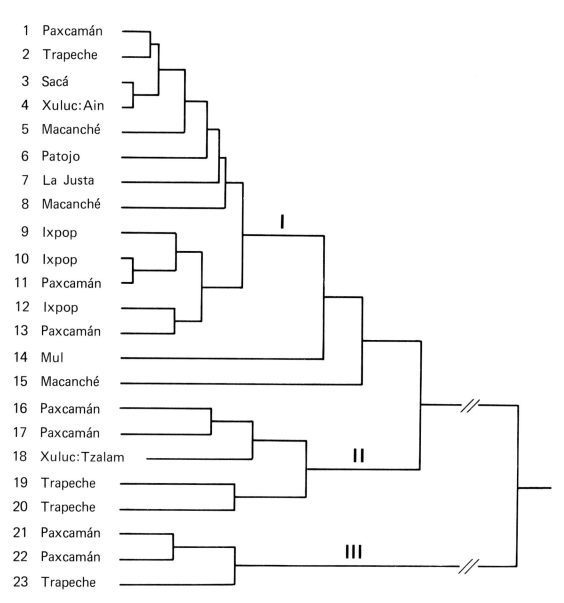

FIGURE 39. Ward's clustering solution using CLUSTAN program for Paxcamán and Trapeche sherds, based on the concentrations of 19 elements (see table 11), using standardized scores. Figures at top of dendrogram indicate dissimilarity. See table 12 for descriptive data on individual sherds.

clay sample that consistently was grouped directly with the sherds, rather than in a separate clay cluster, was the San José sample. Figure 39 (see table 12 for key) presents one clustering solution resulting from running this procedure on snail-inclusion and "odd" paste sherds of the Paxcamán and Trapeche groups, together with two sherds of unslipped (censer) wares. In this dendrogram, it can be seen that the ash pastes form a separate cluster (Cluster III), distinct from the carbonate pastes of the Paxcamán and Trapeche sherds. What was unexpected was the tendency for the monochrome snail paste sherds to form one cluster (Cluster II), and the decorated types and coarser pastes to form another heterogeneous cluster with two separate subclusters (Cluster I). The implications of these results for understanding production cannot be adequately assessed on the basis of the limited data available.

Slip Characteristics

Sherds of the Paxcamán and Trapeche groups from Macanché Island exhibited a distinctive range of variability in slip color. A sizable percentage of the sherds appeared in paste, form, and decoration to belong to the well-known Paxcamán group, but instead of a red or red-orange slip, they bore slips ranging in color from pink to tan to cream. Fire-clouding was very common, and a small proportion of the sherds have well-developed gray surfaces. Recognition of variability in slip color in the snail-inclusion paste pottery from the Tayasal peninsula in Lake Petén-Itzá led Chase (1979) to create a new ceramic group within this paste category, the Trapeche (pink) group. According to his description, Trapeche group pottery bears a cream-to-pink slip, often double-slipped, and stratigraphically underlies Paxcamán group red-slipped sherds in the Early Postclassic in the Tayasal area.

At Macanché the slip color variability could not be so easily accommodated by simply dividing the collection into two groups, red-slipped and cream-pink-slipped. As with snail-inclusion paste color, slip colors at Macanché seemed to exist along a continuum from red to cream, with corresponding variations, though slight, in preservation and luster. A large number of the sherds have slips that are red or red-orange (10R to 2.5YR 4/6–8; color plate 2a1, 3); a very few were dark red (10R 3.5/6). These red slips are generally well preserved and moderately hard, and typically vary from a dull matte appearance to a low luster. Black fire-clouds occur on perhaps one-third of the sherds, most typically at the mouths of dishes and jars. The orange-red slips vary to orange-tan (5YR 6/5; color plate 2b3), and are also dull in luster but often have a "waxy" feel. Relatively small quantities of pink (2.5YR 6/4) slips are present and are often eroded, with a dull or "faded" appearance (color plates 2a2, 2b1). A large portion of the collection has cream or very pale brown (10YR 7/3–4 to 7.5YR 7/4; color plate 2b2) slips; these are generally very eroded, but where present are tactually "waxy" like the orange-tan slips. Fire-clouding is often present, and may be black or reddish. Finally, a very small group of sherds had completely and rather evenly gray-colored slips.

Upon initial examination of the collection, the slip color variation appeared to parallel that of the paste color variation, specifically with respect to degree of oxidation. That is, the better-oxidized red and red-orange slips were more common on better-oxidized brown pastes, while the cream slips occurred principally on the incompletely oxidized dark gray pastes (see P. Rice 1980:77, table 3). Apart from the snail-inclusion paste sherds, sherds of "odd" pastes tend to fall primarily in the middle of the color distribution, with nearly half exhibiting fire-clouding. In the red range, most slips are red-orange rather than clear red, and appear on the yellowish brown ash paste and coarse red paste variants. Coarse gray pastes have slips in the cream and tan color ranges, but fire-clouding is less common than in the red slips.

As noted above, Bullard (1973:233) had remarked these differences in slip and snail

Table 13

Correlation of Paste and Slip Colors in Late Postclassic Paxcamán and Trapeche Group
Pottery from CPHEP 1979 Excavations at Macanché Island

Paste Color	Slip Color					Total
	Cream	Tan	Pink	Red	Fire-clouded	
Dark gray	13	17	33	3	30	96
Light gray	4	49	67	62	27	209
Brown	–	9	26	103	18	156
"Odd"	1	9	4	1	6	21
Total	18	84	130	169	81	482

paste color variation. He suggested that the cream slips may have been Petén imitations of a widely traded Postclassic ware from Yucatán, Slateware. If this were the case, it might be expected that other attributes of the Slateware pottery might have been copied as well, such as vessel forms or decoration, rather than solely the slip characteristics, but such imitation is not readily apparent at Macanché. Another alternative Bullard suggested is that the brown paste sherds with red slips, which were recovered primarily from the upper surface of the mound, may have been later manufactures than the cream-pink-tan-slipped gray paste sherds.

An interpretation of the changes in distribution of the slip colors in the Early Postclassic at Macanché Island has been offered (P. Rice 1980) on the basis of temporal faceting of sherds from CPHEP excavations. Differences in production skills were postulated as the underlying causes of the color changes. In the early facet of the Early Postclassic Aura complex (P. Rice 1980:77, table 4), the potters were apparently trying to achieve two slip colors, a red slip (the Paxcamán group) as well as a cream slip (the Trapeche group). The considerable range of paste and slip colors during this period—for example, the presence of tan and pink slips as well as the high frequency of fire-clouds—suggests that the potters could not reliably and consistently control the atmosphere of their firings. The period may be characterized as one of experimentation or as one in which the potters experienced some difficulties in dealing with local resources that may have been unfamiliar. The prevalence of gray paste colors and fire-clouded surfaces indicates a carryover of the poor firing control that was noted locally in the pottery of the preceding Terminal Classic Romero complex, described in chapter 3.

In the late facet Aura complex (P. Rice 1980:77, table 4), the potters seem to have achieved a more consistent rate of success in producing distinctly red and cream slips. The "intermediate" slip colors, orange-tan and pink, are very rare, and fire-clouding is much less common than in the early facet. Better control of the firing process or more standardized manufacturing practices are evident in the clear association of cream slips with dark gray pastes, although red slips still occur on light gray as well as brown pastes.

This interpretation of the significance of these color variations breaks down in the Late Postclassic Dos Lagos complex because the correlations of paste with slip color are not consistent (table 13). In earlier periods, red and cream slip colors formed the majority categories with pink and tan slips occurring as minority "errors." By contrast, in the Late Postclassic period the cream color was not achieved as consistently; instead there were a greater number of sherds in the intermediate categories, pink and tan.

The cause of these highly variable slip colors of the Trapeche group in the Late Postclassic is a matter of some interest. Imitation of Slatewares is one possible, but untestable, explanation. Another is technological: changes in the composition and/or firing of the slips. A third possible cause is postdepositional alteration. While the entire mound area—top, sides, and base—is covered with midden, that at the base of the mound is particularly thick and black, rich with organic material and large quantities of faunal remains and shell. It is conceivable that a combination of leaching and the presence of organic acids within this heavy midden deposit at the foot of the mound structure could have darkened the original cream colors of the Trapeche slips by reduction, or "bleached" the red slips to pink by preferential removal of the iron colorant.

Evidence for this process as a cause of slip alteration was provided by some of the red-slipped Topoxté group sherds from CPHEP excavations at Macanché. Some of these sherds had an unusually pale creamy pink surface color rarely if ever appearing on the sherds of the Topoxté group from Canté Island in Lake Yaxhá (P. Rice 1979), and virtually all of these were from the midden refuse at the base of the mound. This "fading" was not noted in Topoxté sherds from around the structures on the mound summit. In Bullard's lots, the fading phenomenon in Topoxté sherds was particularly evident in Lot 10 from Operation IA, a mixed midden and fill lot.

Laboratory Experiments

These questions concerning the cause of the variability in color of these Paxcamán and Trapeche slips warranted further investigation, particularly given the possibility of postdepositional alteration as a contributing factor. Testing involved refiring experiments and treating sherd fragments with acid and alkaline solutions; all these procedures were undertaken in the Ceramic Technology Laboratory of the Florida State Museum.

Refiring experiments using an electric kiln were conducted on 31 red-, pink-, and cream-slipped sherds from Bullard's excavations into the island's Late Postclassic midden and from Early Postclassic construction core. Sherds were refired from 500° to 800° C in increments of 50°, with holds of 15 minutes at each increment. The objective was to gain some idea of whether the middle range colors in these slips represented firing variations (oxidation/reduction) of the red or cream slips, if another slip preparation was being used, or if nonfiring factors were largely at work.

Results of the preliminary refiring experiments confirmed that the two general slip color categories, red and cream-pink, evident in Early Postclassic examples of these groups were still being used in the Late Postclassic. Changes in the cream-pink slip were noted with refiring at higher temperatures (750° to 800° C) in complete oxidation: the cream slips became a "golden" or tan color (7.5YR 6–7/6; rarely 8/4).

Investigation of the possibility of postdepositional chemical changes in the slips causing the color variations was carried out by immersing sherd fragments in solutions of different acidity and alkalinity. Six sherds, representing a range of slip and paste colors, were broken into five fragments, of which four were placed into four solutions for seven days (for a total of 24 experimental cases). The solutions used were glacial acetic acid, at pH 2.5 and 3.8, and alkaline solutions of N_2CO_3 (sodium carbonate) at pH 9.5 and 12.3.

These solutions, particularly the acids, had a visible effect on the slip colors of half of the specimens. Of the total of 12 sherd fragments in acid solutions, eight changed color. Three red slips developed a darker or more intense color while one cream sherd turned grayer (acid environments being reducing); the other cream slip fragment became orange-tan in color, as did the three pink sherds. Of the 12 fragments in alkaline solutions, only three changed color; this change was toward lighter or clearer colors in one red and two cream slip samples. None of the four pink-slipped fragments changed color in alkaline conditions.

These experiments were preliminary and extremely simple in structure, and because very few sherds were involved they cannot be regarded as conclusive. Both firing changes and postdepositional alteration (especially by acids, such as are present in the midden) are possible explanations of the variations in slip colors in Late Postclassic Paxcamán and Trapeche group pottery. The effects were most pronounced on the cream-pink slips, as it was noted that both of the experimental variables gave rise to orange-tan colors. It should be noted here that conditions of burial in the midden are not likely to involve simply the effects of high acidity on sherds, but may be complicated by the very salty (magnesium sulfate) composition of the lake waters. Many sherds from the island had whitish surfaces where slips had been eroded off or on broken edges, and this phenomenon (which is very easy to confuse with an eroded slip) is probably a chemical reaction to these salts.

Multiple Slipping

A final note on the Paxcamán/Trapeche slips concerns the question of multiple slipping, which must be treated in three parts.

In the initial description of the Trapeche ceramic group, the distinctive appearance of double slipping was noted: "The underslip has a color value of 5YR 5/8 to 10R 5/8 (yellowish red), while the overslip has a color value of 10YR 7/3 (very pale brown)" (A. Chase 1979:104–105). A small sample of sherds from Macanché was examined under a binocular microscope at magnifications of 10 to 30×. Double-layered surface colors were observed on a small percentage of monochrome, polychrome, and incised types within both the Paxcamán and Trapeche groups. The outermost slips ("overslips") were generally a creamy or very pale brown color, translucent, and often waxy feeling.

The effect of the overslipping was to create a faded pink color by toning down the underlying red, but not all sherds classed as pink-slipped were found to have this double slip. Double slipping was not noted in any of the sherds identified as being of the cream color variant. The same double-slipped effect was noted occasionally where one surface of a

vessel was better oxidized in firing than the other, causing the underlying paste to attain a blush of pinkish orange coloration. If the vessel surfaces had been well smoothed prior to application of the slip, this blush might appear like a reddish orange underslip beneath the upper cream slip. Occasionally the double-slipped effect is visible on only one of two cross-mended sherds, suggesting problems of differential wear or postdepositional alteration.

The reason for the overslipping is difficult to determine: perhaps it was protective of the undercolor, in some way, or added a smoothness, low luster, or impermeability that the colored slip did not provide. Its presence is reminiscent of the post-fire organic coatings that Shepard (1942:264–266) noted were applied to pottery at San José, Belize. She suggests that these coatings acted to preserve grainy pigments (such as those of manganese) from erosion, protect the vessel surface, and add luster.

The second aspect of the question of multiple slipping concerns a cream or white opaque *under*slipping that occurs beneath the red or cream-pink slips. This was first noted in two thin sections of Paxcamán group sherds, in which the primary slip appeared with a birefringence distinct from that of the paste, although it was not clearly demarcated from the paste (see color plate 1a). It is variable in thickness, from 0.05 to 0.30 mm, and seems to have been streakily applied, with numerous small voids. It was more easily detected on exterior vessel surfaces, appearing on a tripod dish and a bowl with outflaring collar.

Related to this white primary slipping is the preparation of the background for polychrome painted decoration in Ixpop and Sacá Polychrome types in the Paxcamán ceramic group, and in Mul Polychrome in the Trapeche group. (This white underslip is also apparent in Chompoxté Red-on-cream type in the Topoxté ceramic group; see color plate 1d.) In many of these painted sherds, the background color of the design band is distinctly different from the underlying paste color. (It is difficult to determine this for the dark gray paste sherds—i.e., most of the Trapeche group—because they are generally heavily eroded.) Six sherds, when examined in cross section under a high power binocular microscope, clearly showed that this background was produced by painting the decorative band area with a white (2.5Y 8/2) to pinkish orange (7.5YR 7.5/3.5) sliplike paint, and then the design was painted over this. The undercoating was apparently applied to an area somewhat larger than the actual design band, so that the red slip of Ixpop Polychrome sometimes partially overlapped it; where this happened the red slip was locally lighter and clearer orange-red in color.

The use of this slip suggests that the potters did not wish a gray-to-brown background color (i.e., the color of the unmodified paste) for at least some of their designs. They seemed to be trying to achieve a lighter, clearer, cream-to-pale orange color by applying this primary slip. More important, this process calls to mind the whitish underslip that forms the background for painting some Late Classic polychromes, especially "Codex Style" vessels (see "Late Classic polychromes," above; also Robicsek and Hales 1981). Three of the Postclassic sherds from Macanché with this primary slip are decorated with painted reptilian motifs.

The third aspect of multiple slipping within the Paxcamán and Trapeche groups also concerns the decorated types. Ixpop and Sacá Polychrome sherds with well-preserved design bands generally have a thin, streaky, translucent orange coating visible over the design. In most cases, this appears to be simply a continuation of a thinner, perhaps diluted, version of the red slip covering the vessel. This overslip is particularly evident on specimens where it was carelessly applied, for the red slip overlaps the black bordering lines of the design and only within the band itself does it streakily thin out. In other instances this continuity with the slip is not so apparent.

A similar sort of translucent light orange overslip was noted on Pastel Polychrome

sherds within the Topoxté ceramic group (P. Rice 1979:25–26). Cowgill (1963:200) noted the same thing on Ixpop samples from Lake Petén-Itzá, and describes it as a "lustrous transparent coat over the 'unslipped' paste areas of black-on-paste bands. In at least some cases, this layer also covered the black." He, too, suggests the possibility that it is a thin version of the main red slip over the body, and notes Shepard's (1957:42; see also 1942) observations concerning a clear protective coating over manganese paints on Classic Maya pottery types.

The relationship of this glossy orange overslip to the waxy semitranslucent "double" slip noted more commonly on sherds of the Trapeche group has not been investigated. Both may represent some modification of the basic slip used to coat the entire vessel, perhaps with organic extracts. It is interesting, however, to note the continuities in decorative technology between these Postclassic ceramic groups and earlier Classic manufactures. The application of a white undercoating in the area to be painted with significant motifs, such as reptiles in the Late Postclassic (see above, chapter 5; also P. Rice 1983a), and the protection of decoration with a glossy overslip, are both techniques used in production of polychrome pottery in the Late Classic period (see P. Rice 1985c).

Summary

The following type descriptions of the Paxcamán and Trapeche ceramic groups represent my efforts to organize these dimensions of variability in slips and pastes into some systematic framework. The sherds that clearly have red and red-orange slip colors were placed into the types and varieties of the Paxcamán ceramic group (color plate 2a). Sherds that have slip colors in the tan, pink, cream (color plate 2b), and gray ranges were more difficult to deal with. The problems occurred in part as a consequence of the subjectivity of color perceptions in this range, but also because frequent fire-clouding resulted in a range of colors on a single sherd. I tried to be consistent in placing "middle range" slip colors into one group or the other, but I acknowledge a bias toward placing questionable (particularly pink) slip colors in the Paxcamán rather than in the Trapeche group.

Because of the different forms, colors, and techniques of slipping and decoration in the Trapeche group at Macanché, I have given all the material different varietal distinctions within the type categories. The small number of distinctive gray to black slips on snail paste were counted here as a third group, apart from Paxcamán and Trapeche, because they cannot be clearly identified as either. I left them as "group unspecified."

With regard to the problem of the classificatory significance of paste variation in the Paxcamán and Trapeche groups, I took a different tack. Because non-snail-inclusion pastes exist in small but significant quantities in both ceramic groups, it does not seem appropriate or consistent to classify the Paxcamán and Trapeche groups in a "snail-inclusion paste ware." Although I favor the identification of paste wares where appropriate (P. Rice 1976), such units are not always felicitously accommodated by the hierarchical classificatory procedures of the type-variety system, particularly in situations where there is as much paste variability as there is in the Paxcamán and Trapeche groups.

I suggest that a more appropriate basis for ware designation is the character (not color) of the slip, as it is for large quantities of Preclassic ("Waxy ware") and Classic ("Gloss ware") pottery. "Volador Dull-Slipped ware" is used here as the ware designation in an effort to accommodate the color range from red to cream and to acknowledge the generally nonglossy, low-luster nature of the Postclassic slips.

CHAPTER 7

Type-Variety Descriptions of the Pottery of the Aura, Dos Lagos, and Ayer Ceramic Complexes

Paxcamán Ceramic Group

Name: **Paxcamán Red: Paxcamán Variety.**

Frequency: 246 sherds, of which 245 were from Macanché Island and 1 from Punta Nimá. Paxcamán Red type represents 15.4 percent of the sherds of the Paxcamán ceramic group in Bullard's collections.

Ware: Volador Dull-Slipped ware.

Complex: Aura, Dos Lagos, and Ayer ceramic complexes.

Established: The Paxcamán type was defined and illustrated by R. E. W. Adams and Trik (1961:125–127) on the basis of the Tikal collections.

Principal identifying modes: Paxcamán Red, the monochrome type within the Paxcamán group, is characterized by red to red-orange slips on a variety of vessel forms, including tripod dishes, jars, and bowls.

Paste and firing: Paxcamán Red type includes much greater paste variability than does any other type in the Paxcamán group (see "Paste Characteristics" in chapter 6 and color plates 1a–c, 1e1–2). The majority of sherds of this type are of snail-inclusion paste, varying from brown to grayish brown in color. Non-snail-inclusion pastes include coarse red, coarse gray, and yellowish brown volcanic-ash-tempered pastes, and these were most commonly used in making tripod dishes. A few sherds show evidence of post-breakage burning.

Surface treatment and decoration: Paxcamán Red sherds have a red to red-orange slip which is highly variable in color and condition (see chapter 6 and color plate 2a). Generally the slips are relatively thin, moderately hard, and have surfaces with a dull lus-

ter; fire-clouding (particularly at the mouths of dishes), fading, and erosion are relatively common.

Forms and dimensions: A variety of vessel forms is present in Paxcamán Red type, including tripod dishes, simple hemispherical bowls, collared bowls, narrow-neck jars with high or medium necks, and neckless jars.

TRIPOD DISH: The most characteristic form of all Postclassic ceramic groups in Petén is the dish or plate (sometimes called a basal break bowl) with three vessel supports. A total of 60 sherds, representing 26 vessels, were recovered from Bullard's excavations on the island. Two vessels were partially reconstructible: one of coarse red paste had cylindrical supports, a groove around the join of wall to base, and a diameter of 21 cm, while the vessel of ash paste had scroll feet and a diameter of 19 cm. The lips of these dishes are often beveled.

Tripod dishes at Macanché differ significantly in size and proportion from those found elsewhere in Petén/Belize, in that they are smaller and often have slightly rounded bases. Vessel diameters at Macanché vary from 19 to 23 cm (average 20.2 cm; eight measurements); wall thickness varies from 5.5 to 7.5 mm (average 6.0 mm; eight measurements).

SIMPLE HEMISPHERICAL BOWL: Fifteen sherds from Bullard's excavations represent three vessels. One partially reconstructible bowl (13 sherds) has a thickened square lip, small round supports with a circular vent, and a dull, eroded, orange-red slip. The diameter is 19 cm, wall thickness is 5 mm, and height (depth) is 9.5 cm. The two other sherds have diameters of 24 and 28 cm; on one the slip extends only partway down the exterior below a rounded lip.

COLLARED BOWL: These are bowls or "jars" with a wide mouth and an outflaring rim or "collar"; 26 sherds from Macanché Island represent 13 vessels. The slip covers the entire interior and exterior, but the form of the body below the join to the rim is not known. The rim or collar is generally thick and heavy, sometimes tapering to the join with the thinner vessel body; the lip is round or slightly beveled. The mouth diameters of four bowls vary between 34 and 36 cm; another, smaller vessel has a diameter of 24 cm. The height of the collar (measured on the vessel interior of four specimens) varies between 4.1 and 6.8 cm, and the thickness ranges from 4.5 mm (where thinned near the join) to more typical measurements of 8 to 10 mm.

NARROW NECK JARS: Jars with narrow neck openings can be divided into those with high necks (17 sherds representing eight vessels), those with medium necks (11 sherds representing four vessels), and those with neck of indeterminate height (18 sherds), of which eight have a lip bolster. The necks of these jars are slipped on the exterior and may or may not be slipped on the interior. The lips are generally rounded, the neck outflaring and thicker at the join with the body.

High-neck jars have neck heights that vary between 8.7 and 12.3 cm, averaging 10.4 cm (seven measurements); wall thickness varies from 7 to 11 mm; mouth diameter ranges from 15 to 19 cm, averaging 17.5 cm (six measurements). Medium-neck jars have neck heights between 4.2 and 7.1 cm (average 6.2 cm), wall thickness 6 to 11 mm, and mouth diameter 9 to 15 cm (average 12.7 cm, based on four measurements).

Six sherds represent the bases of three jars; one of these is flat and was slipped on the exterior (underside). The jars had strap handles placed horizontally on the vessel body (slightly above the point of greatest di-

ameter). Seventeen handles or handle fragments represent 14 vessels; these are generally thick and broad, the width varying between 2.8 and 3.5 cm.

NECKLESS JARS (TECOMATES): Twenty-four sherds, representing two vessels, indicated neckless jar forms. The slip covers the entire exterior, and on one vessel it may also cover the interior. One vessel (two sherds) has a mending hole; the larger partially reconstructible vessel (22 sherds) is very badly fire-clouded, perhaps from use or post-depositional phenomena, and the slip is heavily eroded. The mouth diameter of this vessel is 15.5 cm; the maximum body diameter is 32 cm; wall thickness is 5.5 mm.

HEAVY BOLSTERED RIM: Five sherds, representing three vessels, are rim sherds suggesting an outflaring collar of a thick-walled (1.05 to 1.25 cm) vessel with a very heavy grooved lip bolster. These sherds are quite fire-clouded, and one of them has a mending hole. Although the form of the complete vessel is not clear from these sherds, fragments of a partially restorable vessel with this same heavy bolster were found in a looter's trench during CPHEP mapping operations at Ixlú, and indicated that the vessel was an enormous wide-mouthed jar. The mouth diameters measured on two of the Macanché sherds were 38 and 54 cm.

MISCELLANEOUS RIMS: Forty-six small sherds, a small percentage of them fire-clouded, are from indeterminate vessel forms and most are too small for measurement of vessel diameter.

Illustrations: figures 40 and 41.

Intrasite references: Paxcamán Red: Paxcamán Variety was found in virtually all Postclassic lots from Macanché Island; one handle fragment was found in a Terminal Classic lot. Brown paste sherds are more common on the surface of the mound, while grayish brown paste sherds are slightly more common at the foot of the platform. Three partially reconstructible vessels—a neckless jar, a hemispherical bowl, and a tripod dish (coarse red paste) were recovered in Lot 25 in Bullard's Operation IH.

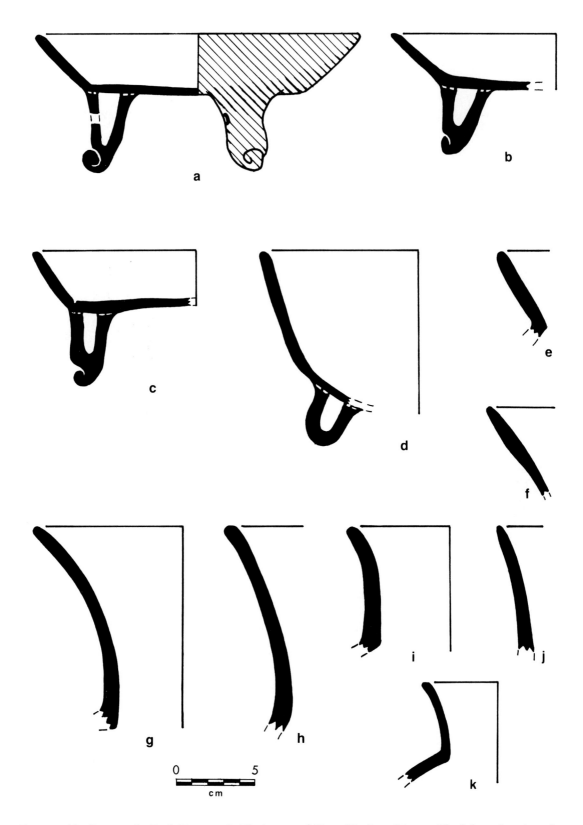

FIGURE 40. Paxcamán Red: Paxcamán Variety, and Type/Variety Unspecified. **b,** volcanic-ash paste.

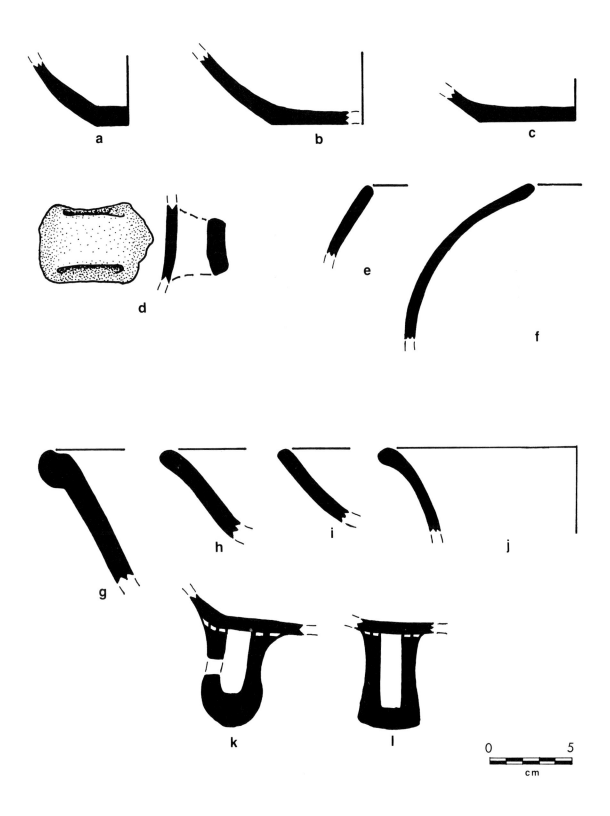

FIGURE 41. Paxcamán Red: Paxcamán Variety, and Type/Variety Unspecified. **k**, **l**, from Punta Nimá. Note: overall slip on **d** not indicated by hachure.

Intersite references: Only one sherd of Paxcamán Variety was included in Bullard's collections from other than Macanché Island, and that was a jar sherd from Punta Nimá. Otherwise, Paxcamán Red is a very abundant and widespread type in the lakes region (especially the central lakes and Lake Petén-Itzá) and adjacent Belize during the Postclassic period. It is virtually absent at Topoxté, only about 30 sherds having been identified at Canté Island (P. Rice 1979). In general, its relative frequency as compared to other Postclassic ceramic groups such as Augustine, Trapeche, and Topoxté varies geographically, with Paxcamán being more common in Petén than in Belize, for example. Six-hundred-odd sherds of the Paxcamán group were identified at Barton Ramie, but these were primarily from one mound. A Paxcamán Red tripod dish is on display at the Field Museum in Chicago, and was recovered from Mountain Cow, Belize. I recently had a chance cursorily to review Thompson's Mountain Cow collection, but I was not able to identify any additional Paxcamán specimens. Sherds of Paxcamán Red are also present at Negroman-Tipú (P. Rice 1984a, 1985a).

The Paxcamán specimens from Macanché Island are unusual in that the vessels are generally smaller than those identified elsewhere. This is particularly true of the tripod dishes, which are small in diameter, have slightly rounded bases and slightly convex rims, and proportionately smaller supports.

The large, thick-walled jars (?) with heavy rim bolsters may be similar to vessels occurring at Santa Rita in Arroba Modeled; there the vessels have blotchy dark slips and appliquéd modeled heads (personal observation; see also D. Chase 1984).

Name: **Paxcamán General: Type and Variety Unspecified.**

Frequency: 1005 sherds, of which 976 were from Macanché Island, 3 from the mainland "center," 12 from Punta Nimá, 1 from San Miguel, and 13 from Ixlú. Variety Unspecified comprises 63.0 percent of the sherds of the Paxcamán ceramic group in Bullard's collections.

Ware: Volador Dull-Slipped ware.

Complex: Aura, Dos Lagos, and Ayer ceramic complexes.

Established: The Paxcamán type was initially defined at Tikal by R. E. W. Adams and Trik (1961).

Principal identifying modes: See Paxcamán Red: Paxcamán Variety. The sherds included here as type and variety unspecifed are body sherds and vessel supports that have the diagnostic pastes and red slips of the Paxcamán group, but can be confidently associated with neither monochrome nor polychrome types.

Paste and firing: See Paxcamán Red: Paxcamán Variety, and chapter 6.

Surface treatment and decoration: See Paxcamán Red: Paxcamán Variety; see also chapter 6. Twenty body sherds from Late Postclassic lots 19 and 20, Bullard's Operation IG, had red slips on what would have been the exteriors of the vessels, and a well-preserved golden-tan (7.5YR 6/5) slip on the interior surface.

Forms and dimensions: A handful of body sherds are extremely thick (1.3 to 1.5 cm), and may be associated with the large bolstered-rim jar described in Paxcamán Variety. Roughly 10 percent of the body sherds were very thin walled, ranging between 4 and 5 mm; these sherds may be part of the body of collared bowls, which tend to be thin walled.

Forty-six vessel supports were unidentifiable as to type or variety or both within the Paxcamán ceramic group. Among these are six bulbous supports; four scroll supports; 14 cylinder supports; five miniature supports; and 17 support fragments whose form could not be determined. These supports are primarily associated with tripod dishes; however, a large Sacá polychrome widemouth jar in a private collection in Petén was also found to have tripod supports (personal observation).

The cylinder supports at Macanché Island are different from those typically noted in Paxcamán pottery elsewhere. Cylindrical supports at Macanché are smaller with straighter sides rather than the "waisted" or trumpet shape associated with Paxcamán samples at Barton Ramie and Lake Petén-Itzá. They are also smaller in proportion to the vessel itself, and are placed closer to the angle of the wall-to-base, rather than fully underneath the dish.

These supports were produced by forming a small hollow tube of clay, perhaps around a finger, and then shaping the actual support and its base—bulbous, scrolled, or flat—over that mold. Unlike the Topoxté vessels, which frequently had multiple vent holes, most of the supports from Macanché had only single circular vents.

Illustrations: figures 40 and 41; see also figure 29.

Intrasite references: See "Intrasite references" for Paxcamán Red: Paxcamán Variety. The red-tan dichrome slips were found on top of the mound (as were most of the well-preserved red slips) primarily in the "Late" Protohistoric levels used to define the provisional Ayer complex. Of the vessel supports, only three were recovered from Early Postclassic lots, and the remainder were from the more heavily sampled Late Postclassic period of occupation of the island.

Intersite references: See above, and also "Intersite references" for Paxcamán Red: Paxcamán Variety. Although the vessel supports at Macanché were generally found to be small in size, the supports in Bullard's collection from Punta Nimá were rather large. A vase or drum-like vessel was said to have been recovered from a cave near Macanché; this vessel, ca. 16 cm in height and with a mouth diameter of 7 cm, was of snail paste and described by Bullard as "Macanché Red Ware" (fig. 29). Blue paint was present on the interior.

Sherds with red and golden tan dichrome slips on the interiors and/or exteriors of vessels were noted at Negroman-Tipú (P. Rice 1984a) as well as at Macanché. At Negroman-Tipú, however, the variant is not found in the snail-inclusion paste Paxcamán group, but rather occurs on reddish orange carbon-ate pastes of the Augustine (red) and Zaczuuz (tan) ceramic groups. Named Lupe Dichrome, this variant has been placed in the Zaczuuz group (P. Rice 1985a). This dichrome treatment also occurs in vessels of San Joaquin Buff ware at Mayapán (R. E. Smith 1971: 229–230).

Name: **Ixpop Polychrome: Ixpop Variety.**
Frequency: 193 sherds, of which 190 are from Macanché Island, 1 from the mainland "center," and 2 from Ixlú. Ixpop Polychrome type comprises 12.1 percent of the sherds of the Paxcamán ceramic group in Bullard's collections.
Ware: Volador Dull-Slipped ware.
Complex: Dos Lagos ceramic complex; in CPHEP excavations Ixpop was also present in the Early Postclassic Aura ceramic complex.
Established: Ixpop Polychrome was defined and illustrated by R. E. W. Adams and Trik (1961:125–127) from excavations at Tikal.
Principal identifying modes: Ixpop Polychrome, the principal decorated type of the Paxcamán ceramic group, is characterized by a band of decoration of black lines on the usually unslipped background paste color of the vessel. A variety of vessel forms are represented, including tripod dishes, bowls, and jars.
Paste and firing: The majority of Ixpop Polychrome vessels are of standard snail-inclusion paste and its firing variants (see chapter 6). One sherd was of a coarse red-brown carbonate paste; the vessel form was a tripod dish. Several dishes looked as if they might have been burned on the interior.
Surface treatment and decoration: Ixpop Polychrome vessels have a red to red-orange slip that is generally of good quality, in terms of both color and preservation. The slips vary from matte to low luster (see chapter 6). Approximately 13 percent of the sherds were double-slipped; their slip color is pinker than is typical for Paxcamán group sherds, and surfaces often have a faint silvery sheen.

The decoration of Ixpop Polychrome is executed in black paint; where the paint is

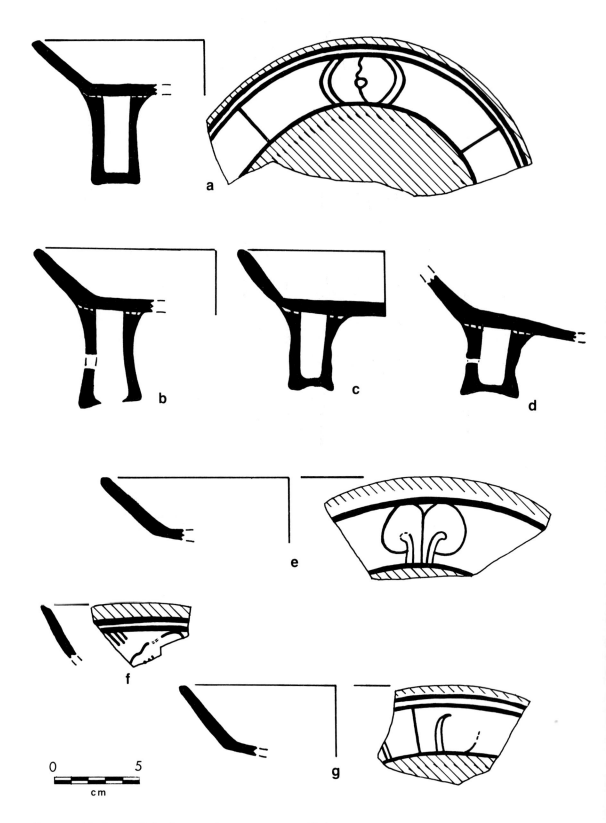

FIGURE 42. Ixpop Polychrome: Ixpop Variety. All decoration on interior of dishes. **b**, from Ixlú.

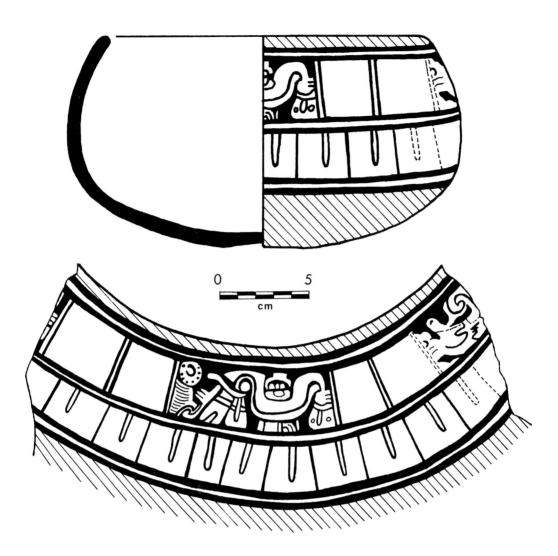

0 ____ 5

cm

FIGURE 43. Ixpop Polychrome: Ixpop Variety. Partially restorable restricted orifice bowl with unusual variant of the "split-representational" reptilian motif in upper panel.

covered by the red slip or an overslip it frequently appears reddish brown (2.5YR 3/2; "dusky red") in color. The paint is used in a narrow unslipped area to form a band, which is usually bounded by two lines at the top and a single line at the bottom. The band varies from 1.8 to 3.5 cm in width on tripod dishes; on jars it is typically wider but is difficult to measure because of breakage (two measurements were 2.5 cm and 4.5 cm). The lines bounding the decorated area are usually 3 to 4 mm in width; lines forming the deco-

ration itself are usually somewhat narrower—2 to 3 mm or so. Execution varies from good to rather careless.

Design motifs (figures 42–44; plate VIII) are similar to those noted for examples of Ixpop Polychrome elsewhere, but a slightly broader range seems to be evident at Macanché. Typically, the design band on tripod dishes is often paneled, either formally (by single or double lines) or informally by the positioning of decorative motifs. These motifs include hook or plumelike elements;

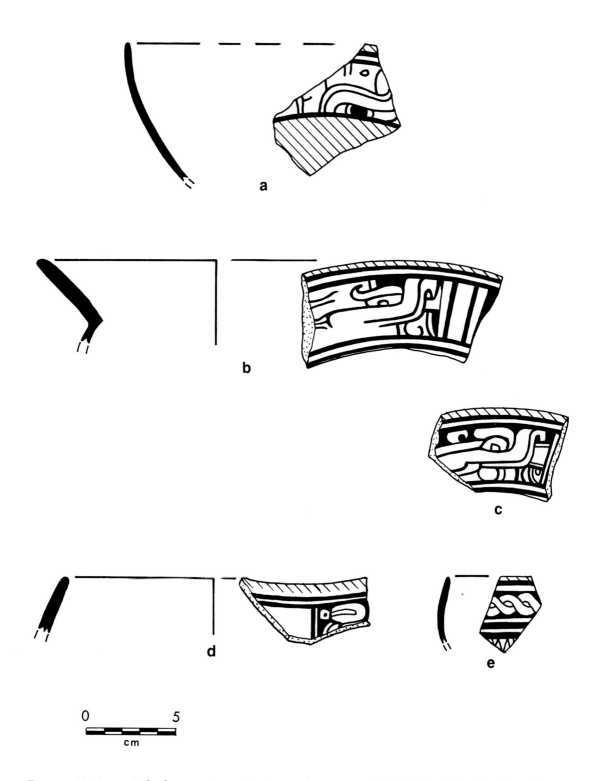

FIGURE 44. Ixpop Polychrome: Ixpop Variety. **a**, fragment with "RE glyph" style of reptile painted on the interior of bowl; **b**, **c**, collared bowl with "profile" style of serpent head on interior collar.

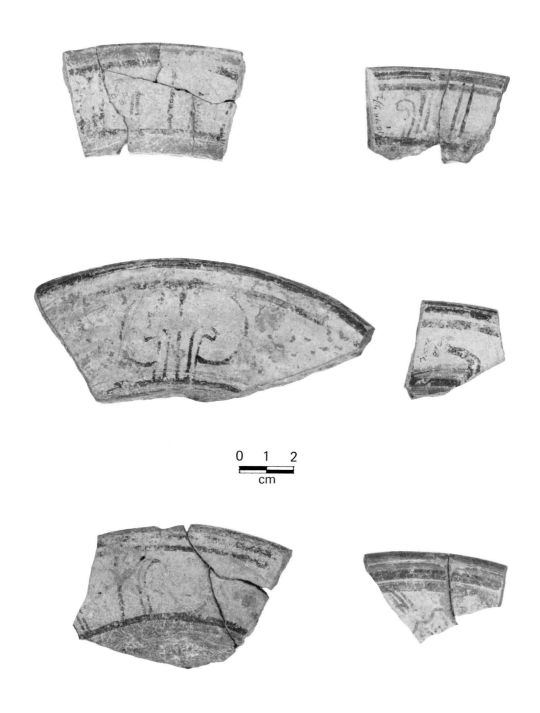

PLATE VIII. Ixpop Polychrome: Ixpop Variety; sherds are all tripod dishes.

PLATE IX. Ixpop Polychrome: Ixpop Variety; restricted orifice bowl, Lot 22.

single or double curved ("parenthesis") lines; a skull (?); a double volute; and a braid or twist. One vessel shows a sort of distorted Eznab symbol (see also R. E. W. Adams and Trik 1961) with a vertical wavy line bisecting the cartouche form. Four vessels, representing dishes and several bowl forms, bear reptilian motifs, including the profiled head and "RE glyph" variants (P. Rice 1983a).

Design motifs on jar body sherds were so highly eroded that no observations could be made. On neckless jars, decoration consisted of multiple (two or three) encircling black lines placed 1 to 1.5 cm below the lip. On one vessel the space between lip and black lines appears to be filled with vertical hachure; on another a band is created with two lines on top and one below; and hachure and semicircles appear indistinctly in the band. One sherd of a probable jar neck shows black bands on an unslipped cream background. Interiors are unslipped except for the zone below the lip in some specimens.

Restricted orifice bowls have slipped interiors, and exteriors are slipped above and below a relatively complex wide design band. One partially reconstructible example shows double bands of panelled decoration, most of the small panels having the stylized feather motif of a narrow "U" pendant from the upper border (fig. 43; plate IX). These flank a large panel with an unusual motif that appears to be a variant of the "quasi-split representational" reptile (P. Rice 1983a). This reptilian motif probably originally appeared two or three times around the circumference of the vessel.

The color of the background of the design band itself is variable (see "Slip Characteristics" in chapter 6). Among the tripod dishes the background varied from white (10YR 8/5) to orange (7.5YR 6.5/3–5) and R. E. W. Adams and Trik (1961:126), in fact, described their Ixpop sample as "black-on-orange." In a few sherds, the band area was clearly painted with a white-to-pale orange primary slip, and the design was painted over this. Three of the sherds exhibiting this primary slip are decorated with reptilian motifs. Unfortunately, this background preparation could be observed in only a very small number of sherds. A thin, streaky, translucent orange coating is visible over the design band of most sherds where there is good preservation (see chapter 6).

The sequence of finishing the vessel may

have been as follows: (1) application of a white undercoat or primary slip in the region of the design band of some vessels; (2) painting the design in black (perhaps manganese) paint over the treated or untreated band area; (3) slipping the entire exterior, the lip, and the interior base, sometimes overlapping the bordering lines of the decorative band; and (4) application of a thin translucent overcoat over the design band. There are some interesting parallels between Ixpop Polychrome decoration and earlier "Codex Style" vessels (see Robicsek and Hales 1981): the cream primary slip; black painted decoration, often bounded by double lines; and the red slip and basal bands. These technological parallels, plus the significant occurrence of reptile representations, suggest important continuities in the technology of polychrome ceramic manufacture in the Petén from the Late Classic to the Postclassic (P. Rice 1985c).

Forms and dimensions: Ixpop Polychrome vessels occur in four major forms at Macanché Island: tripod dishes, round-side bowls, collared bowls, and restricted orifice bowls, plus miscellaneous jar (?) forms.

TRIPOD DISHES: A total of 107 sherds (including one partially reconstructible vessel) were from tripod dishes. These vessels have flat or slightly rounded bases, and very slightly rounded (convex) or straight outflared walls; the lip is rounded or gently bevelled. The mouth diameter, as measured on seven specimens, varies from 17 to 22 cm, averaging 20 cm. Wall thickness varies between 5.5 and 7.5 mm. A small number of sherds (eight, representing four vessels) have very slightly outcurving sides and thin (4 mm) walls. Three small vessels had low walls only 2 cm in height. Two cylinder supports were associated with tripod vessels; neither had vent holes.

ROUND-SIDE BOWLS: Nine sherds, representing three vessels, came from small round-side bowls with rounded lip. On only one sherd could the diameter be measured: 15 cm. The other vessel had an "RE glyph" reptile variant (P. Rice 1983a).

COLLARED BOWL: Nine sherds, representing two vessels, are from a bowl with outflar-

ing collar or neck and slightly bevelled lip. The vessel has a red-orange slip on the exterior of the bowl and collar and on the interior of the vessel body. The interior of the neck or collar has a whitish cream underslip, painted in panels with a reptilian head as the motif. The width of the decorative band is 6.2 cm. Mouth diameter of the collar is 21 cm; the depth and form of the body of the vessel are not known.

RESTRICTED ORIFICE BOWL: Thirty sherds represent eight vessels of this form. One partially reconstructible squat vessel (20 sherds) had a mouth diameter of 17 cm and height of 11 cm. The lip was rounded and the base slightly concave. Slipped on the interior and exterior, the bowl had a design of two contiguous bands of "feather" panels interrupted by larger reptile panels. Another bowl had a diameter of 20 cm.

JARS: Forty-seven miscellaneous jar (?) body sherds showed no sign of interior slipping. They were identified as Ixpop Polychrome by the presence of black lines, usually just the border lines of the decorative band, on the exterior curvature. Several of the sherds appeared to have the white underslip beneath the decorative band. Nine sherds had double-slipped surfaces. Five sherds had very thin walls of 3 to 4 mm.

Illustrations: figures 42–44; plates VIII and IX.

Intrasite references: In Bullard's collection, no Ixpop Polychrome sherds appeared in Early Postclassic lots: the vessels were primarily from "early" Late Postclassic lots, and primarily from the top of the mound rather than the slopes. Two very distinctive partially reconstructible bowls with reptilian motifs were recovered in these deposits in Bullard's Operations IE and IF, on top of the mound to the south of the latest structure.

Intersite references: Ixpop Polychrome has been recovered from a number of locations: Barton Ramie (Sharer and Chase 1976), Tikal (R. E. W. Adams and Trik 1961), the vicinity of Lake Petén-Itzá (G. Cowgill 1963), Flores (Berlin 1955: fig. 1a), and Tayasal (A. Chase 1979), and the general central Petén lakes region (G. Cowgill 1963; P. Rice 1979,

1980). An Ixpop Polychrome dish recovered at Seibal, though not identified as such (Sabloff 1975: fig. 434), was of the general size (diameter 22 cm) and proportions as those from Macanché. In addition, I have noted a specimen of Ixpop Polychrome from Salcajá in the Guatemala Highlands (currently in the National Museum in Guatemala City), which is a very small tripod dish with the "RE glyph" reptile variant. Ixpop Polychrome is also present at the late mission site of Negroman-Tipú, in western Belize (P. Rice 1984a).

The specimens from Macanché extend the range of variability of form and decoration within this type beyond that described for the other sites. Macanché has a variety of forms in Ixpop, including round-side bowls, collared bowls, and restricted orifice bowls.

Tripod dishes at Macanché differ from those at other sites in a number of attributes, principally in their smaller size and general proportions. They are smaller in diameter than similar vessels at Barton Ramie, and tend to have slightly rounded (though not "sagging," as in the Topoxté group dishes) rather than flat bases. Although exact vessel diameters were not given for the Lake Petén-Itzá specimens, the Macanché dishes have slightly different proportions, with smaller diameters in relation to depth. Vessel supports are smaller, too (see above, "Paxcamán General"), more cylindrical in shape, and often unvented. The overall proportions are closer to those of the tripod dishes of the Topoxté ceramic group than to Ixpop at Belize or Lake Petén-Itzá. In addition, vessel walls are less outflaring and more nearly vertical or very slightly convex.

In decoration as in form, the Macanché Ixpop specimens differ to some extent from those of other sites. A small number of Ixpop sherds from Macanché exhibited a white undercoating on the decorative band, a feature not noted previously on Ixpop Polychrome (but present in the polychrome types of the Trapeche group at Macanché; see below). Design motifs and patterning at Macanché include the general repertoire noted at other sites (panelling, braids, double lines, plumes,

volutes) which are common not only in the Paxcamán group but in Late Postclassic pottery throughout the Lowlands (e.g., see R. E. Smith 1971).

The depiction of reptilian creatures on this pottery is unusual, particularly the clearly profiled reptilian head and the "quasi-split representational" form. These appear in the Trapeche group in the lakes area, but are depicted by incising rather than painting (Ain Variety of Xuluc Incised). The "RE glyph variant" seems to have a wider geographic distribution than the other two versions, having been noted in polychrome decoration at Barton Ramie (Sharer and Chase 1976: fig. 196a), Lake Petén-Itzá (G. Cowgill 1963: fig. 4t), Tayasal (Chase and Chase 1983: fig. 27d), and on the vessel from Salcajá.

Black painted polychrome decoration forms a small but consistent percentage of the decorated pottery in all the major Postclassic ceramic groups of Petén-Belize, beginning in the Early Postclassic period. Elsewhere, it seems to be particularly associated with Late Postclassic complexes. To the north, in Yucatán, painted decoration is second in importance to incising in red-slipped wares; painted decoration is more common with the cream or buff slips of San Joaquin Buff and Peto Cream wares. The closest parallel is Pele Polychrome in San Joaquin Buff ware (R. E. Smith 1971:80–81, fig. 54), because it has a red slip and banded decoration. In the Highlands of Guatemala to the south, black-and-white-on-red decoration, usually banded and/or panelled, and frequently depicting reptilian motifs, is an important component of the Late Postclassic pottery of the area; especially noteworthy for comparative purposes is Chinautla Polychrome (Wauchope 1970:110–114; Navarrete 1961:24–45). Although tripod dishes and jars are basic vessel shapes of the polychrome types in all these areas, details of shape and proportions are considerably different.

Name: **Saca Polychrome: Saca Variety.**

Frequency: 18 sherds from Bullard's excavations on Macanché Island. Saca Polychrome accounts for 1.1 percent of the sherds of the Paxcamán ceramic group in Bullard's collections.

Ware: Volador Dull-Slipped ware.

Complex: Aura (?) and Dos Lagos ceramic complexes.

Established: Sacá Polychrome was described by G. Cowgill (1963:237–243) on the basis of his material from the Lake Petén-Itzá region.

Principal identifying modes: Sacá Polychrome may be identified by red-and-black-on-cream polychrome painted decoration; undecorated areas are red-slipped.

Paste and firing: Sacá Polychrome exhibits some variety in pastes (see chapter 6). Most sherds are oxidized brown snail-inclusion paste; five are light gray, one is dark gray, and four are coarse red paste. Sherds seem to be well fired; fire-clouding is very rare.

Surface treatment and decoration: Slips are primarily red-orange or light orange (5YR 6/6) rather than clear red (see chapter 6). One shows fire-clouding. Vessels have a band of decoration executed in black and dark red (10R 3/6, faded or eroded to 4/8), sometimes glossy paint. The red is sometimes heavily eroded to a very faint brown. It is doubtful that a cream to very pale orange underslip, similar to that described for Ixpop Polychrome, is present. Cowgill's original (1963:237–243) type descriptions included both red paint and red-and-black paint within Sacá Polychrome type. At Macanché, Sacá is restricted to red-and-black paint; the presence of red paint alone is a diagnostic trait of a new type, Macanché Red-on-paste(cream) (see below).

Design placement is much like that of Ixpop Polychrome, usually occurring in a band bounded by encircling lines on the interior wall of dishes and exteriors of other vessel forms. Unlike Ixpop, Sacá design bands often are bound by three lines: a red line between two black lines. These may be contiguous or may be separated by 1.5 to 3 mm. The lines are generally 2 to 4 mm in width, but in the borders of jars the red line is frequently considerably broader, 7 to 9 mm.

Within the band it is difficult to identify the design motifs with any accuracy because the sherds are broken. One sherd, a restricted orifice vessel with the design space bounded by two black lines and a red line, shows nested chevrons, pointing to the right, in alternating red and black. The decoration of two tripod dish sherds suggests paired curved lines, executed in red or black, that are similar to paired motifs in Ixpop. No reptile representations were noted.

One unusual vessel is an extremely flaring-sided dish, or perhaps a very large collar on a jar or bowl. The design appears on both interior and exterior whitish (primary slipped?) surfaces of the vessel, with only the lip covered with red-orange slip. On the interior the three boundary lines appear in black-red-black (?) sequence, the black being considerably faded. Within the design band is a "spray" of plumes or curved lines. On the exterior the three border lines are black-red-red, with a more complex (but very eroded) design executed by negative painting in red.

Forms and dimensions: Vessel forms include tripod dishes (four sherds), neckless jars (restricted orifice jars; four sherds), jar body sherds (six sherds), and four sherds of the rim of an unusual lid or outflaring dish.

Tripod dish forms and dimensions appear to fall within the range of tripod dishes of Paxcamán and Ixpop types, but the sherds are generally too small to measure diameter. The four tripod dish rims had interior bevelled lips, which were not noted in significant frequencies in this form in other types. Wall thickness varies from 5 to 7 mm. G. Cowgill (1963:92) noted that his Sacá Polychrome tripod dish specimens have a tendency toward sagging rather than flat bases.

One rim sherd from a restricted orifice bowl is very thin walled (4 mm). The outflaring side dish (collared bowl? lid?) has a mouth diameter of ca. 30 cm and wall thickness of 7.5 mm.

Illustrations: figure 45a–d.

Intrasite references: Sacá Polychrome sherds came primarily from excavations on the top of the mound, rather than in the heavy midden around the slopes. The type was associated primarily with the "early" Late Postclassic, i.e., below 20 cm below sur-

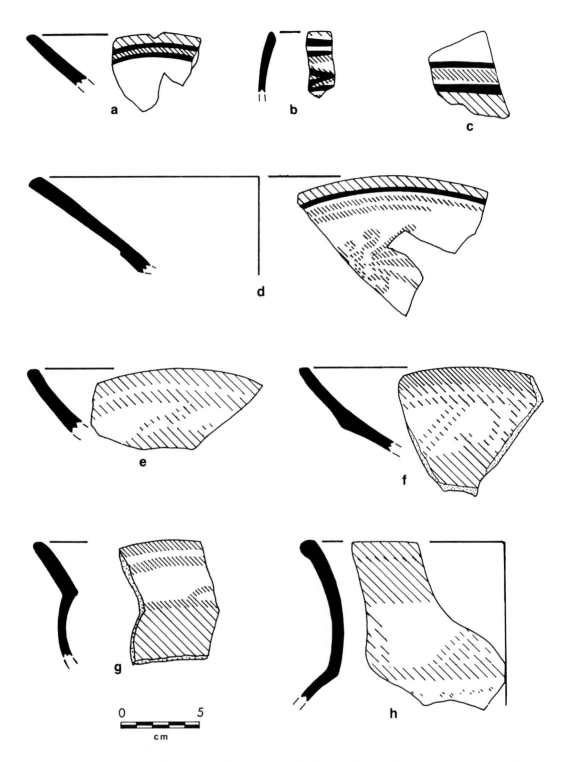

FIGURE 45. **a–c**, Sacá Polychrome: Sacá Variety; **a**, **d**, decoration on interior, a coarse red paste; **b**, **c**, decoration on exterior. **e–h**, Macanché Red-on-paste(cream): Macanché Variety; **e–g**, decoration on interior; **h**, painting on exterior. Paint is light red on **e**, **f**, and **h**, and dark red on **g**.

face in the midden. Although two sherds of Sacá came from Bullard's lots that I have phased as late Early Postclassic, none of the CPHEP excavations into Early Postclassic deposits yielded Sacá Polychrome sherds. The type is extremely rare at Macanché Island.

Intersite references: Sacá Polychrome is not abundant at Postclassic sites in Petén in general. G. Cowgill described the sherds of this type as "minor variants of Ixpop Polychrome" (1963:110) and as "a sort of deluxe Ixpop Polychrome to which an additional color has been added" (ibid.:291). Indeed, ties to Ixpop in decorative motifs, color, and form are significant. The Lake Petén-Itzá/Tayasal region is the only other area besides Macanché where this type has been recovered; it has not been found at Barton Ramie or at Tikal. A large widemouthed jar with tripod supports of Sacá Polychrome type was noted in a private collection in Petén.

Other Postclassic multicolor polychromes in Petén are Dolorido Cream Polychrome in the Trapeche ceramic group (A. Chase 1979) and Canté Polychrome in the Topoxté group (P. Rice 1979), which was originally part of Bullard's (1970) "Topoxté Cream Polychrome" type). There is nothing in these other types, or in the Sacá vessels from other areas, that is similar to the unusual outflaring dish from Macanché.

Outside the Petén area, polychrome painting is very rare in red-slipped wares to the north in the Yucatán Peninsula. To the south at Naco, Honduras, the late facet Late Postclassic (i.e., post-A.D. 1450) sees the appearance of small amounts of Posas, Vagando, and Hidaldo Polychrome types featuring red and black painting on a "white" ground. These types are present in only small amounts (ca. 1 percent of the complex), and Vagando and Posas show ties to Central American styles in particular (Wonderley 1981:191). Vessel forms are different from those in the Southern Lowlands (e.g., in the outflaring walls and shape of the supports of tripod dishes), or represent forms not found at all in Petén polychrome types, such as polychrome ladle censers.

Name: **Macanché Red-on-paste(cream): Macanché Variety.**

Frequency: 26 sherds, of which 25 were from Macanché Island and 1 from Punta Nimá. Macanché Red-on-paste sherds represent 1.6 percent of the sherds of the Paxcamán ceramic group in Bullard's collections.

Ware: Volador Dull-Slipped ware.

Complex: Dos Lagos and Ayer ceramic complexes.

Established: This type was first identified as "provisional" on the basis of the CPHEP material from Canté Island excavations (P. Rice 1979:68). It has not been previously noted in central Petén collections, although red-on-cream decoration was subsumed by G. Cowgill (1963) within Sacá Polychrome type.

Principal identifying modes: Macanché Red-on-paste(cream) type is distinguished by decoration in red paint on a cream-to-gray natural paste color background. Portions of the vessels are red-slipped.

Paste and firing: All but two sherds are of the typical gray snail-inclusion paste (see chapter 6); two are brown paste, and one is coarse gray. Fire-clouding or post-depositional burning is visible on two sherds.

Surface treatment and decoration: Slips are red to red-orange in color; one sherd has a pinkish slip and appears to have been double-slipped (see chapter 6). Decoration consists of encircling lines around the interior rims of tripod dishes and necks of jars, forming a banded design.

Lines and design motifs are executed in red paint on a natural paste background, but the red paint color could prove to be a basis for some varietal distinctions within the type. Ten sherds are painted with a glossy dark or maroon red (10R 3–4/6–8) like that in Sacá Polychrome, but four others have a lighter orange-red paint (2.5YR 5/6) virtually identical to the slip. In one of these sherds, a tripod dish, the slip is a *darker* red than the paint.

Designs, in general fairly eroded, can be identified only in the orange-red paint, and consist of motifs similar to those on Ixpop

Polychrome: paired diagonals, plumelike forms, and so forth. On the jar neck, the red slip occurs on the upper interior 2 cm and exterior 4 cm of the rim. Below that is an unslipped (or possibly cream underslipped) band with paired lines and curvilinear motifs. A line encircles the neck at the join with the jar body. Three sherds have very eroded designs in dark red paint that may resemble the dot-and-line motifs of Chompoxté Red-on-cream: Chompoxté Variety, in the Topoxté ceramic group. On two eroded body sherds it appears that a decorated area was bounded by dark red lines. One painted dish base from CPHEP excavations suggested that the decoration may have covered the entire interior of the dishes, rather than occurring solely in a band on the walls, again paralleling Chompoxté Variety.

These parallels with the Chompoxté Red-on-cream type may suggest varietal distinctions in Macanché Red-on-paste(cream) similar to those in that Topoxté group (see P. Rice 1979). The use of different paints (dark and light) was not apparent in Chompoxté type, however, and in Macanché Red-on-paste it crosscuts the distinctions to be made between banded and unbanded designs, so its significance is difficult to assess at this point.

Forms and dimensions: The vessel forms that can be discerned include dishes or bowls (15 sherds), which are generally fairly large and deep, and jars. One tripod, of dark gray paste with light red orange banded decoration, has a flattened lip, a deep sagging bottom, and a mouth diameter of 24 cm. Another, also with a sagging bottom, has a rounded lip, light gray paste, and eroded decoration in dark red paint; its diameter is 22 cm. The walls of these two vessels are higher than those of tripod dishes in Ixpop or Paxcamán Red types, being roughly 5 cm high as opposed to the more usual 4.0 to 4.5 cm.

Besides the tripod dishes, a jar (four sherds) with a bolstered lip had a high (8 cm) outflaring neck and a mouth diameter of ca. 27 cm. A collared bowl from Punta Nimá had a band of dark red decoration (very eroded) on the interior collar; the slip was red-orange,

and the mouth diameter was 25 cm. Average wall thickness on all forms varies from 5 to 6.5 cm.

Illustrations: figure 45e–h.

Intrasite references: In Bullard's collection, Macanché Red-on-paste(cream) appeared only in Late Postclassic complexes, either in the "late" Protohistoric lots or in "mixed" lots, while in CPHEP excavations three sherds came from late facet Aura Early Postclassic platform construction.

Intersite references: This type had not previously been separated out from Paxcamán collections in earlier material, although a red-on-cream decorative variant had been noted. G. Cowgill (1963) subsumed the red paint decoration under Sacá Polychrome type. Macanché Red-on-paste(cream) has been identifed as part of the late Kauil complex in the Tayasal-Paxcamán zone of Lake Petén-Itzá (Chase and Chase 1983). Vessel forms (the sagging bottom of tripods) and decorative features closely ally this rare type in the central Petén lakes to Chompoxté Red-on-cream type from Topoxté in the northeast. The use of red paint on a cream or "paste color" background suggests slight correspondences with the late Tachís ceramic group from Lake Petén-Itzá (G. Cowgill 1963), but there are considerable differences in form, decorative motifs, and slip colors. The types may, however, be contemporaneous. Small amounts of light red paint on the cream to gray paste colors of the Trapeche group cream-pink-slipped vessels has led to definition of a new type, Picté Red-on-paste (cream) in that group (see below).

Outside of the Petén area and its environs, red-on-cream painting is represented by Tecoh Red-on-buff (San Joaquin Buff ware) to the north in Yucatán, where painted decoration in general has little emphasis as compared to incising. Similarities can be seen in the wide-necked jar forms and in the overall interior decoration in dishes, featuring dots, circles, swirls, and some that looks like imitation resist (R. E. Smith 1971:78–81, fig. 53a and b). To the south, in the western Guatemala Highlands there are numerous white-on-red and red-on-white types of the Late Postclassic period that exhibit banded and unbanded curvilinear motifs, often with dots and ticks (Wauchope 1970). On the southeastern periphery of the Maya Lowlands, at Naco, Honduras, Nolasco Bichrome pottery type begins in the early facet of the Late Postclassic, ca. A.D. 1200. It shows some relationships with Chompoxté Red-on-cream type, and is believed to represent a fusion of a local tradition with this Petén-derived material (Wonderley 1981 : 172, 306).

Name: **Picú Incised: Picú Variety.**

Frequency: 8 sherds, of which 7 were from Bullard's excavations on Macanché Island and 1 from Punta Nimá. Picú Variety of Picú Incised constitutes 0.5 percent of the sherds of the Paxcamán ceramic group in Bullard's collections, and 25 percent of the sherds of Picú Incised type.

Ware: Volador Dull-Slipped ware.

Complex: Dos Lagos ceramic complex.

Established: Picú Incised: Picú Variety was established by G. Cowgill (1963) on the basis of ceramic collections in the vicinity of Lake Petén-Itzá.

Principal identifying modes: Picú Variety of Picú Incised is distinguished by the presence of fine postslip, postfire incising on vessels with the characteristic red slips, pastes, and forms of the Paxcamán ceramic group.

Paste and firing: Picú Variety of Picú Incised typically appears on the snail-inclusion pastes of the Paxcamán group. Most of these sherds are brown pastes, but there are so few of them that it is difficult to say whether this represents a defining characteristic (see chapter 6).

Surface treatment and decoration: Sherds are slipped with a red or red-orange slip (see chapter 6), and decoration appears on a postslip fine incised band. In his notes, Bullard referred to this type as "Picú Plano-relief," in recognition of the use of excising in addition to fine incising. Plano-relief carving or excising is more common on the cream-slipped sherds, however, which have been grouped since Bullard's original work into a different

type and variety within the Trapeche group (see Xuluc Incised: Ain Variety, below).

There are very few sherds of Picú Incised from Macanché and those that were recovered are quite small, so that the motifs are unclear. One dish rim sherd has the incising on the exterior: the decoration consists of a narrow band bounded top and bottom by double lines; the panel itself is crosshatched, while triangles appear above the upper boundary lines.

The sherd from Punta Nimá is a bowl or dish that is an unusual bichrome variant. The exterior seems to have an eroded cream slip (10YR 7/2–3) with seven encircling reddish brown lines (ca. 2 mm wide) placed ca. 2 mm apart. The red-slipped (2.5YR 4–5/8) interior has two panels: the upper panel, 1 cm in width, is bounded with three lines above and below and consists of an encircling braid. Beneath the three lower boundary lines is a complex motif that is probably one of the reptile representations. The paste is light gray-brown snail paste.

Forms and dimensions: The vessels from Macanché are all indeterminate as to dimensions. The dish from Punta Nimá has a diameter of 24 cm, and a thickness of 5.5 mm.

Illustrations: figure 46a and b.

Intrasite references: The sherds from Bullard's excavations come primarily from the "early" Late Postclassic; none of them came from Early Postclassic construction fill, although two sherds of Picú Incised: Picú Variety were recovered by CPHEP test pits into the late facet Early Postclassic platform construction.

Intersite references: Picú Incised was rare at Macanché Island, and also occurs infrequently at other areas. One unusual composite or bichrome variant was noted in Bullard's collection from Punta Nimá. Picú Incised: Picú Variety was present at Tayasal, but incising as a decorative technique was rare by late Middle Postclassic (Cocahmut) times there (Chase and Chase 1983 : 108). In G. Cowgill's excavations in the Lake Petén-Itzá region, Picú Incised showed motifs—reptiles and mats—similar to those in Ain

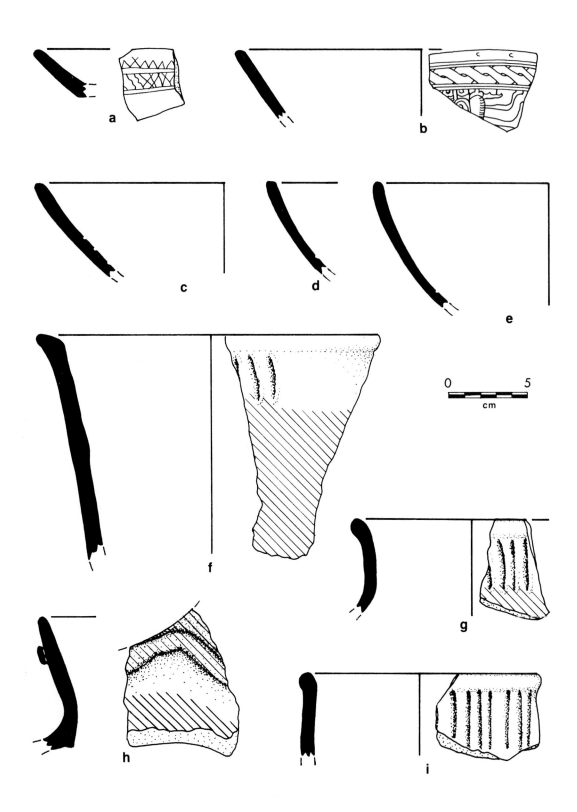

FIGURE 46. **a**, **b**, Picú Incised: Picú Variety (slip is not shown); **a**, decoration on exterior; **b**, incised decoration on interior, exterior has narrow encircling red painted lines. **c–g**, Picú Incised: Thub Variety; **c–e**, grater bowls; **f**, **g**, **i**, "drums" (?). **h**, Chamán Modeled: Variety Unspecified.

Variety of Xuluc Incised (Trapeche group) in the Macanché area. An unusual chalice form in this type (G. Cowgill 1963:fig. 4a) is vaguely reminiscent of vessels from Lamanai (Pendergast 1981:45, fig. 15). Elsewhere in the lakes region, Picú Incised is comparatively uncommon, most incised decoration appearing in Xuluc Incised type. None was found at Barton Ramie.

It is interesting that incising rarely if ever occurs on tripod dishes in Picú Incised or in its homologs, Xuluc Incised and Dulces Incised; instead, incising appears most frequently on collared bowls. This may be a "functional" decision: decoration on tripods is typically on the interior walls which, if incised, would have been difficult to clean after use in serving food.

Incised postslip decoration is common in red-slipped wares of the Northern Maya Lowlands and in northern Belize (R. E. Smith 1971; Sanders 1960; Pendergast 1981), where it appears in banded and panelled arrangements emphasizing abstract plume or feather-like motifs. To the south, in the Maya Highlands and along the southeast periphery (e.g., Naco), incising is rare, with decoration appearing primarily as polychrome painting.

Name: **Picú Incised: Thub Variety.**

Frequency: 24 sherds from Bullard's excavations on Macanché Island. Thub Variety of Picú Incised represents 1.5 percent of the sherds of the Paxcamán ceramic group in Bullard's collections, and 75 percent of the sherds of Picú Incised type.

Ware: Volador Dull-Slipped ware.

Complex: Dos Lagos and Ayer (?) ceramic complexes.

Established: The Thub Variety of Picú Incised was defined by A. Chase (1983) on the basis of the collections from Tayasal.

Principal identifying modes: Thub Variety of Picú Incised is characterized by patterned, prefire-incised lines usually deeply scored into unslipped portions of otherwise red-slipped vessels. Two major forms are known: grater bowls and jar-like vessels (drums?).

Paste and firing: See chapter 6. Eight sherds are of non-snail-inclusion pastes; four of these are volcanic ash paste.

Surface treatment and decoration: Vessels are partially covered with a red slip characteristic of the Paxcamán ceramic group (see chapter 6). On grater bowls the slip reaches only part of the way down the interior wall of the vessel; the unslipped interior portion is incised with one or more encircling lines, and this enclosed area is usually divided into quadrants. Each of the four quadrants is scored with parallel fine lines or shallow grooves, or with cross-hatching. Occasionally the slip covers the encircling boundary lines.

The other vessel category is known from only three jar-like or neck rims. On these, the incising consists of groups of deep parallel vertical slashes, executed while the clay was still rather wet and plastic, between the rim and the upper margin of the red slip. On one of these sherds, the area of the incising may have had a cream slip; the interior is unslipped.

Forms and dimensions: Two forms are known in this type: grater bowls (or molcajetes) and jars or drums (see above). Few of the grater bowls are large enough to include rims and indicate the diameters. One ash paste vessel has a square lip and a diameter of 26 cm; the incising begins 6.1 cm below the slip. The thickness is 5 mm, increasing to 7.5 mm near the thickened rim. Another, also with a square lip, has a thickness of 7 mm and a diameter of roughly 28 cm; the incised motif consists of three circumferential lines placed 4.1 cm below the lip, and the enclosed pattern is of deeply incised lines 0.9 to 1.3 cm apart. A third vessel, 1.1 cm thick, has lines spaced 1.0 to 1.5 cm apart; two sherds of coarse gray paste have incised lines closely spaced at 5 to 7.5 mm distance. One sherd shows that a support had been originally attached to the vessel.

Only three sherds represent the "drum" form, which has a vertical or slightly outflaring neck. One large sherd has a triangular lip bolster, a thickness of 1.0 cm, and a diameter of 24 cm; the sherd suggests a wall (neck?)

greater than 13.8 cm in height. The incised lines on these vessels are carelessly executed, being irregular in length (2.5 to 3.0 cm) and unevenly spaced (0.85 to 1.3 cm). They may be as much as 3 mm in depth.

Illustrations: figure 46c–g.

Intrasite references: Among the fragments of grater bowls, five were recovered from Terminal Classic lots and are regarded as probably intrusive (see chapter 3). The remainder are primarily from "early" Late Postclassic lots and from the top of the mound. The three "drum" sherds were from late mixed surface lots.

Intersite references: Grater bowls are one of the hallmarks of the Postclassic period in the Central Lowlands, and are associated with Fine Orange ware groups in the Boca sphere of the Pasión area of western Petén. Their presence in Terminal Classic lots at Macanché is regarded as intrusive, but given their early occurrence to the southwest, it is possible that this is a genuine association, and an extraordinarily early appearance of the Paxcamán ceramic group.

The "drums" or jars with deeply incised necks appear to be an uncommon but geographically widespread occurrence in Late Postclassic assemblages in the Lowlands. The form was noted in Thub Variety at Tayasal (A. Chase 1983), and in White Creek Incised of the Daylight group at Barton Ramie (Sharer and Chase 1976:fig. 200c), but seems to be more common to the north. The vessel form occurs in Papacal Incised (Mayapán Red ware) at Mayapán (R. E. Smith 1971:64–65, fig. 39), and Ball (1979:fig. 9) also illustrates an example in Slateware. The lines in these Yucatecan examples do not appear to be grouped as are the slashes in Thub Variety at Macanché, however.

Name: **Chamán Modeled: Variety Unspecified.**

Frequency: 3 sherds from Bullard's excavations at Macanché Island. Chamán Modeled type constitutes 0.2 percent of the sherds of the Paxcamán ceramic group in Bullard's collections.

Ware: Volador Dull-Slipped ware.

Complex: Dos Lagos ceramic complex.

Established: A. Chase (1983) defined the type Chamán Modeled in the Tayasal collections.

Principal identifying modes: At Macanché, sherds of Chamán Modeled are distinguished by appliquéd elements on red-slipped vessels of the characteristic pastes of the Paxcamán group.

Paste and firing: All three sherds are snail-inclusion paste (see chapter 6).

Surface treatment and decoration: All sherds are covered with a red slip, which on two sherds covers the appliquéd element. On one sherd of dark gray paste, the appliqué is a narrow fillet in an S-curve along the "neck" (?) of the vessel. On another sherd, the appliqué is a lidded eye; on the third sherd, a small unslipped appliqué pellet has two vertical incised lines 6 mm in length.

Forms and dimensions: The sherd with the appliqué fillet is an unusual rim with an edge that curves vertically to a maximum height of 8 cm; the thickness of the sherd is 1.05 cm. It may be part of the mouth of a double-spouted jar. The sherd with the "eye" may be the base of a vessel, perhaps a potstand.

Illustration: figure 46h.

Intrasite references: These three sherds are all from Late Postclassic lots on Macanché Island.

Intersite references: Chamán Modeled was present at Tayasal, where it was first defined, but there is no indication of these modeled or appliquéd variations occurring in G. Cowgill's collection from Lake Petén-Itzá.

Name: **Unidentified Polychrome: Type and Variety Unspecified.**

Frequency: 71 sherds, of which 67 are from Bullard's excavations on Macanché Island and 4 from Ixlú. Unidentified Polychrome sherds comprise 4.5 percent of the sherds from the Paxcamán ceramic group in Bullard's collections.

Ware: Volador Dull-Slipped ware.

Complex: Dos Lagos (and Ayer?) ceramic complexes.

Principal identifying modes: This is a residual category for eroded sherds that show the traces of red slip or design boundaries, or both, characteristic of polychrome types in the Paxcamán ceramic group, but are eroded to such an extent that the specific colors (and hence the type identifications) cannot be determined.

Paste and firing: One of these sherds is volcanic ash paste, while the remainder are of snail-inclusion paste variants (see chapter 6). Most of the sherds are very fire-clouded.

Surface treatment and dimensions: Sherds are covered with a red to red-orange slip (see chapter 6). They all show a line or break in the slip, which marks the beginning of the banded polychrome decoration, but the decorative band itself is sufficiently eroded that the colors, motifs, and classificatory categories cannot be determined. Two sherds were apparently double-slipped.

Forms and dimensions: All but eight of these sherds represent dishes (probably tripods) or bowls. One dish has a diameter of 22 cm; two of the sherds are thin-walled. Two rims suggest vessels that are unusually deep, with wall heights measuring 5.4 and 5.5 cm; these are probably bowls.

Illustrations: None.

Intrasite references: All but four of these sherds are from the Late Postclassic midden deposit on the island; nearly two-thirds of the sherds are from the "early" levels. Three reconstructible tripod dishes came from Lot 22, on the top of the mound.

Intersite references: Four of these eroded unidentifiable polychrome sherds were from Ixlú. For comparative occurrences, see "Intersite references" for Ixpop and Sacá Polychromes, and Macanché Red-on-paste(cream) types, above.

Trapeche Ceramic Group

Name: Trapeche Pink: Tramite Variety.

Frequency: 368 sherds from Bullard's excavations on Macanché Island. Tramite Variety sherds comprise 19.1 percent of the

sherds of the Trapeche ceramic group in Bullard's collections.

Ware: Volador Dull-Slipped ware.

Complex: Aura, Dos Lagos, and Ayer (?) ceramic complexes.

Established: The Tramite Variety of Trapeche Pink is established in the present work. The Trapeche ceramic group and its constituent types were originally given definition and illustration by A. Chase (1979: 104–105) on the basis of material from Tayasal.

Principal identifying modes: Tramite Variety of Trapeche Pink, the monochrome-slipped type within the Trapeche group, is characterized by slip colors varying from cream to pink to orange-tan, which are found on a variety of vessel forms. Paste and form characteristics parallel those of the Paxcamán group.

Paste and firing: The Tramite Variety of Trapeche Pink pottery typically is of the same gray to grayish-brown snail-inclusion paste that is found in the Paxcamán ceramic group (see chapter 6 and color plates 1a–1c, 1e3). The mouths of dishes are often darkened by fire-clouds, a characteristic also noted in Paxcamán tripod dishes.

As in the Paxcamán group, "odd" pastes occur primarily in the monochrome-slipped type of the group, and within the Tramite Variety of Trapeche Pink at Macanché they are most common in tripod dishes (55 sherds, or 40.4 percent). Eleven sherds were of yellowish brown volcanic ash paste, five of which represented a reconstructible vessel with scroll supports. Twenty-two sherds, including one partially reconstructible vessel, were of coarse gray paste, while 19 sherds were of a coarse dark brown "crystalline"-appearing paste that had rare snail shell fragments. Three sherds were of the relatively coarse reddish brown paste that probably corresponds to A. Chase's original (1979) "Halal Variety" in "Red-brown Paste Ware."

Surface treatment and decoration: Tramite Variety sherds have slipped surfaces varying in color from cream (10YR 7/3–4) to pinkish (5YR 7/3) to orange-tan (7.5YR 7/4) (color plate 2b). Fire-clouding to gray or pink is relatively common. Occasionally the sherds are double-slipped: a reddish orange underslip is covered by a thicker, semi-translucent cream-colored slip. The slips are soft, relatively thick, and matte-finished. When well preserved, the surface has a dull waxy luster and feel; the possibility of some organic post-fire coating is suggested by similarities with Shepard's observations on San José pottery (1942:264–266; see chapter 6, above). The slip tends to erode easily, both as a single slip and as an overslip, flaking off in patches.

Forms and dimensions: A wide variety of forms is represented in Tramite Variety of Trapeche Pink at Macanché, paralleling the range of shapes found in Paxcamán Red. Major form categories include tripod dishes, hemispherical bowls, collared bowls (widemouthed jars), narrow-necked jars, neckless jars, and some miscellaneous forms.

TRIPOD DISH: A total of 136 sherds were from tripod dishes; of these, 81 sherds (representing 44 vessels) were of snail-inclusion paste and 55 sherds (34 vessels) were of "odd" pastes. Tripod dishes in Tramite Variety have flat or very slightly convex bases, and walls vary from very slightly convex to slightly outflaring. The lip is generally rounded, though internal bevels and thinning are occasionally visible. A few sherds have a groove marking the join of the wall to the base.

Vessel diameters range from 20 to 24 cm (average 21 cm; 18 measurements), and the height of the interior wall ranges from 3.8 to 4.6 cm (mean 4.1 cm; 12 measurements). Wall thickness averages 6.8 mm, with a range of 5.5 to 7.9 mm (12 measurements). One very small vessel, represented by seven sherds, had a wall height of about 3 cm and a diameter of 15 cm. There is no evident difference in dimensions or proportions between snail-inclusion-paste vessels and those of other pastes. Six vessels had scroll supports and six had cylindrical supports.

HEMISPHERICAL BOWLS: Nineteen sherds come from round-sided bowls. The sherds are generally too small for reliable estimates of vessel diameter, but the thickness and

curvature suggest a range approximating that of tripod dishes. The bowls are hemispherical with rounded, slightly beveled, or tapered lips. Twelve sherds come from what is probably a single vessel, a large hemispherical bowl (diameter 41 cm) with internal rim thickening and bevel. Both interior and exterior surfaces are slipped.

COLLARED BOWL (OR WIDEMOUTHED JARS): Fifty-seven sherds represent vessels with a short to medium-high neck that is either approximately vertical in orientation or outflaring at an angle of about 30° from the vertical. Because the vessel body form of these variants is unknown, I have grouped them together as "widemouthed jars" (or collared bowls). Twenty-seven sherds have short necks or collars, which vary from 3.1 to 4.1 cm in height (four measurements), and may be nearly vertical or outflaring. The mouth diameters vary from 20 to 30 cm (three vessels). In the 30 sherds (26 vessels) of bowls or jars with high necks or collars, the collar height varies from 4.8 to 7.0 cm (average 5.1 cm; 12 measurements). The collar is generally outflaring, and occasionally is recurved and thinned near the join with the vessel body; in thickness it ranges from 6.9 to 9.5 mm (average 8.2 mm; 12 measurements) and is generally greater than that of the body of the bowl. The lip is rounded, or rarely has a slight interior bevel; the mouth diameter could be measured on only two vessels, and the measurements obtained were 38 and 40 cm. The form of the vessel body is not entirely certain, nor is the presence of an interior slip.

NARROW-NECKED JARS: Seventy sherds are from jars with narrow neck openings, and these have been subdivided into high-neck, medium-neck, and height-indeterminate categories. High-necked jars are indicated by 26 sherds, representing eight vessels. Three relatively complete specimens have neck heights ranging from 9.3 to 12.3 cm. Mouth diameters vary between 19 and 20 cm; the interior neck diameter ranges from 9.75 to 10 cm; and the maximum wall thickness varies from 1.1 to 1.4 cm. The slip continues from 5 to 6 cm below the edge of the lip on the interior of the neck. Medium-neck jars are represented by 11 sherds (seven vessels): neck heights vary from 4.4 to 6.9 cm (seven measurements) and mouth diameters from 11.5 to 12 cm (three measurements). Thirty-three sherds are fragments of the necks of jars, the height of which is indeterminate; mouth diameters vary from 14 to 20 cm—probably at least four of these represent high-neck jars.

Besides these jar necks, the bases and strap handles of jars can also be identified. Twenty-seven strap handle fragments were noted in Tramite Variety. These varied in length from 5.5 to 9.0 cm (average 7.5 cm; seven measurements); width varied from 2.2 to 4.25 cm (average 3.2 cm; 12 measurements); thickness ranged between 7 and 13 mm (average 10 mm). It was not known whether the handles were from narrow or widemouthed jars, but presumably the former. Besides the strap handles, one small ring handle was noted.

Fifteen jar bases were recovered, but the overall jar form could not be determined. Many of the bases appeared to have slight indentations, or at least thinning of the exterior. One had a pronounced concavity. Diameters of the bases vary from 8 to 10.5 cm.

NECKLESS JAR: Ten sherds, representing seven vessels, are from neckless jars (tecomates). Two vessels have mouth diameters of 18 and 22 cm. Most slips are pink in color, and only one sherd is slipped on the interior.

HEAVY BOLSTERED RIM: Five sherds are from the necks or rims of very large jars or basins. Two sherds are from the rim of such a vessel; the lip has a heavy bolster with a shallow indentation or groove on its upper surface. The mouth diameter is 50 cm, and average wall thickness is 1.1 cm. The sherds have holes drilled on each edge, suggesting that the original vessel may have been mended, but it is not known whether the vessel in question was a basin or a very large jar (similarities with a vessel in Paxcamán Red suggest the latter; see above). Three other sherds are from the lower neck of a large wide-mouthed jar or bowl, perhaps the same vessel form. The original height of the neck

of the vessel would have been greater than 11 cm; exterior neck diameter is 26 cm, and average wall thickness is 1.1 cm.

MISCELLANEOUS: Twenty-eight sherds are from unusual or unidentifiable vessel forms.

Miniature vessel—A miniature wide-mouthed jar has a cream slip; mouth diameter is ca. 6.5 cm, and neck height is 1.75 cm.

Pedestal base—Six sherds formed a reconstructible pedestal base with a diameter of ca. 12 cm. Traces of pink-orange slip could be seen on the very eroded vessel interior; the exterior appeared to have a cream-to-orange slip.

Drum—One small sherd with a pinkish slip may be from a drum; the basis for this suggestion is an abrupt "shoulder angle" just below the join of the neck with the body, a characteristic not found in ordinary jar necks.

Rims—Twenty small rim sherds, one of which had a small lip bolster, were recovered in this type. They are too small for determination of vessel form, but most likely represent wide-mouthed jars and tripods.

Illustrations: figures 47–49.

Intrasite references: Ten sherds of Tramite Variety of Trapeche Pink (including a partially reconstructible vessel) were recovered from Terminal Classic lots in Bullard's excavations, and are probably intrusive. Thirty-four sherds were from Early Postclassic lots, and the remainder (324 sherds, or 88.0 percent) were from the Late Postclassic Dos Lagos complex. Of the latter, only one sherd came from on top of the mound; virtually all the Late Postclassic sherds, in other words, were from the mixed midden material on the mound slopes. Three partially reconstructible vessels came from these deposits: a hemispherical bowl from Operation IH, a tripod dish of ash paste from Operation IA, and a tripod dish of snail-inclusion paste from Operation IB. The Trapeche group in general declined in frequency in late or Protohistoric deposits on the island (see table 8).

The forms of the Trapeche cream-to-pink-slipped ceramic group parallel those of the red-slipped Paxcamán group, but it is inter-

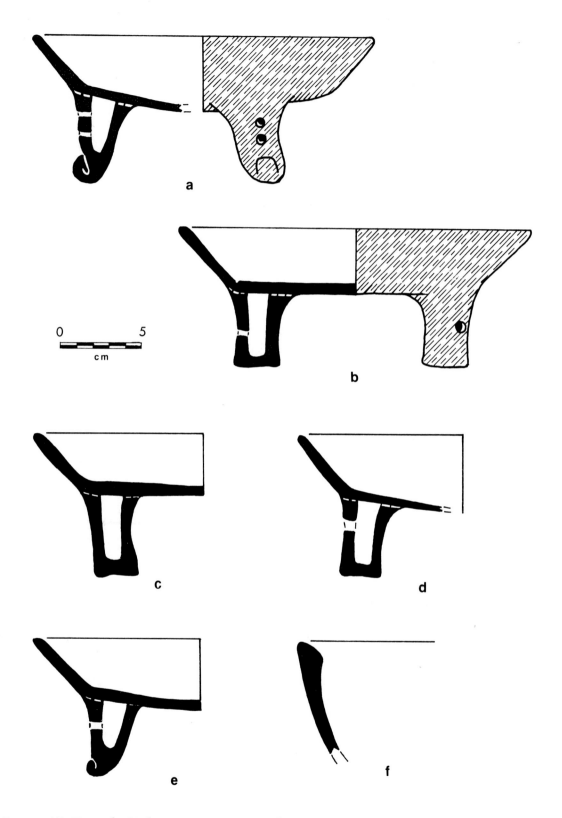

FIGURE 47. Trapeche Pink: Tramite Variety, and Type/Variety Unspecified. **b**, coarse red paste; **e**, volcanic-ash paste.

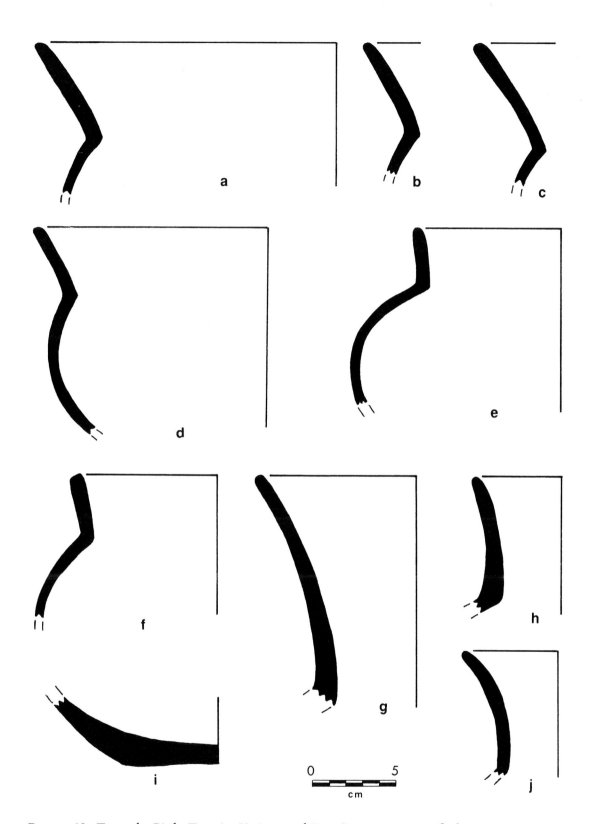

FIGURE 48. Trapeche Pink: Tramite Variety, and Type/Variety Unspecified.

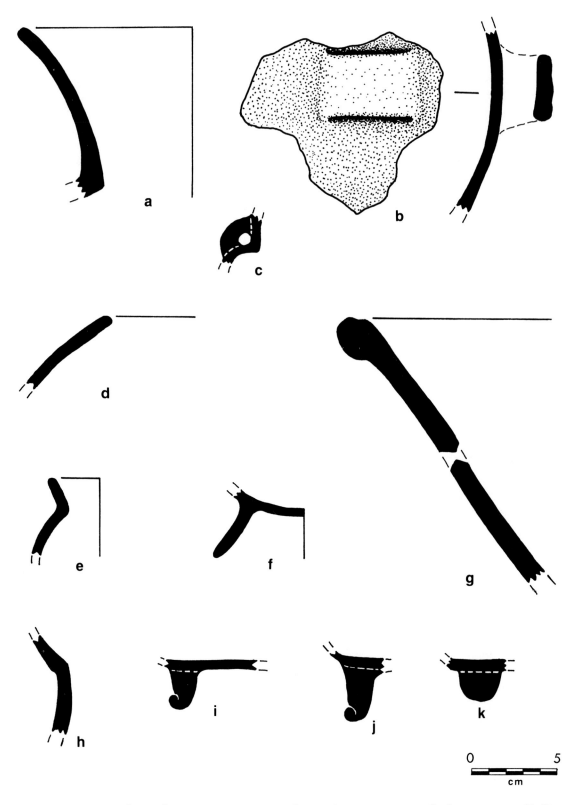

FIGURE 49. Trapeche Pink: Tramite Variety, and Type/Variety Unspecified. Note: overall slip on **b** not indicated by hachure.

esting that there seems to be a dichotomous distribution of the two with respect to contexts at the top and at the bottom of the mound (table 9): Trapeche is virtually absent in lots from the upper surface of the mound, whereas Paxcamán is more abundant there.

Intersite references: Tramite Variety of Trapeche Pink type has a relatively restricted distribution in the lakes area of Petén, having been found in large quantities only at Macanché, although it also occurred at Salpetén and Quexil. No Trapeche group sherds were recovered from Bullard's excavations in the mainland "center," at Ixlú, or in his Punta Nimá collection. The Trapeche ceramic group was absent to the east at Topoxté, and was not found at Barton Ramie (although a jar rim of Yaha Creek Cream [Gifford 1976: fig. 177a] is very similar to Postclassic jar rims of the Trapeche group). At Negroman-Tipú, in western Belize, golden tan slips occur on red-orange pastes in the Early Postclassic Zaczuuz (tan) ceramic group (P. Rice 1985c).

Cream- or pink-slipped sherds were not identified in G. Cowgill's analysis of the Lake Petén materials, although the Trapeche ceramic group received its initial definition as an exclusively Early Postclassic ceramic group from the Tayasal collections. No plate forms or cylinder feet were identified there, however (A. Chase 1979:110–111). Differences in forms and slip colors, together with a longer temporal range of the material at Macanché as compared with Tayasal, led to separation of a distinct variety, the Tramite Variety, at Macanché.

Two intriguing possibilities can be raised as the stimulus for the development and elaboration of this ceramic group (see chapter 6). One is that Trapeche may be a development out of the Terminal Classic cream-slipped Harina ceramic group. The other is that the Trapeche group—especially the Tramite Variety—bears some relationship to the creamy-gray-to-tan waxy slips of slatewares in the Cehpech Terminal Classic complex of the Puuc area of Yucatán, especially Puuc Slate and Thin Slate (R. E. Smith 1971:

164–165). In later periods, in the Hocabá and Tases complexes (A.D. 1200–1450), a monochrome-slipped type, Kukula Cream, occurs within Peto Cream ware in northern Yucatán. Ties can also be seen with San Joaquin Buff ware in this area. The variations in slip color in the Late Postclassic Tramite Variety sherds at Macanché (see chapter 6) are paralleled in the late San Joaquin Buff ware, in which the slip varies from cream through gray, beige, buff, and "pinkish cinnamon" (R. E. Smith 1971:229). The vessel forms of this "buff" ware match those of Mayapán Red ware in much the same way that Trapeche parallels Paxcamán.

Name: **Trapeche General: Type and Variety Unspecified.**

Frequency: 1162 sherds from Bullard's excavations on Macanché Island. The type and variety unspecified sherds of the Trapeche ceramic group represent 60.5 percent of that group in Bullard's collections.

Ware: Volador Dull-Slipped ware.

Complex: Aura and Dos Lagos ceramic complexes.

Established: The Trapeche ceramic group and its constituent types was established by A. Chase (1979:110–112) on the basis of the ceramics of Tayasal.

Principal identifying modes: The sherds grouped into the "Trapeche General" category are those classified on the basis of slip (cream-pink-tan) and paste characteristics as belonging to the Trapeche ceramic group, but lacking sufficient data on other attributes to permit determination of type or variety membership.

Paste and firing: See chapter 6. Thirteen sherds are of "odd" (i.e., non-snail-inclusion) pastes.

Surface treatment and decoration: Sherds are covered with a slip varying in color from cream to pinkish to tan (chapter 6).

Forms and dimensions: Sherds grouped in the Trapeche General category are either vessel supports or body sherds.

SUPPORTS: Eighty-eight vessel supports were recovered, and it is assumed that they all originally were part of tripod dishes. In snail-inclusion paste, five supports were of the scroll form; eight were bulbous; 48 were cylindrical, and one was an unusual solid conical foot with a vertical slash. Of the cylindrical supports, 11 were open at the bottom, 14 had a single circular vent hole in the side, and 23 were not vented. Twelve supports, representing all forms, were of "odd" pastes, including coarse gray, yellow ash, and red-brown pastes. Four miniature feet were recovered: two scroll and two bulbous. The remaining supports were broken fragments of indeterminate form. On the basis of analysis of the vessel forms and pastes in the various types of the Trapeche ceramic group, it is probable that all the scroll feet and most of the odd paste supports belonged to the monochrome Trapeche Pink type; the cylindrical supports lacking vent holes were likely from Mul Polychrome vessels.

BODY SHERDS: A total of 1074 miscellaneous body sherds occurred with the characteristic slips and pastes of the Trapeche ceramic group, but could not be further classified as to type or form. One of these was reddish brown paste. Twenty-one sherds (2 percent) had double slips; 19 were thick-walled, while 30 were thin-walled.

Illustrations: figures 47–49.

Intrasite references: Twenty-seven sherds were recovered from Terminal Classic deposits on Macanché Island, and 108 sherds came from Early Postclassic lots. The largest quantity of Trapeche General sherds, 1027 sherds (or 88.4 percent of the total), were Late Postclassic in date. Of these Late Postclassic sherds, only 21 (or 2 percent) came from the mound summit; the remainder came from the excavations around the slopes of the mound. (See also the various types within the Trapeche ceramic group.)

Intersite references: See the various types within the Trapeche ceramic group.

Name: **Mul Polychrome: Manax Variety.**

Frequency: 155 sherds from Bullard's excavations on Macanché Island. Mul Polychrome constitutes 8.1 percent of the sherds of the Trapeche ceramic group in Bullard's collections.

Ware: Volador Dull-Slipped ware.

Complex: Aura (late facet) and Dos Lagos ceramic complexes.

Established: The Manax Variety of Mul Polychrome is established in the present work. The Trapeche group and its constituent types, including Mul Polychrome, were given definition by A. Chase (1979: 110–112) on the basis of material from Tayasal.

Principal identifying modes: Manax Variety of Mul Polychrome features the same slip and paste, and many of the same forms as Tramite Variety of Trapeche Pink monochrome type, but it is distinguished by the presence of a design band of reddish brown to black paint on an unslipped or cream-slipped surface.

Paste and firing: See Trapeche Pink: Tramite Variety, and chapter 6.

Surface treatment and decoration: Sherds of Manax Variety of Mul Polychrome have the same range of slip colors that are found in Tramite Variety of Trapeche Pink (see above and chapter 6). Double slipping occurs on 11 sherds.

Decoration consists of reddish brown (2.5YR 3–4/2) to black paint that is applied in an encircling band around the vessel circumference. Although the sherds from Tayasal were described as having only reddish brown paint, at Macanché 41 sherds (including one reconstructible tripod dish) had black paint. Unlike the Tayasal examples (A. Chase 1979:110), the paint was clearly applied under (i.e., before) the cream-pink slip. This band appears on the interior wall of tripod dishes and on the exterior of jars, including tecomates. As in Ixpop Polychrome (above), the design band is not covered with the overall slip (cream to pink, in this case) of the vessel, and it may sometimes have an opaque cream or white primary slip or underslip. Similarly, just as the red slip overlapping the black painted lines of Ixpop Polychrome caused the black to appear dark reddish brown, so the cream or orange-tan slips of the Trapeche group cause the black lines

0   1   2
cm

PLATE x. Mul Polychrome: Manax Variety; tripod dish, Lot 25.

of Mul Polychrome to be somewhat reddish in color.

The decoration itself is bounded by two circumferential lines at the top and one at the bottom of the band. On only two of the Mul Polychrome: Manax Variety sherds from Macanché was this design band sufficiently well preserved to provide information on motifs; and these suggested similarities with Ixpop Polychrome. One had a double curved line, while the other had an unknown curvilinear motif. No designs on jars could be determined, save the double line borders.

Forms and dimensions: Three forms are represented: tripod dishes (130 sherds) with cylindrical supports, jars (21 sherds), and neckless jars (four sherds). Tripod dishes (plate x) have mouth diameters varying from 18 to 24 cm (average 19.8 cm; 19 measurements). The base is flat to slightly convex, and the lip form varies from round to slightly flattened. Five partially reconstructible vessels of this form were found. All supports in Manax Variety are cylindrical; only two vessels had supports with vents, the remainder being unvented. Supports are typically somewhat asymmetrical, and their bases do not rest flat on the surfaces on which the vessel stands.

Jars are represented primarily by body sherds with evidence of painting on their ex-

terior surfaces. Because no rims were recovered it is impossible to say whether the jars are wide- or narrow-necked, or neckless. One neckless jar rim sherd has an unslipped interior, and a design band beginning approximately 1.5 cm below the lip on the exterior.

Illustrations: figure 50a–g; plate x.

Intrasite references: One sherd of Manax Variety of Mul Polychrome was recovered from a Terminal Classic lot, and is regarded as intrusive. Five Manax Variety sherds were found in lots phased to the Early Postclassic (these all had black rather than red-brown paint); Manax Variety sherds were also recovered in CPHEP excavations into late facet Early Postclassic fill contexts. Only two sherds came from the summit of the mound: most of the sherds came from the mixed midden deposits excavated on the mound slopes. Three partially reconstructible tripod dishes were recovered from Lot 25, in Operation IH; in addition, one each came from Operations IA and IB.

Intersite references: Brown or black painted decoration on cream-slipped wares is not common in the lakes area of Petén, and no sherds of Mul Polychrome were recovered in any of Bullard's other excavations or collections. Mul Polychrome: Mul Variety is associated only with the Early Postclassic

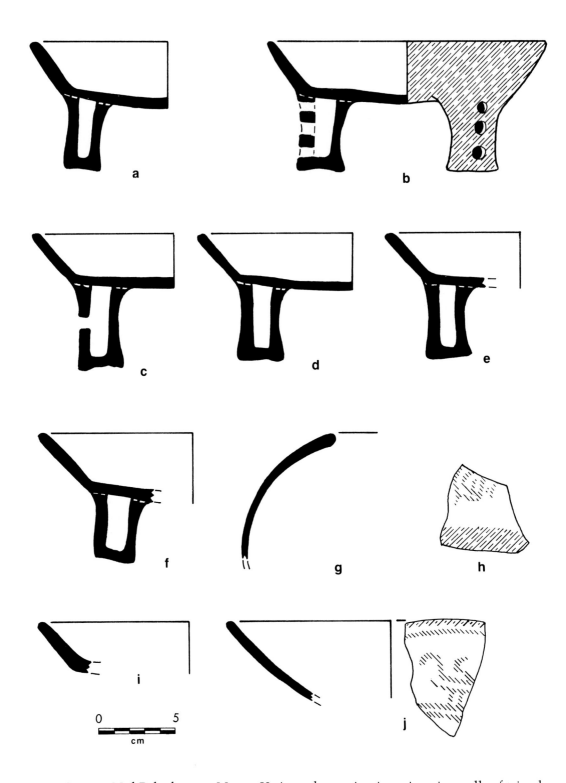

FIGURE 50. **a–g**, Mul Polychrome: Manax Variety; decoration is on interior walls of tripod dishes, and exterior of neckless jar, but is too faint to be discerned. **h–j**, Picté Red-on-paste(cream): Picté Variety; **h**, decoration on exterior; **i, j**, decoration on interior. Painted decoration of **h** and **j** is light red paint, rather than dark red as shown.

Chilcob complex at Tayasal (Chase and Chase 1983), whereas at Macanché the Manax Variety is both Early and Late Postclassic.

The color variations of the paint of the Mul Polychrome type, as it occurred at Tayasal and Macanché, are of some interest. I imagine the pigment was probably a manganese paint which may vary in color between brown and black. Similar brown-to-black color variations occurred in the decoration of Ixpop Polychrome, though it was not as pronounced; the color is especially likely to be reddish brown if the slip overlies it.

Generally comparable painted types can be identified outside of the central Lowlands, both to the north and to the south. Northward, in Yucatán, Xcanchakan Black-on-cream is a common type within Peto Cream ware during the Hocabá and Tases phases at Mayapán. Aside from the black-on-cream colors, the vessels of this type are dissimilar to the Petén examples because the tripod dishes have primarily recurved walls, and the decoration is typically non-banded trickle paint (R. E. Smith 1971: fig. 52). To the south, at Naco, Forastero Bichrome is a black-on-cream painted type, but again there are significant differences: the dishes have recurved walls, and the decoration is a busy combination of straight and curving lines appearing on both the interior and exterior of the vessels (Wonderley 1981: 182–186, fig. 39). Cream slipping has not been noted in the Maya Highlands of Guatemala.

Name: **Picté Red-on-paste(cream): Picté Variety.**

Frequency: 6 sherds from Bullard's excavations on Macanché Island. Picté Red-on-paste(cream) constitutes 0.3 percent of the sherds of the Trapeche ceramic group in Bullard's collections.

Ware: Volador Dull-Slipped ware.

Complex: Aura (late facet) and Dos Lagos ceramic complexes.

Established: Picté Red-on-paste(cream): Picté Variety is described in the present work on the basis of the Macanché ceramic collection.

Principal identifying modes: Picté Red-on-paste(cream) is characterized by a band of red painted decoration on tripod dishes, on bowls, and on jars having a slip color varying from cream to pink to orange-tan.

Paste and firing: See chapter 6.

Surface treatment and decoration: For slip characteristics, see chapter 6. The decoration in this type apparently parallels that of Macanché Red-on-paste(cream) in placement and structure, and in being executed in red paint, which often is light orange-red in color (10R 5/8 to 2.5YR 5/8). A few sherds had a creamy white primary slip applied in the area of the design band. In general, the preservation of the sherds is so poor that little can be distinguished of the design save the encircling bands at the top and bottom, which often remain only as a faint pink color. A jar sherd appeared to have two concentric circles on the exterior. A hemispherical bowl had a faintly painted motif in a broad band on the interior, bounded by two lines on both top and bottom. The uppermost of these lines is either fire-clouded or painted in black paint.

Forms and dimensions: Tripod dishes are represented by three sherds; two sherds are from a hemispherical bowl with a diameter of 21 cm; two sherds are from jars.

Illustrations: figure 50h–j.

Intrasite references: All of the sherds of Picté Red-on-paste(cream) in Bullard's collection were recovered from the Late Postclassic midden on the slopes of the mound. Five Picté Red-on-paste(cream) sherds were recovered in late facet Early Postclassic construction fill in CPHEP pit 6.

Intersite references: Red painted decoration usually occurs on the creamy gray unslipped background color of the snail-inclusion paste; there is little to no evidence of primary slipping in this type. The decoration of Picté type is similar to that of Macanché Red-on-paste(cream) in the Paxcamán ceramic group, especially in the use of the light red paint. Both of these uncommon types seem to derive their inspiration from the dark red painted decoration on the cream paste of Chompoxté Red-on-cream in the To-poxté ceramic group, which was imported into Macanché Island in some quantities, particularly in the Late Postclassic period. At Tayasal, no red-on-cream decorated type was formally separated out, although the illustrated vessel of Dolorido Cream Polychrome (A. Chase 1979: fig. 4e) is red-on-cream.

Elsewhere, red painted decoration combined with cream or buff background colors or slips occurs in small but distinctive quantities. At Mayapán, Tecoh Red-on-buff is a late-occurring type in San Joaquin Buff ware, featuring red paint on "buff" slipped surfaces (R. E. Smith 1971:fig. 53), while red paint on slatewares is an earlier treatment. Red-on-white painting is also found in the Maya Highlands (Wauchope 1970), and at Naco, Honduras, Nolasco Bichrome is a red-on-cream painted type dating to the Late Postclassic (Wonderley 1981).

Name: **Xuluc Incised: Ain Variety.**
Frequency: 33 sherds from Bullard's excavations at Macanché Island. Ain Variety of Xuluc Incised constitutes 1.7 percent of the sherds of the Trapeche ceramic group in Bullard's collections, and 45.2 percent of the sherd of Xuluc Incised type.
Ware: Volador Dull-Slipped ware.
Complex: Aura (?) and Dos Lagos ceramic complexes.
Established: The Ain Variety of Xuluc Incised is established in the present work on the basis of the Macanché material. Xuluc Incised type was originally established by A. Chase (1979:106–110) in the Tayasal collection. One vessel of what is now Ain Variety was illustrated by Bullard (1973:235) as "Picú Plano-Relief."
Principal identifying modes: Ain Variety of Xuluc Incised is characterized by post-slip incising on vessels covered with a cream, pink, or orange-tan slip.
Paste and firing: See chapter 6.
Surface treatment and decoration: For characteristics of the slip, see chapter 6. The incised decoration of Ain Variety is applied through the slip and consists of post-slip,

post-polish, post-fire fine incised or excised bands or both. Reptilian creatures are a common motif of the design, as are mat-like woven segments or braids (P. Rice 1983a).

On a collared bowl with a pink-tan slip, the design appears on the interior collar, and nearly the entire design can be reconstructed (fig. 51; see Bullard 1973:235). The design is set off by two encircling lines, spaced 3 to 5 mm apart. The band itself has been divided into panels featuring reptilian creatures (the "profile representation," P. Rice 1983a), separated by narrow vertical panels of braids and "bow-knots." The design is executed very neatly and clearly, with fine detailing, and emphasized by excising (Bullard's "plano-relief carving"). On another collared bowl sherd, fire-clouded to black at the lip, the decoration is a mat motif.

A different kind of design, and more careless execution, appears on two neckless jars. The designs are incomplete, owing to breakage, but on one vessel the incising is in a band on the upper exterior, beginning 1.5 cm below the lip. A narrow band with an angular braid or guilloche motif, set off by two horizontal lines, surmounts an incomplete area of geometric rectilinear designs. The second vessel has the band beginning 6 mm below the lip, and the decorated area consists of probable reptilian motifs.

CPHEP excavations at Macanché recovered additional examples of Ain Variety of Xuluc Incised that broadened the range of forms and motifs of this variety. On a carelessly incised "collared bowl," panels of reptiles alternated with panels featuring nested rectangles; the two motifs were separated by three pairs of vertical lines. On a shallow bowl with outflaring sides, a design on the exterior wall features a paneled band in which elaborate reptilian creatures alternate with a braided "mat" segment. A jar with a high outcurving neck had an incised panel on the upper exterior neck. The design is apparently paneled as on other vessels, but only a portion of the design was visible on the sherd. An elaborate reptile (the "quasi-split representational" version) appeared in a

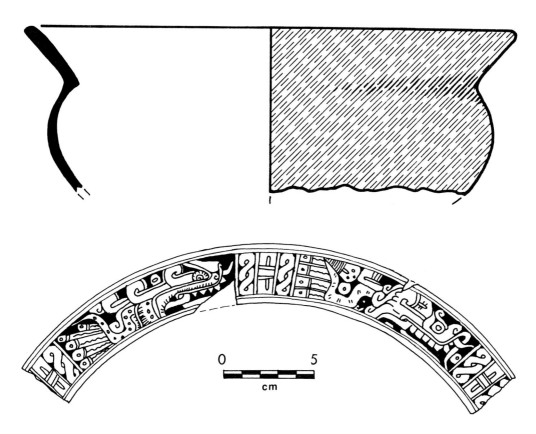

FIGURE 51. Xuluc Incised: Ain Variety. Collared bowl with incised and excised band on collar interior, which features profiled reptilian heads and twists. Slip on interior not indicated by hachure.

panel bounded by three incised lines above and below. Under the panel, three narrow black painted lines encircle the neck.

Forms and dimensions: Ain Variety of Xuluc Incised occurs in bowls, collared bowls, neckless jars, and a high-neck jar. One bowl with outflaring sides and a rounded lip had a mouth diameter of 21.5 cm. Two collared bowls had mouth diameters of 22 and 28 cm. The mouth diameter of the neckless jar was 21 cm, while the diameter of the high-neck jar was 22 cm. No tripod dishes were noted in Xuluc Incised: Ain Variety.

Illustrations: figure 51, 52a–d.

Intrasite references: Only one sherd was recovered from Early Postclassic lots, the bulk of the material being from the Late Postclassic. No sherds came from Bullard's excavations at the top of the mound. A partially

reconstructible collared bowl with a reptile motif was recovered from Operation IH.

Intersite references: Incised cream-to-pink-slipped vessels are not common in the Petén area as a whole. Although the Xuluc type and variety received definition as members of the Early Postclassic Chilcob complex at Tayasal, cream-slipped incised sherds were not characteristic of the Middle or Late Postclassic there: incising was said to be rare by Late Cocahmut (Middle Postclassic) times, and was not characteristic of the Kauil complex (A. Chase 1979:108, 112). In addition, incised cream slips were not noted by G. Cowgill at Lake Petén-Itzá. Banded and paneled postslip incised decoration in the red-slipped Picú Incised type from Lake Petén-Itzá did include motifs similar to those of Xuluc Incised: Ain Variety, however, particu-

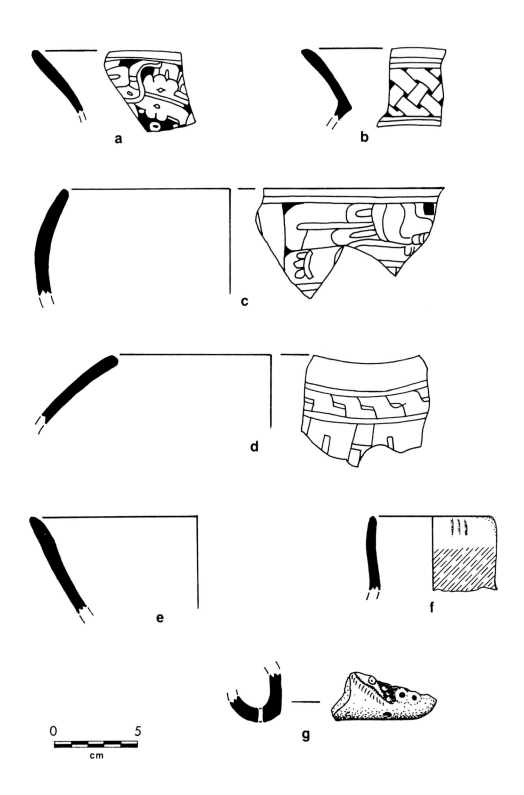

FIGURE 52. **a–d**, Xuluc Incised: Ain Variety; **a**, **b**, decoration on interior of collar; **c**, **d**, decoration on exterior. **e**, **f**, Xuluc Incised: Tzalam Variety; **e**, grater bowl; **f**, "drum" (?). **g**, Chuntuci Composite: Variety Unspecified; censer handle. Slip on **a–d**, **g**, not indicated by hachure.

larly the combination of reptiles with mats (G. Cowgill 1963:fig. 4b, d, e, h, i, m). A small but distinctive presence of Ain Variety of Xuluc Incised was noted at Lakes Salpetén and Quexil, but none was recovered at Topoxté. The absence of tripod dishes in Xuluc Incised: Ain Variety is also paralleled in Dulces Incised in the Topoxté ceramic group (P. Rice 1979:46) and, apparently, also in Picú Incised in the Paxcamán group.

In Yucatán, incising, while very common in red-slipped wares, is rare in cream-buff-slipped wares, which more typically have painted decoration. Incising does occur occasionally in San Joaquin Buff ware (see Tzalam Variety of Xuluc Incised, below), but not in Peto Cream ware.

Name: **Xuluc Incised: Tzalam Variety.**

Frequency: 40 sherds from Bullard's excavations at Macanché Island. Tzalam Variety of Xuluc Incised comprises 2.1 percent of the sherds of the Trapeche ceramic group in Bullard's collections, and 54.8 percent of the sherds of Xuluc Incised type.

Ware: Volador Dull-Slipped ware.

Complex: Aura and Dos Lagos ceramic complexes.

Established: The Tzalam Variety of Xuluc Incised is established in the present work on the basis of material from Macanché. The Xuluc Incised type was established by A. Chase (1979:106–110) using Tayasal materials.

Principal identifying modes: The Tzalam Variety of Xuluc Incised may be identified by deep prefire incising on unslipped areas of sherds of the Trapeche ceramic group.

Paste and firing: See chapter 6. One sherd was of a relatively coarse red-brown paste lacking snail inclusions. Two sherds have a darkened interior, as though from burning in use.

Surface treatment and decoration: Sherds in the Tzalam Variety of Xuluc Incised are characterized by patterns of fairly deep, often groove-incised lines on unslipped areas of vessels that are otherwise covered with the typical cream-to-pink slips of the Trapeche group (see chapter 6). Two vessel forms are

known in this variety of Xuluc Incised, and each has its own kind of incising.

Grater bowls are slipped on the exterior and on the interior down to (or just below) the beginning of the incised pattern. The pattern is generally executed by fine incising (three sherds had groove incising), and begins approximately 5 cm below the rounded lip of the bowl. One or two lines bound the circumference of the design, which usually consists of crosshatching or perpendicularly incised quadrants of the bowl's interior base. The lines appear to have been done with a finely pointed instrument, and vary in separation from 0.8 to 1.2 cm.

Narrow-mouthed, straight-neck rim sherds may belong to jars or to drums. Deep vertical groove-incised lines, occurring in groups of threes, extend downward approximately 1 cm from the lip. The sherds are eroded, but it appears that the slip was applied irregularly beginning about 5 to 10 mm below these lines. On one vessel having an outflaring neck with lip bolster, the very deeply incised lines are approximately 3 cm long; they appear on the neck below the bolster, and may occur in groups.

Forms and dimensions: Thirty-two sherds are from grater bowls, relatively deep round-sided bowls with (usually) tripod supports and an incised pattern on the interior base. Two of the vessel supports are scroll form, and one is more or less conical. The sherds are small, and no measurements of diameters were possible.

Eight sherds were from drums/jars: six of these were from vessels with short straight necks, and one was a vessel with an outflaring neck and lip bolster. Five of the short neck rims are from a single vessel having a mouth diameter of 7 cm and a neck height of 4 cm. One sherd is from a slightly larger vessel with a neck height of 5.25 cm and a mouth diameter of 10 cm.

Illustrations: figure 52e–f.

Intrasite references: Two grater sherds of Tzalam Variety of Xuluc Incised were recovered from Bullard's excavations into Terminal Classic contexts on the island, eight were from Early Postclassic lots, and the remainder were from the Late Postclassic, primarily from midden on the mound slopes. One was from the top of the mound. The "drums" were from Late Postclassic lots only, all but one being Operation IH.

Intersite references: The Tzalam Variety of Xuluc Incised is similar to the Tan Variety identified at Tayasal, but has been distinguished on the basis of slip, form, and temporal duration of the Trapeche group at Macanché. Grater bowls occur in Zanahoria Scored type in the cream-slipped Dolorido ceramic group in the early facet Terminal Classic Xcocom complex at Becan (Ball 1977: 90, fig. 32f). In Yucatán, graters in cream- or buff-slipped wares occur in both San Joaquin Buff ware (Pencuyut Incised; R. E. Smith 1971:fig. 51r) and Peto Cream ware (Xcanchakan Black-on-cream; R. E. Smith 1971: fig. 52s), as well as in Chichén Slate ware (R. E. Smith 1971: fig. 13m, n). The "drum" form is common in the red-slipped Mayapán Red ware, but also occurs in Slatewares: Ball illustrates a Sacalum Black-on-slateware drum (1979: fig. 9). One vessel of Tekit Incised, in Puuc Slate, has a lip bolster and may be a jar rather than a drum (R. E. Smith 1971: fig 54p).

Name: **Chuntuci Composite: Variety Unspecified.**

Frequency: 2 sherds from Bullard's excavations on Macanché Island. Chuntuci Composite constitutes 0.1 percent of the sherds of the Trapeche ceramic group in Bullard's collections.

Ware: Volador Dull-Slipped ware.

Complex: Aura ceramic complex.

Established: Chuntuci Composite type has been identified on the basis of the Tayasal materials (A. Chase 1983).

Principal identifying modes: The sherds from Macanché that are tentatively identified as Chuntuci Composite are thought to be ladle censer handles with modeled elements and the characteristic cream-tan-pink slip of the Trapeche group.

Paste and firing: See chapter 6.

Surface treatment and decoration: See chapter 6 for a discussion of slip characteristics. One sherd is a fragment of what was apparently a hollow tube with incised, punctated, and modeled elements on it, which was then covered with a largely eroded cream slip. The other is a small curving fragment with an appliqué pellet. These both probably represent the ends of ladle censer handles.

Forms and dimensions: Judging from the curvature, the two sherds appear to represent ladle censer handles, but this is not certain. The larger tube-like fragment had a circular perforation that appeared to be a vent hole in its side.

Illustration: figure 52g.

Intrasite references: Both sherds of Chuntuci Composite were recovered from Early Postclassic construction fill on the island. No sherds of Chuntuci Composite were identified in CPHEP excavations.

Intersite references: Chuntuci Composite was identified at Tayasal (Chase and Chase 1983). This type was not noted in any of the other lake basins surveyed by CPHEP.

Name: **Trapeche Group Polychromes: Type and Variety Unspecified.**

Frequency: 155 sherds from Bullard's excavations on Macanché Island. Unidentified polychromes represent 8.1 percent of the sherds of the Trapeche ceramic group in Bullard's collection.

Ware: Volador Dull-Slipped ware.

Complex: Aura and Dos Lagos ceramic complexes.

Principal identifying attributes: Sherds of this residual category are classified as members of the Trapeche ceramic group on the basis of their cream-to-pink slips. They are classed as polychromes because of the break in slip application on the interior walls (of tripod dishes) or exteriors (of jars). They could not, however, be given specific type identifications because of erosion of the paint colors.

Paste and firing: See chapter 6.

Surface treatment and decoration: See chapter 6 for discussion of slip characteristics. On these sherds, the slip was applied on tripod dishes over the exterior surface, but only on the upper and lower portions of the interior wall, and the interior floor. Between the clearly bounded lines of slip application, either the original paste surface or sometimes a white underslip appears. Neither brown-black nor red painted decoration could be clearly identified in the unslipped portion of the tripod dishes, or in similar areas of jar body sherds. Twenty-nine sherds have double slips.

Forms and dimensions: Most sherds (147) were from tripod dishes. Diameters range from 18 to 22 cm, with an average of 19.6 cm (14 measurements). Seven of the sherds have attached cylindrical vessel supports: six are unvented (two of these are solid) while one has a line of three holes. Wall form varies from straight to slightly convex. In addition to the tripod dishes, seven sherds are from jars, to judge from their curvature and location of exterior decoration; one sherd is from a hemispherical bowl.

Illustrations: None.

Intrasite references: Two sherds were from Early Postclassic lots, and the remainder were from Late Postclassic midden material; only one sherd was from the top of the mound. Three reconstructible tripod dishes were from Operation IH.

Intersite references: See "Intersite references" for the polychrome types, Mul and Picté, within the Trapeche ceramic group.

Gray Group Unspecified

Name: **Unnamed Gray Slipped.**

Frequency: 61 sherds from Bullard's excavations on Macanché Island.

Ware: Volador Dull-Slipped ware.

Complex: Dos Lagos ceramic complex.

Established: Neither a group nor a type is established here; rather, the sherds are separated as an indeterminate ceramic group related to Paxcamán, Trapeche, or both.

Principal identifying modes: Sherds of this unspecified provisional grouping are distinguished by having the pastes and forms of the Paxcamán and Trapeche ceramic groups, but the slips are gray in color.

Paste and firing: See chapter 6. The sherds are virtually all of snail-inclusion paste. The gray slip colors show some fire-clouding, but are generally fairly even in coloration.

Surface treatment and decoration: Sherds are covered with a gray slip that varies from dark gray (2.5YR 4/0) to light grayish brown (10YR 5/1–2). Fire-clouds appear as either cream or pink blotches, as do rootlet blemishes. The coloring is generally fairly even, making it difficult to determine if the gray results from accidental firing of Paxcamán and Trapeche vessels, or if an overall gray slip was the intended result.

On only one vessel (four sherds) can decoration be determined: this is a restricted orifice bowl which has a 5-cm-wide band of incised decoration, bounded by two lines above and two below. Within the band is a large, relatively undetailed and carelessly executed reptilian creature. Two other sherds have indeterminate incised motifs; these both represent collared bowls. Twenty-one sherds probably had banded polychrome painted decoration on them, but are now eroded. Vessel supports, not always clearly slipped, were fire-clouded gray.

Forms and dimensions: Eighteen sherds represent tripod dishes, including one miniature with a diameter of 12 cm and wall height of 2.1 cm. The dimensions of the others could not be determined owing to their small size. Four sherds represent collared bowls; four sherds represent a single restricted orifice bowl with a diameter of 22 cm and wall thickness of 8 mm. A polychrome restricted orifice vessel (barrel-shaped jar?) likewise had a mouth diameter of 22 cm, but was somewhat thinner walled at 6 mm. Seven other jar rims were noted. Vessel supports include one cylindrical foot, one miniature solid cylinder, one scroll foot, one bulbous, and three supports of indeterminate form.

Illustration: figure 53.

Intrasite references: Nine of these sherds were recovered from Terminal Classic Lot 38 on the island; none was from an Early Postclassic lot. Fifty-two sherds were Late Postclassic, and of these, 13 were from around the structures on the summit of the mound.

Intersite references: Gray-slipped Postclassic sherds were not encountered at the

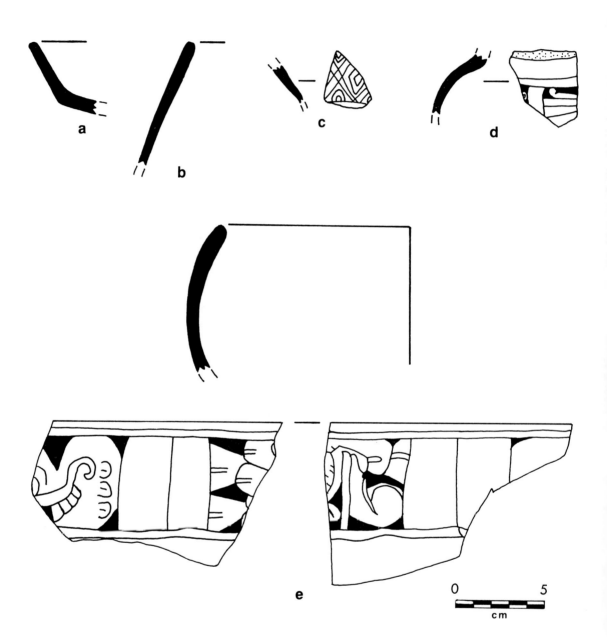

FIGURE 53. Group Unspecified Gray. **c**, decoration on interior of collar of bowl; **d**, **e**, decoration on exterior. Note: gray slip not indicated by hachure.

mainland "center," at Ixlú, or in Bullard's collections from Punta Nimá. A formal gray-slipped group has not been identified at other areas in Petén, but it is not known if this is because the sherds did not occur in abundance or because they were clearly examples of fire-clouding. Given the latter possibility, I refrained from naming these as a separate group, preferring simply to isolate them informally for descriptive and comparative purposes. Elsewhere, gray seems to have been a significant slip color variant in Yucatecan slatewares, as well as in the Late Postclassic San Joaquin Buff ware (R. E. Smith 1971).

Topoxté Ceramic Group

Name: **Topoxté Red: Topoxté Variety.**

Frequency: 126 sherds from Bullard's excavations on Macanché Island. Topoxté Variety represents 24.4 percent of the sherds of the Topoxté ceramic group in Bullard's collections, and 33.6 percent of the sherds of the Topoxté Red type.

Ware: Clemencia Cream Paste ware.

Complex: Aura, Dos Lagos, and Ayer ceramic complexes.

Established: Topoxté Red: Topoxté Variety, as the principal member of the red-slipped group in Clemencia Cream Paste ware, was identified and described on the basis of the pottery from the Topoxté islands in Lake Yaxhá (P. Rice 1979:15–21; see also Bullard 1970).

Principal identifying modes: Topoxté Red is a monochrome-slipped type featuring a red slip on a distinctive cream-colored marly paste, and occurs in a variety of dish, bowl, and jar forms.

Paste and firing: The paste of Topoxté Red is Clemencia Cream Paste ware (P. Rice 1979: 13–15), a fine textured marly paste that is cream or very pale brown (10YR 7/3) in color, rarely slightly more orange (7.5YR 6–7/4) (color plates 1d, 1e5, 1e6). Inclusions are generally fine in size and not readily apparent to the naked eye except as light gray particles (dirty calcite). Pastes are usually well oxidized, and fire-clouding appears on about 10 percent of the sherds. At Macanché, 50

sherds have an unusual light gray paste (10YR 6/1; rarely 7.5YR 5/0).

Surface treatment and decoration: Surfaces are covered with a red or red-orange (10YR 4–5/8) slip that typically has a matte or low luster finish (see P. Rice 1979:16). Because of the cream paste background, slips are a clearer red (color plate 2c) than is characteristically found on Paxcamán sherds, and fire-clouds are not common. Slips are thinly applied, and faint fine striations from finger-wiping (?) the vessel surfaces are often still visible through the slip. Pink or very pale red slips (10R 6/3) occasionally occur, perhaps as a result of use or post-depositional alteration; these show some association with grayish pastes.

Forms and dimensions: The sherds of Topoxté Red recovered from Macanché Island are generally very small, and it is difficult to determine vessel forms and dimensions from them. The vessels appear to be primarily jars of one sort or another. It is possible that some of the jar rims should have been placed in the "Topoxté General: Type Unspecified" category below, because the vessels may have had decoration on the vessel body below the join with the rim.

Jars of the Topoxté ceramic group differ from jars in other Postclassic slipped ceramic groups in frequently having a round lip bolster. Forty sherds (including 14 of gray paste) were necks with lip bolsters; the bolster varied from 1 to 1.2 cm in height. One widemouth jar had a vertical neck 4.5 cm high with a 1.0-cm lip bolster, and a mouth diameter of 30 cm; the wall thickness was 6.5 mm, and the slip appearing on interior and exterior surfaces was a faded pinkish red (10R 6/4). A neckless jar with a wide (1.6 cm) bolster, mouth diameter of 40 cm, and wall thickness of 5.2 mm had a well-preserved orange-red (2.5YR 5/8) slip over the interior and exterior. Twenty-nine rims suggested narrow-neck jars with mouth diameters of 20–30 cm (mean 24.2 cm; five measurements), and wall thickness of 4 to 8.5 mm.

Five strap handles (width 2.7 to 2.9 cm) and two base sherds were also found.

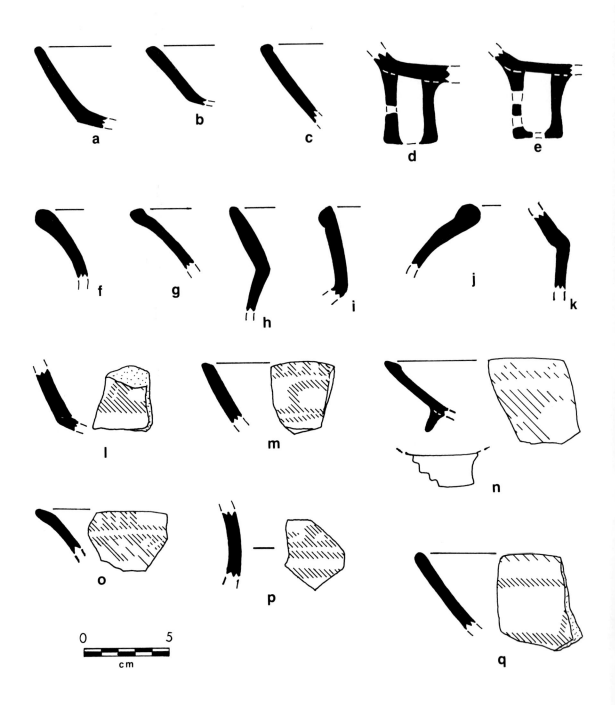

FIGURE 54. **a–k**, Topoxté Red: Topoxté Variety, and Type/Variety Unspecified. **l–p**, Chompoxté Red-on-cream: Chompoxté Variety. **q**, Chompoxté Red-on-cream: Akalché Variety. **l–o**, **q**, decoration on interior; **p**, decoration on exterior. **n**, decoration is painted in light red paint.

Only 12 sherds of tripod dishes were identified, and no diameters are available. Tripod dishes of the Topoxté ceramic group are distinctive in that the interior has no break or angle between the wall and floor: it is typically a smooth curve, and the angle appears only on the exterior.

Twenty-four bowl sherds, all of light gray paste, were recovered; one of these has a diameter of 19 cm. Two collared bowl sherds were identified as Topoxté Red.

Illustrations: figure 54a–k.

Intrasite references: One intrusive sherd of Topoxté Red was recovered in Bullard's Terminal Classic lot 38. Although no Topoxté sherds were present in Early Postclassic construction fill lots, four sherds were recovered from CPHEP excavations into early facet Early Postclassic contexts in pit 5B, and a dozen came from late facet Early Postclassic platform construction in pits 3 and 6. In Bullard's lots, most of the Topoxté Red sherds are from the heavy Late Postclassic midden that covers the mound.

The Topoxté ceramic group is unusual as compared to some of the other slipped Postclassic materials (particularly the Trapeche group) at Macanché Island in that the sherds occur in significant quantities on the top of the mound rather than simply along the slopes. In connection with problems of functional and post-depositional effects on paste and slip variability of Postclassic sherds (see chapter 6), the gray paste sherds of Topoxté Red were recovered almost exclusively from the slope lots rather than from the summit lots. Pink slip colors were noted particularly in Lot 10, from Operation IA.

Intersite references: No sherds of Topoxté Red were recovered from Bullard's excavations at the mainland "center," at Ixlú, or in his Punta Nimá collections. Topoxté Red has been found to occur only rarely in the Lake Petén-Itzá area (it is present at Tayasal [Chase and Chase 1983: fig. 30a]), and was not common in the excavations by CPHEP at the other central Petén lakes. Macanché Island seems to have the largest quantities of Topoxté pottery apart from the Topoxté Is-

land site itself. Topoxté group pottery is present in amounts approximately equal to Paxcamán group sherds in the Postclassic ceramics collection from Negroman-Tipú, in western Belize (P. Rice 1984a, 1985a), and one sherd was noted in the Barton Ramie collection (personal observation). It is of interest that although variable (but generally small) quantities of Topoxté group pottery were traded out of the Topoxté islands to neighboring areas, there was evidently no ceramic trade balance through importation of Paxcamán or Trapeche types into Topoxté, because only approximately 30 sherds of the Paxcamán group were recovered at Canté Island (P. Rice 1979:64)

Name: **Topoxté General: Type and Variety Unspecified.**

Frequency: 249 sherds were recovered from Bullard's excavations on Macanché Island. "Topoxté General" sherds comprise 48.2 percent of sherds of the Topoxté ceramic group in Bullard's collection.

Ware: Clemencia Cream Paste ware.

Complex: Dos Lagos ceramic complex.

Established: The Topoxté ceramic group was established on the basis of collections from Topoxté and Canté islands in Lake Yaxhá (see P. Rice 1979; Bullard 1970).

Principal identifying modes: The "Topoxté General" category used here designates pottery with the distinctive cream paste and forms of the Topoxté group, but the absence of slips or decoration precludes specific type identification.

Paste and firing: See Topoxté Red: Topoxté Variety, above. Fifty-five of the "type unspecified" sherds had gray pastes.

Surface treatment and decoration: See Topoxté Red: Topoxté Variety, above. Slips were generally eroded from the surfaces of these sherds, precluding specific type identifications.

Forms and dimensions: Vessel forms identified here are miscellaneous rims, supports, and body sherds. Ten rims could not be clearly identified as of Topoxté Red monochrome type; eight of these were gray paste jar rims, two having a flange-like lip. Thirty-eight sherds (12 of gray paste) were vessel supports: ten were bulbous in form, seven were cylinders, one was a small scroll—the distinctive "turned-up toe" or "Turkish slipper" form of the Topoxté group—and 18 were of indeterminate form. Two of the indeterminate sherds were dish bases with broken supports that may have been modeled into actual human feet, or nonstandard forms.

The remaining 200 sherds were miscellaneous body sherds. Of these, two sherds had a slip on the interior surface only, 17 had the slip on both surfaces, four had the slip only part of the way down the exterior, and the remainder were indeterminate as to slip occurrence. No extremely thick-walled sherds (such as were found in Paxcamán Red and Trapeche Pink types) were noted in Topoxté Red, although very thin-walled sherds did occur.

Illustrations: figure 54a–k.

Intrasite references: See Topoxté Red: Topoxté Variety. It is possible that some of the jar rims that were included as Topoxté Red monochrome should have been included here as "type unspecified," because some of these could have had decoration on the body below the neck join.

Intersite references: See Topoxté Red: Topoxté Variety. In situations where the slips and/or decoration are eroded, sherds of the Topoxté ceramic group can normally be easily recognized by the distinctive cream-colored Clemencia paste. The light gray paste sherds, especially the body sherds, pose problems because they are very similar to light gray Paxcamán pastes (which do not always have conspicuous snail inclusions). Neither the gray paste nor the faded red slips were consistently noticed in the original type identifications at Canté Island, nor were they common in the Topoxté material from other sites.

Name: **Pastel Polychrome: Pastel Variety.**

Frequency: 2 sherds from Bullard's excavations at Macanché Island. Pastel Polychrome constitutes 0.4 percent of the sherds of the Topoxté ceramic group in Bullard's collections.

Ware: Clemencia Cream Paste ware.

Complex: Dos Lagos and Ayer ceramic complexes.

Established: Pastel Polychrome was defined as a member of the Topoxté ceramic group on the basis of materials from Canté Island (P. Rice 1979:21–28).

Principal identifying modes: Pastel Polychrome is identified by the presence of black painted decoration on unslipped areas of red-slipped Topoxté group vessels.

Paste and firing: See Topoxté Red: Topoxté Variety.

Surface treatment and decoration: Vessels of Pastel Polychrome are typically covered in the red to red-orange slip of the Topoxté ceramic group. Decoration occurs in an unslipped banded area on the interior wall of tripod dishes and the exterior of jar bodies. This area is bounded by black painted lines, with a design in black paint executed within it (P. Rice 1979: figs. 5 and 6). In the two sherds from Macanché Island, nothing could be discerned about the decoration save the black paint.

Forms and dimensions: One sherd from Macanché was a tripod dish rim (diameter unknown), while the other was a jar body sherd.

Illustrations: None.

Intrasite references: These sherds were from Late Postclassic deposits, one on top of the mound and one on the slope. Thirty-eight sherds of Pastel Polychrome were recovered in CPHEP excavations into Late Postclassic–Protohistoric contexts on the top of the mound on the island.

Intersite references: Pastel Polychrome is part of the tradition of black painted decoration in Petén that includes Ixpop Polychrome in the Paxcamán ceramic group, Mul Polychrome in the Trapeche group, and Pek Polychrome in the Augustine group. Although the motifs in the two Macanché examples could not be identified specifically, the Pastel type as a whole shares the range of restrained banded decoration noted for the other Petén types. Reptile representations, such as the "RE-glyph variant" noted in Ixpop Polychrome (P. Rice 1983a), have not been observed in Pastel Polychrome, however, but this may simply be a function of the fact that Pastel Polychrome is very much a minority decorated type within the Topoxté ceramic group. As such, Pastel Polychrome is also infrequently identified outside the Topoxté site, although it has been identified at Negroman-Tipú (personal observation). The more commonly occurring decorated type of the Topoxté group is Chompoxté Red-on-cream.

Name: **Chompoxté Red-on-cream: Chompoxté Variety.**

Frequency: 20 sherds from Bullard's excavations on Macanché Island. Chompoxté Variety of Chompoxté Red-on-cream type represents 3.9 percent of the sherds of the Topoxté ceramic group in Bullard's collection, and 66.6 percent of the Chompoxté type.

Ware: Clemencia Cream Paste ware.

Complex: Dos Lagos and Ayer ceramic complexes.

Established: The Chompoxté Variety of Chompoxté Red-on-cream type was established in the ceramic collections from the Topoxté islands (P. Rice 1979:31–42). It was originally the principal component of what Bullard (1970) called "Topoxté Cream Polychrome."

Principal identifying modes: The Chompoxté Variety of Chompoxté Red-on-cream is distinguished by a non-banded complex decoration painted in dark red paint on the interior walls and floors of tripod dishes, and on the exteriors of jars.

Paste and firing: See Topoxté Red: Topoxté Variety.

Surface finish and decoration: Tripod dishes are slipped on the exterior surfaces with the typical red or red-orange slip of the Topoxté ceramic group (see Topoxté Red: Topoxté Variety). Decoration occurs in a dark red (10R 3/6) glossy paint, and includes a variety of dots, circles, plumes, and indefinite

curvilinear motifs (plate XI). These elements appear over the entire interior surface of dishes, not just on a band around the wall, and the rims of dishes and jars are usually also decorated with chevrons, ticks, or dots (see P. Rice 1979: figs. 9 and 10). At Macanché Island, the specific motifs are virtually impossible to discern, and the Chompoxté Variety is identified either by the rim decoration or by the painting on the interior floor of dishes. One collared bowl had a mat motif. Two sherds have paint that is an atypical light red rather than dark red color (see Macanché Red-on-paste(cream) in the Paxcamán ceramic group).

Forms and dimensions: Eight tripod dishes were of Chompoxté Variety; one had a diameter of 24 cm and thin walls 4 mm thick. Tripod dishes in the Topoxté ceramic group typically lack a break or angle between the wall and floor on the interior, and instead the wall curves gently. At Macanché, one dish had a stepped flange applied to the exterior at the basal angle. One sherd was a collared bowl, diameter 26 cm, that was heavily fire-clouded; the exterior slip was nearly black in color, and ticks were painted on the beveled lip. A neckless jar had a mouth diameter of 10 cm. Five other sherds represented jars with exterior decoration in dark red paint. Three had thin walls (4 mm in thickness).

Illustrations: figure 54l–p, plate XI.

Intrasite references: Chompoxté Variety occurred in Late Postclassic midden (in both "early" and "late" Protohistoric lots) on the island. The Chompoxté Red-on-cream type (both varieties) is unusual among the decorated types of Postclassic ceramic groups because it occurs in quantities at the top of the mound rather than solely on the mound slopes: nearly one-third of the decorated sherds in Bullard's collection were recovered from around the structures on top of the mound.

Intersite references: Chompoxté Red-on-cream is an abundantly occurring decorated ware at the Topoxté islands in Lake Yaxhá (see Bullard 1970), and is the principal type

PLATE XI. Chompoxté Red-on-cream: Chompoxté and Akalché Varieties; rim and body sherds.

of the Topoxté ceramic group that is found outside the Topoxté islands (although it is usually difficult to determine the variety of this type because of surface erosion). This type, which was made and used in both the Early and Late Postclassic period at Topoxté (P. Rice 1983), seems to have been the inspiration for the small quantities of red-on-paste(cream) decoration appearing in the Paxcamán ceramic group (Macanché Red-on-paste) and in the Trapeche ceramic group (Picté Red-on-paste). Macanché Red-on-paste seems to be a late facet Early Postclassic decorative innovation in the area, and shows the same distinction between banded and non-banded decorative arrangements that formed the basis for the Chompoxté-Akalché varietal distinctions. The light and dark red paints used in Macanché and Picté types, and the few examples in Chompoxté Variety, do not occur with sufficient frequency to permit generalizations about their significance.

Chompoxté Red-on-cream (either Chompoxté or Akalché Variety) was not found in Bullard's excavations in the mainland "center," at Ixlú, or in the Punta Nimá collection. The Chompoxté Variety is present in the Lake Petén-Itzá region (A. Chase 1983), and at Negroman-Tipú, in western Belize (personal observation).

Red-on-cream or -buff painting is found in small quantities to the north, in the late Postclassic Tecoh Red-on-buff type at Mayapán (R. E. Smith 1971) for example, and the distinctive red-on-cream painting in Nolasco Bichrome at Naco, Honduras, bears a number of close resemblances to the decoration of Chompoxté Red-on-cream (see Wonderley 1981 : 167).

Name: **Chompoxté Red-on-cream: Akalché Variety.**
Frequency: 10 sherds from Bullard's excavations on Macanché Island. Akalché Variety of Chompoxté Red-on-cream represents 1.9 percent of the sherds of the Topoxté ceramic group in Bullard's collections, and 33.3 percent of the Chompoxté type.
Ware: Clemencia Cream Paste ware.

Complex: Dos Lagos ceramic complex.
Established: The Akalché Variety of Chompoxté Red-on-cream type was defined and described on the basis of the ceramic materials from the Topoxté islands (P. Rice 1979 : 28–31; see also Bullard 1970).
Principal identifying modes: Akalché Variety of Chompoxté Red-on-cream type is distinguished by a band of dark red painted decoration on the unslipped cream paste of red-slipped dishes and jars of the Topoxté ceramic group.
Paste and firing: See Topoxté Red: Topoxté Variety.
Surface treatment and decoration: Decoration consists of a band of decoration in dark red (10R 3/6) paint on the inside wall of tripod dishes or bowls, and in a band on the exterior body of jars. The remaining portions of the vessel are slipped in the red to red-orange slip of the Topoxté group (see Topoxté Red: Topoxté Variety, above), tripod dishes on the exterior and interior lip and floor, and jars on the body and neck. The sherds at Macanché Island are small and eroded, and specific decorative motifs cannot be identified (see P. Rice 1979: fig. 7). They were identified as Akalché Variety primarily by recognition of the dark red lines against lighter red slip that form the boundary of the decorative band, because Chompoxté Variety is unbanded. On one sherd, the paint is an eroded light orange-red rather than the typical dark red color, but it joins with another sherd having the design continuation in dark red paint. The light red paint color may be a consequence of post-depositional alteration.
Forms and dimensions: Four sherds, representing two vessels, are from tripod dishes. On one of these, the mouth diameter is 24 cm, the wall height is 4.9 cm, and the wall thickness is 6.8 mm. Six are jar body sherds.
Illustration: figure 54q.
Intrasite references: See Chompoxté Red-on-cream: Chompoxté Variety.
Intersite references: See Chompoxté Red-on-cream: Chompoxté Variety. Akalché Variety is the decorative variant of this type that shows continuities of structure and arrange-

ment with the very common black painted polychrome types Ixpop and Mul. The banded, often paneled arrangements and simple, spare motifs of Akalché Variety are similar to the common Paxcamán and Trapeche group polychromes.

Name: **Topoxté Group Polychromes: Type and Variety Unspecified.**

Frequency: 109 sherds from Bullard's excavations at Macanché Island. Unidentified polychromes represent 21.1 percent of the sherds of the Topoxté ceramic group in Bullard's collections.

Ware: Clemencia Cream Paste ware.

Complex: Dos Lagos and Ayer ceramic complexes.

Principal identifying modes: The "Type and Variety Unspecified" category of the Topoxté ceramic group is used here as a residual category for those sherds having the characteristic forms, pastes, slips, and traces of the paint (usually dark red, as in Chompoxté Red-on-cream type) typically found on Topoxté group polychromes. The sherds lack sufficient evidence of the decorative structure to permit type or varietal assignment.

Paste and firing: See Topoxté Red: Topoxté Variety. Twenty-five sherds are of gray paste.

Surface treatment and decoration: Sherds have indefinite and eroded traces of paint, primarily the vestiges of typical dark red Chompoxté Red-on-cream decoration, and often have some of the characteristic red or red-orange slip remaining (see Topoxté Red: Topoxté Variety). Ten sherds are rims with dots, ticks, and stripes on the lip, but the rest of the forms and decoration cannot be discerned.

Forms and dimensions: Eighty-seven sherds were fragments of dish rims; one had evidence of a foot attachment. Only one diameter measurement could be obtained, and that was a mouth of 25 cm. Wall thickness varied from 5.4 to 7.7 mm; exterior wall height varied from 4.1 to 5.3 cm. One small thin-walled dish appeared to be a miniature vessel. Seven sherds were jar body sherds; 15 sherds represented miscellaneous rims.

Illustrations: None.

Intrasite references: See Pastel Polychrome and Chompoxté Red-on-cream: Chompoxté Variety.

Intersite references: See Pastel Polychrome and Chompoxté Red-on-cream: Chompoxté Variety.

Name: **Dulces Incised: Dulces Variety.**

Frequency: 1 sherd from Bullard's excavations on Macanché Island. Dulces Incised represents 0.2 percent of the sherds of the Topoxté ceramic group from Bullard's collections.

Ware: Clemencia Cream Paste ware.

Complex: Dos Lagos ceramic complex.

Established: The Dulces Incised type was established in the collections from the Topoxté islands (see P. Rice 1979:45–49).

Principal identifying modes: Dulces Incised may be identified by the presence of postslip fine incising in vessels with the red slips and cream pastes of the Topoxté ceramic group.

Paste and firing: See Topoxté Red: Topoxté Variety. The interior of this dish sherd was fire-clouded.

Surface finish and decoration: The single sherd from Macanché Island had the typical red slip of the Topoxté group. The exterior was incised with a crosshatched pattern of fine postslip incised lines; the interior is eroded and fire-clouded, but may have been painted.

Forms and dimensions: The sherd from Macanché Island represents a bowl or dish; dimensions were not recorded.

Illustrations: None.

Intrasite references: The sherd was recovered from Bullard's excavations at the top of the mound on Macanché Island in Late Postclassic midden. One Dulces Incised sherd was also recovered from CPHEP midden excavations in pit 3.

Intersite references: Dulces Incised falls into the Postclassic tradition of incised decoration in slipped wares, which is represented by Picú and Xuluc types in the Paxcamán and Trapeche ceramic groups. Dulces Incised was a very rare type at Canté Island, in Lake

Yaxhá, and it appears that incising was not as significant a decorative mode in the pottery in that area as it was in the central Petén. Dulces Incised was not encountered at the other lake basins, the representatives of the Topoxté ceramic group at these locations being monochrome or polychrome painted types.

In general, there appear to be, both within Petén and in surrounding areas, dichotomous distributions of the relative importance of incised versus painted decoration, and elaboration of "cream"- (or "pink"-) versus red-slipped types. The relative importance of one or another of these decorative alternatives in Petén may be informative as to contacts with other areas that share similar decorative emphases. For example, outside of Petén, incising is a common decorative technique throughout the Postclassic in red-slipped types in Yucatán and northern Belize, and painting is little emphasized except in the Late Postclassic Tases complex (after A.D. 1300). In the Highlands and southeastern peripheries, polychrome painting is far more common, and incising is very rare. The emphasis on red and cream painting in this region seems to be echoed at Topoxté, while the elaborate incised vessels in red- (Picú) and cream-pink-slipped (Ain Variety of Xuluc) wares at the central lakes suggest stronger links in ceramic decorative technology with Yucatán.

Augustine Ceramic Group

Name: **Augustine Red: Variety Unspecified.**

Frequency: 64 sherds, of which 53 sherds were from Bullard's excavations at Macanché Island, 1 from Ixlú, and 10 from Punta Nimá.

Ware: Vitzil Orange-Red ware.

Complex: Aura and Dos Lagos ceramic complexes.

Established: The Augustine Red type was established by R. E. W. Adams and Trik (1961:125–127) on the basis of material from Tikal.

Principal identifying modes: Augustine Red is characterized by a glossy orange-red slip on relatively thick and coarse reddish brown carbonate paste. Forms include jars and dishes with distinctive hollow effigy supports.

Paste and firing: The paste of the Augustine group is reddish brown (2.5YR 5/6–8, varying to 5YR 5/5–6) in color (color plate 1e4), with abundant white and gray crystalline calcite inclusions, as well as occasional hematite lumps and rare shell fragments. Inclusions are generally less than 0.5 mm in size, but may be as large as 1.2 mm. The vessels are generally well fired, the pastes rarely if ever exhibiting dark coring. Paste firing variations associated with fire-clouds usually occur on basal portions of dishes and on supports, where the color varies to light tan or gray (10YR 6/2–3). Fire-clouds are tan rather than black.

Surface treatment and decoration: The vessels were well smoothed prior to application of a low luster to glossy red-orange slip. Where well preserved, the slip is approximately the same color as the paste (10YR 5/6–8), occasionally varying to more orange (2.5YR 4/8) in color, with a distinctly waxy tactual quality. Fire-clouds are evident as tan areas (10YR 6.5/3.5), most typically occurring on the bases of dishes and on the vessel supports. The slips were extremely eroded in the Macanché examples, but were well preserved in the sherds from Punta Nimá.

No decorated (i.e., polychrome or incised) Augustine group sherds were noted in these collections. The only decoration evident consists of the modeling of the hollow effigy supports, which have a pronounced snout-like scroll and two large incised circles for eyes, sometimes with modeled brow ridges. Vents for the supports consist of long diagonal slashes on the rear of the foot.

Forms and dimensions: The sherds at Macanché are primarily small body sherds, and do not permit determination of form. One sherd appears to represent a hemispherical bowl with a flat bolster; the bowl has a diameter of 18 cm, the thickness is 6 mm, and the bolster is 6.4 mm high.

The sherds from Punta Nimá are better preserved as to slips, and also are larger, providing more information on forms. Three

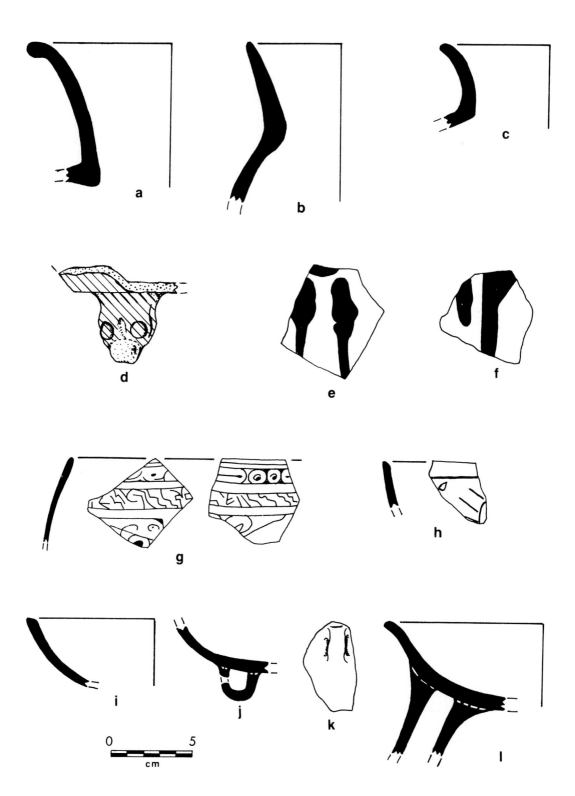

FIGURE 55. Miscellaneous Postclassic types. **a–d**, Augustine Red: Variety Unspecified, from Punta Nimá. **e**, **f**, Trickle Slateware. **g**, **h**, Fine Orange; incised decoration appears on the exteriors. **i–k**, Pulpería Red: Pulpería Variety (slip on **k** not indicated by hachure). **l**, unidentified special.

jars are represented. One has a high, markedly outflaring neck, thinned toward the lip, with a slight lip bolster. The slip extends down 3.7 cm in the neck interior. The mouth diameter is 19 cm, the interior neck diameter is 9 cm, neck height (exterior) is 7.7 cm, and thickness ranges from 7.8 to 9.4 mm. A jar with a low neck and outcurving rim is slipped on the exterior and interior all the way to the neck-body join. The neck height is 4.2 cm, the mouth diameter is 14 cm, and the thickness is 8 mm. A medium-high-necked jar has a gently outflaring neck that joins the body without a sharp angle, and was thinned to a direct lip. The mouth diameter is 19 cm, and the wall thickness ranges from 8 mm in the body to a maximum of 1.1 cm at the neck.

Besides these jars, a fragment of a dish base with an effigy foot was found. This vessel lacks the rim, so that the diameter at the mouth could not be measured; the basal (exterior) diameter is approximately 28 cm, and wall thickness is 7 mm. A groove on the interior accentuates the join of the wall to the base. Another small rim sherd has an outflaring wall and beveled lip; it could not be determined whether it was from a dish or a jar, and it was too small to determine the diameter.

Illustrations: figure 55a–d.

Intrasite references: Three support fragments were recovered from Bullard's lots phased to the Terminal Classic period at Macanché Island, and are regarded as intrusive. One sherd was recovered from Early Postclassic lots, and the remainder were from the Late Postclassic midden, mostly from the top of the mound. In CPHEP excavations on Macanché Island, the Augustine sherds were from the late facet of the Early Postclassic Aura complex or later in date.

Intersite references: The Augustine sherds most informative as to vessel forms and slips were from Punta Nimá, rather than from Macanché, and this points up an interesting phenomenon relative to this ceramic group: its unusual geographical distribution. Augustine group sherds, including decorated types,

are found in abundance at Barton Ramie in the New Town (Early Postclassic) complex (Sharer and Chase 1976:291–294), and also in quantities in the Lake Petén-Itzá region (G. Cowgill 1963; A. Chase 1983; see also Berlin 1955: fig. 1b), where its appearance begins in the early facet of the Early Postclassic Chilcob complex.

In the intervening area—the Petén lakes region—its distribution is irregular but generally infrequent. No sherds of Augustine were identified at the excavations of the Topoxté islands in Lake Yaxhá, and its appearance is uncommon at Macanché and Salpetén; at Macanché, in fact, it cannot be clearly associated with the early facet of the Early Postclassic, as it can elsewhere, except perhaps for the apparently intrusive (?) support fragments in Bullard's Terminal Classic lots. In the CPHEP excavations in the lakes area, Augustine appeared in significant quantities only on the islands in Lake Quexil, and there it did occur in the early facet Early Postclassic. Perhaps the proximity of Quexil to Tayasal accounts for the parallel occurrence. Bullard commented (1973:226, 227) on the difficulty of recognizing Augustine as a classificatory entity at Macanché, and this seems to be generally true in the lakes area, a problem that is exacerbated by the generally poor preservation of the slips in sherds from nonconstruction lots.

Pottery of the Augustine ceramic group is abundant at Negroman-Tipú, on the Macal River in western Belize, from the Early Postclassic period through the Late Postclassic and apparently into the Historic period. From the Middle Postclassic onward, the Augustine pottery at this site showed more similarities to Paxcamán group vessels from Petén than to Augustine group vessels from Barton Ramie, and has been classified into new varieties (P. Rice 1985a).

Slateware Group Unspecified

Name: **Unnamed Trickle-on-gray Slate.**

Frequency: 2 sherds from Bullard's excavations on Macanché Island.

Ware: Unspecified Slateware.

Complex: Aura ceramic complex.

Principal identifying modes: These sherds are identified as Trickle Slate wares by the presence of gray-black broad wavy lines on a gray surface of coarse carbonate-tempered sherds.

Paste and firing: The paste is gray to brown in color, moderate in texture, and has crystalline calcite inclusions. The calcite is light gray to white, and "twinkles" as light reflects off the faces of the crystals. Particles range up to 1 mm in size, but are primarily less than 0.5 mm.

Surface treatment and decoration: One sherd has three uneven broad "stripes" or blobs of dark gray paint. The sherd surface is somewhat leached, and has no luster. Slip color varies from light to medium gray (10YR 5–7/1), and the paint is dark gray (7.5YR 4/0). Shepard (1962:260) comments that the pigment on Trickle Slate wares is an organic plant extract, rather than a mineralic paint, applied to a carbon-retentive montmorillonite clay-based slip.

Forms and dimensions: The vessel form is unknown, but the slight curvature of the sherds and location of the decoration on the exterior curve suggests that it was probably a bowl or jar. The sherd thickness is 5.5 cm.

Illustrations: figure 55e, f.

Intrasite references: One of the Trickle sherds came from the lowest construction levels in Operation IB, while the other came from mixed midden and fill in Lot 10, Operation IA. One additional Trickle Slate ware sherd and 42 additional miscellaneous non-Trickle Slate wares were recovered from CPHEP excavations, primarily dating to the late facet Early Postclassic (Aura complex) platform construction fill on the island.

Intersite references: "Trickle" decoration is typically associated with the Northern Lowlands of the Yucatán Peninsula, and with slatewares in particular (see R. E. Smith 1971; Ball 1977). Ball (1977:63) describes a Pixtun Trickle-on-gray type from Becan dating to the Late Chintok–Early Xcocom phases, which may be the type represented by the three Trickle sherds from Macanché

Island. Trickle ware was not found elsewhere in the CPHEP investigations in the lakes region. Slateware (Ticul Thin Slate) was recovered at Tayasal in the Hobo Terminal Classic complex (A. Chase 1983).

Fine Paste Ware Ceramic Groups

Name: **Fine Orange Group Unspecified.**

Frequency: 8 sherds from Bullard's excavations into Postclassic contexts on Macanché Island.

Ware: Fine Orange ware.

Complex: Aura and Dos Lagos ceramic complexes (?).

Principal identifying modes: Fine Orange ware is characterized by extremely fine-textured orange-colored pastes, generally with very thin walls and often having dark cores. No slip remains on the sherds. Vessels at Macanché occur in bowl and pyriform shapes, and are decorated with incising.

Paste and firing: Fine Orange paste is extremely fine textured, dense, orange (5YR 5–6/6–8) in color, and usually with no inclusions visible to the naked eye. Very fine mica particles may be visible on the eroded surfaces of the sherds. The vessels were generally well fired, as fire-clouds are rare, but dark gray cores are common in cross section.

Surface treatment and decoration: Surfaces are very well smoothed, but because of erosion it is impossible to determine if a slip originally had been present. Generally the surfaces are lighter in color than the pastes, varying from 5YR 6/3–4 to 7.5YR 7–8/4.

Four sherds have incised decoration. One is the incised interior of a grater bowl, and may represent Trapiche Incised: Decorated Interior Variety of the Altar group (see Sabloff 1975:194–195). Another incised sherd has relatively deep incised lines forming an indistinct pattern on the exterior of a hemispherical bowl. Traces of a white coating on the exterior may be a slip. The surfaces of both these sherds have extremely fine mica particles present.

The remaining two incised sherds are from a pyriform vessel. The incising is very fine, faint, and shallow (although there may be some gouge-incising plano relief carving as well); it is very carelessly executed. The decoration consists of two bands, the upper one having circles with central dots, while the lower band has step-frets (modified *grecas*?). Below the bands an unclear decoration appears to be arranged in a panel. This vessel may be of Villahermosa Incised of the Matillas group (see R. E. Smith 1971: fig. 55b9).

Forms and dimensions: The grater bowl sherd has no rim; its thickness is 4.7 mm. The hemispherical bowl sherd is too small to obtain a diameter; the rim is square, the walls appear to be vertical, and it is 6.8 mm thick. The pyriform jar is very thin walled at 2.5 to 5 mm, and the mouth diameter is 12 cm. In addition to these forms, the Fine Orange sherds at Macanché included a fragment of an annular base, a rounded bulbous foot fragment, a small ring handle, and a body sherd.

Illustrations: figure 55g–h.

Intrasite references: All of these Fine Orange sherds were from Late Postclassic midden on Macanché Island; the incised pyriform vase was from the top of the mound. A few Fine Orange sherds were recovered from CPHEP excavations on the island: one Sahcabá Modeled-carved sherd was found in the Late Postclassic midden, and two miscellaneous Fine Orange sherds came from early facet Early Postclassic proveniences. In addition, five Islas Gouge-incised sherds were recovered in Terminal Classic deposits (see chapter 4 above).

The placement of these sherds in the Aura and Dos Lagos ceramic complexes at Macanché may be questioned, because some of the sherds included here may be of the earlier Altar ceramic group. Thus they may be present in these late deposits as a result of mixing in of earlier materials. In view of the overall uncertainties regarding the typology of these sherds, however, plus the fact that they were recovered from late contexts, I have chosen to leave them in the Aura–Dos Lagos type descriptions.

Intersite references: Fine Orange sherds were rare in occurrence in the lake areas investigated by CPHEP; the most frequently encountered specimens were modeled-carved vessels or their imitations, and only at Yaxhá were they found in amounts greater than "extremely rare" (see P. Rice 1986). The same holds true for the large centers to the north, with modeled-carved vessels being found in small quantities at Uaxactún, and Fine Orange at Tikal being described as "scattered" in its occurrence (Culbert 1973b:81). At Tayasal, Tumba Black-on-orange is the only type specified among the Fine Orange sherds recovered there (A. Chase 1983); at Macanché no painted types were noted. In general, Fine Orange wares seem to be common in Petén only in the Pasión area, where they were a major diagnostic of the Boca Terminal Classic ceramic sphere, and may have been manufactured there (Bishop and Rands 1982:314).

Name: **Poité Incised: Poité Variety (?).**

Frequency: 1 sherd from Bullard's excavations at Macanché Island.

Ware: Fine Gray ware (Tres Naciones ceramic group).

Complex: Aura and/or Dos Lagos ceramic complex (?).

Established: The Poité Incised type and Poité Variety were described and illustrated by R. E. W. Adams (1971:45) on the basis of the ceramics of Altar de Sacrificios.

Principal identifying modes: Poité Incised is characterized by extremely fine-textured gray paste, fine postslip incising, and a thin dark gray exterior slip.

Paste and firing: The paste of Poité Incised is like that of Fine Orange in being extremely fine textured and lacking visible inclusions, but differs in being fired in an incompletely oxidizing atmosphere to produce a gray color (10YR 6/1).

Surface treatment and decoration: The surface of the sherd is very well smoothed and polished, and covered with a streaky low-luster slip that varies in color from dark gray (10YR 4/1) to brown (10YR 5/3). The fine line postslip incising suggests that the decoration had a banded arrangement.

Forms and dimensions: The form of this vessel is unknown; it may have been a bowl or pyriform vessel; thickness is 3.5–4.0 mm.

Illustrations: None.

Intrasite references: Seven sherds tentatively identified as Fine Gray were encountered in CPHEP excavations into early facet Early Postclassic deposits in pit 6 at Macanché Island. For stratigraphic and temporal distribution of fine paste wares, see Fine Orange wares, above.

Intersite references: Fine Gray has not been recovered in CPHEP excavations elsewhere in the lakes area, nor was it mentioned as occurring at Tayasal (A. Chase 1983). Fine Gray was noted at Uaxactún (R. E. Smith 1955: fig. 75b4, 9) and Tikal (Culbert 1973b: 81), but generally it is more common at sites in the Pasión area (see Sabloff 1975:211–213). In the Pasión area most of the illustrated vessels are grater bowls.

Tachís Ceramic Group

Name: **Pulpería Red: Pulpería Variety.**
Frequency: 6 sherds from Punta Nimá.
Ware: Unspecified.
Complex: Unknown.

Established: The Tachís ceramic group and Tachís Red type were originally named by G. Cowgill (1963:112–115). A. Chase (1983) has used "Tachís" to refer to a red-on-paste decorated type at Tayasal (Cowgill's illustrations are also red-on-paste), so I have named a new monochrome red type, Pulpería Red, within the group.

Principal identifying modes: Pulpería Red is characterized by an unusually dark red slip on gray-to-brown pastes.

Paste and firing: The paste of Pulpería Red is the characteristic fine-textured gray-to-brown carbonate paste containing snail inclusions that was used for the Paxcamán and Trapeche ceramic groups (see chapter 6).

Surface treatment and decoration: Surfaces are covered with a dark red slip that varies in the range of 7.5–10R 3–4/6 in color. As compared to Paxcamán sherds, the slip is thicker and lacks the double slipping occa-

sionally noted (see chapter 6). One sherd is rather carelessly burnished. No decoration is visible on these sherds, although one sherd of a hemispherical bowl has an eroded interior that may be indicative of a decorative band.

Forms and dimensions: Sherds are generally thin-walled as compared to Paxcamán and Trapeche group vessels. A hemispherical bowl has a diameter of 16 cm and a slightly bevelled lip; the wall thickness varies from 4 to 6.4 mm. Another vessel—a bowl?—has a rounded base and a small round support with a single vent hole; the slip is fire-clouded to a very dark reddish brown. One sherd has a small strap handle 1.2 cm wide and 2.4 cm long; the wall is 3.5 mm in thickness.

Illustrations: figure 55i–k.

Intrasite references: No sherds of the Tachís group could be clearly identified in Bullard's collections from Macanché Island. The sherds described here were from Bullard's unprovenienced collection from the Punta Nimá sand pits on the north shore of the Tayasal peninsula.

Intersite references: The Tachís ceramic group is not well defined anywhere in Petén, and has not been securely identified in any of the CPHEP excavations in the lakes area. Tachís Red-on-paste has been identified at Tayasal in the Kauil Late Postclassic–Historic complex, and the group may be largely confined to the Lake Petén-Itzá region.

Pozo Ceramic Group

Name: **Pozo Unslipped: Pozo Variety.**
Frequency: 2836 sherds, of which 2796 were from Bullard's collections and excavations at Macanché Island, 2 from the mainland "center" at Lake Macanché, 31 from Ixlú, and 7 in the Punta Nimá collection. Pozo Unslipped constitutes 99 percent of the sherds of the Pozo ceramic group in Bullard's collections.

Ware: Montículo Unslipped ware.
Complex: Aura, Dos Lagos, and Ayer ceramic complexes.

Established: The Pozo Unslipped type

was first described in the Postclassic collections from Canté Island in Lake Yaxhá (P. Rice 1979:56–62).

Principal identifying modes: Pozo Unslipped type consists of unslipped vessels of medium- to coarse-textured gray carbonate paste, with surfaces that are generally rather poorly smoothed. Vessel forms include a wide-mouthed jar with short vertical or outflaring neck, and shallow bowls with square lip.

Paste and firing: Pozo Unslipped vessels have a moderate to coarse textured paste, bearing abundant calcite particles. The calcite varies from semi-translucent (comparatively rare) to whitish, pinkish, and yellowish in color, and the particles are usually subrounded or subangular. Particle sizes are most typically 1.0 mm or less in diameter, but occasionally are as large as 2.0 mm. Approximately 10 percent of the sherds have small fragments of snail shell visible on the surfaces or in broken cross section. These appear to be the same kinds of shell that are present in the gray-to-brown paste of the Paxcamán and Trapeche ceramic groups (see chapter 6).

The vessels were not fully oxidized in firing. Paste colors vary from dark gray (5YR 4/1) to light gray (2.5YR 7.2) or, very rarely, light brown (10YR 6/4). Surface colors are more variable, with a greater proportion of the sherds having lighter (i.e., higher in value) surface colors. The range is from the same dark grays of the paste to 10YR 7/1, and occasionally 2.5YR 8/2. Sherds with lighter colored surfaces often have dark cores. The tendency for Pozo Unslipped vessels to have grayer interior and browner exterior surface colors, noted at Topoxté (P. Rice 1979), was not observed in the Macanché sherds.

Approximately 3 percent of the sherds (n = 88) have a paste that is more reddish brown (5YR 6/4 to 7.5YR 6/4–6) and better oxidized than the typical Pozo Unslipped paste. Fire-clouding is almost nonexistent. A few of these sherds have inclusions of snail shell. The interior and exterior surfaces

of these reddish brown sherds are better smoothed than are those of the typical coarse gray paste.

Finally, 41 sherds have a very dark gray paste that is frequently fire-clouded or sooted black or both; these sherds are typically somewhat more thin-walled than are the standard Pozo sherds.

Surface treatment and decoration: Little care was taken in finishing the vessel surfaces. Generally the interiors are smoother and more evenly finished than are the exteriors, a characteristic also evident in Late Classic period unslipped jars, and this may suggest manufacture by means of molds. Exterior surfaces show striations, marks from inclusions having been dragged across the surface during scraping, ridges from scraping the body when it was too dry, careless finishing of the join of the neck to the body, and pockmarking.

The only "decoration" evident in these sherds is the presence on one sherd of a "bird head" effigy lug handle.

Forms and dimensions: The most common form in Pozo Unslipped is a wide-mouthed jar or olla, but bowls are also present in this type.

WIDEMOUTHED OLLAS: This form is represented by 735 sherds of Pozo Unslipped, and vessels may have either a vertical (517 rimsherds) or outflaring (213 rims) neck. On the latter, the rim angles out 8° to 40° from the vertical. Rarely—on five sherds—are the necks inslanted. A small number of jars (n = 49) with vertical necks also had exterior lip bolsters.

Most of the necks are short to medium high, their height (measured above the join on the exterior) varying between 1.7 and 3.5 cm (mean 2.9 cm). Higher—up to 4.7 cm— necks occur in less than 10 percent of the vertical neck jars, and in slightly over 25 percent of the outflaring neck jars.

On ollas with outflaring necks the lip is often slightly flattened or bevelled; on vertical neck jars the lip may be very slightly thinned and rounded, or squared. The rims are often rather poorly made and slightly asymmetrical, making it difficult to obtain reliable diameter measurements. Mouth diameters range between 15 and 44 cm, with most varying between 20 and 26 cm. There is a considerable overlap in the range of diameters in short, medium, and high neck categories, but in general the vessels with higher necks have larger diameters. Vessels with vertical necks are most abundant and seem to be somewhat more standardized as to form: fewer than 10 percent of the necks are classed as "high," and there is less variation in diameters, which have a mean value of 22.2 cm. Ollas with outflaring necks are more variable in height, angle, and diameter, but are generally slightly larger, averaging 24 cm in mouth diameter. Lip bolsters are more common on vertical necks, however, perhaps to allow more secure closure.

The jars are thickest at the rim and just below the neck-body join, becoming rapidly thinner at the shoulder or just above the vessel's widest diameter. The thickness of the neck varies from 5.2 mm to 11.5 mm, with a mean of 8.1 mm. Many of the rims that have part of the body present obviously broke at this weak thin point on the shoulder. The most common point of breakage, however, is the join of the collar or neck to the body, suggesting that perhaps in manufacture the neck edge was a bit too dry when the collar was added.

A subset of these wide-necked ollas consists of unusually small vessels, mouth diameter ca. 12–14.5 cm, with very short (ca. 1.0 to 1.5 cm) outflaring or vertical necks. These are typically dark gray (sometimes sooted) and thin-walled, although often the interior neck is lighter gray than other portions of the vessel, interior or exterior.

Besides these plain widemouthed ollas, other rim styles are present. Jars with bolstered lips occur infrequently (n = 49). The bolsters are generally round, although six sherds have flattened ones or bolsters with shallow grooves on the upper surface. On five sherds from which diameter measurements could be obtained, dimensions varied

from 30 to 34 cm. The vessels generally have high vertical necks, and the angle of join between neck and body typically is not as pronounced or as defined as on jars without bolsters.

HANDLES: Nine sherds represent handles of vessels: of these, seven are strap handles and one is a small, thin lug handle. Four of the strap handles are of finer textured paste that resembles some of the varieties in the Paxcamán ceramic group, and it is possible that these belong to that group but the slip has completely worn off. Alternatively, the same pastes may have been used for some unslipped vessels.

Six unslipped widemouth rims, plus 13 additional sherds of unknown form but presumably jars, have "flap handles." These are formed of small lumps of clay pressed against the vessel shoulder 1.0 to 1.5 cm below the join with the neck. The middle of the lump appears to have been drawn and tapered downward and pressed against the wall to form the lower handle attachment, the end result being a short, broad, T-shaped "flap." These handles do not project outward from the body sufficiently to allow a finger to be inserted for a grip, although on some a cord could have been passed through for hanging. The ollas with these "handles" have both short and medium-high necks, which may be either vertical or outflaring in orientation. A variety of pastes are represented, including the typical coarse gray paste, as well as two sherds of the reddish brown paste.

One vessel was a small thin-walled dark gray jar (?) with an unusual effigy appliqué on the shoulder forming a lug handle. An elongate spike was split vertically, then a "plug" was placed between the halves and two small appliqué "eyes" were placed on either side. The effect is one of an effigy bird or turtle head with something in its mouth. The vessel has a short (2.7 cm), slightly outflaring neck with thinned, slightly pointed lip. The thickness of the neck is 6.5 mm, while the body is 4.0 mm thick.

BOWLS: Simple bowl forms are also represented by 51 sherds of Pozo Unslipped. These vary from deep bowls with nearly straight sides to shallow dishes with flaring or curved sides. Except for two sherds with small lip bolsters, rims are direct, with either flattened or squared lips; bevelled lips occur on four sherds from shallow open bowls with outflared sides, and seven sherds have simple rounded rims. Mouth diameters vary from 20 to 26 cm (six measurements) with 20 cm being the modal value. Wall thickness varies from 3.8 to 9.5 mm. The finishing of the vessels is careless, as is that of jars, with pockmarks, drag marks, striations, ridges, and other imperfections common. Generally, the interiors are better smoothed than are the exteriors.

GRATERS: Two sherds represented unslipped, relatively coarse-textured grater bowls. No dimensions were measured.

BODY SHERDS: The remaining sherds are miscellaneous body sherds, unidentifiable as to form. It should be noted that some of these sherds may represent the vase-like censers of La Justa Composite, many of which are manufactured of a paste virtually identical to that of Pozo Unslipped (in Montículo Unslipped ware).

Illustrations: figures 56 and 57.

Intrasite references: Twenty sherds of Pozo Unslipped type were recovered from Terminal Classic lots in Bullard's excavations; 42 sherds came from Early Postclassic lots, and the remainder were from the Late Postclassic and/or Protohistoric complexes. No substantial differences in size of the ollas can be determined between the early and late facets of the Late Postclassic materials.

Outflaring neck ollas are virtually absent from the "late" Late Postclassic or Protohistoric midden lots on the island. Most of the sherds of this form variant are "early" Late Postclassic; they are especially abundant in Lot 25 in Operation IH. The reddish brown paste variant of the ollas was recovered primarily from the summit of the mound rather than from the slopes, and is primarily "early" Late Postclassic in date. In CPHEP excavations, the red-brown paste variant, flap handles, and graters all were encoun-

tered in Early Postclassic platform fill on the island. Bowl sherds rarely occurred in lots from Bullard's excavations on the top of the mound, being found more frequently in the midden on the mound slopes. One partially reconstructible vessel was found in Bullard's Lot 5, in Operation IA.

Intersite references: Pozo Unslipped jars were recovered at the mainland "center" at Lake Macanché, at Ixlú, and in the collections from Punta Nimá. Pozo Unslipped was also recovered at Canté Island, one of the Topoxté islands in Lake Yaxhá (P. Rice 1979), although Bullard did not report similar jars in his excavations. The vessels from Macanché are more poorly finished and darker in color than the Topoxté specimens, but the differences are not sufficiently striking or consistent to warrant naming a new variety at Macanché.

The widemouthed jar or olla form, with a vertical, inslanting, or outflaring neck, seems to be the standard unslipped jar form in the Postclassic period in the Southern Lowlands. Similar forms were encountered at Lake Petén-Itzá (G. Cowgill 1963:fig. 6m, n) and at Tayasal in all Postclassic complexes. At the latter location, they were given the Barton Ramie type designation of Maskall Unslipped in the Chilcob Early Postclassic complex, and a new type, Nohpek, was named for the Cocahmut through Kauil complexes (A. Chase 1983). No distinctive Postclassic jar forms are described or illustrated as being present in the collections from Seibal.

These same olla forms occured at Barton Ramie in the types Rio Juan Unslipped and in Maskall Unslipped (Sharer and Chase 1976: fig. 201, fig. 205f–l). The red and dark gray paste variations noted in Pozo Unslipped at Macanché have some correspondences to these two types (reddish in Rio Juan and black in Maskall) at Barton Ramie, and it is likely that the thin-walled dark gray sherds should be classified as Maskall Unslipped. Rio Juan, however, has less variation in diameter, and bolsters are not common in that type.

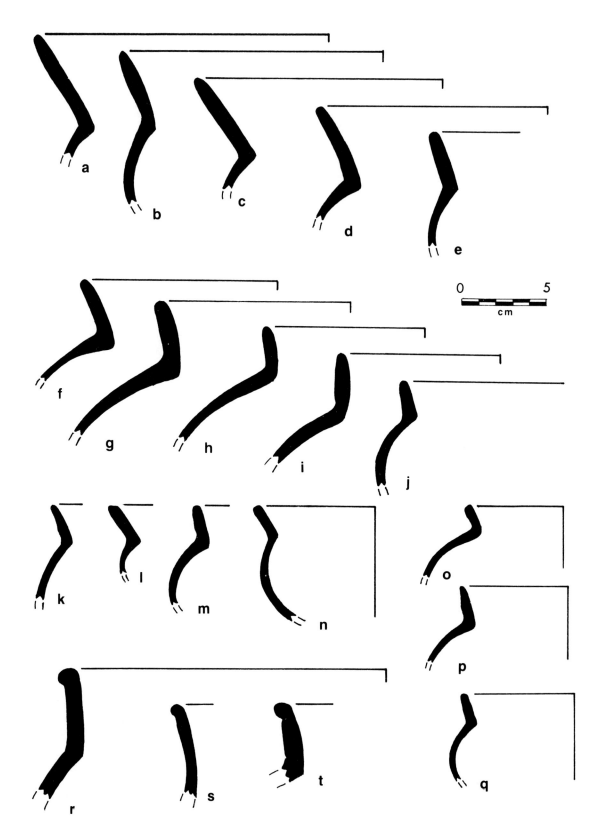

FIGURE 56. Pozo Unslipped: Pozo Variety.

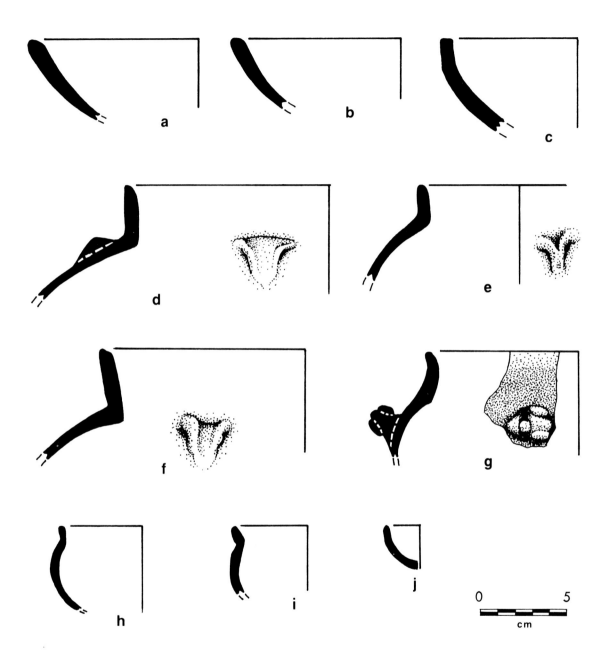

FIGURE 57. Pozo Unslipped: Pozo Variety.

It is intriguing that the "bird head" effigy lug handle seems to occur rarely but consistently in unslipped Postclassic vessels throughout the Lowlands. This appliqué was noted in Pozo Unslipped at Canté Island (P. Rice 1979: fig. 14b), in Rio Juan Unslipped: Variety Unspecified and More Force Unslipped at Barton Ramie (Sharer and Chase 1976: figs. 206f and 204l, respectively), in Thul Appliqué at Mayapán (R. E. Smith 1971: fig. 28a21, 23), and on an unslipped bowl at Lamanai (Pendergast, personal communication).

Similar widemouthed jars occur at Mayapán in the Postclassic period in Panabá Unslipped, which also includes bowl forms (see R. E. Smith 1971:figs. 28b2, 29a–e, 61a5), but lip bolsters seem to be rare at that site. The jars also are found in Yacmán Striated type (see R. E. Smith 1971: figs. 28a1–12 and 28b1, 3), but striation is virtually nonexistent in Petén Postclassic assemblages.

Two things are of interest with respect to these Postclassic unslipped jars or ollas. One is that there is no narrow-necked unslipped jar component in Pozo Unslipped at Macanché Island, although there were narrow-necked jars in Pozo at Topoxté and in Mayapán Unslipped ware (e.g., Panabá Unslipped) at Mayapán. Narrow-necked jars or tinajas at Macanché are present in the slipped Paxcamán and Trapeche ceramic groups, but in general there is no equivalent in the Postclassic assemblages of the unslipped narrow-necked jar that was so common in the Classic period.

The second observation is that if the vessel dimensions of Macanché Island are compared with those of other sites, it is evident that the diameters of unslipped ollas are approximately the same as those of Barton Ramie, and they fall within the lower range of similar vessels at Mayapán. Yet the diameters of the tripod dishes of the slipped Paxcamán and Trapeche groups, for example, at Macanché are considerably smaller than those of the dishes of the Paxcamán and Augustine groups at Barton Ramie. The reasons for the similarities and differences in vessel dimensions between the slipped and unslipped subcomplexes must be a function of both dietary variations as well as differences in the composition of the food-consuming unit(s) in these locations, but unfortunately they cannot be specified on the basis of present evidence.

Name: **La Justa Composite: La Justa Variety.**

Frequency: 33 sherds, of which 32 are from Bullard's excavations on Macanché Island and 1 from Punta Nimá. La Justa Composite comprises 1 percent of the sherds of the Pozo ceramic group included in Bullard's collections.

Ware: Montículo Unslipped ware.

Complex: Dos Lagos and Ayer ceramic complexes.

Established: Present work.

Principal identifying modes: La Justa Composite type includes a variety of censers of unslipped, relatively coarse gray paste occurring primarily in three forms. One is a pedestal based vase with finger impressed decoration; another is a cylindrical or hourglass-shaped vessel with appliqué spikes; the third is a ladle censer form.

Paste and firing: The paste is variable, but is generally the dark gray-to-brown relatively coarse calcite paste used in Pozo Unslipped ollas (see Pozo Unslipped). Surface colors vary from light brown (10YR 6.5/3) to dark gray. One sherd had several large snail shell fragments and ferruginous lumps.

Surface treatment and decoration: Surfaces are not very well smoothed in general (see Pozo Unslipped). Some of the sherds are pockmarked from leaching of the calcite inclusions. Interiors are sometimes smoke-darkened gray.

On 12 sherds (eight vessels), decoration consists of a band of finger impressions around the neck of the vessel, generally at the point of maximum constriction of the neck, which may be from 1.5 to 4.7 cm below the lip. The impressions may be placed on an appliquéd fillet 1.1 to 1.5 cm in width, or directly into the vessel wall; they are usu-

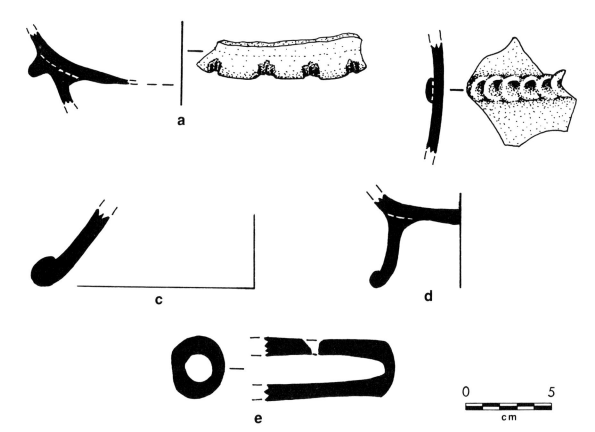

FIGURE 58. La Justa Composite: La Justa Variety. **a**, from Punta Nimá.

ally made with the ball of the finger, and are spaced 1.0 to 1.5 cm apart. Appliqué spikes were applied to the exterior of six sherds.

One sherd from Punta Nimá is an hourglass censer with a flange 1.15 cm deep; groups of three small incised lines indent the edge of the flange at intervals of 2.6 to 3.3 cm. The middle incision is deeper than the ones on either side, the effect being to create stepped notches 5 to 8 mm wide along this flange.

Forms and dimensions: Rimsherds of these vessels suggest, by analogy with Bullard's (1970) impressed censers at Topoxté, tall vases with slightly outflared rims and squared or rounded lip; one impressed vase

has a diameter of 18 cm. An extremely outflaring rim has a 2-cm-high bolster, and a mouth diameter of 26 cm. The height of the vessels could not be obtained.

The hourglass censer from Punta Nimá is relatively thin walled, at 4 to 6 mm in thickness; neither the mouth nor the body diameter can be measured because of their fragmentary condition, but the diameter of the flange is 18 cm. Traces of the pedestal base suggest it is vertical rather than flaring, and has slashes or vent holes.

Four sherds are pedestal bases, representing the bases of vase or hourglass censers. One almost complete base (two sherds) has an irregularly folded-over lip forming a round bolster 8 to 9 mm in height, and a diameter of 11 cm; the base is 4.35 cm high. Another sherd is a base with a direct squared lip; the diameter is 14 cm, and the pedestal is 3.5 cm high.

Two sherds are from ladle censers: one vessel is of dark gray paste with an outflared wall and a thinned lip, and only an unusual break suggests a handle attachment. A complete handle is 7.9 cm long, 3.2 cm in diameter, and 8 to 9 mm in wall thickness; a small vent was placed 2.5 cm from the join with the bowl. The paste is dark and dense gray, although the surfaces vary to light brown. No information is available as to the form of the bowl of the censer.

Illustration: figure 58.

Intrasite references: One impressed sherd from Bullard's excavations was from an Early Postclassic lot; the remainder were from Late Postclassic midden material, primarily from the mound slopes and principally from Operation IH, both "early" and "late" levels. Six impressed fillet sherds were recovered in CPHEP excavations into Late Postclassic contexts; none of these was from the top of the mound. A ladle censer fragment was recovered in an early facet Early Postclassic context of CPHEP excavations.

Intersite references: The three censer forms represented by these sherds at Macanché—impressed vase, spike hourglass, and ladle—are widespread in occurrence in the Maya Lowlands beginning in the Terminal Classic period and extending through the Postclassic. They are manufactured in a range of localized forms and decorative variants that have been classified into a multitude of categories—"composite," "appliquéd," "modeled," and so forth—in a variety of unslipped wares and groups. In the material from Macanché, Punta Nimá, and Ixlú, contained in Bullard's collection, I have classified the relatively small quantities of similar noneffigy censer materials by separating ware categories (Montículo or Uapake) as the first division. Within each ware and each unslipped ceramic group (Pozo and Chilo, respectively), a diverse lot of censer form and decorative treatments was combined into a single "composite" type. A third composite type category is present in the Patojo ceramic group (ware unspecified), which contains a modeled type that includes effigy censers.

I decided upon this solution because the technical and distributional characteristics of the Montículo and Uapake wares are sufficiently distinct in the lakes area that in my judgment they warrant more attention than does the decorative mode of applying appliqué spikes, for example. It is interesting, I think, that these paste divisions of the censer groups do not appear to be localized to particular areas, but instead are widespread, suggesting a variety of sites of manufacture of the censers as well as some exchange of the finished product.

Censers with appliquéd elements or impressed fillets or both are known in Petén from a Caban burial in Temple 1 at Tikal (R. E. W. Adams and Trik 1961: fig. 42a, b) as well as in the Lake Petén-Itzá area (G. Cowgill 1963: fig. 60, p, t). Hourglass censers are known from Tayasal in the Cocahmut complex (Puxteal Modeled; A. Chase 1983). These vessels were not identified at Barton Ramie, but impressed censers were present at Topoxté, where they were classified within the Pozo Unslipped ceramic group as Extranjeras Impressed type (P. Rice 1979: 62–64).

Similar forms are present at Seibal, where "several vessels have finger impressed fillets and circular button adornos" (Sabloff 1975: 175); one appliquéd fillet censer with a bolstered lip was mislabeled as Chaquiste Impressed (Sabloff 1975: fig. 326a). Most of the late censers at Seibal are classified as Miseria Appliquéd type (unspecified variety), and are assigned to the Bayal sphere although it is likely that many are later in date. These are primarily hourglass censers with spike appliqués and are usually associated with Fine Paste ceramics or stelae with a 10.1.0.0.0 date (Sabloff 1975: 176). They occur occasionally with basal flanges, which may sometimes be notched (Sabloff 1975: fig. 335a, c).

Vase or hourglass censers with appliquéd spike or disc elements, sometimes combined with impressed fillets, are common in Terminal Classic censer subcomplexes over the peninsula, occurring in Petén at Uaxactún and Seibal, as well as to the north at Becan, and to the south in the Motagua valley (A. L. Smith and Kidder 1943: fig. 22c,d,e,g). At Becan, flat-bottomed, often footed, bowls are particularly elaborated in the Xcocom type Pastelaría Composite, with combinations of fillets and patterned spike appliqués (Ball 1977: figs. 43–44).

The spiked hourglass censers at Macanché are not at all contemporaneous with these Terminal Classic prototypes, but instead are a Late Postclassic development, occurring in both La Justa Composite type in Montículo Unslipped ware and in Gotas Composite in Uapake Unslipped ware (Chilo ceramic group, see below). Censers with impressed fillet, plus appliquéd discs or spikes, are common at Negroman-Tipú (P. Rice 1984a), and seem to be of general occurrence in the Cayo District of Belize (Schmidt 1976/77: figs. 2 and 3). Temporally, then, the Macanché vessels show closer relationships to late censers with impressed fillets or appliquéd elements (buttons, spikes, etc.) from Mayapán in Thul Appliqué or Cehac-Hunacti Composite types in the Hocabá complex (see R. E. Smith 1971: fig. 30d, e, g–l, o, r, t; fig. 31a–c, e, h, i, l–p; fig. 62a–e), than to the earlier Petén Classic materials.

Ladle censers are not particularly common in Petén. The form was not widely noted in the lakes area, although a modeled censer handle was found in the Early Postclassic at Macanché in Chuntuci Composite: Variety Unspecified (Trapeche group), and a modeled human head, probably from a ladle censer handle, was identified in Patojo Modeled. A "Mixtec" handled censer in the Paxcamán ceramic group is noted at Tayasal in the early Cocahmut complex (A. Chase 1983), and G. Cowgill illustrates a ladle censer from Lake Petén-Itzá (1963: fig. 6u). Outside Petén, ladle censers tend to be very elaborate with modelling, appliqué elements, or effigy heads (for example at Becan), while at Naco (Wonderley 1981) and in the Guatemalan Highlands (Wauchope 1970) the ladle censers may also be painted. Plain ladle censer handles are noted at Mayapán in Navula Unslipped (R. E. Smith 1971: fig. 33a–e), at Becan (Ball 1977: fig. 46a, d), and at Negroman-Tipú (P. Rice 1984a).

Chilo Ceramic Group

Name: **Chilo Unslipped: Chilo Variety.**
Frequency: 522 sherds, of which 510 were from Bullard's excavations on Macanché Island; also 1 sherd from the mainland "center" and 11 sherds from Ixlú. Chilo Unslipped constitutes 94.9 percent of the sherds of the Chilo ceramic group in Bullard's collections.
Ware: Uapake Unslipped ware.
Complex: Dos Lagos and Ayer ceramic complexes.
Established: Present work. The name "Chilo" was given to this collection of material by Bullard, who did not complete the type descriptions.
Principal identifying modes: Chilo Unslipped type consists of reddish brown to dark gray jars, calcite tempered, often rather poorly made. Bowls, tecomates, and short-neck jars (lacking the definite angle between body and neck of Pozo group vessels) are the principal vessel forms; horizontal strap handles may occur on these vessels.
Paste and firing: Chilo Unslipped is manufactured in Uapake Unslipped ware, the paste and surface characteristics of which are described here. The paste of Chilo Unslipped is typically yellowish red or brown in color (5YR 5/6; 5YR 6/5), and occasionally moderately well oxidized. Some sherds are of a dark fire-clouded gray paste similar to that of Pozo Unslipped sherds. Surface colors range from light gray (10YR 7/1–2) through light reddish brown to dark gray (5YR 4/1), or light brown or pinkish gray (7.5YR–5YR 6/4–2). By far the most common colors are in the mottled orange to brown range, and the color continuum between these sherds and the reddish brown sherds of Pozo occa-

sionally causes difficulties in distinguishing the two. Fire-clouding and poor firing control are frequently noted.

Gray, white, and semitranslucent calcite are the most common kinds of inclusions found in the paste; most appear to be approximately 1 mm in size. Many sherds have one or more particles as large as 3 to 4 mm, and one pebble was 7 mm in length. Ferruginous and manganese lumps are occasionally noted. Snail fragments are only rarely present in this paste.

Surface treatment and decoration: The surface finish on the vessels of Chilo Unslipped is extremely poor. Unlike the Pozo ollas, which had fairly well-smoothed interiors despite the condition of the exterior surfaces, Chilo sherds are carelessly finished on both interior and exterior. Pockmarks, striations, drag-lines, and highly irregular wall thickness and rim contours are invariably characteristic of these vessels. In most sherds the temper particles are visible on the surfaces. The pockmarking appears to be from post-depositional leaching of the calcite, for it may be observed on the fractured edges of many sherds.

Forms and dimensions: The most common vessel form consists of subglobular widemouthed jars or olla (plate XII) which are considerably different from the forms in Pozo Unslipped. The principal difference is the lack of a definite angle at the join of the neck to the body in Chilo Unslipped. In most sherds the neck-to-body join is marked on the interior by a slight angle, ridge, or "corner," but this is smoothed out on the exteriors. Also, the shoulder is much less pronounced in the Chilo jars, resulting in a low ratio of mouth diameter to body diameter. The necks of the vessels vary from inslanting to vertical to very slightly outflaring. Mouth diameters are difficult to measure accurately, because vessels are often highly asymmetrical, but seem to range from 18 to 28 cm, with a mean of 21 cm (seven measurements). Rims are sometimes slightly thinned to the lip, which is rounded or roughly squared, or very rarely bolstered. Another

vessel form of Chilo Unslipped is a jar with a relatively high and narrow neck, and horizontal strap handles. One partially reconstructible vessel was recovered from Macanché; the neck is approximately 8.5 cm high, the mouth diameter is 20 cm, and the body diameter is estimated at 30 cm. The wall thickness varies from 5.5 mm in the body of the vessel to 8 mm at the neck (it is noteworthy that although the vessels of Chilo Unslipped are singularly poorly finished, they are not unusually thick-walled). On one partially reconstructible vessel, the mouth diameter is 28 cm.

A neckless jar with a slightly upturned handle came from Macanché Island. The mouth diameter is 14 cm; the handle is irregularly shaped but has a maximum width of 2.9 cm, and was applied 4.5 cm below the square lip. The wall thickness is about 6 mm.

Illustrations: figure 59, and plate XII.

Intrasite references: Chilo Unslipped is very common in the Late Postclassic midden levels at Macanché Island; one sherd from Bullard's Terminal Classic lots and one sherd from Early Postclassic fill are believed to be intrusive. In CPHEP excavations, Chilo was found to be particularly abundant in the upper 20 to 30 cm of the midden, and as such is hypothesized to be a diagnostic of the "late" Postclassic/Protohistoric Ayer complex in the lakes region. This same stratigraphic relationship was not readily apparent in the lot separations maintained in Bullard's excavations, however, where Chilo was present in significant quantities in levels 30–50 cm below surface as well.

The type is particularly common on the top of the mound, in excavations around the structures situated there, and three partially reconstructible vessels were recovered in Bullard's Operations ID and IE. Three other partially reconstructible vessels came from excavations in midden on the mound slopes in Operations IA and IB.

Intersite references: Vessels of the Chilo group, diagnostic of very late habitation of the lakes area, are found in varying quantities in this region. They were noted in the

PLATE XII. Chilo Unslipped: Chilo Variety; olla, fragments from lots 8, 9, and 17.

Kauil complex at Tayasal (A. Chase 1983), but nothing clearly similar can be identified in Cowgill's descriptions of the Lake Petén-Itzá material; no sherds of Chilo were included in Bullard's collection from Punta Nimá, and the type was not identified at the Topoxté islands. At the peninsular site of Zacpetén, in Lake Salpetén, the Chilo group sherds included a few with a faint red painted decoration. Chilo was also present in Bullard's collection from Ixlú, and rare examples were noted at Negroman-Tipú (personal observation).

One of the most interesting aspects of the Chilo ceramic group in the Petén lakes region is that it shows clear continuities with vessels made in the twentieth century in the community of San José, on the north shore of Lake Petén-Itzá. Bullard, in fact, referred in his notes to the sherds of these Chilo vessels as "recent." There is a virtual identity between the forms illustrated here from Macanché Island and those of modern San José (Reina and Hill 1978: fig. 41a, b, d, and f).

Name: **Gotas Composite: Gotas Variety.**
Frequency: 28 sherds, of which 25 were from Bullard's excavations on Macanché Island, 1 from Ixlú, and 2 from Punta Nimá. Gotas Composite represents 5.1 percent of the sherds of the Chilo ceramic group in Bullard's collections.

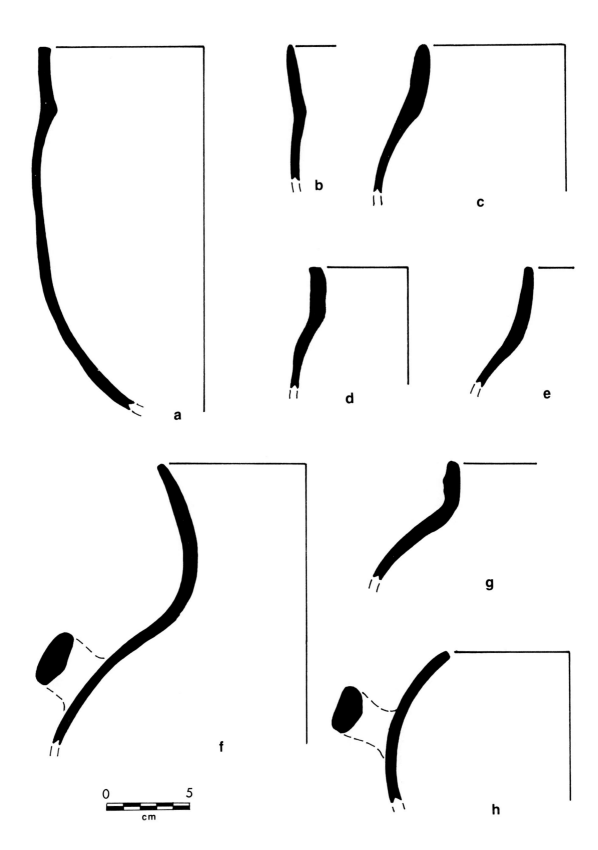

FIGURE 59. Chilo Unslipped: Chilo Variety.

Ware: Uapake Unslipped ware.

Complex: Dos Lagos and Ayer ceramic complexes.

Established: Present work.

Principal identifying modes: The Gotas Composite type is identified by coarse reddish brown paste unslipped vessels most commonly bearing spike appliqués, but also occasional impressions and/or effigy appliquéd elements.

Paste and firing: See Chilo Unslipped. Vessels appear to be incompletely oxidized in firing. Pastes are generally coarse and vary in color from gray with orange undertones, to dark gray-brown, and reddish brown (5YR 6/4). Interiors are almost invariably fire-darkened.

Surface treatment and decoration: Surfaces are not very well finished: pockmarks from calcite leaching, drag-marks of inclusions, scrape marks, and general irregularities of surface treatment and wall thickness are common.

Decoration consists primarily of appliquéd spikes. One partially reconstructible vessel (nine sherds) is an hourglass censer with three rows of blunt-conical spikes, 1.5 cm long, arranged in widely spaced columns (there probably would have been eight columns on the complete vessel) over the exterior receptacle. The interior shows deep scrape marks and is heavily fire-clouded; there is also fire-clouding on part of the exterior base. A vessel from Punta Nimá has a single vertical column of appliquéd spikes; this vessel is cylindrical rather than hourglass-shaped. Two sherd fragments are circular modeled appliquéd elements.

Five sherds are from vessels with a line of finger-impressed decoration. One sherd from Punta Nimá has very deep impressions directly into the clay (rather than into an applied fillet), and directly below the impressions is a spike appliqué. The impressions are approximately 1.3 cm apart, and the pairs of fingernail marks suggest that each impression was made by poking the clay twice. Another vessel, represented by two sherds, is very poorly made and has a line of irregularly spaced finger impressions (1.1 to 2.1 cm apart) roughly 1.5 cm below the rounded lip. A third vessel has a fillet applied 3.4 cm below the lip, and finger impressions on that are 1.1 to 1.3 cm apart.

Forms and dimensions: Three vessels with impressed decoration have mouth diameters of 10, 16, and 24 cm; wall thickness ranges from 5.5 to 8.2 mm. The spike appliqué hourglass censer is 17 cm high, with a 6-cm-high pedestal base. The mouth of the vessel has a square lip and a diameter of roughly 20.5 cm, while the diameter of the pedestal base is approximately 15 cm. Wall thickness is uneven, but varies from 1.1 to 1.4 cm.

An unusual censer sherd from Ixlú is a basal fragment that appears to be oval rather than circular in the shape of its pedestal base. One spike effigy censer from Punta Nimá is cylindrical rather than hourglass shaped, and has unusually thin walls at 4.5 mm. A small bowl or pedestal base (the lines of attachment of an upper portion of the vessel are unclear) has outflaring sides and a square lip, with a mouth diameter of 12 cm; the wall height is 4.25 cm, while the thickness is 6.2 mm.

Illustration: figure 60.

Intrasite references: The partially reconstructible spike appliqué censer came from Operation IH in lots 24 and 28 associated with Ídolos Modeled. In addition, one partially reconstructible censer with appliqué spikes and an incised flange came from "early" Late Postclassic debris in CPHEP excavation pit 3. Although spike hourglass censers are Terminal Classic in date throughout the Lowlands (see La Justa Composite, above), at Macanché Island the form is most commonly Late Postclassic. Two spike censer fragments were recovered from Early Postclassic lots.

Intersite references: See La Justa Composite, above. Besides the Macanché material, two censer fragments were included in Bullard's collection from Punta Nimá: a cylindrical vessel with appliqué spikes and a sherd with both spikes and impressed fillet.

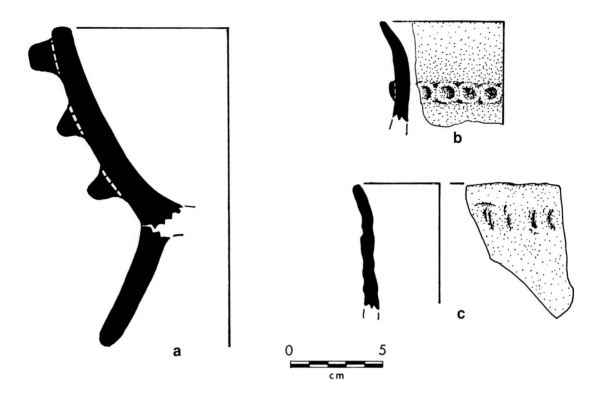

FIGURE 60. Gotas Composite: Gotas Variety.

An hourglass censer fragment was recovered from Ixlú.

Patojo Ceramic Group

Name: **Patojo Modeled: Patojo Variety.**

Frequency: 59 sherds, of which 52 were from Bullard's excavations at Macanché Island and 7 were from Punta Nimá. Patojo Modeled comprises 59.0 percent of the Patojo ceramic group in Bullard's collections.

Ware: Unspecified.

Complex: Dos Lagos ceramic complex.

Established: Present work.

Principal identifying modes: Patojo Modeled type and variety consists of effigy censers and other modeled or appliquéd forms in an unslipped fine-to-coarse-textured paste, which is usually gray but varies to light tan or orange-brown in color.

Paste and firing: Patojo Modeled sherds are manufactured of at least three distinct pastes, but because of the variability in the vessels, and the relatively small quantities of occurrence, these paste differences were not used as a basis for type or varietal classes.

SNAIL-INCLUSION PASTE: Nine sherds from Macanché are of dark gray, dense, fine-textured paste, identical to the predominant paste used in the Paxcamán and Trapeche slipped ceramic groups (see chapter 6). It is soft, dense, and heavy, with small snail-shell fragments as inclusions. Exteriors appear to be unslipped, and if they had ever been painted (as the modeled censers often were), no trace remains at present. One modeled snail-paste sherd from Punta Nimá was oxidized to an orange-brown color (5YR 6/5), although a gray core remained.

COARSE GRAY PASTE: Thirty-six sherds are of a coarse dark gray paste, relatively thick and heavy, with translucent or opaque white-to-pinkish calcite inclusions, sometimes rounded, sometimes with cleavage faces visible. Occasionally snail shells are evident in the paste. Surfaces are unslipped and vary within the color range of light gray or brown, but generally with orange undertones (10YR 7–8/3 to 7.5YR 7–8/2, 7/4). The colors are often mottled and the surfaces frequently are speckled with white, presumably from rehydration of calcite particles after firing.

ORANGE PASTE: Effigy censer fragments at Punta Nimá seem to be characterized by a coarse and sandy, better oxidized, more orange-brown or reddish brown paste, in the color range 5YR 6/4–5).

Surface treatment, decoration, and forms: Surfaces are smoothed; snail pastes are generally well finished, the coarse paste sherds being somewhat more rough textured. Vessels may have had paint or stucco applied to the effigy figures or to the associated vases, but except for faint stucco traces this is generally not apparent.

The censer vessels have modeled human figures attached to cylindrical vase forms, and these figures generally are elaborated with a variety of appliquéd pellets, feather-, flower-, and flangelike elements attached (plate XIII). Three faces have open mouths, and rather protruding, heavy lidded eyes with punched pupils (fig. 61a; plate XIV, upper right). Ears have been broken off, as have any indications of a headdress.

The four fragments of hands and five of feet are made with sausagelike rolls of clay, forming the fingers or toes, protruding from under a flap of clay. Wrists and ankles have encircling "bracelets" of ovoid appliquéd pellets set side to side (fig. 62). Feet (fig. 63) rest on a short thin slab of clay that ends just before the tips of the toes, forming the sole of the figure's sandals. One sandal has a V-shaped thong across the instep. A curious feature of these fragments is that on the feet, fragments of toenails are indicated by appliquéd rounds or ovals of clay; on the hands, only the thumbnail is so indicated, and the nails on the other digits are not represented.

A small round human head, which could have been the end of a ladle censer, is manu-factured of snail paste (fig. 61b; plate XIV, lower right). The face is extremely round and wide, with almost no forehead; the mouth is open, eyes are closed, and there are earplugs in the ears. The head was modeled over a small globular clay foundation, almost as though it was formed over a miniature jar. Broken at the base of the neck, the head is 4.5 cm high and 5 cm wide.

A small modeled bird's head, with large curving beak and round eyes, was found in the coarse paste. Birds' heads were placed on the headdresses of some of the figures in the Mayapán censers.

At Punta Nimá, the orange paste censers included a high broad fanlike feathered element, which may have been a headdress or an ornament placed behind the effigy figure (fig. 64). Five heavy bolstered rims, which appear to be of the vase portion of these effigy censer vessels, were found. One of these from Punta Nimá has a diameter of approximately 34 cm, and a thickness (below the bolster) of 1.45 cm; the interior is fire-clouded. Another rim has traces of stucco on it.

Illustrations: figures 61–64; plates XIII, and XIV, upper and lower right.

Intrasite references: All the sherds from Macanché Island were from Late Postclassic midden, and all but two of them were from Bullard's Operation IH, on the west side of the mound. In CPHEP excavations, only a few effigy censer fragments were recovered in Patojo Modeled; four of the sherds were of snail paste.

Intersite references: Human effigy censers are one of the horizon markers for the Late Postclassic period in Yucatán, and they are found in Petén as well. Effigy censers of Ídolos Modeled type (originally "Topoxté censer ware," Bullard 1970), in the distinctive Clemencia Cream Paste ware, were identified and described at Topoxté (P. Rice 1979), and this type is present at Macanché Island as well (see below). Many of the censers at Topoxté were not of this cream paste ware, however, but instead were of a heavier, coarser brown paste that would be classified

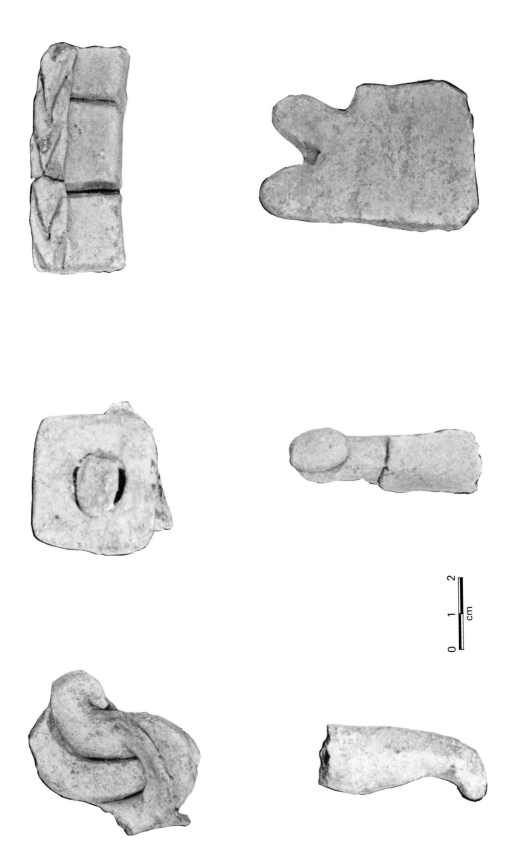

PLATE XIII. Patojo Modeled: Patojo Variety; censer fragments and adornos.

0 1 2
cm

PLATE XIV. Figurine (left) and Patojo Modeled heads; upper right, effigy censer; lower right, ladle censer.

here as Patojo Modeled. This classificatory category also includes the censer from Topoxté that is on display in the Peabody Museum in Cambridge, Massachusetts.

Besides the Patojo censers identified here in the collection from Punta Nimá, effigy censers are known from the Lake Petén-Itzá region (G. Cowgill 1963) and from Taysal (A. Chase 1983). No effigy censers were identified at Seibal, but the adorno fragments classified as Late Classic Pedregal Modeled at that site (e.g., Sabloff 1975: fig. 225b, d, e) are virtually identical to those appearing on the effigy censers in the Late Postclassic period. No effigy censers are known from Tikal or from Barton Ramie, but they are present at Negroman-Tipú (P. Rice 1984a).

Effigy censers are also reported in Campeche (Ball 1985), at Isla Cilvituk (Andrews 1943), at Tulum on the east coast (Sanders 1960), and of course in Chen Mul Modeled

type at Mayapán (R. E. Smith 1971: fig. 32e–pp). The widespread occurrence of these vessels throughout the Maya Lowlands in the Postclassic period suggests a widespread religious unity over the northern Lowland Maya area during this period (Sanders 1960: 245).

Their manufacture and use in ritual activities apparently continued well into the Historic period, and these censers probably constituted some of the "idols" that the Spaniards decried and smashed when they visited Maya temples. It is possible that with increasing Spanish control in Yucatán and Belize during the sixteenth and seventeenth centuries, the Itzá communities deep in the forests of the Petén lakes region came to be regarded by the Maya as the surviving centers of traditional religion and ritual. The fate of the manufacture and use of these effigy censers during this stressful time, and the relationship between them, the spike

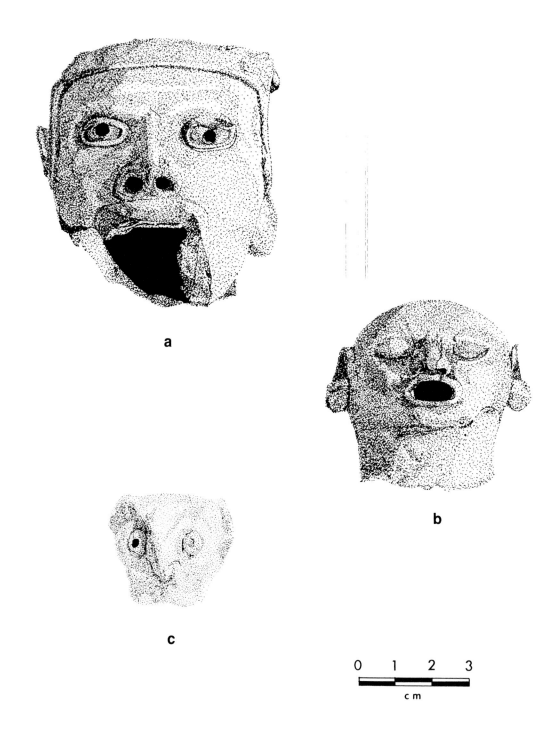

a

b

c

0 1 2 3
c m

FIGURE 61. Patojo Modeled: Patojo Variety. **a**, human effigy censer head; **b**, head of ladle
censer; **c**, bird head. **a** and **b** of snail-inclusion paste. Drawing by Jill Loucks.

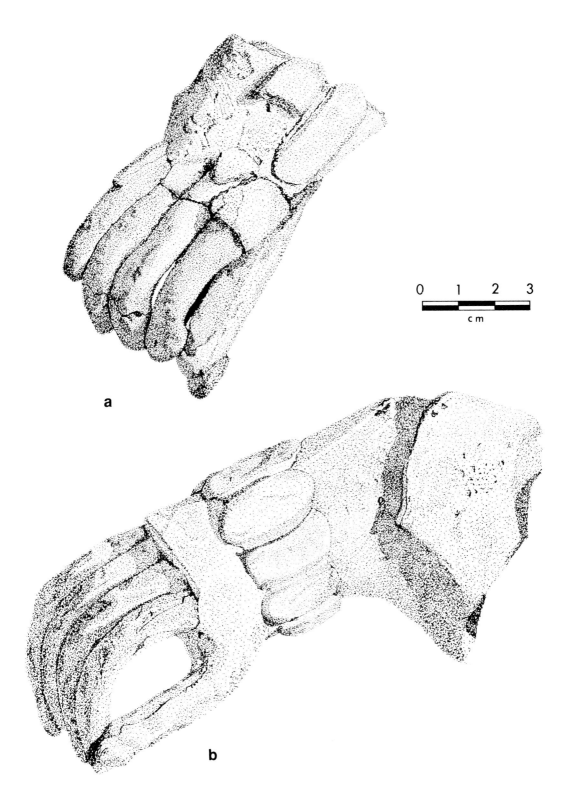

FIGURE 62. Patojo Modeled: Patojo Variety, hands of human effigy censers; note details of nails and bracelet. Drawing by Jill Loucks.

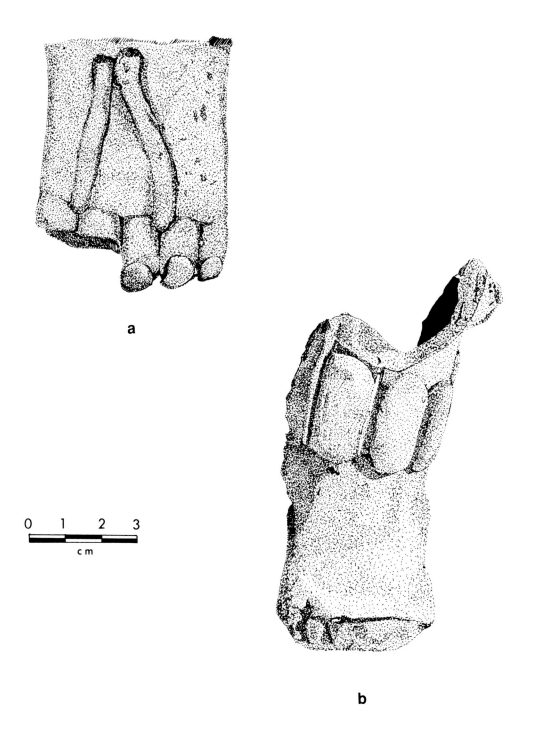

a

b

0 1 2 3
c m

FIGURE 63. Patojo Modeled: Patojo Variety. **a**, foot with V-shaped sandal thong; **b**, ankle with "anklet" of appliqué pellets. Drawing by Jill Loucks.

0 1 2 3
cm

FIGURE 64. Patojo Modeled: Patojo Variety, fan-like feathered headdress from Punta Nimá in orange paste. Drawing by Jill Loucks.

appliquéd hourglass censers, and the later "Lacandón type" hourglass censers (J.E.S. Thompson 1977) with appliquéd faces, is not at all understood.

Name: **Mumúl Composite: Mumúl Variety.**

Frequency: 40 sherds, of which 26 were from Bullard's excavations at Macanché Island, 4 from Ixlú and 10 from Punta Nimá. Mumúl Composite represents 41.0 percent of the sherds of the Patojo ceramic group included in Bullard's collections.

Ware: Unspecified.

Complex: Dos Lagos ceramic complex.

Established: Present work.

Principal identifying modes: Mumúl Composite vessels are noneffigy censer vessels characterized by a diverse range of modeled, appliquéd, incised, or stuccoed decoration, and especially flanges. They are manufactured of pastes that are thick, heavy, coarse, dense, and generally gray in color.

Paste and firing: See Patojo Modeled: Patojo Variety. The paste is generally coarse gray, with abundant calcite inclusions; snail inclusions and ferruginous lumps are occasionally present. A few sherds are of snail-inclusion paste, like that of the Paxcamán and Trapeche slipped ceramic groups, and a few of the Patojo Modeled sherds. Although many of the forms parallel those of La Justa and Gotas composite, the Mumúl type is distinguished by being thicker, denser or heavier, and generally more solid. In addition, surface colors tend to be mottled but slightly better oxidized to pale orange or brown (10YR 7–8/3, 7.5YR 7–8/2–4). Two sherds are of a moderately fine but very friable (almost vesicular) red paste, while one is an equally friable dark gray paste.

Surface treatment and decoration: Twenty sherds represent fragments of one or two vessels of probable hourglass shape with one or more encircling incised flanges on the exterior. Seven sherds represent flanges, apparently from a single vessel, which vary in breadth from 2.65 to 3.55 cm, and are segmented by deep incised grooves at intervals

of 3 to 4.3 cm. Five sherds that apparently belong to the same vessel have hooked spike appliqués, but owing to the fragmentary nature of the sherds nothing can be said about either the arrangement of the spikes or their relationship to the flanges. The interior of these sherds is heavily fire-darkened.

A pedestal base fragment, stuccoed on both interior and exterior surfaces, is of snail-inclusion paste. Three rim sherds are bolstered: one is of snail-inclusion paste; another is stuccoed.

One flat, probably vertically applied, flange fragment has an open-mouthed fanged creature, probably a serpent, depicted in groove-incising.

One sherd from Punta Nimá has a large thick impressed fillet, and appears to have been stuccoed.

Forms and dimensions: Four rim sherds are known from Macanché; three are the mouths of vessels and have diameters of 20, 24, and 30 cm; wall thickness varies between 9.5 and 14 mm. Two of these are bolstered (the bolster is 2.4 to 2.8 cm high), and one is extremely outflaring. The other rim is stuccoed. The pedestal base fragment of snail-inclusion paste has a diameter of 38 cm, the walls are 8.5 mm thick, and the base is 6.8 cm in height. It is stuccoed on both the interior and exterior.

The diameters of body sherds of the partially reconstructible flanged and spiked vessel or vessels range between 24 and 28 cm; thickness ranges between 9.5 and 1.45 mm.

A number of unusual vessel forms are represented by the sherds from Punta Nimá. Three sherds represent vases with vertical flanges on the sides. One vessel (two sherds) has a diameter of approximately 12 cm and a thickness of 7–8 mm; the flange projects out 4 cm and is perforated, presumably as part of the decoration. The shape of the other vessel cannot be determined; the flange is 2.5 cm wide, and four appliquéd balls, 1.5– 1.7 cm in diameter, were applied in a line.

One vessel from Punta Nimá is a cylinder, 20 cm in diameter and 1.0–1.2 cm thick; it had a thick interior platform, formed of

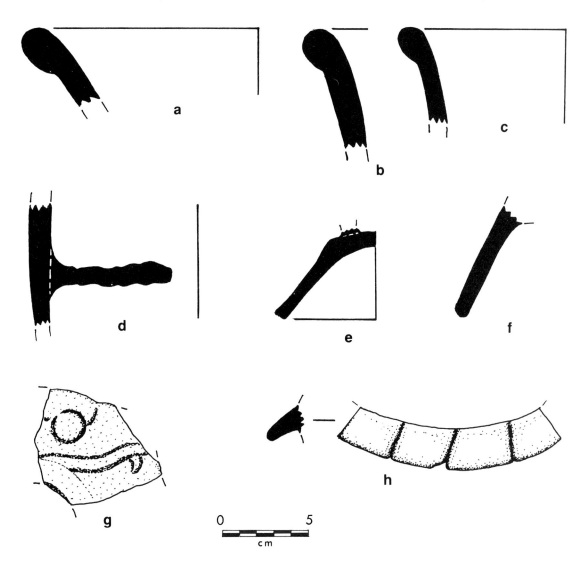

FIGURE 65. Mumúl Composite: Mumúl Variety, censer fragments. **d**, from Punta Nimá.

three broad coils of clay, with a central hole roughly 3.7 cm in diameter. The surface colors vary from dark gray to orange, but there is no clear evidence of burning.

Finally, an unusual large, heavy, square panel is part of Bullard's Punta Nimá collection. This panel, 17 by 15.5 cm in size, is 1.3 cm thick, and had been attached to a vessel the internal diameter of which was approximately 40 cm. The panel is scored with four horizontal lines 2.8 to 3.5 cm apart, and apparently an appliqué of some sort had been attached to it. The area of appliqué is marked by two dark gray ovals, one above the other, 8.5 by 10.5 cm in size.

Illustration: figure 65.

Intrasite references: All but two of the vessels from Macanché Island were from Late Postclassic midden material in Bullard's Operation IH. The other two were from the

PLATE XV. Ídolos Modeled: Ídolos Variety; censer fragments and adornos.

top of the mound. One partially reconstructible flanged censer of Mumúl Composite was recovered from CPHEP excavations in pit 3, in Late Postclassic midden outside the structure on the northwest corner of the mound.

Intersite references: See La Justa Composite above. Mumúl Composite censer material was recovered from Ixlú and Punta Nimá, in addition to Macanché Island.

Ídolos Ceramic Group

Name: **Ídolos Modeled: Ídolos Variety.**

Frequency: 49 sherds from Bullard's excavations on Macanché Island.

Ware: Clemencia Cream Paste ware.

Complex: Dos Lagos and Ayer ceramic complexes.

Established: The Ídolos group, type, and variety were described on the basis of the material from the Topoxté islands in Lake Yaxhá (P. Rice 1979:50–56). These censers were previously referred to as "Topoxté Censer" type by Bullard (1970).

Principal identifying modes: Ídolos Modeled type consists of appliquéd and modeled human effigy censers, unslipped, of a fine cream-colored paste. Red paint is occasionally present.

Paste and firing: Ídolos Modeled effigy censers are manufactured of characteristic fine-textured, cream-colored marly paste (Clemencia Cream Paste ware) that is associated with the red-slipped and polychrome types of the Topoxté ceramic group (see above). These censer fragments characteristically feel unusually light in weight relative to their mass. Thirteen sherds are smudged or fire-clouded on the exterior, but this fire-darkening is not visible on vessel interiors; two sherds are of light grayish paste.

Surface treatment and decoration: Surfaces are generally eroded and pockmarked, and it may be that the erosion and leaching of the calcite inclusions are responsible for the light weight and porous characteristics of the sherds. Fifteen sherds have traces of red paint or a red slip: this occurs on four sherds that are fragments of pedestal bases.

On six sherds the paint is present on one side of flat flange elements that have appliquéd features on the obverse side (plate xv).

No whole vessels were found at Macanché. The sherds that have been recovered include four fragments of the dress or kiltlike garment worn by the figure, showing a braided panel down the front and a beaded hem. One leg shows anklets and leggings. Another fragment shows a portion of a face, with punched holes for eye pupils, an open mouth, and ear plugs. The remaining fragments are from various portions of the censer receptacle or the attached figurine and flanges.

The materials from Macanché Island were incorporated into the original type descriptions of Ídolos Modeled (P. Rice 1979:51). Bullard (1970:281–285) gives a more complete description of the larger quantities of material he recovered from Topoxté Island in Lake Yaxhá, but his censer descriptions include vessels that would now be classified as Patojo Modeled.

Forms and dimensions: The fragments recovered are too small for estimates of height of the figures, and thickness is variable depending on the nature of the fragment. Bullard (1970:281) estimated that one effigy figure from Topoxté was 45 cm in height, but this censer would now be classified as Patojo Modeled rather than Ídolos Modeled type. In general, the fragments of the figures of Ídolos Modeled are smaller and more delicate than are those of Patojo Modeled, and I would imagine a height closer to 30 or 35 cm.

Five sherds, all with red paint, were probably from the bases of the censer receptacle rather than the attached effigy figure. Three of these are pedestal base fragments. It is also possible that they represent some other kind of slipped censer form that may or may not have attached effigy figures.

Illustrations: figure 66, and plate xv.

Intrasite references: All but three sherds of Ídolos Modeled from Bullard's excavations were from the uppermost levels of his Operation IH. Although this single excavation unit yielded nearly all the censer sherds, and particularly the effigy censer fragments, that

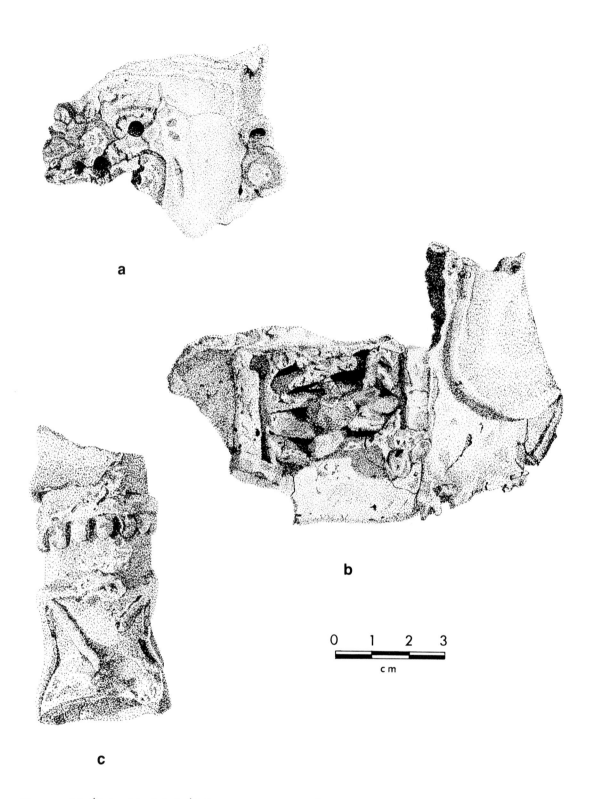

a

b

c

FIGURE 66. Ídolos Modeled: Ídolos Variety, censer fragments. **a**, fragment of a head and face;
b, lower skirted garment with braided front; **c**, lower leg with anklet, from an
unidentified location in Bullard's collections (possibly Topoxté). Drawings by Jill
Loucks.

were recovered in his operations on the island, it is significant that the Ídolos group sherds were recovered in different portions of that trench from the other material. That is, Ídolos Modeled, like Gotas Composite, was primarily from lots 24 and 28, the uppermost and latest levels of the excavation (28 being higher on the slope of the mound on the eastern half of the trench). The censers of the Patojo ceramic group, on the other hand, were recovered from the lower levels of midden primarily at the bottom of the mound overlying marl (lots 25, 30, and 35). One sherd of Ídolos Modeled was from an Early Postclassic construction fill lot.

Intersite references: Ídolos Modeled human effigy censers have been identified in El Petén only at Macanché Island and at the Topoxté islands. Fragments are present, but extremely rare, at Negroman-Tipú in western Belize (P. Rice 1984a). Ball (1985:74) has identified Ídolos at the site of El Chorro in eastern Campeche. See "Intersite references" for Patojo Modeled: Patojo Variety.

Unslipped Group Unspecified

Name: **Hubelna Unslipped: Hubelna Variety.**

Frequency: 3 sherds from Bullard's excavations on Macanché Island.

Ware: Unspecified.

Complex: Dos Lagos Late Postclassic ceramic complex.

Established: Present work (plus additional information from Negroman-Tipú, Belize).

Principal identifying modes: Hubelna Unslipped may be identified by its very coarse, open, gray or reddish paste and thick triangular bolstered rims.

Paste and firing: The paste of Hubelna Unslipped is distinctive, being very coarse, open-textured, and almost "vesicular" in appearance. Colors vary from dark gray to reddish brown.

Surface treatment and decoration: Only rim sherds are known in this type, and they exhibit no embellishment. Surfaces are generally smoothed, but preserve the coarse, open, "vesicular" character of the paste. The

rims are thick, elongated triangular bolsters, smoothed on the upper surface and slightly irregular on the underside.

Forms and dimensions: The only sherds known of this type are thick, heavy rim sherds, rarely with any portion of the wall remaining attached. Where a small portion of the unusually thin wall exists, the form seems to be that of a large shallow bowl or basin. Rims are generally too small to measure diameter, but a large size (well over 30 cm) is evident.

It is possible that these Hubelna Unslipped vessels served as comales, or griddles for toasting tortillas. This function is suggested by the shallow depth, large diameter, and the contrast between the thickness of the rim and body. More important is the "vesicular" quality of the paste: the open, porous texture would provide resistance to the thermal stresses of placement of the vessel over a fire for dry toasting (as opposed to liquid containment, which disperses the heat). Many of these characteristics are also to be found in modern-day comales, which are, in addition, extremely fragile (personal observation).

Other uses are of course possible, and in the absence of large wall sherds, the exact shape of these vessels is somewhat uncertain. It was first thought that these few large triangular bolsters at Macanché were flanges on censers, until the greater quantities of fragments from Negroman-Tipú suggested the possibility that they represented comales.

Illustrations: None.

Intrasite references: Only three sherds of Hubelna Unslipped: Hubelna Variety were recovered from Macanché Island; two of these came from Late Postclassic midden debris on top of the mound (lots 20 and 21), while one was from mixed material at the base of the mound (Lot 35).

Intersite references: Considerable quantities of Hubelna Unslipped: Hubelna Variety rim sherds were recovered at Negroman-Tipú, in western Belize (P. Rice 1985a). Although they were present from the Early

Postclassic on, they seemed to be most abundant in the Late Postclassic period.

Unidentified Specials

A fragment of a well-made bowl with a long cylindrical support (fig. 55l) could not be identified with any local Petén ceramic types. The paste is fine, dense, and gray in color; it looks very much like the paste typically used in manufacture of pottery of the Paxcamán and Trapeche ceramic groups, but lacking snail shells. A large manganese nodule was visible on one edge. The surface is well smoothed and lacks any trace of a slip, but it is possible that a slip could have been originally present and eroded off. Surfaces are mottled and rootlet marked; the color is approximately 7.5YR 7.5/2 (very light brown).

The sherd suggests that the original vessel was a relatively shallow bowl with an outcurving wall; there is a very slight basal angle on the exterior of the vessel, but the interior curves smoothly from wall to base. The support is broken, and it is not known how long (or high) it might originally have been; at least one vent hole was present, and the breakage occurred in a line with this orifice. The diameter of the bowl is approximately 18 cm, with a wall thickness of 6.4 mm, while the thickness at the base is 7.6 mm. The support has a diameter of 3.2 cm.

Although the paste of this vessel is similar to those of locally manufactured Postclassic slipped wares, the form is highly atypical. The closest similarities can be found in the polychrome dishes with outcurving walls and long cylindrical effigy supports in the Guatemalan Highlands (Wauchope 1970).

Part III

Ceramic and Nonceramic Artifacts from Macanché Island

CHAPTER 8

Ceramic Artifacts

IN ADDITION to the large quantities of pottery vessel fragments proceeding from Bullard's excavations on Macanché Island, small numbers of other kinds of ceramic artifacts were recovered from the island, as well as being present in his collections from Punta Nimá and Ixlú. These artifacts include miniature vessels, figurines, mold fragments, pestles, notched sherds and pellets, and miscellaneous objects, including worked sherds.

Miniature Vessels

Thirteen miniature vessels were recovered in Bullard's excavations at Macanché Island. These vessels were not all present in his collection at the Florida State Museum, and so some of the following descriptions are based only on his notes and measurements.

One vessel (fig. 67a) is a very small bowl with an everted lip. It is not clear if the vessel was slipped or not. The mouth diameter is 3.2 cm, while the height is 2.1 cm; the wall thickness measures 3 mm. This bowl is described as "dark gray paste, medium sand temper," with a Munsell color reading of 10YR 7/1. It was recovered in the Late Postclassic midden in Lot 35, Operation IH.

A larger hemispherical bowl (fig. 67b) had a mouth diameter of 8.5 cm and a height of 4 cm, with walls 5 mm thick. The color varied around 10YR 7/1–3, and the paste was also described as dark gray with medium sand temper. This bowl came from Terminal Classic Lot 41 in Operation IH. It is not clear whether or not the vessel was slipped.

A miniature jar with handles (fig. 67c) is 6.5 cm high, with a maximum body diame-

ter of 5.1 cm. The vessel has a relatively high and slightly outflaring neck, with two horizontal ring handles placed at the widest part of the asymmetrical body. The color is described as 10YR 7/3 (very pale brown), and according to Bullard's notes the vessel may originally have been slipped. This miniature jar came from Lot 7, in Operation IA.

Ten other sherds of miniature vessels were included in Bullard's collections at the Florida State Museum; six of these would be classified as Chilo Unslipped type on the basis of paste, color, and technological characteristics, while four would be Pozo Unslipped.

The six "Chilo" sherds represent four vessels, two of which are bowls: one gray bowl has a diameter of 10 cm and a wall thickness of 4.5 mm, another gray bowl, represented by three sherds, has a diameter of 8 cm and a wall thickness of 5.3 mm. A sherd of a flat dishlike vessel is orange-brown in color with an irregular outline; its diameter is roughly 8 cm, with 4.5 mm wall thickness. A jar with a relatively high outflaring neck varies in color from brown to fire-clouded dark gray; its diameter is 4 cm and wall thickness is 3 mm. These last two vessels were recovered from midden at the mound summit, while the others were from debris on the slopes.

The four "Pozo" sherds (fig. 57h–j) represent three vessels, one of which is a light gray (10YR 7.5/2) bowl with a diameter of 4.5 cm and a wall thickness of 4.3 mm. The other two vessels are ollas with short wide necks; diameters measure 9 and 10 cm, while wall thickness measures 5.0 and 3.7 mm, re-

201

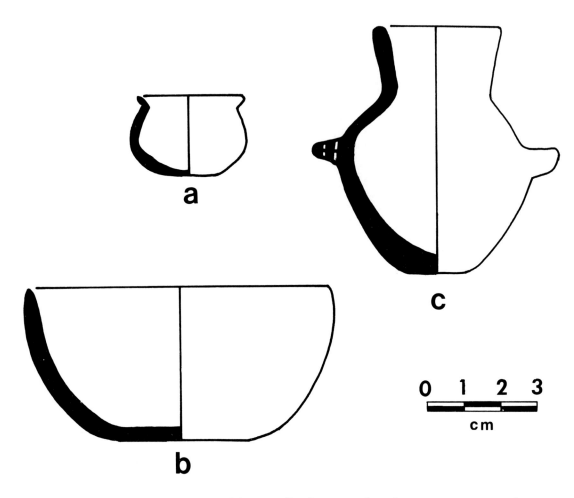

FIGURE 67. Miniature vessels, traced from Bullard's originals in his notes. **a**, Lot 35; **b**, Lot 41; **c**, Lot 7.

spectively. These sherds all came from midden debris on the mound slopes.

Figurines

Two figurine fragments were recovered from Macanché Island. One, from Lot 5 in Operation IA, was small and very eroded; made of gray snail-inclusion paste, it measured 11.2 cm in height (fig. 68; plate XIV, left). The figurine was made by impressing a thick slab of clay into a mold to form the face, arms, and costume. A thinner slab of clay then appears to have been added to form the back of the figurine, leaving a small open shaft down the interior of the figure, so that

it is, in effect, hollow. The figurine seems to bear some of the same general features of costuming as the censers: a flap headdress, earplugs, a necklace or collar, and beaded skirt, but details are obliterated by erosion. No traces of slip or paint are indicated; the figurine has the pinkish white coating that was commonly seen on severely eroded sherds of the Paxcamán and Trapeche groups.

A second figurine fragment is broken to such an extent that little can be said to describe it; rather than being a figurine fragment, it may be part of an adorno or effigy appendage on a vessel of some sort. It is a broken human head, of which all that is

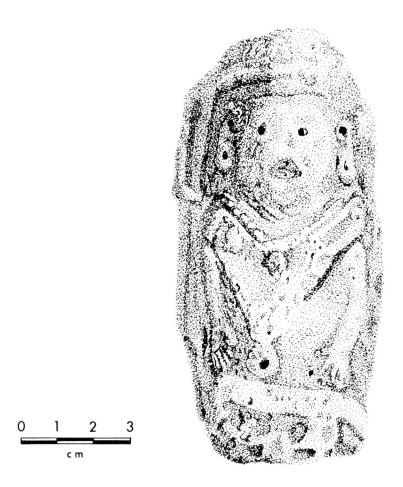

0   1   2   3
c m

FIGURE 68. Moldmade figurine, Lot 5. Drawing by Jill Loucks.

identifiable is the upper part of the face: the forehead and the eyes. Nothing is suggestive of a headdress. The fragment is of a light red/tan ash paste, and came from Lot 9 in Operation IB.

Mold Fragment

One fragment of a clay mold was recovered (fig. 69), which was intended for manufacture of a human face such as those found on the Postclassic effigy censers. The fragment is from the lower right portion of the face and includes half of the mouth, the chin, and the bulbous portion of the nose. This mold, which is fire-clouded on its exterior, was manufactured of the dense gray snail-inclusion paste similar to that used in making pottery of the slipped Paxcamán and Tra-

peche ceramic groups. The fragment measures 4.8 cm long, 3.6 cm wide, and varies between 8.5 and 13 mm in thickness. The mold fragment was recovered from Lot 21, which is a Late Postclassic midden lot from the mound summit.

Two other fragments of molds for Postclassic effigy censers were recovered in CPHEP excavations in the lakes area, one at Lake Quexil and one at Zacpetén, in Lake Salpetén. Molds for censers were also recovered at Mayapán (R. E. Smith 1971: fig. 66a1–5).

Pestles

Two effigy pestles (fig. 70) were in Bullard's collections, one from Lot 16 (mixed Late Postclassic) and one from Punta Nimá. These

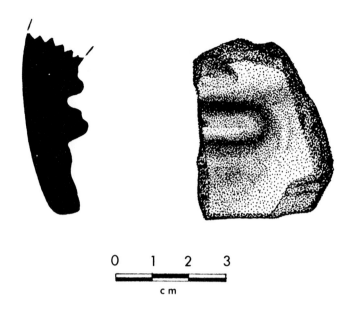

0   1   2   3
cm

FIGURE 69. Fragment of a mold for making the faces of Postclassic human effigy censers, Lot 21.

are cylindrical or slightly conical clay objects, varying from 7.1 to 7.4 cm in height; they have a gently rounded base marked with deep circular or oval punctations. The opposing end of the pestle is modeled into an effigy face of some unknown animal, the eyes and nostrils being punched or punctated, and the mouth indicated by an incised slash. One creature looks simian while the other looks more reptilian. The colors are light yellowish brown (10YR 6/4) and white (7.5YR 8/0).

Several similar artifacts have been recovered from Negroman-Tipú (personal observation). On one, the base was flat and lacked the punctations of the Macanché examples, and it may have been an applique adorno of some sort.

Notched Sherds and Pellets

Fifty clay pellets and worked sherds had rounded or oval shapes and notched ends (plate xvi). Nine of these artifacts are formed clay ovoids, varying in length from 1.65 to 3.0 cm and in width from 1.7 to 1.9 cm.

Forty-one are formed from potsherds by notching the ends and smoothing the sides; they vary in size from tiny sherds measuring 1.45 by 1.25 cm, up to relatively large artifacts measuring 3.92 by 2.73 cm, the average being 2.28 by 1.72 cm. Thirty of these objects came from identifiable pottery types, one of which (from an Early Postclassic lot) was Subín Red; three others were sherds of the Topoxté ceramic group, one was Trapeche, and the remainder were Paxcamán. One of the formed oval weights was of a fine-textured orange clay similar to that of Fine Orange pottery.

The weights of these notched pieces are as variable as their sizes. The weight of the formed pellets ranges from 1.60 to 5.88 grams, with a mean of 3.76 grams. The 41 sinkers made from sherds vary in weight from 0.98 grams to 12.62 grams, but the weights are clearly skewed toward the lower end of the range, with 32 of the artifacts weighing less than four grams. The mean of the notched sherds is 2.78 grams; the mean of the total set of 50 artifacts is 2.96 grams.

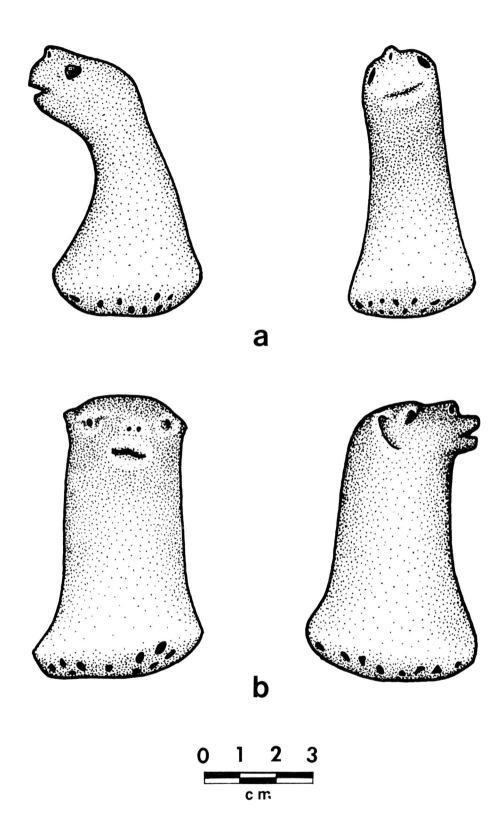

FIGURE 70. Pestles, traced from Bullard's original drawings. **a**, Lot 3 (Punta Nimá); **b**, Lot 16.

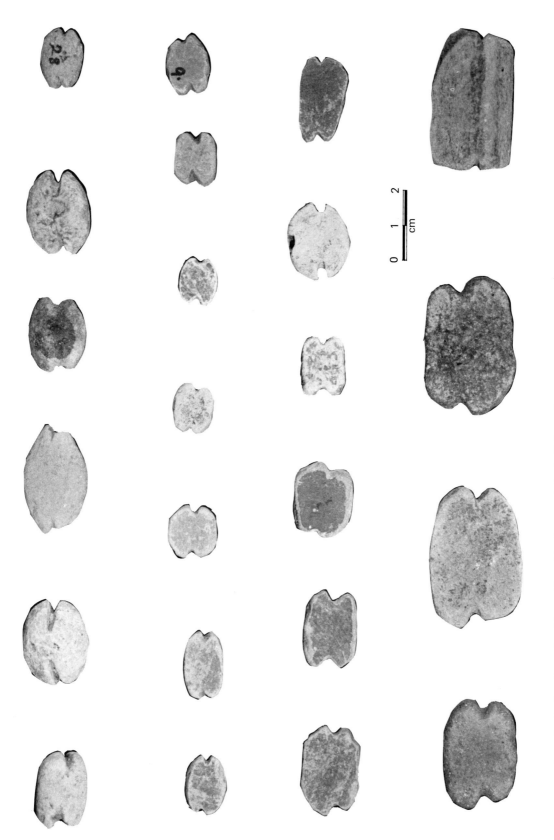

PLATE XVI. Notched sherds and pellets. Sherd in lower right is 3.8 cm long.

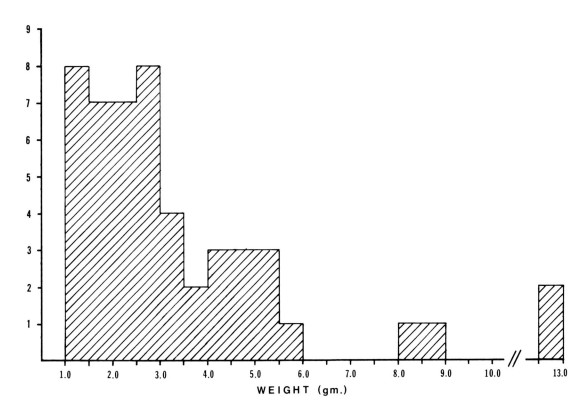

FIGURE 71. Frequency distribution of ceramic line sinkers at Macanché Island by weight (grouped into 0.5 gram intervals).

Figure 71 is a frequency diagram showing the distribution of the weights of these artifacts.

Two of the notched sherds in Bullard's collection were recovered from Terminal Classic lots (and are probably intrusive; see chapter 2), and one was from Early Postclassic platform construction fill. The remainder were all from the Late Postclassic midden, and were evenly divided by whether they came from the top of the mound or from the slopes. Most of them were from the "early" Late Postclassic deposit.

In CPHEP excavations on Macanché Island, 14 notched sherds were found; six were from Early Postclassic lots, while eight were from Late Postclassic contexts, and most of these were also mostly "early" rather than "Protohistoric." The CPHEP specimens range in length from 1.49 to 3.52 cm, with an average of 2.39 cm; in width the range is from 1.1 to 2.74 cm, with an average of 1.84.

These means are very close to the corresponding averages measured on the Bullard collection. Notched sherds and pellets were also widely found at the other Postclassic areas excavated in the lakes region. No weights are available on the CPHEP artifacts.

Notched sherds are present all over the Maya area (table 14), from Yucatán into Chiapas and even Tehuantepec, and are especially common in the Postclassic period (see, for example, Eaton 1976; Phillips 1979:13–14; Wonderley 1981:281–282). They are generally presumed to be items of fishing technology, tied as weights to fishing nets or lines; other possible uses are as loom weights in weaving, or as pendants. There is considerable variation in form in these objects, some having notches on all four sides rather than at the two ends of the long axis, and some (e.g. at Naco) may be grooved around the circumference or edge of the sherd.

Table 14

Comparative Measurements on Notched Sherd Sinkers in the Maya Lowlands

Location	N	Length range (cm)	Width range (cm)	Weight range (g)	References
North Coastal Yucatán	58	2.0–8.5	2.0–4.5	1–138	Eaton 1978
Lubaantún	4	2.2–5.9	1.9–5.0	8.5 –35	Hammond 1975
Barton Ramie	10	2.1–3.8	1.7–2.4	—	Willey et al. 1965
Seibal	11	3.0–4.0	2.8–3.8	—	Willey 1978
Cozumel	1,068	1.0–10.0	–	1 –36	Phillips 1979
Kakalché, Belize	119	1.5–6.0	1.0–4.0	—	Graham 1983
Watson's Island, Belize	280	1.5–5.0	1.0–4.5	—	Graham 1983
Negroman-Tipú	86	1.4–4.4	0.7–3.3	.85–13.0	Paine 1981
Naco, Honduras	3	1.3–3.0	1.5–2.6	—	Wonderley 1981
Macanché Island	50	1.4–3.9	1.2–2.7	.98–12.6	Rice (this volume)

As compared to the notched sherds from Cozumel, Yucatán, the artifacts from Macanché Island (and the lakes area in general) are small and light in weight. The specimens from Cozumel ranged in length from less than 1 cm to more than 10 cm, and 528 specimens averaged 6.6 g in weight, with a range of 1 to 36 g (Phillips 1979:2, 4, and fig. 2). These differences in size between the two areas suggest variations in the function of the sinkers in central Petén and in Cozumel. For example, Eaton (1976) noted that Maya fishermen use 1 g split shot or 3–4 g hollow lead weights for shallow water, and 54 g and 117 g lead weights for deeper water; the range of weights from coastal Yucatán sites corresponds closely to these modern data. The small sinkers in the lakes area fall at the low end of this range, doubtless reflecting their use in calm, relatively shallow water rather than the rougher waters of the coast, and as line rather than net sinkers. It is interesting that the 86 notched and/or formed sherds from Negroman-Tipú, on the Macal River in western Belize, have dimensions that are very comparable to those from the lakes: length—mean 2.2 cm, range 1.4–4.4 cm; width—mean 1.54 cm, range 0.7–3.1 cm; weight—mean 3.27 g, range 0.85–13.0 g (Paine 1981). These small, light-weight sinkers could only have been effective in areas where the river "pools."

It is also possible that some of these ar-

tifacts could have been used in weaving, as loom weights (see Kent and Nelson 1976) or as bobbins, rather than in fishing. This possibility is not unlikely given the reputation of Petén as a cotton cloth producing area in the early Historic period.

Miscellaneous Worked Sherds

Fifteen worked sherds were included in Bullard's collection; 14 of these were from Macanché Island. Two of the sherds, discs with central perforations, are probably fragments of spindle whorls. The diameters are approximately 6.2 and 5.6 cm, thicknesses 8.5 and 7.0 mm. The largest of the two spindle whorls is from Early Postclassic Lot 26. One sherd has an incompletely drilled central hole (a "spindle rest?"); rather more square than round in shape, its diameter varies between 3.95 and 4.48 cm, and the thickness is 5.5 mm. This sherd, and the smaller of the two spindle whorls, are from Late Postclassic midden lots. It is interesting that no specially formed clay spindle whorls were found at Macanché (as they were at Topoxté), although whorls of stone were noted (see chapter 10).

Seven other sherd discs have no evidence of drilling; diameters range from 2.6–2.7 cm (a Paxcamán sherd) up to 5.1–5.3 cm. One of these sherds is from Ixlú, another (slightly rectangular) is from Early Postclassic fill, and the remainder are from Late Postclassic midden debris on the island. These may have served as lids (see Garber 1984) or as "gaming pieces."

Three smaller sherds, all of the Paxcamán ceramic group, are chipped into roughly circular shapes but the edges are not ground and smoothed. Diameters range from 1.7 to 2.6 cm; these are all from the top of the mound.

One small oval sherd of Topoxté Red type may be an unnotched line sinker; its dimensions are 2.16 cm long and 1.47 cm wide.

One irregular thick oval sherd is of the Paxcamán ceramic group; the edges are smoothed, but because it is broken its complete form and possible function cannot be ascertained.

Two beadlike artifacts were in Bullard's collection at the Florida State Museum, both from Late Postclassic midden. One broken bead is oval in shape and made of coarse dark gray clay; it is 3.28 cm long and 2.08 cm in diameter, and the drilling hole in the center is 4.7 mm in diameter. The second bead is round, and made of a very fine textured orange-red clay; it measures 1.4 cm long and 1.58 cm in diameter, with a 3.8 mm drilling hole. In addition, Bullard's notes contain the description of "3 unslipped pottery beads . . . rather crudely made, not polished nor perfectly symmetrical." They measure 3.6, 3.6, and 3.2 cm in length; 2.0, 1.9, and 1.7 cm in width; and the diameter of the hole varies between 5 and 6 mm. These are all from Lot 35.

CHAPTER 9

Chipped Stone Artifacts

CHIPPED stone artifacts recovered during Bullard's excavations on Macanché Island were not saved for shipment to the United States along with the ceramic materials. Instead, they were measured, drawn, and photographed, and then discarded. The descriptions of the tools included here are quoted from Bullard's notes, and the accompanying figures are traced directly from his field sketches. No lithic materials were mentioned in his notes on the collections from Punta Nimá, Ixlú, and the mainland "center."

Chert

Seventy-one flakes and chipped tools of chert were counted by Bullard. In addition to these artifacts, two probable "caches" accounted for at least 723 pieces of chert, one cache consisting of "about 78 flakes" and the other composed of "550+ flint chips." Eight of the 71 chert tools were from Terminal Classic lots, five were from Early Postclassic fill, and the remainder (58) were from the Late Postclassic midden. Within this midden, most of the artifacts (40 of 58) came from the slopes of the mound.

Of the two caches, the smaller came from Lot 21 (Operation IE) in Late Postclassic midden on top of the mound, west of the structure. The only information available in Bullard's notes reads "about 78 flint flakes, probably a cache." According to his profile drawing of the pit, the cache was located at a depth of approximately 40 to 50 cm, and lay 50 cm west of a possible platform wall running north-south across the center of the pit (see figure 10). There is no information on the extent of the actual deposit or whether it

was associated with any distinct soil matrix. The cache was photographed (plate xviiа) and discarded; no measurements on the sizes, shapes, or other characteristics of the flakes were recorded. From the photograph, however, it appears that many of the flakes were fairly large decortication flakes, and this "cache" may therefore represent some locus of primary nodule preparation. No tools or obsidians are noted in association with this cache, although eight small projectile points and 27 flakes were found in Lot 17, the surface lot of this pit (see below; it should be noted, however, that Lot 21 comprised material from the western half of the trench only, while Lot 17 covered its entire extent, and there was no mention of finding the cherts in any sort of concentration in Lot 17).

The larger cache (plate xviib) is from Late Postclassic–Protohistoric Lot 24, in Operation IH, on the western slope of the mound. Bullard's notes read: "Deposit of 550+ flint chips, found just under surface next to 0 [eastern] stake of trench. Chips are about same size, smaller than the deposit in IE, ave. 2–3 cm across. Include 3 obsidian flake blades and 11 [chert] arrow points, mostly apparently partly made and perhaps rejects."

There is no information on the actual deposit itself, i.e., the area within which the chips were found or if there were any associated distinct soil changes. One obsidian core (see below) was also recovered from this lot, although it was not identified specifically as being part of the cache. In addition to the cache in Lot 24, large quantities of censer sherds were also recovered, particularly of the late Gotas Composite and Ídolos Modeled

A

0 1 2 3
cm

B

PLATE XVII. Chert caches, Bullard's original field photograph. **a**, Lot 21. **b**, Lot 24; matchbox in lower right is for scale.

PLATE XVIII. Chipped arrow points, Lot 17. Specimen in upper left is 3.8 cm in length. All are of chert except point in lower left, which is obsidian.

Table 15

Distribution of Chipped Stone Artifacts in Bullard's Excavation Units on Macanché Island

Period	Chert			Obsidian
	Points	Bifaces	Flakes	
Terminal Classic	–	5	3	7
Early Postclassic	2	–	3	7
Late Postclassic	23	5	30	46
Total	25	10	36	60

types. It is possible that there is some significance to the association of these censers with the deposition of the chert cache.

Aside from these caches, the cherts from Bullard's excavations on Macanché Island can be described in terms of three categories of artifacts: points, large bifaces, and utilized flakes (table 15).

Points

Twenty-five points were recovered, of which two were from Early Postclassic platform fill and 23 from the late midden. By far the majority of the points were from the upper levels of the "late" or Protohistoric midden deposit, with seven from Lot 17 (on top of the mound in Operation IE) and 11 from the cache in Lot 24 (Operation IH).

The eleven points in Lot 24, associated with the cache, are described as being only partly made. Four of them are side-notched, with round or straight bases (see plate XVIIb): lengths vary from 2.0 to 2.7 cm, and widths vary from 1.1 to 1.5 cm. Two points are "tanged"; one measures 3.9 cm long, 1.3 cm wide, and 6 mm thick, while the other is 3.4 cm long, 1.2 cm wide, and 3 mm thick. No measurements are available on the remaining five points in the cache, or whether the specimens are unifacially or bifacially flaked.

Of the points in Lot 17 (plate XVIII), Bullard wrote: "8 arrow points. 7 flint, 1 obsidian. Side notched. Base notched (2), straight (3), and rounded (3)." It is not mentioned if they were unifacially or bifacially flaked. Two complete chert points measured 2.7 and 3.8 cm in length, and 1.9 and 1.6 cm in width. Three other specimens had broken

tips: the estimated lengths ranged from 3.0 to 3.7 cm, and all widths were 1.4 cm.

Two large tanged points were recovered in Early Postclassic Lot 26. The smaller of the two (fig. 72a; plate XIX, near left) is described as "bifacial flint point. Well-flaked. Secondary retouch along edge." Measurements are length 7.1 cm, width 3.4 cm, and thickness 5 mm. The larger point (fig. 72b; plate XIX, near right) is "plano-convex. Secondary retouch along edges"; length is 7.5 cm, width 3.7 cm, and thickness 1.1 cm.

A point similar to the tanged points in Lot 24 came from Lot 14, and is illustrated in figure 72c (plate XIX, far right). The measurements given for this artifact are length 3.7 cm, width 2.1 cm, thickness 4 mm.

In Lot 25 was found a large "leaf-shaped blade of dark flint. Good flat flaking, with secondary chipping along edges. Bifacial." This point (fig. 73c), which measured 9.7 cm in length, 3.9 cm in width, and 6 mm in thickness, may be of northern Belize (Colha) chert.

Tiny sidenotched points are common artifacts in the Maya area in the Postclassic period, being noted at Altar de Sacrificios (Willey 1972: fig. 140a, b; 141), Colha (Hester 1982: fig. 3), and Naco (Wonderley 1981: fig. 43), as well as elsewhere in the lakes region including Topoxté (Bullard 1970:278; also in CPHEP excavations). They are typically unifacially flaked (it is not known whether Bullard's examples were unifacially or bifacially flaked), and may be manufactured from chert or obsidian. Besides these examples recovered by Bullard's excavations, three points were also noted in CPHEP excava-

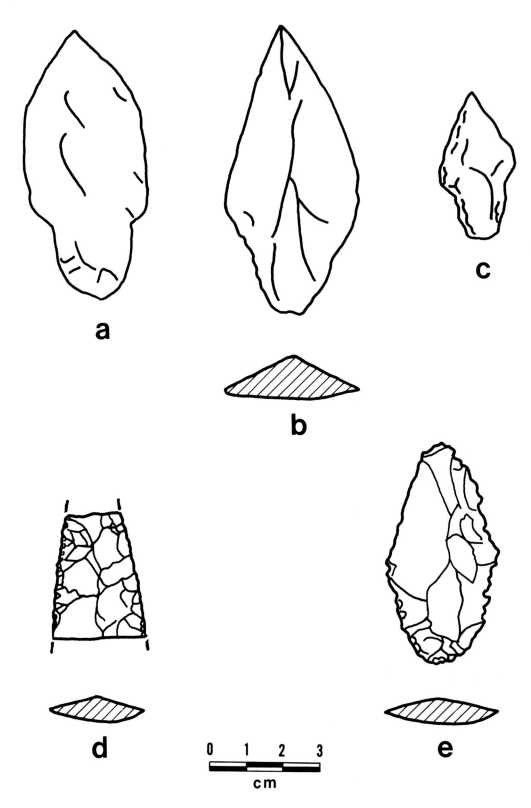

FIGURE 72. Projectile points, traced from Bullard's original drawings. **a–d**, chert; **d**, **e**, obsidian.

PLATE XIX. Chipped lance or spear points. Far left, obsidian, Lot 17; near left, chert, Lot 26; near right, chert, lot 26, length 7.5 cm; far right, chert, Lot 14, length 3.7 cm.

tions on Macanché Island, two of chert and one of obsidian.

The dating of the earliest appearance of these points is variable, but is a matter of some interest because it may relate to the beginning of use of the bow and arrow in Petén. At Seibal a small side-notched point is Terminal Classic (Bayal) in date (Willey 1978: 127), and at Macanché one tiny side-notched point of chert was recovered by CPHEP in Terminal Classic tierra blanca. At Colha, Belize, these points are dated to the early facet of the Early Postclassic (A.D. 900–1050). These dates correlate the appearance of the bow and arrow with the "Mexican" intrusions at the end of the Classic in the western area; Wonderley (1981:237–238) notes that these small points are not common in the Maya Highlands, but are instead typical of the Gulf coast and Central Mexican region. Regardless of the date of their introduction into Petén, they apparently continued to be in use throughout the Postclassic and during the period of latest occupation of the lakes area.

The larger "leaf-shaped" and "tanged" points Bullard noted correspond to the "lenticular" and "lozenge" shaped points dated to the late facet of the Early Postclassic (A.D. 1050–1250) at Colha (Hester 1982: fig. 3; see also Willey 1978:108–112). Six generally similar points were recovered in CPHEP excavations in late facet Early Postclassic platform construction fill, as well as in Late Postclassic midden on Macanché Island (three were from "Protohistoric" contexts in the area of Pits 5A and 5B). These points were also recovered by CPHEP in Postclassic contexts elsewhere in the lakes region (see Aldenderfer 1982, n.d.).

Utility Bifaces

This is a catchall category for the ten large bifacially flaked tools recovered in Bullard's excavations on the island.

Three objects were found in mixed Lot 10. One (fig. 73a; plate xx, near right) is a "pick. Percussion chipped, bifacial. Does not show use polishing." This pick measured 3.7 cm in length, 2.2 cm in width, and 1.5 cm in thick-

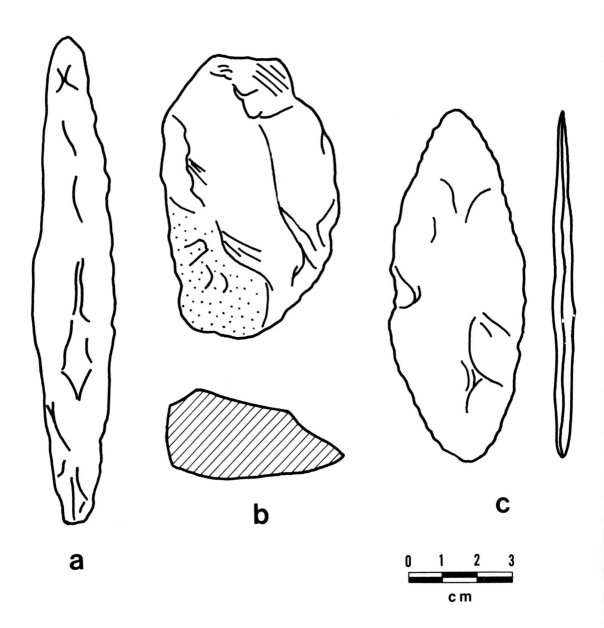

FIGURE 73. Chipped chert tools, traced from Bullard's originals. **a**, **b**, Lot 10; **c**, Lot 25, may be northern Belize zone chert.

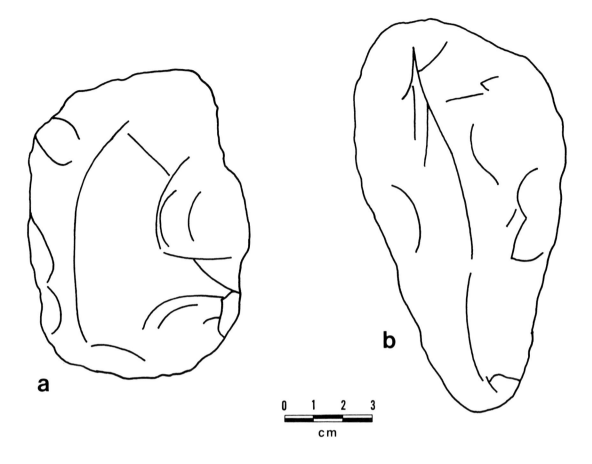

FIGURE 74. Chipped chert tools, traced from Bullard's originals. **a**, Lot 10; **b**, Lot 6.

ness. Another chipped stone tool (fig. 73b; plate xx, upper far right), not clearly described as a biface, was a "'chopper.' Flint. Percussion chipped. Plano-convex. Battering at sharp edge. Matrix on broad edge." The only measurement given is the length, 8 cm. The third object from Lot 10 (fig. 74a; plate xx, lower far right) is a "rectangular chipped flint implement. Percussion chipped, bifacial. Edges battered to shape, are not sharp." Measurements are 9.9 cm long, 7.4 cm wide, and 3.2 cm thick.

One item (fig. 74b; plate xx, near left) from Terminal Classic Lot 6, Operation IA, is described as a "core axe, percussion chipped, bifacial. Does not show use polishing." Measurements are 13.5 cm in length,

7.2 cm in width, and 3.0 cm in thickness. Although not strictly speaking a "biface," a "roughly chipped flint hammerstone" from Lot 6 (plate xx, far left) can also be noted here.

From Late Postclassic midden in Lot 14, a "fragment of chopper or butt of core axe" was recovered, but was not illustrated in Bullard's notes.

Three core axe fragments were noted as coming from Terminal Classic lots 38 and 40. Measurements on the two fragments from Lot 40 were 4.5 and 5 cm wide, and 3.0 and 1.1 cm thick, respectively.

A "bifacial quadranguloid chipped flint" object, perhaps similar to the rectangular tool with battered edges described above,

PLATE XX. Bifacial tools. Far left, Lot 6; near left, core axe, Lot 6; near right, pick, Lot 10; upper far right, "chopper," Lot 10; lower far right, Lot 10.

was found in Lot 7. This artifact measured 4.9 cm by 4.3 cm; no thickness was given.

In CPHEP excavations on the island, large bifaces were generally uncommon. The only items at all similar to those recovered by Bullard were three hammerstones, plus a chert core from Early Postclassic platform construction fill and Late Postclassic midden. Large bifacial tools—similar to the "choppers," "celts," or "axes" so common in the Classic period— were infrequent in Postclassic lithic assemblages of the lakes area in general (Aldenderfer, personal communication). These utility or "standard" biface tools are typically assumed to have had some function in swidden agriculture—for example, in forest clearance and/or as hoes—or in construction (see Stoltman 1978 : 21–25). Their notable absence in the lakes area suggests a major change in the technology of either or both of these activities in the Postclassic period.

Utilized Flakes

Thirty-six utilized chert flakes were recovered in Bullard's excavations on Macanché Island. Three of these were from Terminal Classic lots, three were from Early Postclassic platform construction fill, and the remainder (30) were from Late Postclassic deposits. Most of the Late Postclassic flakes (22) came from the slopes rather than the summit of the mound, but the distribution is evenly divided with respect to Late Postclassic versus "Protohistoric" contexts. There is virtually no additional information on these objects in Bullard's notes. One flake from Lot 6 is described as an "unshaped flake with use chipping on edge. Length 6.7 cm." Another one from Lot 6 is described as having secondary chipping.

Without the actual artifacts themselves, it is difficult to say anything about raw materials and styles of manufacture of the tools recovered by Bullard. It was noted that among the tools recovered by CPHEP on Macanché Island, the cherts from the early facet of the Early Postclassic were generally poor quality gray materials, while in the late facet Early Postclassic and thereafter there was a greater variety of raw materials (Aldenderfer 1982, also personal communication; see also P. Rice 1980 : 81). Brown cherts from the northern Belize chert zone were increasingly available in the lakes area in the Terminal Classic and Postclassic periods (P. Rice n.d. b), but there is little information in Bullard's notes as to whether any of his material consisted of this distinctive fine brown stone. His note that one well-flaked blade in Lot 25 (fig. 73c) is "dark flint" suggests that this particular artifact may be of Belizean chert.

Obsidian

Sixty pieces of obsidian were recovered in Bullard's excavations on Macanché Island. Among these items were three points or blades, one core, and two flakes (one utilized); the remainder (54) were "flake blades." Seven obsidians were recovered in Terminal Classic deposits, seven in Early Postclassic deposits, and 46 of the artifacts came from the Late Postclassic midden (table 15). Obsidians were found more commonly in the "early" Late Postclassic midden, and in the tests on the mound slopes, with only 12 specimens being from the "late" or Protohistoric period deposit.

One small sidenotched arrow point was found in late Lot 17 (plate xviii, lower left); it measures 2.3 cm in length, 1.0 cm wide, and 3 mm thick. Another point, described as a "lancet," was recovered from Terminal Classic Lot 11, but measurements were not given in Bullard's notes. The midsection of a "blade. Bifacial. Fine flat flaking with secondary retouch" came from Lot 8 (fig. 72d). It measured 3.4 cm in length, with a width of 2.6 cm and a thickness of 6 mm.

A large flake was used to make a point (fig. 72e; plate xix, far left), which is described as "plano-convex. Rather crudely shaped and flaked. Secondary chipping on flat edge." This artifact came from Lot 17, and measured 5.7 cm long, 2.9 cm wide, and 5 mm thick. Its "tanged" shape makes it similar to the "lozenge"-shaped Postclassic points from Colha described above (Hester 1982: fig. 3).

The obsidian core was found in "late" or

Protohistoric Lot 24, the same lot that contained the large cache of chert chips, although it is not specified whether this core is directly associated with the cache. The core was not drawn or photographed, but it is assumed that it is one of the exhausted prismatic or polyhedral cores typical of obsidian blade production. It measured 5.1 cm in length, and its width (diameter) varied from 1.1 to 1.5 cm.

Of the obsidian "flake blades" at Macanché Island, Bullard wrote the following: "Black obsidian, cloudy or streaked; few pieces are clear. No differentiation by level noted. Largest flake blades 10 cm long, 2.0 wide; typical blade: length 6.0, width 1.1."

CPHEP excavations at Macanché Island led to recovery of 41 pieces of obsidian: six were from Terminal Classic lots and 35 were from Postclassic contexts. None of these objects were prismatic core fragments. One was a projectile point, and the remainder were blades. The blades from CPHEP excavations were considerably smaller than those from Bullard's operations. In length the blades ranged from 0.79 to 6.8 cm, and only seven of them were longer than 4.0 cm. The average dimensions of 67 Postclassic blade fragments from the Lake Macanché basin as a whole were 2.79 cm in length and 1.17 cm in width. Similar figures obtain for Postclassic obsidian blades from CPHEP excavations at the other Petén lake basins, which have average lengths of 2.5 to 2.7 cm. In CPHEP excavations at Macanché Island, blades seemed to occur in smaller quantities in the upper 20 cm or so of the late midden (the Protohistoric phase) than in the Early and Late Postclassic periods. This may indicate changes in the availability of this commodity during Protohistoric times, resulting from stresses on long distance trade caused by Spanish contact, or it may relate to the changing economic status of Petén relative to other contemporaneous sites.

Studies of obsidians recovered by CPHEP excavations throughout the lakes area (P. Rice 1984b, n.d. b) have revealed that obsidian was available in this region in significantly greater quantities in the Postclassic period as compared to the Classic period. As in other areas of the Maya Lowlands, the principal supplier of obsidian to the lakes area in the Postclassic period was the Ixtepeque quarry located in eastern Guatemala (P. Rice, Michel, Asaro, and Stross 1985).

CHAPTER 10

Ground Stone Artifacts

GROUND stone items recovered from Bullard's excavations at Macanché Island were of four kinds: manos and metates, bark beaters, spindle whorls, and beads. As with chipped stone tools, these artifacts were measured, drawn, and photographed by Bullard, but were not saved for further analysis. In consequence, the following descriptions are limited to the data included in Bullard's notes.

Manos and Metates

Twenty-seven fragments of manos, metates, and related stone tools were counted in Bullard's notes (table 16). Fourteen of these were manos or mano fragments, 11 were metate fragments, and the remaining items were a "pounder" and a "pestle." By far the most common of the raw materials for these tools was limestone, which Bullard often described as "hard gray" limestone.

Of the 14 manos or fragments, 11 were of limestone, one was granite, and two were not identified as to stone type. The manos occurred in a variety of shapes and sizes (fig. 75, plate XXI), even within a single category of raw material. Of the eight limestone manos illustrated by Bullard in his notes, one is circular in cross section, two are triangular, one is rhombohedral, and the remaining four are roughly squarish or rectangular in section.

The single granite mano is likewise approximately square in cross section.

Two whole square/rectangular specimens of limestone measured 20 cm in length, while a shorter artifact, "4 sided with 2 sides used more than the others," measured only 14 cm in length. Maximum widths varied from 6 to 7 cm for the square-rectangular and triangular ones; a flat rectangular mano measured 5 cm in width. One rather large implement is circular in cross section and is described as a "'mano' or roller of hard limestone. Surface does not show grinding but is the naturally slightly rough surface of the stone." The length is 24.5 cm, and the diameter varies between 10 and 11 cm. A small mano of granite (fig. 75e) is square in cross section and plano-convex in longitudinal section; described as having "all 4 surfaces ground," its length is 12 cm and width is approximately 5 cm.

The remaining manos are broken fragments and lengths are unknown. The widths are in the same general range of 6 to 7 cm; one triangular fragment is smaller in section, its three sides measuring only 5 cm.

With respect to the temporal distribution of these objects, one limestone mano (no illustration in Bullard's notes) came from Terminal Classic "marl" deposits, the limestone mano with four worn sides came from the Early Postclassic, and the remainder of the artifacts were from the Late Postclassic midden. Only three of these late mano fragments were from the summit of the mound.

Unlike the mano fragments from Bullard's excavation, which were primarily made of limestone, the eleven metate fragments were of a variety of stones: three were of limestone, three of granite, and five of "scoria" or vesicular basalt. Bullard provides data on five metates: three of limestone and two of scoria.

The limestone metate fragments (fig. 76a and b; plate XXI) are relatively large and thick,

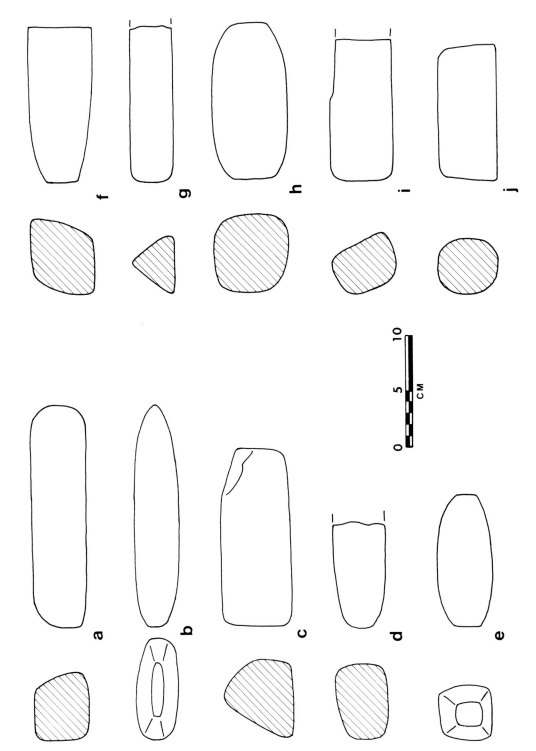

FIGURE 75. Manos, cross sections and longitudinal sections, traced from Bullard's originals. **a–d**, **f–g**, hard limestone; **e** is said to be granite; **j**, not to scale, is twice the size of **a–i**.

Table 16
Distribution of Mano and Metate Fragments in Bullard's Excavations at Macanché Island

Period	Limestone	"Scoria"	Granite	Other	Total
Terminal Classic	1	–	1	–	2
Early Postclassic	1	–	–	1	2
Late Postclassic	12	5	3	1	21
Total	14	5	4	2	25

measuring 4.5 to 8.5 cm in thickness in their grinding areas. The grinding surfaces of two, from lots 24 and 28, are deeply concave, described as "trough-shaped," while the third, from Lot 24, is shallower and described as "basin-shaped." This last (fig. 76a; plate XXII, left) is the largest fragment, and measures approximately 36 cm in length, 28 cm in width, and 8.5 cm thick.

Two of the metates of "scoria" or vesicular basalt (fig. 76c and d; plate XXIII) are rela-

tively flat slabs with small, low (probably tripod) supports. The fragments are smaller than those of limestone, measuring 2.2 to 2.6 cm in thickness. Because of breakage, no estimate of length and width can be given.

One metate fragment, described as "rotten granite," was from Terminal Classic Lot 40; all the remaining fragments were from the Late Postclassic midden, and all were from the mound slopes.

Besides the mano and metate fragments,

PLATE XXI. Manos and fragments. All are hard limestone except center specimen, which is said to be granite. For scale, see fig. 75 (plate XXI shows specimens [left to right], fig. 75a, 75f, 75e, 75h, and 75g).

PLATE XXII. Metate fragments, limestone. Left and center, Lot 24; right, Lot 28. For scale, see fig. 76a, b.

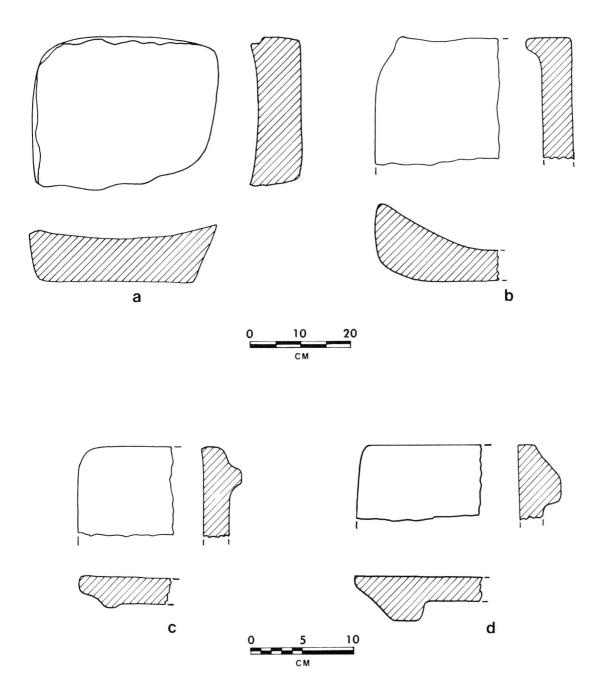

FIGURE 76. Plan and cross-sections of metate fragments, traced from Bullard's originals. **a**, **b**, Lot 24, hard limestone, **a** is 36 cm long; **c**, Lot 7, and **d**, Lot 10, vesicular basalt ("scoria"). Direction of grinding is in long (horizontal) axis of figure.

PLATE XXIII. Metate fragments, vesicular basalt ("scoria"). For scale, see fig. 76c, d.

two functionally similar ground stone tools, both of limestone, were noted. One is described as a "pounder?" It is circular in plan, and the "lower surface shows peck marks. Other surfaces smooth." It measures 6.3 cm in diameter and 4.3 cm in height, and came from Early Postclassic construction fill. The second item, from mixed Late Postclassic midden material, is a "pestle, hard gray limestone, same stone as used for many manos. Rectangular in section, ground to shape. Butt end shows pecking and polishing probably due to use." The artifact measures 9.2 cm high, with a cross section 4.6 by 3.5 cm.

Eight mano/metate fragments were recovered by CPHEP excavations on the island, including one of limestone, three of vesicular basalt, two of granite, and two of quartzite (or crystalline limestone?). Two of these were from the Late Postclassic debris around the structure in pit 3 (including one of vesicular basalt), and three were from late facet Early Postclassic platform construction fill (including one specimen of vesicular basalt).

The occurrence of basalt among these materials at Macanché Island is of some interest, in part because the footed metates in Bullard's excavations are similar to modern artifacts made and used in Highland areas. It is also interesting in light of the popular thesis (Rathje 1972) that basalt metates were, like obsidian, essential commodities for

maintenance of the Classic Lowland lifestyle, and they had to be procured continuously from the Highlands in order to satisfy these important needs. Vesicular basalt ("scoria") fragments have been found only in Postclassic contexts in the lakes area, and were not noted at all in the Classic period. The other raw materials used to manufacture these grinding stones can be classed as nonlocal, for example quartzite and granite, but even with their inclusion it is clear that roughly half of the grinding stones at Macanché Island are from local sources (limestones).

Bark Beaters

Four bark-beater fragments were recovered from Macanché Island in Bullard's excavations. One of these is from Early Postclassic platform construction fill, and is described as "edge grooved for hafting. One surface has grooves 4 to 5 mm apart; opposite side has grooves parallel with above spaced 2–3 mm apart and grooves are narrower." The length of the incomplete fragment is 6.5 cm, the width is 8 cm, and the thickness is 5 cm. The type of stone is not specified, but is probably limestone.

Another fragment of "fine-grained gray limestone" came from "late"/Protohistoric Lot 8. It is described as being "edge-grooved for hafting. Surface groovings on both sides.

0   1   2
cm

PLATE XXIV. Bark beater, Lot 25, showing different incised patterns on surfaces.

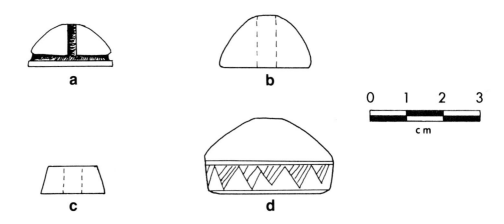

FIGURE 77. Stone spindle whorls, traced from Bullard's originals. **a**, Lot 6; **b**, Lot 41; **c**, Lot 26; **d**, Lot 20.

On one side grooves are at right angles to above, are only preserved in one corner where they appear to be more widely spaced than the above." The length of the fragment is 7 cm, the incomplete width is 3.6 cm, and the thickness is 4.5 cm.

A bark beater fragment of "hard white limestone" came from mixed Lot 25; as with the others, this fragment is "edge grooved for hafting. One surface [plate XXIV, top] has grooves 3–4 mm apart; opposite surface [plate XXIV, bottom] has diamond and dot pattern. Diamonds are 8 mm across." The length of the fragment (incomplete) is 4.5 cm, the width of the tool is about 8 cm, and the thickness is 4.0 cm.

From surface Lot 4 came a fragment of "fine grained gray limestone." Unlike the other specimens, the "edge does not show hafting groove. Only one side is grooved. Grooves are about 3 mm apart." The length is 8.3 cm, the width (incomplete) is 4.2 cm, and the thickness is 3.5 cm.

No bark beaters were encountered in CPHEP excavations on Macanché Island.

Spindle Whorls

Four stone spindle whorls were found at Macanché Island (fig. 77): two from Terminal Classic "marl," one from Early Post-classic platform construction fill, and one from the Late Postclassic midden. The two from Terminal Classic deposits are both of hard white stone and are roughly hemispherical in shape. One is plain, measuring 2.5 cm in diameter and 1.4 cm high, with a central hole 5 mm in diameter. The second is described as being of white "marble" and measures 2.3 cm in diameter and 1.1 cm high, with a central hole 5 mm in diameter. There is a single circumferential groove just above the base, and four vertical grooves around the top.

The Early Postclassic whorl appears to be a truncated conical shape, with a flat top and base. It is manufactured of "fine grained white stone," and measures 1.7 cm in basal diameter and 7 mm in height, with a central hole 5 mm in diameter.

The specimen from the Late Postclassic midden is larger, measuring 3.5 cm in diameter, 2 cm in height, and with a central hole 7 mm in diameter. It is described as being of "gray stone . . . with lightly incised hatched triangle decoration around edge. Decoration has 1 boundary line at bottom, 2 at top."

No stone spindle whorls were noted in CPHEP excavations at Macanché Island, spindle whorls being manufactured only from modified sherds. At Topoxté, however, spindle whorls were made both of fired clay and of stone.

Stone Bead

A fragment of a rectangular stone bead of "hard white limestone" was found in "late" Protohistoric midden. The measured length of the fragment is 2.7 cm, and its width is 1.2 cm; the drill hole measures 3.5 mm in diameter.

Chapter 11

Miscellaneous Materials

Worked Bone

Four artifacts made of bone were recovered by Bullard at Macanché Island. One was a bone awl from the Terminal Classic "marl" deposit in Lot 6 (fig. 78a). It is described as being "from split cannon bone. Point and surfaces handled are well polished." The length is 11.6 cm. A broken tip of a similar awl was found in another Terminal Classic lot, and measured 6.0 cm in length.

A bone tube was found in Late Postclassic midden. It was "made from a long bone. Marrow removed to make tube. Edges of ends well smoothed." The tube measured 17 cm long, the ends measured 2.5 by 1.7 cm, and 1.8 by 1.5 cm.

A bone disc spindle whorl came from Late Postclassic midden debris in Lot 7 (fig. 78b). It measured 3.4 cm in diameter, 4.0 mm in thickness, and had a central hole 7 mm in diameter.

Six pieces of worked bone were identified in CPHEP excavations, including two awls in Late Postclassic deposits and one needle in late facet Early Postclassic construction fill.

Shell

Large quantities of snail shells, primarily the large round *Pomacea* but also smaller amounts of jute (*Pachychilus*), were present in the Late Postclassic midden on Macanché Island, occurring in reduced quantities in Early Postclassic and Terminal Classic contexts. In addition to this material, which probably represents food debris, there were small amounts of worked shell and rare pieces of marine shell.

Bullard noted two pieces of "cut shell" in Late Postclassic midden lots, plus one "bivalve with a hole (drilled or made by parasite?) near hinge." Three pieces of conch shell were found in Late Postclassic midden, while one piece of shell described only as "burned" was in Early Postclassic platform construction fill.

In CPHEP excavations, one *Pomacea* shell with a circular hole cleanly removed, perhaps for a disc bead, was noted. Five pieces of marine shell were found, with distributions in all temporal contexts; one of these was an intact conch shell trumpet in Terminal Classic midden underlying platform construction in pit 6. A bead and "button" of indeterminate shell were also noted, these in Late Postclassic midden.

Miscellaneous Faunal Remains

Although Bullard counted over 148 pieces of bone, antler, teeth, and turtle carapace in his excavations, 177 pieces were identified by Mary Pohl (Florida State University) in the collection Bullard sent her (table 17). More than half of the bone reached Pohl lacking provenience information, unfortunately, but of those provenienced specimens (67), most were from the Late Postclassic midden.

Because of the skewed distributions, it is difficult to draw any conclusions about faunal exploitation at the site from the species identifications (table 18). Of the 19 Terminal Classic bones, five were white tailed deer (*Odocoileus,* which is generally present in greater quantities than the smaller brocket deer *Mazama*), and eight bones represented three turtle species. The three Early Postclassic bones represented only deer, but the

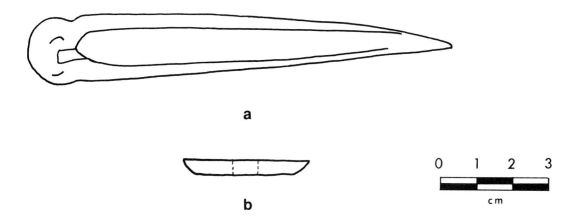

a

b

0   1   2   3

cm

FIGURE 78. Bone tools, traced from Bullard's originals. **a**, Lot 6, awl of deer cannon bone; **b**, Lot 7, spindle whorl, upper surface is smoothed outer surface of bone.

Table 17

Distribution of Faunal Remains in Bullard's
Excavations at Macanché Island

Period	Recorded in Bullard's notes	Identified by Pohl[a]
Terminal Classic	36	19
Early Postclassic	2	3
Late Postclassic	110+	44
Unknown	—	110
Total	148+	176

a. See table 18.

lack of other species can probably be attributed to the small sample size.

If the Late Postclassic faunal sample is compared with that of the Terminal Classic, the only meaningful observations that might be drawn concern the appearance of brocket deer and the presence of both white-lipped and collared peccary in the former assemblage. The relative de-emphasis of turtle in the Late Postclassic (and the absence of one species, *Staurotypus*) is probably more apparent than real, being a function of the lack of provenience data for much of the collection: nearly half of the unprovenienced bones represent turtle, and given the nature of Bullard's excavations at least 35 of them probably are from Late Postclassic midden contexts. One bone of domesticated dog was identified in Lot 7, but because of the modern disturbance on the island this could be a relatively recent intrusion.

A final observation may be made relative to the fauna on Macanché Island. Considering the importance of reptiles in the iconography of the Late Postclassic pottery (see chapter 5; P. Rice 1983a), it is interesting that only one crocodilian bone fragment was noted in the Late Postclassic collection, that one coming from the midden in Lot 25.

Human Remains

Two bone fragments from Lot 35 were described by Bullard as "probably human," and one human tooth, drilled through the root, was noted in Lot 30. These all are from Late Postclassic midden in Operation IH. They apparently were not among the materials sent to Pohl.

Other

Two pieces of red ochre were noted in Lots 19 and 22 on top of the mound.

Table 18

Faunal Remains from Bullard's Excavations on Macanché Island
(Identifications by Mary Pohl)

Lot no.:	7	25	30	5	27	22	16	19	9	28	10	24	34	33	31	6	41	40	38	No lot number	Species total
		Late Postclassic[a]											Early Postclassic[b]			Terminal Classic[c]					
White-tailed deer	3	8		1	[d]	4	1					4		1	1	4		1		26	54
Brocket deer		2			[d]	1						1	1							12	17
Sematemys			1							1							3	1	1	51	58
Chrysemys								1								1				3	5
Other turtle																1			1		2
W.-l. peccary	1	1										1									3
Collared peccary				1					1		1										3
Armadillo	1								1		1							1		7	11
Howler monkey									1												1
Ocel. turkey																1				3	4
Currasow	1															1					2
Tapir												1					1			1	3
Crocodile		1														1		1			3
Cervid						1				1											2
Domestic dog	1																				1
Paca																				2	2
Tayassid																				5	5
Lot total	7	12	1	2	1	5	1	1	3	2	2	7	1	1	1	9	4	4	2	110	176

a. Subtotal for Late Postclassic period = 44.
b. Subtotal for Early Postclassic = 3.
c. Subtotal for Terminal Classic = 19.
d. Deer present, species and number of animals unspecified.

PART IV

SUMMARY AND CONCLUSIONS

CHAPTER 12

Macanché Island and the Petén Postclassic

TWO EXCAVATION projects on the island in Lake Macanché, Bullard's trenching operations in 1968 and the Central Petén Historical Ecology Project test pits in 1979, have focused on the aboriginal platform constructed on the northern end of the island in Lake Macanché. Although the island itself is small, with a single large platform supporting perhaps only two structures, the construction and midden sequencing provided a great deal of information that is important for reconstruction of Petén Postclassic history.

Two features of the island's occupation can be highlighted with respect to the broader view of the Petén Postclassic. One is that the island shows apparent continuity of settlement from the end of the Late Classic period through the Postclassic period and probably throughout the sixteenth century. Second, with this long history of occupation, Macanché Island is one of the few locations in Petén to provide a stratigraphic basis for separation of phases of Postclassic period chronology and shorter temporal facets within those intervals. The stratigraphic dating at Macanché Island has been supported by radiocarbon and obsidian hydration dates.

Each period of Postclassic occupation poses its own particular problems for archaeologists, and these excavations and analyses at Macanché Island have by no means resolved all of them. Indeed, the data from these two projects have in some cases only thrown the issues into murkier depths. Nonetheless, it is useful here to summarize the findings of archaeological research on the island as a way of drawing attention to what is and is not known about the Petén Postclassic.

The Terminal Classic period, which I am dating here between approximately A.D. 830 and 950, is a particularly difficult period to comprehend in Petén. Macanché Island has a Terminal Classic occupation represented by a ceramic assemblage that is not only distinct from that of any other area in Petén, but distinct from other assemblages in the lakes area and, most perplexingly, different from that on the Lake Macanché mainland. One subset of the material in the Romero complex—red-slipped serving wares—shows particular ties in paste and form to the Pasión area, but there are no parallels within other ceramic categories, such as censers and trade wares (e.g., Fine Orange), to indicate that these relationships may have existed on a sustained basis.

There seems to be a significant technological continuity between the pottery of the Terminal Classic period and the Postclassic. The gray carbonate pastes and streaky slips, especially cream slips, of much of the Terminal Classic pottery show clear ties to later material within the Paxcamán and Trapeche ceramic groups. Similar continuities are not so readily apparent between Late Classic and Terminal Classic ceramics in the lakes area, however. Although the Terminal Classic inhabitants of Macanché Island appeared to have continued access to some volcanic-ash-tempered wares characteristic of the Late Classic in central Petén, polychromes are absent. Some continuities exist in polychrome decorative techniques between Classic and Postclassic pottery, including the use of a white underslip and a translucent overslip.

The Terminal Classic period seems to represent a series of relatively localized or regionalized developments throughout the southern Lowlands, with evidence of only diffuse ties to other locales. (This situation contrasts with Terminal Classic events in the north, in Yucatán, however.) In Petén, the demographic continuities between the Late Classic and Postclassic periods that are revealed by excavations in the lakes area suggest that this region served in some senses as a focus of resettlement (perhaps as a refuge?) during the economic and political upheavals at the close of the Classic era (see also D. Rice 1986 for a discussion of Postclassic architecture and settlement at Macanché and elsewhere in the Petén lakes district). There are some indications of discontinuities, however. The deposition of quantities of partially reconstructible vessels in Terminal Classic tierra blanca contexts as part of what seems to have been a major cleanup of the island coincided with remodeling of the earlier Late Classic mound on the island. These activities, combined with the distinctions between island and mainland ceramic assemblages in the basin, suggest that the occupants of the island were making conscious efforts at establishing separateness. Some sort of "renewal"/desecration ritual activity may be indicated along the lines suggested by Fry (1985) for sites in the vicinity of Tikal in the Terminal Classic period. One curious and inexplicable aspect of the Macanché Island Romero complex is the absence of censers.

The Postclassic occupation of Macanché Island is divided into two periods, the Early and Late Postclassic; the probable extension of that settlement into the sixteenth century and perhaps beyond is accommodated by the identification of a provisional Protohistoric ceramic complex at the island.

The Early Postclassic period, which I am dating approximately A.D. 950 to 1200, is still poorly understood. The early part of this

period sees the continuation of characteristic Terminal Classic pottery types in the Aura complex, plus the beginning of manufacture of characteristic Postclassic slipped and unslipped wares. The two important slipped groups, Paxcamán and Trapeche, are relatively poorly fired when they first appear in the sequence, with heavy fire-clouding evident on the slips, but by the late facet of the Early Postclassic there seems to have been better control of the firing of these wares. At the same time, the use of earlier Terminal Classic pottery types ends in the late facet.

The Early Postclassic period is very poorly known at Macanché Island, the early facet being particularly underrepresented and reconstructed from only a few thin midden areas probed by CPHEP test pits. The late facet is somewhat better sampled, with both CPHEP and Bullard excavations into the late facet Early Postclassic platform on the island. The pottery of the late facet reveals—perhaps in part because it is better represented in the collections—a broader sampling of types and forms than was evident in the early facet. Included among these late Aura materials are a few sherds of the Topoxté group, manufactured in the area of Lake Yaxhá some distance to the east, as well as some composite censer fragments.

Topoxté pottery is present in much greater quantities in the Late Postclassic than in the Early Postclassic at Macanché, an occurrence which has been the basis for the traditionally late dating of this ceramic group in Petén. The recovery of sherds of this group in late facet Early Postclassic construction fill at Macanché Island, together with the Early and Late Postclassic phasing at Topoxté itself (P. Rice 1986), indicates that any hiatus that may have existed between Terminal Classic and Postclassic occupation of the Lake Yaxhá basin was of very short duration. An intriguing but inexplicable observation on the role of the Topoxté Island site in Postclassic Petén concerns the fact that although appreciable quantities of Topoxté sherds were moved into Macanché and elsewhere in the lakes area, there is no corresponding presence of Paxcamán or Augustine sherds at Topoxté. The nature of the economic relationships or distributional mechanisms underlying this occurrence is unknown.

The Late Postclassic period is the phase of occupation of Macanché Island that is best known, at least in terms of excavation volumes. All of the CPHEP test pits and all of Bullard's trenches sampled debris from this period, which is represented primarily by a mantle of thick dark midden material over the entire mound. Large quantities of ceramics in this midden, particularly along the western and southern slopes of the mound, include quantities of partially reconstructible serving vessels as well as both effigy and composite censers.

There is virtually nothing that can be said about particular activity areas around the mound on the basis of either the pottery or other kinds of artifacts. These assemblages do, however, by virtue of innovations or dimensional changes, provide a very general picture of material technologies that is considerably altered from that of the Classic period. This has significant implications for understanding the nature of the Classic-to-Postclassic transition and the overall character of the Postclassic period in Petén. With respect to pottery vessels, the tripod plate or dish, which was a standard serving form since the Classic period, is considerably reduced in depth, diameter, and volume in the Postclassic period. At the same time, the manufacture and use of large slipped incurved rim bowls or basins ceased in the Postclassic. The typical narrow-necked unslipped "water jar" of the Classic period was no longer produced, the Postclassic unslipped vessels being widemouthed ollas that were somewhat smaller in capacity. A new ceramic form in Postclassic assemblages throughout the Lowlands was the grater bowl or molcajete, a small bowl with a deeply incised surface characteristically interpreted as having been used for grinding chiles. Another new form seems to be the comal, a shallow griddle for toasting tortillas; although these ves-

sels are rare at Macanché, and impossible to date, evidence from Negroman-Tipú suggests an Early Postclassic appearance (P. Rice 1985a).

Changes can be noted in other artifact categories as well. Net or line sinkers, formed either by modification of potsherds or by special manufacture of notched clay pellets, were widespread in Postclassic deposits not only at Macanché but all over the Lowlands. In chipped stone, the large "utility" or "standard" biface so common in Classic assemblages ceased to be found in the Postclassic. Projectile points were also transformed, being small "lozenge-shaped" projectiles or tiny side-notched arrow points.

There seems to have been a major change in subsistence production or in the social composition of the consuming unit, or in both, between the Late Classic and the Postclassic period in Petén. The smaller serving vessel sizes and general infrequency of large vessels for food preparation and storage suggest that domestic units of food consumption were smaller and perhaps less specialized or more directly involved in day-to-day production activities than in the Classic period.

The artifacts also indicate an emphasis on the production and collection of different kinds of food in the Postclassic as compared to the Classic, although the paucity of data on the Early Postclassic makes it difficult to postulate a temporal sequence. The Postclassic line sinkers register an increased emphasis on fishing or obtaining other kinds of aquatic resources, and this is supported in part by the quantities of turtle carapace and bone found in the Late Postclassic midden at the site. The absence of large chipped stone bifaces—assumed to have been used in forest clearance and/or as hoes—in the Postclassic period bespeaks a changed agricultural technology. Whether this is further argument for the inadequacy of the swidden model for Lowland Maya agriculture in general, or denotes changed circumstances peculiar to the ecological situation in the Terminal Classic period in the lakes area, is impossible to say at present. Similarly, the use of small arrow points may correlate with altered hunting practices, but the faunal data from excavations at Macanché are inadequate at present for examining this hypothesis. It is unfortunate that the artifact categories from the excavations cannot be directly associated with two economic pursuits in the Postclassic period in Petén, cloth weaving and cacao production. The notched sherds may have been used as loom weights, but a function in fishing activities is much more likely.

Evidence for ties between Petén and its neighbors is very tenuous in the Postclassic period. Obsidian (primarily from the Ixtepeque source), basalt, and other nonlocal stone reached the lakes region, but in small amounts. Likewise, virtually all of the pottery in the area seems to be locally made, and evidence of actual imports (such as Plumbate or Fine Orange) from outside Petén is very slim. Nonetheless, it is clear that Macanché Island and Petén in general were sharing ceramic styles that were fairly widespread in the Postclassic period in Mesoamerica. One example is the effigy censers, which were common all over the Maya Lowlands: mold fragments found at Macanché Island and elsewhere in the lakes region, together with a variety of pastes in this form, suggest that these vessels were manufactured locally.

The polychrome and incised decoration on some of the slipped pottery from the central Petén lakes region suggests a sharing of decorative motifs, arrangements, and stylistic identities between this relatively remote Lowland area and the more populous and complex Postclassic societies of Central Mexico. At the same time, there is a widespread display of certain themes, common to Mesoamerican elites, which focus on reptilian motifs and may play a role in legitimizing rulership (P. Rice 1983a, b). Within the overall context of Petén Postclassic political and economic relationships, it is significant that these motifs and styles are shared among the central Petén lakes (Macanché, Salpetén, Quexil, and Lake Petén-

Itzá), but they are not present in the Topoxté area, which has a very different stylistic repertoire. These variations in style at Topoxté, coupled with the apparently one-way ceramic exchange between that site and the rest of Petén, are not at all understood at present. They appear to be, minimally, a continuation of the regionalization evident in the area since Terminal Classic times. On the other hand, there is a curious dichotomization of ceramic styles *within* regions that is structurally comparable between regions throughout the Maya area. This dichotomization is evident in the occurrence of polychrome and dichrome painted decoration, painted and incised decoration, and the kinds of decoration appearing on red-slipped and cream-slipped wares, and it can be noted in the Late Postclassic ceramic manufactures of the northern Lowlands, the southern Lowlands (Petén), and the Maya Highlands. It is impossible, at present, to hazard a guess as to the significance of these distributions.

Ethnohistoric data suggest that occupation of the Petén lakes area continued well into the sixteenth and seventeenth centuries. Verification of this late occupation is nearly impossible in Petén, because of the absence of diagnostic materials that are exclusive to this period: the traditional Petén Postclassic ceramic groups, Paxcamán and Trapeche, appear to continue relatively unchanged into this period, and no examples of European artifacts—olive jars or majolica, for example—were recovered in the excavations by either Bullard or CPHEP in the lakes region. A few obsidian hydration dates from the lakes area, however, support the existence of populations in this area in the sixteenth century, and for this reason (as well as differences in frequencies of particular types) a provisional Protohistoric Ayer ceramic complex was identified.

At Macanché, as elsewhere in the other lake basins save at Topoxté, this very late occupation was associated with the presence of a distinctive, poorly made unslipped ceramic classified as Chilo Unslipped. Chilo Unslipped not only demonstrates some of the characteristics frequently associated with ceramic production in conditions of acculturative stress—a decline in overall technological qualities, and surface finishing in particular—but the forms in which it occurs are very similar to shapes manufactured in central Petén in the twentieth century. This ceramic category is the only indication of material continuities between Postclassic and modern populations in Petén; other possible ties may be identified in skull veneration, given the skull burials at some Postclassic sites and the practices of the twentieth century inhabitants of San José, Petén (Reina 1961:219).

At Macanché Island, Chilo Unslipped occurs in greatest quantities in the upper 20–30 cm of midden on the island, and is particularly common at the mound summit. The material from this location provides the basis for description of the Protohistoric Ayer complex, which is additionally characterized by the continued presence of Topoxté group pottery, a decline in decorated wares, a decline in quantities of obsidian, and the apparent continued manufacture of censers, both composite and effigy types.

Two "caches" or deposits of relatively large quantities of chert flakes are associated with Late Postclassic–Protohistoric occupation of the island, both occurring on the upper western slope of the mound. There is no information to tie these to other kinds of specific activities of the island's inhabitants, however.

The precise date at which the occupation of the Lake Macanché basin and Macanché Island ceased is unknown. The Itzá populations of Tayasal (Lake Petén-Itzá) were conquered in 1697 by Martin de Ursua, and in the following years there were major translocations of populations in the central Lowlands to the Lake Petén-Itzá area. The population of Tipú, in western Belize, was moved to this locale in 1707, and it is likely that settlements in closer proximity to Tayasal, such as at Macanché, might have suffered *reducción* somewhat earlier. Today, the Lake Macanché basin is the location of a thriving modern population, primarily emigrés from the Highlands, who are engaged in farming, cattle-ranching, and a variety of other economic pursuits.

APPENDIX 1

Sherd Type Frequencies by Lot

Lot 1

Operation: Punta Nimá
Context: None (collection purchased)

Paxcamán Red: Paxcamán Variety, plus Gen.	10
Macanché Red-on-paste: Macanché Variety	1
Augustine Red: Variety Unspecified	9
Pulpería Red: Pulpería Variety	6
Pozo Unslipped: Pozo Variety	5
La Justa Composite: La Justa Variety	1
Gotas Composite: Gotas Variety	2
Patojo Modeled: Patojo Variety	7
Mumúl Composite: Mumúl Variety	10
Tinaja Red: Variety Unspec.	3
Subín Red: Variety Unspec.	3
Chaquiste Impressed: Variety Unspec.	2
Pantano Impressed: Pantano Variety	2
Buff Late Classic Polychrome	1
Cream Late Classic Polychrome	2
Orange Late Classic Polychrome	2
Buff/Orange Late Classic Polychrome	28
Encanto Striated: Variety Unspec.	2
Polvero Black: Variety Unspec.	1
Cambio Unslipped: Variety Unspec.	9
Total	106

Lots 2 and 3

Operation: San Miguel
Context: None (collections purchased)

Paxcamán Red: Paxcamán Variety, plus Gen.	3
Picú Incised: Picú Variety	1
Augustine Red: Variety Unspec.	1
Buff Late Classic Polychrome	1
Pozo Unslipped: Pozo Variety	2
Modern modeled horse or mule	1
Total	9

Lot 4

Operation: Macanché Island
Context: General surface collection

Paxcamán Red: Paxcamán Variety, plus Gen.	1
Picú Incised: Picú Variety	1
Picú Incised: Thub Variety	4
Trapeche Pink: Tramite Variety, plus Gen.	4
Topoxté Red: Topoxté Variety, plus Gen.	1
Pozo Unslipped: Pozo Variety	1
Chilo Unslipped: Chilo Variety	2
Largo Red-on-cream: Largo Variety	3
Classic ash pastes	2
Miscellaneous unidentified	2
Total	21

Lot 5

Operation: IA, Macanché Island
Context: Late Postclassic plus Protohistoric, mixed midden

Paxcamán Red: Paxcamán Variety, plus Gen.	100
Ixpop Polychrome: Ixpop Variety	7
Macanché Red-on-paste: Macanché Variety	8
Picú Incised: Picú Variety	1
Picú Incised: Thub Variety	1
Chamán Modeled: Variety Unspec.	1
Unidentified Paxcamán Group Polychrome	4
Trapeche Pink: Tramite Variety, plus Gen.	256
Mul Polychrome: Manax Variety	22
Picté Red-on-paste: Picté Variety	2
Xuluc Incised: Ain Variety	5
Xuluc Incised: Tzalam Variety	1
Unidentified Trapeche Group Polychrome	27
Unidentified Gray Slipped Group	7
Topoxté Red: Topoxté Variety, plus Gen.	28
Unidentified Topoxté Group Polychrome	12
Pozo Unslipped: Pozo Variety	331

Chilo Unslipped: Chilo Variety	89
Ídolos Modeled: Ídolos Variety	2
Unidentified Postclassic Special	1
Tinaja Red: Variety Unspec.	2
Subín Red: Variety Unspec.	3
Achote Black: Variety Unspec.	1
Encanto Striated: Variety Unspecified	2
Classic ash pastes	22
Total	935

Lot 6

Operation: IA, Macanché Island
Context: Terminal Classic "marl" deposit

Paxcamán Red: Paxcamán Variety, plus Gen.	2
Trapeche Pink: Tramite Variety, plus Gen.	2
Xuluc Incised: Tzalam Variety	2
Pozo Unslipped: Pozo Variety	2
Daylight Orange: Darknight Variety	8
Tinaja Red: Variety Unspec.	13
Subín Red: Variety Unspec.	4
Harina Cream: Harina Variety	12
Largo Red-on-cream: Largo Variety	3
Payaso Orange-brown: Payaso Variety	24
Achote Black: Variety Unspec.	26
Cambio Unslipped: Coarse Gray Variety	111
Encanto Striated: Variety Unspec.	4
Classic ash pastes	59
Miscellaneous unidentified	77
Total	349

Lot 7

Operation: IA, Macanché Island
Context: Late Postclassic and Protohistoric
midden (mixed with fill?)

Paxcamán Red: Paxcamán Variety, plus Gen.	11
Macanché Red-on-paste: Macanché Variety	1
Trapeche Pink: Tramite Variety, plus Gen.	91
Mul Polychrome: Manax Variety	7
Xuluc Incised: Tzalam Variety	1
Unidentified Trapeche Group Polychrome	10
Unidentified Gray Slipped Group	2
Topoxté Red: Topoxté Variety, plus Gen.	7
Fine Orange Group Unspec.	1
Pozo Unslipped: Pozo Variety	233
Patojo Modeled: Patojo Variety	1
Subín Red: Variety Unspec.	3
Cameron Incised: Variety Unspec.	1

Encanto Striated: Variety Unspec.	1
Classic ash pastes	17
Miscellaneous unidentified	4
Total	391

Lot 8

Operation: IB, Macanché Island
Context: Late Postclassic/Protohistoric
midden

Paxcamán Red: Paxcamán Variety, plus Gen.	58
Ixpop Polychrome: Ixpop Variety	11
Macanché Red-on-paste: Macanché Variety	3
Picú Incised: Picú Variety	1
Picú Incised: Thub Variety	1
Chamán Modeled: Variety Unspec.	1
Unidentified Paxcamán Group Polychrome	3
Mul Polychrome: Manax Variety	3
Xuluc Incised: Ain Variety	2
Unidentified Gray Slipped Group	2
Topoxté Red: Topoxté Variety, plus Gen.	35
Chompoxté Red-on-cream: Akalché Variety	1
Chompoxté Red-on-cream: Chompoxté Variety	1
Unidentified Topoxté Group Polychrome	3
Augustine Red: Variety Unspec.	6
Pozo Unslipped: Pozo Variety	207
Chilo Unslipped: Chilo Variety	19
Tinaja Red: Variety Unspec.	9
Cameron Incised: Variety Unspec.	1
Achote Black: Variety Unspec.	1
Encanto Striated: Variety Unspec.	4
Classic ash pastes	25
Total	397

Lot 9

Operation: IB, Macanché Island
Context: Late Postclassic/Protohistoric
midden

Paxcamán Red: Paxcamán Variety, plus Gen.	162
Ixpop Polychrome: Ixpop Variety	31
Macanché Red-on-paste: Macanché Variety	1
Picú Incised: Picú Variety	1
Picú Incised: Thub Variety	2
Unidentified Paxcamán Group Polychrome	17
Mul Polychrome: Manax Variety	1
Unidentified Gray Slipped Group	2

Topoxté Red: Topoxté Variety, plus Gen.	68
Chompoxté Red-on-cream: Akalché Variety	5
Chompoxté Red-on-cream: Chompoxté Variety	2
Chompoxté Red-on-cream: Varieties Unspec.	12
Pastel Polychrome: Pastel Variety	1
Unidentified Topoxté Group Polychrome	7
Augustine Red: Variety Unspec.	2
Trapeche Incised: Decorated Interior Var.(?)	1
Fine Orange Group Unspec.	2
Pozo Unslipped: Pozo Variety	66
La Justa Composite: La Justa Variety	3
Chilo Unslipped: Chilo Variety	53
Gotas Composite: Gotas Variety	1
Tinaja Red: Variety Unspec.	6
Achote Black: Variety Unspec.	1
Encanto Striated: Variety Unspec.	3
Classic ash pastes	52
Sierra Red: Variety Unspec.	1
Miscellaneous unidentified	197
Total	700

Lot 10

Operation: IA, Macanché Island
Context: Late Postclassic and Protohistoric midden mixed with construction fill

Paxcamán Red: Paxcamán Variety, plus Gen.	33
Paxcamán Red-on-paste: Macanché Variety	2
Trapeche Pink: Tramite Variety, plus Gen.	95
Mul Polychrome: Manax Variety	15
Xuluc Incised: Tzalam Variety	1
Unidentified Trapeche Group Polychrome	8
Unidentified Gray Slipped Group	11
Topoxté Red: Topoxté Variety, plus Gen.	39
Chompoxté Red-on-cream: Akalché Variety	1
Chompoxté Red-on-cream: Chompoxté Variety	3
Chompoxté Red-on-cream: Varieties Unspec.	11
Unidentified Topoxté Group Polychromes	2
Slateware	1
Daylight Orange: Darknight Variety	2
Augustine Red: Variety Unspec.	2
Pozo Unslipped: Pozo Variety	58
La Justa Composite: La Justa Variety	2

Chilo Unslipped: Chilo Variety	2
Tinaja Red: Variety Unspec.	7
Subín Red: Variety Unspec.	8
Harina Cream: Harina Variety	1
Encanto Striated: Variety Unspec.	4
Classic ash pastes	33
Miscellaneous unidentified	191
Total	532

Lot 11

Operation: IA, Macanché Island
Context: Terminal Classic "marl" deposit

Augustine Red: Variety Unspec.	2
Pozo Unslipped: Pozo Variety	5
Daylight Orange: Darknight Variety	6
Tinaja Red: Variety Unspec.	136
Subín Red: Variety Unspec.	25
Harina Cream: Harina Variety	21
Largo Red-on-cream: Largo Variety	7
Payaso Orange-brown: Payaso Variety	49
Achote Black: Variety Unspec.	22
Cambio Unslipped: Coarse Gray Variety	384
Encanto Striated: Variety Unspec.	11
Classic ash paste	131
Late Classic special	1
Miscellaneous unidentified	9
Total	809

Lot 12

Operation: IA, Macanché Island
Context: Terminal Classic "marl" deposit

Paxcamán Red: Paxcamán Variety, plus Gen.	1
Trapeche Pink: Tramite Variety, plus Gen.	6
Tinaja Red: Variety Unspec.	2
Harina Cream: Harina Variety	16
Achote Black: Variety Unspec.	18
Cambio Unslipped: Coarse Gray Variety	30
Total	73

Lot 13

Operation: IC, Macanché Island
Context: Late Postclassic/Protohistoric midden

Paxcamán Red: Paxcamán Variety, plus Gen.	27
Trapeche Pink: Tramite Variety, plus Gen.	15

Xuluc Incised: Ain Variety	1
Unidentified Trapeche Group Polychrome	3
Fine Orange (Villahermosa Incised?)	1
Pozo Unslipped: Pozo Variety	35
Chilo Unslipped: Chilo Variety	8
Patojo Modeled: Patojo Variety	1
Total	91

Lot 14

Operation: IC, Macanché Island
Context: Late Postclassic midden

Paxcamán Red: Paxcamán Variety, plus Gen.	15
Trapeche Pink: Tramite Variety, plus Gen.	4
Unidentified Trapeche Group Polychrome	12
Topoxté Red: Topoxté Variety, plus Gen.	1
Fine Orange (Villahermosa Incised?)	1
Pozo Unslipped: Pozo Variety	4
Chilo Unslipped: Chilo Variety	1
Tinaja Red: Variety Unspec.	3
Chaquiste Impressed: Variety Unspec.	1
Miscellaneous unidentified	30
Total	72

Lot 15

Operation: ID, Macanché Island
Context: Late Postclassic/Protohistoric
            midden

Paxcamán Red: Paxcamán Variety, plus Gen.	14
Ixpop Polychrome: Ixpop Variety	2
Macanché Red-on-cream: Macanché Variety	3
Unidentified Paxcamán Group Polychrome	5
Topoxté Red: Topoxté Variety, plus Gen.	4
Unidentified Topoxté Group Polychrome	4
Augustine Red: Variety Unspec.	1
Pozo Unslipped: Pozo Variety	3
Chilo Unslipped: Chilo Variety	77
Gotas Composite: Gotas Variety	2
Subín Red: Variety Unspecified	5
Cameron Incised: Variety Unspecified	1
Encanto Striated: Variety Unspecified	2
Classic ash paste	13
Miscellaneous unidentified	48
Total	184

Lot 16

Operation: IB, Macanché Island
Context: Mixed Late Postclassic midden and
            platform fill

Paxcamán Red: Paxcamán Variety, plus Gen.	46
Ixpop Polychrome: Ixpop Variety	8
Unidentified Paxcamán Group Polychrome	3
Trapeche Pink: Tramite Variety, plus Gen.	104
Mul Polychrome: Manax Variety	21
Picté Red-on-paste: Picté Variety	2
Xuluc Incised: Tzalam Variety	1
Unidentified Trapeche Group Polychrome	6
Unidentified Gray Slipped Group	1
Topoxté Red: Topoxté Variety, plus Gen.	7
Chompoxté Red-on-cream: Chompoxté Variety	2
Unidentified Topoxté Group Polychrome	5
Augustine Red: Variety Unspec.	2
Pozo Unslipped: Pozo Variety	40
Tinaja Red: Variety Unspecified	3
Encanto Striated: Variety Unspecified	3
Classic ash pastes	25
Miscellaneous unidentified	175
Total	454

Lot 17

Operation: IE, Macanché Island
Complex: Late Postclassic/Protohistoric
            midden

Paxcamán Red: Paxcamán Variety, plus Gen.	49
Ixpop Polychrome: Ixpop Variety	6
Picú Incised: Thub Variety	1
Unidentified Paxcamán Group Polychrome	2
Trapeche Pink: Tramite Variety, plus Gen.	2
Topoxté Red: Topoxté Variety, plus Gen.	34
Chompoxté Red-on-cream: Chompoxté Variety	1
Chompoxté Red-on-cream: Varieties Unspec.	12
Unidentified Topoxté Group Polychrome	6
Dulces Incised: Dulces Variety	1
Fine Gray (Poité Incised?)	1
Pozo Unslipped: Pozo Variety	22
Chilo Unslipped: Chilo Variety	100
Encanto Striated: Variety Unspec.	4
Cambio Unslipped: Variety Unspec.	1
Classic ash pastes	16
Miscellaneous unidentified	92
Total	350

Lot 18

Operation: IF, Macanché Island
Complex: Late Postclassic/Protohistoric
          midden

Paxcamán Red: Paxcamán Variety, plus Gen.	15
Macanché Red-on-paste: Macanché Variety	2
Mul Polychrome: Manax Variety	1
Unidentified Gray Slipped Group	3
Augustine Red: Variety Unspec.	1
Pozo Unslipped: Pozo Variety	4
Chilo Unslipped: Chilo Variety	58
Tinaja Red: Variety Unspec.	1
Classic ash pastes	1
Miscellaneous unidentified	19
Total	105

Lot 19

Operation: IG, Macanché Island
Context: Late Postclassic/Protohistoric
          midden

Paxcamán Red: Paxcamán Variety, plus Gen.	108
Ixpop Polychrome: Ixpop Variety	23
Sacá Polychrome: Sacá Variety	4
Macanché Red-on-paste: Macanché Variety	1
Picú Incised: Picú Variety	1
Unidentified Paxcamán Group Polychrome	2
Trapeche Pink: Tramite Variety, plus Gen.	7
Unidentified Gray Slipped Group	2
Topoxté Red: Topoxté Variety, plus Gen.	8
Chompoxté Red-on-cream: Variety Unspec.	1
Unidentified Topoxté Group Polychrome	2
Augustine Red: Variety Unspec.	1
Pozo Unslipped: Pozo Variety	32
Chilo Unslipped: Chilo Variety	20
Gotas Composite: Gotas Variety	1
Tinaja Red: Variety Unspec.	9
Encanto Striated: Variety Unspec.	3
Classic ash paste	13
Miscellaneous unidentified	368
Total	606

Lot 20

Operation: IG, Macanché Island
Context: Late Postclassic midden

Paxcamán Red: Paxcamán Variety, plus Gen.	134
Ixpop Polychrome: Ixpop Variety	16
Sacá Polychrome: Sacá Variety	4

Picú Incised: Thub Variety	4
Chamán Modeled: Variety Unspec.	1
Unidentified Paxcamán Group Polychrome	2
Trapeche Pink: Tramite Variety, plus Gen.	7
Xuluc Incised: Tzalam Variety	1
Topoxté Red: Topoxté Variety, plus Gen.	1
Augustine Red: Variety Unspec.	17
Fine Orange Group Unspec.	2
Pozo Unslipped: Pozo Variety	59
Chilo Unslipped: Chilo Variety	2
Hubelna Unslipped: Hubelna Variety	1
Tinaja Red: Variety Unspec.	14
Subín Red: Variety Unspec.	4
Cameron Incised: Variety Unspec.	2
Harina Cream: Harina Variety	9
Encanto Striated: Variety Unspec.	8
Classic Polychrome	2
Classic ash pastes	176
Miscellaneous unidentified	330
Total	796

Lot 21

Operation: IE, Macanché Island
Complex: Late Postclassic midden

Paxcamán Red: Paxcamán Variety, plus Gen.	96
Ixpop Polychrome: Ixpop Variety	29
Sacá Polychrome: Sacá Variety	5
Picú Incised: Picú Variety	1
Picú Incised: Thub Variety	2
Unidentified Paxcamán Group Polychrome	5
Trapeche Pink: Tramite Variety, plus Gen.	5
Mul Polychrome: Manax Variety	1
Unidentified Gray Slipped Group	3
Topoxté Red: Topoxté Variety, plus Gen.	17
Pastel Polychrome: Pastel Variety	1
Chompoxté Red-on-cream: Akalché Variety	3
Chompoxté Red-on-cream: Chompoxté Variety	4
Chompoxté Red-on-cream: Varieties Unspec.	5
Augustine Red: Variety Unspec.	1
Pozo Unslipped: Pozo Variety	140
Hubelna Unslipped: Hubelna Variety	1
Tinaja Red: Variety Unspec.	3
Subín Red: Variety Unspec.	2
Achote Black: Variety Unspec.	1
Classic Polychrome	1
Classic ash pastes	23
Miscellaneous unidentified	1
Total	350

Lot 22

Operation: IF, Macanché Island
Complex: Late Postclassic midden

Paxcamán Red: Paxcamán Variety, plus Gen.	44
Ixpop Polychrome: Ixpop Variety	52
Sacá Polychrome: Sacá Variety	1
Picú Incised: Picú Variety	1
Picú Incised: Thub Variety	1
Unidentified Paxcamán Group Polychrome	6
Trapeche Pink: Tramite Variety, plus Gen.	1
Unidentified Gray Slipped Group	1
Topoxté Red: Topoxté Variety, plus Gen.	2
Chompoxté Red-on-cream: Varieties Unspec.	2
Unidentified Topoxté Group Polychrome	1
Augustine Red: Variety Unspec.	3
Pozo Unslipped: Pozo Variety	26
Chilo Unslipped: Chilo Variety	19
Encanto Striated: Variety Unspec.	3
Classic ash pastes	18
Miscellaneous unidentified	291
Total	472

Lot 23

Operation: ID, Macanché Island
Context: Late Postclassic midden

Paxcamán Red: Paxcamán Variety, plus Gen.	9
Ixpop Polychrome: Ixpop Variety	3
Picú Incised: Thub Variety	2
Unidentified Paxcamán Group Polychrome	3
Unidentified Gray Slipped Group	4
Topoxté Red: Topoxté Variety, plus Gen.	3
Chompoxté Red-on-cream: Chompoxté Variety	3
Chompoxté Red-on-cream: Variety Unspec.	2
Pozo Unslipped: Pozo Variety	11
Tinaja Red: Variety Unspec.	1
Classic Polychrome	1
Cambio Unslipped: Variety Unspec.	1
Encanto Striated: Variety Unspec.	2
Classic ash pastes	5
Miscellaneous unidentified	44
Total	94

Lot 24

Operation: IH, Macanché Island
Context: Late Postclassic/Protohistoric midden

Paxcamán Red: Paxcamán Variety, plus Gen.	44
Ixpop Polychrome: Ixpop Variety	3
Macanché Red-on-paste: Macanché Variety	2
Unidentified Paxcamán Group Polychrome	4
Trapeche Pink: Tramite Variety, plus Gen.	40
Xuluc Incised: Ain Variety	2
Unidentified Trapeche Group Polychrome	2
Unidentified Gray Slipped Group	2
Topoxté Red: Topoxté Variety, plus Gen.	60
Unidentified Topoxté Group Polychromes	10
Augustine Red: Variety Unspec.	1
Pozo Unslipped: Pozo Variety	76
La Justa Composite: La Justa Variety	16
Chilo Unslipped: Chilo Variety	42
Gotas Composite: Gotas Variety	14
Patojo Modeled: Patojo Variety	1
Ídolos Modeled: Ídolos Variety	34
Tinaja Red: Variety Unspec.	2
Subín Red: Variety Unspec.	1
Harina Cream: Harina Variety	1
Cambio Unslipped: Variety Unspec.	1
Encanto Striated: Variety Unspec.	1
Classic ash pastes	32
Miscellaneous unidentified	153
Total	544

Lot 25

Operation: IH, Macanché Island
Context: Late Postclassic mixed midden

Paxcamán Red: Paxcamán Variety, plus Gen.	71
Ixpop Polychrome: Ixpop Variety	7
Unidentified Paxcamán Group Polychrome	1
Trapeche Pink: Tramite Variety, plus Gen.	329
Mul Polychrome: Manax Variety	48
Picté Red-on-paste: Picté Variety	2
Xuluc Incised: Ain Variety	5
Xuluc Incised: Tzalam Variety	8
Unidentified Trapeche Group Polychrome	61
Unidentified Gray Slipped Group	5
Topoxté Red: Topoxté Variety, plus Gen.	28
Chompoxté Red-on-cream: Chompoxté Variety	1
Chompoxté Red-on-cream: Variety Unspec.	1
Unidentified Topoxté Group Polychrome	6
Pozo Unslipped: Pozo Variety	761
La Justa Composite: La Justa Variety	2
Chilo Unslipped: Chilo Variety	5
Gotas Composite: Gotas Variety	5
Patojo Modeled: Patojo Variety	33
Mumúl Composite: Mumúl Variety	19
Harina Cream: Harina Variety	8
Payaso Orange-brown: Payaso Variety	1

Achote Black: Variety Unspec. 1
Cambio Unslipped: Variety Unspec. 7
Encanto Striated: Variety Unspec. 1
Classic ash pastes 22
Miscellaneous unidentified 27
Total 1465

Lot 26

Operation: IG, Macanché Island
Context: Early Postclassic (early facet?)
platform construction fill

Paxcamán Red: Paxcamán Variety, plus Gen. 3
Trapeche Pink: Tramite Variety, plus Gen. 12
Xuluc Incised: Tzalam Variety 1
Topoxté Red: Topoxté Variety, plus Gen. 1
Augustine Red: Variety Unspec. 1
Slateware 1
Tinaja Red: Variety Unspec. 126
Subín Red: Variety Unspec. 13
Cameron Incised: Variety Unspec. 7
Harina Cream: Harina Variety 46
Achote Black: Variety Unspec. 1
Cambio Unslipped: Variety Unspec. 39
Cambio Unslipped: Coarse Gray Variety 11
Encanto Striated: Variety Unspec. 14
Classic ash pastes 26
Miscellaneous unidentified 210
Total 512

Lot 27

Operation: IH, Macanché Island
Complex: Late Postclassic midden

Paxcamán Red: Paxcamán Variety, plus Gen. 5
Trapeche Pink: Tramite Variety, plus Gen. 85
Mul Polychrome: Manax Variety 5
Xuluc Incised: Ain Variety 7
Xuluc Incised: Tzalam Variety 3
Unidentified Trapeche Group Polychrome 2
Unidentified Gray Slipped Group 1
Topoxté Red: Topoxté Variety, plus Gen. 6
Pozo Unslipped: Pozo Variety 37
Chilo Unslipped: Chilo Variety 1
Patojo Modeled: Patojo Variety 3
Mumúl Composite: Mumúl Variety 1
Ídolos Modeled: Ídolos Variety 1
Tinaja Red: Variety Unspec. 2
Miscellaneous unidentified 153
Total 312

Lot 28

Operation: IH, Macanché Island
Context: Late Postclassic midden

Paxcamán Red: Paxcamán Variety, plus Gen. 52
Ixpop Polychrome: Ixpop Variety 5
Sacá Polychrome: Sacá Variety 2
Macanché Red-on-paste: Macanché Variety 1
Picú Incised: Thub Variety 1
Unidentified Paxcamán Group Polychrome 6
Trapeche Pink: Tramite Variety, plus Gen. 49
Mul Polychrome: Manax Variety 6
Xuluc Incised: Ain Variety 1
Xuluc Incised: Tzalam Variety 1
Unidentified Trapeche Group Polychrome 3
Unidentified Gray Slipped Group 1
Topoxté Red: Topoxté Variety, plus Gen. 7
Unidentified Topoxté Group Polychrome 1
Pozo Unslipped: Pozo Variety 46
La Justa Composite: La Justa Variety 1
Chilo Unslipped: Chilo Variety 8
Gotas Composite: Gotas Variety 2
Ídolos Modeled: Ídolos Variety 8
Tinaja Red: Variety Unspec. 6
Harina Cream: Harina Variety 3
Encanto Striated: Variety Unspec. 2
Classic ash paste 26
Miscellaneous unidentified 127
Total 365

Lot 29

Operation: Small "ceremonial center," Lake
Macanché mainland
Context: Mixed

Paxcamán Red: Paxcamán Variety, plus Gen. 3
Ixpop Polychrome: Ixpop Variety 1
Pozo Unslipped: Pozo Variety 2
Chilo Unslipped: Chilo Variety 1
Tinaja Red: Variety Unspec. 17
Chaquiste Impressed: Variety Unspec. 1
Achote Black: Variety Unspec. 1
Encanto Striated: Variety Unspec. 2
Sierra Red: Variety Unspec. 4
Flor Cream: Variety Unspec. 1
Polvero Black: Variety Unspec. 3
Miscellaneous unidentified 32
Total 68

Lot 30

Operation: IH, Macanché Island
Context: Late Postclassic mixed midden

Paxcamán Red: Paxcamán Variety, plus Gen.	37
Trapeche Pink: Tramite Variety, plus Gen.	231
Mul Polychrome: Manax Variety	21
Xuluc Incised: Ain Variety	8
Xuluc Incised: Tzalam Variety	10
Unidentified Trapeche Group Polychrome	19
Unidentified Gray Slipped Group	5
Topoxté Red: Topoxté Variety, plus Gen.	1
Pozo Unslipped: Pozo Variety	512
Patojo Modeled: Patojo Variety	5
Mumúl Composite: Mumúl Variety	1
Tinaja Red: Variety Unspec.	2
Harina Cream: Harina Variety	2
Cambio Unslipped: Variety Unspec.	2
Encanto Striated: Variety Unspec.	2
Classic ash pastes	1
Total	859

Lot 31

Operation: IH, Macanché Island
Context: Early Postclassic (late facet) platform construction fill

Paxcamán Red: Paxcamán Variety, plus Gen.	16
Trapeche Pink: Tramite Variety, plus Gen.	73
Mul Polychrome: Manax Variety	2
Xuluc Incised: Ain Variety	1
Xuluc Incised: Tzalam Variety	5
Chuntuci Composite: Variety Unspec.	1
Unidentified Trapeche Group Polychrome	1
Pozo Unslipped: Pozo Variety	20
La Justa Composite: La Justa Variety	1
Chilo Unslipped: Chilo Variety	1
Ídolos Modeled: Ídolos Variety	1
Tinaja Red: Variety Unspec.	8
Encanto Striated: Variety Unspec.	5
Classic ash pastes	35
Miscellaneous unidentified	166
Total	336

Lot 32

Operation: IG, Macanché Island
Context: Late Classic platform construction fill

Chaquiste Impressed: Variety Unspec.	1
Achote Black: Variety Unspec.	1

Cambio Unslipped: Variety Unspec.	2
Classic ash pastes	9
Miscellaneous unidentified	18
Total	31

Lot 33

Operation: IH, Macanché Island
Context: Early Postclassic (late facet) platform construction fill

Paxcamán Red: Paxcamán Variety, plus Gen.	9
Sacá Polychrome: Sacá Variety	1
Trapeche Pink: Tramite Variety, plus Gen.	24
Chuntuci Composite: Variety Unspec.	1
Augustine Red: Variety Unspec.	12
Tinaja Red: Variety Unspec.	2
Encanto Striated: Variety Unspec.	1
Classic ash pastes	16
Miscellaneous unidentified	57
Total	123

Lot 34

Operation: IH, Macanché Island
Complex: Early Postclassic (late facet) platform construction fill

Paxcamán Red: Paxcamán Variety, plus Gen.	6
Trapeche Pink: Tramite Variety, plus Gen.	8
Xuluc Incised: Tzalam Variety	1
Pozo Unslipped: Pozo Variety	9
La Justa Composite: La Justa Variety	1
Classic ash pastes	3
Miscellaneous unidentified	29
Total	57

Lot 35

Operation: IH, Macanché Island
Complex: Late Postclassic midden (selected sherds only)

Paxcamán Red: Paxcamán Variety, plus Gen.	2
Ixpop Polychrome: Ixpop Variety	1
Unidentified Paxcamán Group Polychrome	1
Trapeche Pink: Tramite Variety, plus Gen.	13
Mul Polychrome: Manax Variety	1
Picté Red-on-paste: Picté Variety	1
Xuluc Incised: Ain Variety	1
Xuluc Incised: Tzalam Variety	3
Topoxté Red: Topoxté Variety, plus Gen.	2

Pozo Unslipped: Pozo Variety	1
La Justa Composite: La Justa Variety	2
Patojo Modeled: Patojo Variety	1
Mumúl Composite: Mumúl Variety	5
Hubelna Unslipped: Hubelna Variety	1
Ídolos Modeled: Ídolos Variety	2
Miscellaneous unidentified	2
Total	39

Lot 36

Operation: IH, Macanché Island
Context: Early Postclassic (late facet) platform
 construction fill

Paxcamán Red: Paxcamán Variety, plus Gen.	6
Trapeche Pink: Tramite Variety, plus Gen.	18
Pozo Unslipped: Pozo Variety	1
Classic ash pastes	4
Miscellaneous unidentified	34
Total	63

Lot 37

Operation: IH, Macanché Island
Context: Early Postclassic (late facet) platform
 construction fill

Paxcamán Red: Paxcamán Variety, plus Gen.	6
Sacá Polychrome: Sacá Variety	1
Trapeche Pink: Tramite Variety, plus Gen.	7
Xuluc Incised: Tzalam Variety	1
Unidentified Trapeche Group Polychrome	1
Pozo Unslipped: Pozo Variety	6
La Justa Composite: La Justa Variety	1
Tinaja Red: Variety Unspec.	2
Harina Cream: Harina Variety	2
Achote Black: Variety Unspec.	2
Encanto Striated: Variety Unspec.	3
Classic ash pastes	17
Balanza Black: Variety Unspecified	2
Miscellaneous unidentified	56
Total	107

Lot 38

Operation: IH, Macanché Island
Context: Mixed deposit, Terminal Classic
 "marl," plus some Postclassic rock
 fill

Paxcamán Red: Paxcamán Variety, plus Gen.	10
Picú Incised: Thub Variety	1

Unidentified Paxcamán Group Polychrome	1
Trapeche Pink: Tramite Variety, plus Gen.	3
Unidentified Gray Slipped Group	9
Unidentified Topoxté Group Polychrome	1
Augustine Red: Variety Unspec.	1
Fine Orange Group Unspec.	1
Pozo Unslipped: Pozo Variety	8
La Justa Composite: La Justa Variety	2
Tinaja Red: Variety Unspec.	65
Subín Red: Variety Unspec.	17
Harina Cream: Harina Variety	67
Payaso Orange-brown: Payaso Variety	13
Achote Black: Variety Unspec.	56
Cambio Unslipped: Variety Unspec.	220
Cambio Unslipped: Coarse Gray Variety	234
Encanto Striated: Variety Unspec.	124
Classic ash pastes	327
Flor Cream: Variety Unspec.	1
Balanza Black: Variety Unspec.	5
Total	1166

Lot 39

Operation: IE, Macanché Island
Context: Mixed, Early Postclassic construction
 fill plus Late Postclassic midden

Paxcamán Red: Paxcamán Variety, plus Gen.	3
Pozo Unslipped: Pozo Variety	6
Tinaja Red: Variety Unspec.	8
Pantano Impressed: Pantano Var.	1
Harina Cream: Harina Variety	1
Encanto Striated: Variety Unspec.	4
Classic ash pastes	38
Miscellaneous unidentified	39
Total	100

Lot 40

Operation: IH, Macanché Island
Context: Terminal Classic "marl" deposit
 (mixed with Postclassic)

Paxcamán Red: Paxcamán Variety, plus Gen.	12
Unidentified Paxcamán Group Polychrome	3
Trapeche Pink: Tramite Variety, plus Gen.	26
Mul Polychrome: Manax Variety	1
Pozo Unslipped: Pozo Variety	5
Tinaja Red: Variety Unspec.	30
Subín Red: Variety Unspec.	7
Harina Cream: Harina Variety	3
Achote Black: Variety Unspec.	12
Cambio Unslipped: Variety Unspec.	2

Cambio Unslipped: Coarse Gray Variety	119
Encanto Striated: Variety Unspec.	8
Classic ash pastes	94
Miscellaneous unidentified	4
Total	326

Lot 41

Operation: IH, Macanché Island
Context: Terminal Classic "marl" deposit

Picú Incised: Thub Variety	4
Chilo Unslipped: Chilo Variety	1
Tinaja Red: Variety Unspec.	69
Subín Red: Variety Unspec.	4
Harina Cream: Harina Variety	7
Largo Red-on-cream: Largo Variety	17
Payaso Orange-brown: Payaso Variety	19
Achote Black: Variety Unspec.	32
Jato Black-on-gray: Variety Unspec.	1
Classic Polychrome	2
Cambio Unslipped: Variety Unspec.	27
Cambio Unslipped: Coarse Gray Variety	122
Encanto Striated: Variety Unspec.	16
Classic ash pastes	24
Flor Cream: Variety Unspec.	2
Unidentified Late Classic special	2
Miscellaneous unidentified	1
Total	350

Lot 42

Operation: IH, Macanché Island
Context: Terminal Classic "marl" deposit

Cambio Unslipped: Variety Unspec.	4
Encanto Striated: Variety Unspec.	1
Total	5

Lot 43

Operation: Test 1, in front of Main Pyramid, Ixlú
Context: Postclassic midden and collapse
            above plaza floor

Paxcamán Red: Paxcamán Variety, plus Gen.	13
Ixpop Polychrome: Ixpop Variety	2
Unidentified Paxcamán Group Polychrome	4
Augustine Red: Variety Unspec.	1
Pozo Unslipped: Pozo Variety	31
Chilo Unslipped: Chilo Variety	11

Gotas Composite: Gotas Variety	1
Mumúl Composite: Mumúl Variety	2
Tinaja Red: Variety Unspec.	20
Orange Late Classic Polychrome	1
Buff Late Classic Polychrome	6
Cream Late Classic Polychrome	2
Miscellaneous Late Classic Polychrome	8
Encanto Striated: Variety Unspec.	6
Classic ash pastes	29
Sierra Red: Variety Unspec.	9
Joventud Red: Variety Unspec.	2
Flor Cream: Variety Unspec.	1
Polvero Black: Variety Unspec.	3
Miscellaneous unidentified	49
Total	201

Lot 44

Operation: Test 1, in front of Main Pyramid, Ixlú
Context: Late Classic plaza construction fill

Tinaja Red: Variety Unspec.	3
Subín Red: Variety Unspec.	1
Orange Late Classic Polychrome	8
Buff Late Classic Polychrome	4
Miscellaneous Late Classic Polychrome	11
Encanto Striated: Variety Unspec.	1
Miscellaneous unidentified	23
Total	51

Lot 45

Operation: Test 1, in front of Main Pyramid, Ixlú
Context: Late Classic plaza construction fill

Tinaja Red: Variety Unspec.	11
Orange Late Classic Polychrome	7
Buff Late Classic Polychrome	3
Cream Late Classic Polychrome	10
Miscellaneous Late Classic Polychrome	2
Achote Black: Variety Unspec.	6
Encanto Striated: Variety Unspec.	2
Sierra Red: Variety Unspec.	1
Calam Buff: Variety Unspec.	1
Miscellaneous unidentified	15
Total	58

Lot 46

Operation: Test 1, in front of Main Pyramid, Ixlú
Context: Late Classic plaza construction fill

Tinaja Red: Variety Unspec.	10
Subín Red: Variety Unspec.	1
Late Classic Polychrome	4
Sierra Red: Variety Unspec.	2
Polvero Black: Variety Unspec.	1
Balanza Black: Variety Unspec.	1
Miscellaneous unidentified	23
Total	42

Lot 47

Lot 47 contained one item, the stone "idol" shown in figure 27.

Lot 48

Operation: San Francisco, Petén (?)
Context: None (collection purchased in Santa Elena)

Paxcamán Red (?)	1
Patojo Modeled (?)—mask	1
Total	2

Lot 49

Operation: ID and/or IE, Macanché Island
Context: Surface

Paxcamán Red: Paxcamán Variety, plus Gen.	14
Ixpop Polychrome: Ixpop Variety	4
Macanché Red-on-paste: Macanché Variety	1
Unidentified Paxcamán Group Polychrome	1
Trapeche Pink: Tramite Variety, plus Gen.	13
Topoxté Red: Topoxté Variety, plus Gen.	14
Chompoxté Red-on-cream: Chompoxté Variety	3
Chompoxté Red-on-cream: Variety Unspec.	2
Unidentified Topoxté Group Polychrome	2
Pozo Unslipped: Pozo Variety	29
La Justa Composite: La Justa Variety	1
Chilo Unslipped: Chilo Variety	2
Total	86

APPENDIX 2

Directory of Ceramic Typological Units at Macanché Island

Achote Black	Group and Type, Petén Gloss Ware
Ain Variety	Variety of Xuluc Incised (Trapeche Ceramic Group)
Akalché Variety	Variety of Chompoxté Red-on-cream (Topoxté Ceramic Group)
Altar Orange	Group and Type (Fine Orange Paste Ware)
Appliqué Variety	Variety of Chamán Modeled (Paxcamán Ceramic Group)
Augustine Red	Group, Type, and Variety (Vitzil Orange-red Ware)
Cambio Unslipped	Group, Type, Variety (Uaxactún Unslipped Ware)
Cameron Incised	Type in Tinaja Ceramic Group
Canjil Variant	Paste variant in Tinaja Ceramic Group
Chaquiste Impressed	Type in Tinaja Ceramic Group
Chilo Unslipped	Group, Type, Variety (Uapake Unslipped Ware)
Chompoxté Red-on-cream	Type and Variety (Topoxté Ceramic Group)
Chuntuci Modeled	Type in Trapeche Ceramic Group
Clemencia Cream Paste Ware	Ware (Topoxté and Ídolos Ceramic Groups)
Coarse Gray Variety	Variety in Cambio Unslipped
Danta Group	Group (Petén Gloss Ware)
Darknight Variety	Variety in Daylight Orange
Daylight Orange	Type and Group (San Pablo Gloss Ware)
Dulces Incised	Type and Variety in Topoxté Group
Encanto Striated	Type in Cambio Group
Fine Orange Ware	Ware
Gotas Composite	Type and Variety in Chilo Group
Harina Cream	Group, Type, and Variety (ware unspecified)
Ídolos Modeled	Group, Type, and Variety (Clemencia Cream Paste Ware)
Ixpop Polychrome	Type and Variety (Paxcamán Group)
Jato Black-on-gray	Type in Danta Group
La Justa Composite	Type and Variety in Pozo Group
Largo Red-on-cream	Type and Variety in Harina Group
Macanché Red-on-paste (cream)	Type and Variety in Paxcamán Group
Manax Variety	Variety in Mul Polychrome (Trapeche Group)
Montículo Unslipped Ware	Ware (Pozo Group)

Mul Polychrome	Type in Trapeche Group
Mumúl Composite	Type and Variety (ware unspecified)
Palmar Orange Polychrome	Group and Type in Petén Gloss Ware
Pantano Impressed	Type and Variety in Tinaja Group
Pastel Polychrome	Type and Variety in Topoxté Group
Patojo Modeled	Type and Variety (ware unspecified)
Paxcamán Red	Group, Type, and Variety (Volador Dull Ware)
Payaso Orange-brown	Group, Type, and Variety (ware unspec.)
Petén Gloss Ware	Ware
Picté Red-on-paste	Type and Variety in Trapeche Group
Picú Incised	Type and Variety in Paxcamán Group
Pixtún Trickle-on-slate	Type in Slateware
Poité Incised	Type in Tres Naciones Group (Fine Gray Ware)
Pozo Unslipped	Group, Type, and Variety (Montículo Unslipped Ware)
Pulpería Red	Type and Variety in Tachís Group
Sacá Polychrome	Type and Variety in Paxcamán Group
San Pablo Gloss Ware	Ware (Daylight Group)
Slateware	Ware
Subín Red	Type in Tinaja Group
Tachís Group	Group (ware unspecified)
Thub Variety	Variety of Picú Incised (Paxcamán Group)
Tinaja Red	Group, Type, and Variety (Petén Gloss Ware)
Topoxté Red	Group, Type, and Variety (Clemencia Cream Paste Ware)
Tramite Variety	Variety in Trapeche Pink (Trapeche Group)
Trapeche Pink	Group and Type (Volador Dull Ware)
Trapiche Incised	Type in Altar Group
Tres Naciones Gray	Group in Fine Gray Ware
Trickle-on-gray	Type in Slateware
Tzalam Variety	Variety in Xuluc Incised (Trapeche Group)
Uapake Unslipped Ware	Ware (Chilo Group)
Uaxactún Unslipped Ware	Ware (Cambio Group)
Villahermosa Incised	Type in Matillas Group
Vitzil Orange-Red Ware	Ware (Augustine Group)
Volador Dull-Slipped Ware	Ware (Paxcamán and Trapeche Groups)
Xuluc Incised	Type (Trapeche Group)

References

Adams, R. E. W.
  1971   *The Ceramics of Altar de Sacrificios, Guatemala.* Papers of the Peabody Museum of Archaeology and Ethnology, vol. 63 (1). Cambridge: Harvard University.
  1973   Maya collapse: transformation and termination in the ceramic sequence at Altar de Sacrificios. In, *The Classic Maya Collapse*, T. P. Culbert, ed. Albuquerque: University of New Mexico Press. Pp. 133–163.

Adams, R. E. W. and A. S. Trik
  1961   Temple I (Str. 5-1): Post-constructional activities. *Tikal Reports* no. 7. Museum Monographs. Philadelphia: University Museum.

Adams, W. Y.
  1979   On the argument from ceramics to history: a challenge based on evidence from Medieval Nubia. *Current Anthropology* 20: 727–734.

Aldenderfer, M. S.
  1982   The structure of domestic lithic assemblages in the Late Classic and Postclassic of the Central Petén lakes region. Paper presented at the 2nd Maya Lithics Conference, San Antonio, Texas.
  n.d.   The structure of rural lithic assemblages of the Late Classic in the Central Petén lakes region, Guatemala. In, *Stone Tools and Maya Civilization*, T. Hester and H. Shafer, eds. (in press)

Andrews, E. W. IV
  1943   The archaeology of southwestern Campeche. *Contributions to American Anthropology and History* 8 (49), Carnegie Institution of Washington, Pub. 546.

Ball, J. W.
  1977   *The Archaeological Ceramics of Becan, Campeche, Mexico.* Middle American Research Institute Pub. 32. New Orleans: Tulane University.
  1979   Ceramics, culture history, and the Puuc tradition: some alternative possibilities. In, *The Puuc: New Perspectives*, L. Mills, ed. Pella, Iowa: Central College Press. Pp. 46–51.
  1982   The Tancah ceramic situation: cultural and historical insights from an alternative material. Appendix I in *On the Edge of the Sea: Mural Painting at Tancah-Tulum*, A. Miller, ed. Washington, D.C.: Dumbarton Oaks. Pp. 105–113.
  1985   The Postclassic that wasn't: the 13th through 17th century archaeology of central eastern Campeche, Mexico. In, *The Lowland Maya Postclassic*, A. F. Chase and P. M. Rice, eds. Austin: University of Texas Press. Pp. 73–84.

Berlin, H.
  1955   Apuntes sobre vasijas de Flores (El Petén). *Antropología e Historia de Guatemala* 7: 15–17.

Bishop, R. L., and R. L. Rands
  1982   Maya Fine Paste ceramics: a compositional perspective. In, *Excavations at Seibal, Department of Petén, Guatemala. Analyses of Fine Paste Ceramics*, Peabody Museum of Archaeology and Ethnology, Memoirs vol. 15, no. 2, pp. 283–314. Cambridge: Harvard University.

255

Bullard, W. R., Jr.
1970   Topoxté: a Postclassic Maya site in Petén, Guatemala. *Monographs and Papers in Maya Archaeology*, W. R. Bullard, Jr., ed. Papers of the Peabody Museum of Archaeology and Ethnology, vol. 61: 245–308. Cambridge: Harvard University.
1973   Postclassic culture in Central Petén and adjacent British Honduras. In, *The Classic Maya Collapse*, T. P. Culbert, ed. Albuquerque: University of New Mexico Press. Pp. 225–242.

Charlton, T. H.
1968   Post-conquest Aztec ceramics: implications for archaeological interpretation. *Florida Anthropologist* 21: 96–101.

Chase, A. F.
1979   Regional development in the Tayasal-Paxcamán zone, El Petén, Guatemala: a preliminary statement. *Cerámica de Cultura Maya* 11: 86–119.
1983   A Contextual Consideration of the Tayasal-Paxcamán Zone, El Petén, Guatemala. Ph.D. Dissertation, University of Pennsylvania.

Chase, A. F., and D. Z. Chase
1983   *La Cerámica de la Zona Tayasal-Paxcamán, Lago Petén-Itzá, Guatemala.* Philadelphia: University Museum.

Chase, D. Z.
1984   The Late Postclassic pottery of Santa Rita Corozal, Belize: the Xabalxab ceramic complex. *Cerámica de Cultura Maya* 14 (in press)

Cowgill, G. L.
1963   Postclassic Period Culture in the Vicinity of Flores, Petén, Guatemala. Ph.D. Dissertation, Harvard University.

Cowgill, U., and G. E. Hutchinson
1963a   A chemical and mineralogical examination of the ceramic sequence from Tikal, El Petén, Guatemala. *American Journal of Science* 267: 465–477.
1963b   El Bajo de Santa Fe. *Transactions of the American Philosophical Society* 53.

Culbert, T. P.
1973a   (ed.) *The Classic Maya Collapse.* Albuquerque: University of New Mexico Press.
1973b   The Maya downfall at Tikal. In, *The Classic Maya Collapse*, T. P. Culbert, ed. Albuquerque: University of New Mexico Press. Pp. 63–92.

Deevey, E. S., Jr., M. Brenner, and M. W. Binford
1983   Paleolimnology of the Petén lake district, Guatemala. III. Late Pleistocene and Gamblian environments of the Maya area. *Hydrobiologia* 103: 211–216.

Eaton, J. D.
1976   Ancient fishing technology on the Gulf Coast of Yucatán, Mexico. *Bulletin of the Texas Archaeological Society* 47: 231–243.
1978   Studies in the archaeology of coastal Yucatán and Campeche, Mexico. Middle American Research Institute Pub. 46.

Farriss, N. M.
1984   *Maya Society Under Colonial Rule: The Collective Enterprise of Survival.* Princeton, N.J.: Princeton University Press.

Foster, G. M.
1959   The Coyotepec molde and some associated problems of the potters wheel. *Southwest Journal of Anthropology* 15: 53–63.

Fry, R. E.
1985   Revitalization movements among the Postclassic Lowland Maya. In, *The Lowland Maya Postclassic*, A. F. Chase and P. M. Rice, eds. Austin: University of Texas Press. Pp. 126–141.

Garber, J. F.
1984   A functional assessment and contextual analysis of the sherd disks from Cerros, northern Belize. *Ceramica de Cultura Maya* 13:76–83.

Gifford, J. C.
1976   *Prehistoric Pottery Analysis and the Ceramics of Barton Ramie in the Belize Valley.* Peabody Museum of Archaeology and Ethnology, Memoirs vol. 18. Cambridge: Harvard University.

Graham, E.
1983   The Highlands of the Lowlands:
        Environment and Archaeology in
        the Stann Creek District, Belize,
        Central America. Ph.D.
        Dissertation, University of
        Cambridge.
Hammond, N.
1975   *Lubaantun. A Classic Maya Realm.*
        Peabody Museum of Archaeology
        and Ethnology, Monograph no. 2.
        Cambridge: Harvard University.
Hester, T. R.
1982   The Maya lithic sequence in
        northern Belize. In, *Archaeology at
        Colha, Belize: The 1981 Interim
        Report*, T. R. Hester, H. J. Shafer,
        and J. D. Eaton, eds. San Antonio:
        Center for Archaeological Research,
        University of Texas, and Centro
        Studi e Ricerche Ligabue, Venezia.
Jones, G., D., D. S. Rice, and P. M. Rice
1981   The location of Tayasal: a
        reconsideration in light of Petén
        Maya ethnohistory and archaeology.
        American Antiquity 46: 530–547.
Kent, K. P., and S. M. Nelson
1976   Net sinkers or weft weights?
        Current Anthropology 17 (1): 152.
Loten, H. S., and D. M. Pendergast
1984   A lexicon for Maya architecture.
        Royal Ontario Museum *Archaeology
        Monograph* 8. Toronto.
Miller, A. G.
1985   The Postclassic sequence at Tancah
        and Tulum, Quintana Roo, Mexico.
        In, *The Lowland Maya Postclassic*,
        A. F. Chase and P. M. Rice, eds.
        Austin: University of Texas Press.
        Pp. 31–49.
Morley, S. G.
1937–38 *The Inscriptions of Petén,
        Guatemala.* Carnegie Institution of
        Washington, Pub. 437.
Navarrete, C.
1961   La cerámica de Mixco Viejo.
        Humanidades vol. 3, no. 6.
        Guatemala: University of San
        Carlos.
Pagden, A. R. (trans. and ed.)
1971   *Hernán Cortés—Letters from
        Mexico.* New York: Grossman.
Paine, S. E. S.
1981   The mariposas of Macal Tipu. Ms.,

        Department of Anthropology,
        Hamilton College.
Pendergast, D. M.
1981   Lamanai, Belize: summary of
        excavation results, 1974–1980.
        Journal of Field Archaeology 8 (1):
        31–53.
Phillips, D. A.
1979   Pesas de pesca de Cozumel,
        Quintana Roo. *Boletin de la Escuela
        de Ciencias Antropológicas de la
        Universidad de Yucatán*, año 6, no.
        36: 2–18. Merida.
Ralph, E. K., H. N. Michael, and M. C. Han
1973   Radiocarbon dates and reality.
        MASCA Newsletter 9 (1): 1–20.
Rands, R. L., R. L. Bishop, and J. A. Sabloff
1982   Maya fine paste ceramics: an
        archaeological perspective. In,
        *Excavations at Seibal, Department
        of Petén, Guatemala. Analyses of
        Fine Paste Ceramics.* Peabody
        Museum of Archaeology and
        Ethnology, Memoirs vol. 15, no. 2.
        Pp. 315–343. Cambridge: Harvard
        University.
Rathje, W. L.
1972   Praise the gods and pass the metates:
        a hypothesis of the development of
        Lowland rainforest civilizations in
        Mesoamerica. In, *Contemporary
        Archaeology*, M. P. Leone, ed.
        Carbondale: Southern Illinois
        University Press. Pp. 365–392.
Reina, R. E.
1961   The abandonment of Primicias by
        Itzá of San José, Guatemala, and
        Socotz, British Honduras. *Tikal
        Reports* no. 10. Philadelphia:
        University Museum.
Reina, R. E., and R. M. Hill II
1978   *The Traditional Pottery of
        Guatemala.* Austin: University of
        Texas Press.
Rice, D. S.
1986   The Petén Postclassic: a settlement
        perspective. In, *Late Lowland Maya
        Civilization: Classic to Postclassic*,
        J. A. Sabloff and E. W. Andrews V,
        eds. Albuquerque: University of
        New Mexico Press. Pp. 301–344.
Rice, D. S. and P. M. Rice
1980   Informe preliminar, Proyecto
        Lacustre, Primera Temporada, 1979,

Boletin de la Escuela de Ciencias Antropologicas de la Universidad de Yucatán 7: 75–90. Merida.

1981   Muralla de León: a Lowland Maya fortification. *Journal of Field Archaeology* 8 (3): 271–288.

1982   Informe preliminar, Proyecto Lacustre, Segunda Temporada, 1980. *Boletin* de la Escuela de Ciencias Antropologicas de la Universidad de Yucatán 10 (56): 17–38. Merida.

1984   Collapse to conquest: Postclassic archaeology of the Petén Maya. *Archaeology* 36: 46–51.

n.d.   Final summary report, 1979, 1980, and 1981 field seasons of Proyecto Lacustre. Manuscript, 96 pp.

Rice, P. M.

1976   Rethinking the ware concept. *American Antiquity* 41: 538–543.

1978   Postclassic pottery production and exchange in the Central Petén, Guatemala. Paper presented at the Society for American Archaeology meeting, Tucson, Arizona.

1979   Ceramic and non-ceramic artifacts of Lakes Yaxhá and Sacnab, El Petén, Guatemala. Part I, The Ceramics; Section B, Postclassic Pottery from Topoxté. *Cerámica de Cultura Maya* 11: 1–86. Philadelphia.

1980   Petén Postclassic pottery production and exchange: a view from Macanché. In, *Models and Methods in Regional Exchange*, R. E. Fry, ed. Occasional Papers of the Society for American Archaeology 1: 67–82.

1983a   Serpents and styles in Petén Postclassic pottery. *American Anthropologist* 85 (4): 866–880.

1983b   Reptiles and rulership in the Central Petén Postclassic. Paper presented at the American Anthropological Association meeting, Chicago.

1984a   The ceramics of Negroman-Tipú: a preliminary overview. Paper presented at the annual meeting of the Northeastern Anthropological Association, Hartford.

1984b   Obsidian procurement in the Central Petén lakes region, Guatemala. *Journal of Field Archaeology* 11 (2): 181–194.

1984c   Some reflections on change in pottery-producing systems. In, *The Many Dimensions of Pottery: Ceramics in Archaeology and Anthropology*, S. E. van der Leeuw and A. Pritchard, eds. CINGULA series no. 7. Amsterdam: Institute for Pre- and Protohistory, University of Amsterdam. Pp. 231–293.

1985a   Postclassic and Historic period pottery from Negroman-Tipú, Belize. Paper presented at the 5oth annual meeting of the Society for American Archaeology, Denver.

1985b   Reptilian images and vessel function in Petén Postclassic pottery: a preliminary view. *Quinta Mesa Redonda de Palenque*, vol. 7, M. G. Robertson and V. Fields, eds. San Francisco: Pre-Columbian Art Research Institute. Pp. 115–122.

1985c   Maya pottery techniques and technology. In, *Ceramics and Civilization*, W. D. Kingery, ed. Advances in Ceramics Series, no. 1. Columbus, Ohio: American Ceramic Society. Pp. 113–132.

1986   The Petén Postclassic: perspectives from the Central Petén lakes. In, *Late Lowland Maya Civilization: Classic to Postclassic*, J. A. Sabloff and E. W. Andrews V, eds. Albuquerque: University of New Mexico Press. Pp. 251–299.

n.d. a   An obsidian hydration dating sequence from the Maya Lowlands. *Journal of New World Archaeology.* (in press)

n.d. b   Economic change in the Lowland Maya Late Classic period. In, *Production, Exchange, and Complex Societies*, E. Brumfiel and T. Earle, eds. Cambridge: Cambridge University Press. (in press)

Rice, P. M., and D. S. Rice

1979   The Postclassic at Topoxté and Macanché, El Petén, Guatemala. Paper presented at the American Anthropological Association meetings, Cincinnati.

1985   Topoxté, Macanché, and the Central Petén Postclassic. In, *The Lowland Maya Postclassic*, A. F. Chase and P. M. Rice, eds. Austin: University of Texas Press. Pp. 166–183.

Rice, P. M., H. V. Michel, F. Asaro, and F. Stross
1985 Provenience analysis of obsidians from the Central Petén lakes, Guatemala. *American Antiquity* 50 (3): 591–604.
Robicsek, F., and R. Hales
1981 *The Maya Book of the Dead, The Ceramic Codex.* Charlottesville: University of Virginia Art Museum.
Sabloff, J. A.
1975 Ceramics. In, *Excavations at Seibal, Department of Petén, Guatemala.* Peabody Museum of Archaeology and Ethnology, Memoirs vol. 13, no. 2. Cambridge: Harvard University.
Sanders, W. T.
1960 *Prehistoric Ceramics and Settlement Patterns in Quintana Roo, Mexico.* Contributions to American Anthropology and History, 12 (60). Carnegie Institution of Washington Pub. 606.
Schmidt, P. J.
1976/77 Postclassic finds in the Cayo District, Belize. *Estudios de Cultura Maya* 10: 103–114.
Sharer, R. J., and A. F. Chase
1976 New Town ceramic complex: New Town ceramic sphere. In, *Prehistoric Pottery Analysis and the Ceramics of Barton Ramie in the Belize Valley.* Peabody Museum of Archaeology and Ethnology, Memoirs vol. 18: 288–315.
Shepard, A. O.
1942 Technological notes on the pottery from San José. Appendix B in *Excavations at San José*, by J. E. S. Thompson. C.I.W. Publication 506: 251–271.
1957 *Ceramics for the Archaeologist.* Carnegie Institution of Washington Pub. 609.
1962 Ceramic development of the Lowland and Highland Maya. *XXXV Congreso Int. de Americanistas,* pp. 249–262. Mexico.
Smith, A. L., and A. V. Kidder
1943 *Explorations in the Motagua Valley, Guatemala.* Carnegie Institution of Washington Pub. 546, Contribution 41.
Smith, R. E.
1955 *Ceramic Sequence at Uaxactún, Guatemala.* Middle American Research Institute Pub. 20. New Orleans: Tulane University.
1971 *The Pottery of Mayapán.* Papers of the Peabody Museum of Archaeology and Ethnology, vol. 66. Cambridge: Harvard University.
Smith, R. E., and J. C. Gifford
1966 Maya ceramic varieties, types, and wares at Uaxactún: supplement to "Ceramic Sequence at Uaxactún, Guatemala." Middle American Research Institute Pub. 28: 125–174. New Orleans: Tulane University.
Stoltman, J. B.
1978 Lithic artifacts from a complex society: the chipped stone tools of Becan, Campeche, Mexico. Middle American Research Institute *Occasional Paper* 2. New Orleans: Tulane University.
Thompson, J. E. S.
1940 *Late Ceramic Horizons at Benque Viejo, British Honduras.* Carnegie Institution of Washington Pub. 528, Contribution 35.
1977 A proposal for constituting a Maya subgroup, cultural and linguistic, in the Petén and adjacent regions. In, *Anthropology and History in Yucatán,* G. Jones, ed. Austin: University of Texas Press. Pp. 3–42.
Thompson, R. H.
1958 Modern Yucatecan Maya pottery making. Society for American Archaeology Memoirs 15. *American Antiquity* 23 (no. 4, part 2).
Tschopik, H.
1951 An Andean ceramic tradition in historical perspective. *American Antiquity* 15: 196–218.
Villagutierre Soto Mayor, Don J. de
1933 [1701] *Historia de la Conquista de la Provincia de el Itzá, Guatemala.*
Wauchope, R.
1970 Protohistoric pottery of the Guatemala Highlands. In, *Monographs and Papers in Maya Archaeology,* W. R. Bullard, Jr., ed. Papers of the Peabody Museum of Archaeology and Ethnology, vol. 61: 89–244. Cambridge: Harvard University.

Willey, G. R.
1972   *The Artifacts of Altar de Sacrificios.*
        Papers of the Peabody Museum of
        Archaeology and Ethnology, vol. 64
        (1). Cambridge: Harvard University.
1973   Certain aspects of the Late Classic
        to Postclassic periods in the Belize
        valley. In, *The Classic Maya
        Collapse*, T. P. Culbert, ed.
        Albuquerque: University of New
        Mexico Press. Pp. 93–106.
1978   Artifacts. In, *Excavations at Seibal,
        Department of Petén, Guatemala.*
        Peabody Museum of Archaeology
        and Ethnology, Memoirs vol. 14, no.
        1. Cambridge: Harvard University.
Willey, G. R., T. P. Culbert, and R. E. W. Adams
1967   Maya Lowland ceramics: a report
        from the 1965 Guatemala City
        conference. *American Antiquity* 32:
        289–315.

Willey, G. R., W. R. Bullard, Jr., J. B. Glass, and
J. C. Gifford
1965   *Prehistoric Maya Settlement in
        Belize Valley.* Papers of the Peabody
        Museum of Archaeology and
        Ethnology, vol. 54. Cambridge:
        Harvard University.
Wishart, D.
1978   CLUSTAN User Manual, 3rd
        edition. Edinburgh: Edinburgh
        University.
Wonderley, A. P.
1981   *Late Postclassic Excavations at
        Naco, Honduras.* Latin American
        Studies Program Dissertation Series
        86. Ithaca: Cornell University.
1985   The land of Ulua: Postclassic
        research in the Naco and Sula
        valleys, Honduras. In, *The Lowland
        Maya Postclassic*, A. F. Chase and
        P. M. Rice, eds. Austin: University
        of Texas Press. Pp. 254–269.

Index

Achote ceramic group, 55, 58, 59, 60 *(table 3)*, 74–76
   Achote Black type, 56, 59, 60 *(table 3)*, 72, 74–76 *(fig. 34)*
Adams, R.E.W., 69
Alain. *See* Yalain
Altar de Sacrificios, 64, 65, 67, 69, 70, 71, 82
   lithics, 213
Altar Orange ceramic group, 84, 168
   Altar Orange: Variety Unspecified, 60 *(table 3)*, 84
Animal bone. *See* Bone, animal
Arroba Modeled type, 122
Arrow points. *See* Projectile points, sidenotched (arrow)
Ash (tempered) paste
   Classic and Terminal Classic, 40, 55, 56, 58, 59, 61, 63, 64, 65, 71, 76, 82, 84–85, 91, 95, 235. *See also* Canjil firing variant
   Postclassic, 56, 105, 107, 109 *(table 11)*, 112, 118. *See also* individual type and variety descriptions
Augustine ceramic group, 40, 47, 56, 85, 90, 91, 93 *(table 4)*, 94 *(table 5)*, 95, 96 *(table 6)*, 99, 123, 165–67 *(fig. 55)*, 237
   Augustine Red type, 42, 93 *(table 4)*, 94 *(table 5)*, 96 *(table 6)*
Aura complex/phase, 37 *(table 1)*, 40–42, 59, 91, 94 *(table 5)*, 95, 97 *(table 7)*, 113, 235. *See also* individual group and type descriptions
   early facet, definition, 40, 91
   late facet, definition, 42
Ayer complex/phase, 36 *(table 1)*, 102, 238, 239. *See also* individual group and type descriptions
   definition, 43, 103 *(table 10)*

Balanza Black type, 89
Ball, Joseph, 77, 154
Bark beaters, 43, 226, 227 *(pl. XXIV)*, 228
Barton Ramie, 60, 72, 77, 79, 80, 83, 85, 95, 99, 105, 107, 108, 122, 123, 129, 130, 133, 137, 138, 145, 159, 167, 173, 176, 178, 187
Basalt ("scoria"), 221, 223 *(table 16)*, 225 *(fig. 76)*, 226, 238
Bayal complex/sphere, 70, 72, 74, 178, 215
Beads
   shell, 230
   stone, 43, 229
Becan, 56, 72, 74, 76, 77, 82, 154, 179
Bejuco complex, 74
Benque Viejo, 79
Bifaces, chipped stone, 100, 215–19 *(figs. 73, 74; pl. XX)*, 237
Boca complex/sphere, 56, 57, 64, 67, 70, 72, 82, 138
Bone
   animal, 43, 230–31 *(table 17)*, 232 *(table 18)*
   human, 231
   worked, 27, 39, 230, 231 *(fig. 78)*
Bullard, William R., Jr.
   analyses of Macanché artifacts, 3, 4, 104, 107, 113, 167
   excavations at Macanché, 2, 4, 9
   interpretation of Postclassic, 90. *See also* Central Petén Postclassic Tradition
   interpretation of Terminal Classic Romero phase, 61, 82

Cache, chert, 17, 21, 43, 210–11 *(pl. XVII)*, 213, 220, 239
Calam Buff type, 89

Cambio ceramic group, 39, 77–82
  Cambio Unslipped: Coarse Gray Variety,
    39, 40, 55, 57, 58, 59, 60 (table 3), 78
    (fig. 35), 79–80, 82, 84, 91
  Cambio Unslipped type, 39, 40, 59, 77–80
    (fig. 35), 100
Cameron Incised type, 60 (table 3), 63, 68
    (fig. 32), 69–70, 91, 100
Canjil firing variant, 57, 58, 59, 63, 64, 67, 69
Canté Island, 95, 103, 114, 122, 159, 160,
    164, 173, 176
Canté Polychrome type, 133
Carbonate paste
  Classic period, 56, 58, 61, 63, 64, 65, 72,
    75, 77, 79, 80, 83, 91, 235
  Postclassic period. See Snail inclusions
    (in paste); individual type and variety
    descriptions
Cayo Unslipped: Cayo Variety, 80
Cehac-Hunacti Composite, 179
Censers, 27, 33, 43, 44, 97 (tables 7, 8), 99
    (table 9), 101, 202, 210, 235, 236
  effigy, 42, 43, 98, 101, 102, 178, 184–92,
    195–97, 203, 238, 239
  ladle, 154, 176, 177 (fig. 58), 178, 179, 185
  noneffigy (composite, hourglass, vase),
    42, 43, 60, 94, 101, 176–79 (fig. 58),
    183–84, 192, 239
  Terminal Classic lack of, 39, 60
Central Petén Historical Ecology Project
    (CPHEP). See Macanché Island, CPHEP
    excavations; Macanché, Lake, CPHEP
    operations
Central Petén Postclassic Tradition, 9, 61,
    90, 91, 102
Cerro Ortiz, 9, 44
Chamán Modeled: Variety Unspecified, 92
    (table 4), 96 (table 6), 136 (fig. 46), 138
Chaquiste Impressed type, 39, 60 (table 3),
    63, 68 (fig. 32), 69, 70, 71, 99, 178
Chase, Arlen, 83, 105, 107, 112, 139
Chen Mul Modeled type, 187
Chichén Itzá, 2
Chichén Slate ware, 154
Chilcob complex, 95, 108, 149, 151, 167, 173
Chilo ceramic group, 42, 43, 44, 47, 93
    (table 4), 96 (table 6), 97 (table 8), 98,
    99 (table 9), 101, 102, 103 (table 10),
    179–84

Chilo Unslipped: Chilo Variety, 43, 47,
    93 (table 4), 94, 96 (table 6), 98, 103
    (table 10), 178, 179–81 (pl. XII, fig. 59),
    201, 238, 239
Chinautla Polychrome type, 130
Chintok complex, 74, 168
Chompoxté Red-on-cream type, 74, 115,
    134, 135, 150
  Akalché Variety, 92 (table 4), 96 (table 6),
    162 (pl. XI), 163–64
  Chompoxté Variety, 92 (table 4), 96 (table
    6), 103 (table 10), 134, 161–63 (pl. XI)
Chuntuci Composite: Variety Unspecified,
    92 (table 4), 94 (table 5), 152 (fig. 52),
    154, 179
Clemencia Cream Paste ware, 92 (table 4),
    94 (table 5), 96 (table 6), 103 (table
    10), 198. See also Ídolos ceramic group;
    Topoxté ceramic group
Cocahmut complex, 101, 102, 135, 151, 173,
    178, 179
Codex Style pottery, 86, 101, 116, 129
Colha, 213, 215
Collapse, of Maya civilization, 1–2
Colonas, 197, 237. See also Hubelna
    Unslipped type
Conch shell, 39
Cortés, Hernán, 2
Cowgill, George, 90, 104, 105, 106, 107,
    134, 138, 145, 151, 179, 181
Cozumel, 208
Culbert, T. Patrick, 55, 64
Cycle Ten dates, 44, 57, 178

Danta ceramic group, 82–83
Daylight ceramic group, 56, 60 (table 3),
    83–84, 95, 138
  Daylight Orange, 56, 60 (table 3), 83–84
  Daylight Orange: Darknight Variety, 56,
    60 (table 3), 81 (fig. 36), 83–84
Dolorido ceramic group, 56, 154
  Dolorido Cream Polychrome, 74, 133, 150
Dos Lagos complex/phase, 37 (table 1),
    42–43, 95–102 (tables 7–9), 113
  definition, 42, 96 (table 6)
Droga Red-on-cream type, 74
Dulces Incised: Dulces Variety, 92 (table 4),
    96 (table 6), 137, 153, 164–65

Ejército Red type, 64
Encanto Striated type, 55, 57, 59, 60 (table 3), 80–82 (fig. 36)
  Encanto Variety, 82
  Pisote Variety, 82
Extranjeras Impressed type, 178
Eznab sphere, 39, 46, 55, 56, 57, 70, 82

Figurines, 202–3 (fig. 68)
Fine Gray ware, 94 (table 5), 96 (table 6), 169–70
Fine Orange ware, 57, 58, 60 (table 3), 61, 70, 94 (table 5), 96 (table 6), 138, 168–69, 204, 235, 238. See also Altar Orange ceramic group
Flor Cream type, 89
Forastero Bichrome type, 149

Gifford, James C., 60
Gotas Composite: Gotas Variety, 93 (table 4), 96 (table 6), 103 (table 10), 179, 181, 183–84 (fig. 60), 192, 210
Grater bowl, 56, 100, 137, 138, 153, 154, 168, 169, 170, 173, 237
Gray ceramic group, unspecified, 92 (table 4), 96 (table 6), 97 (table 8), 98, 99 (table 9), 117, 155–57 (fig. 53)
Ground stone, 99, 221–29. See also Manos/ metates

Hammerstone, 219
Harina ceramic group, 39, 55, 57, 58, 59, 60 (table 3), 61, 64, 71–74, 76
  Harina Cream type, 60 (table 3), 71–72, 73 (fig. 33), 80, 91
  as predecessor to the Trapeche group, 59, 63, 145
Hidaldo Polychrome type, 133
Hobo complex, 168
Hocabá complex, 145, 149, 179
Hubelna Unslipped: Hubelna Variety, 93 (table 4), 197–98

Ídolos ceramic group, 93 (table 4), 96 (table 6), 103 (table 10), 194–97
  Ídolos Modeled: Idolos Variety, 93 (table 4), 94, 95, 96 (table 6), 103 (table 10), 183, 185, 194 (pl. XV), 195–97 (fig. 66), 210
Isla Cilvituk, 187
Isla complex/phase/sphere, 95, 101, 102

Islas Gouged-incised type, 84
Itzá, 2, 9
Ixlú, 74, 80, 82, 85, 86, 87, 89, 139, 145, 157, 159, 163, 173, 178, 181, 183, 184, 195, 208
  Bullard excavations, 2, 3, 44, 46–47, 57, 58, 65, 67, 70, 72
Ixpop Polychrome: Ixpop Variety, 92 (table 4), 94 (table 5), 96 (table 6), 101, 115, 116, 123–30 (figs. 42–44; pls. VIII, IX), 131, 133, 134, 146, 147, 149, 164
Ixtepeque, 220, 238

Jato Black-on-gray type, 57, 58, 81 (fig. 36), 82–83, 85
Joventud Red type, 89
Joyac Cream Polychrome type, 74

Kauil complex, 101, 102, 134, 151, 170, 173, 181
Kukula Cream type, 145

La Justa Composite: La Justa Variety, 93 (table 4), 94, 96 (table 6), 103 (table 10), 173, 176–79 (fig. 58), 192
Lake Petén-Itzá. See Petén-Itzá, Lake
Lake Macanché. See Macanché, Lake
Lake Salpetén. See Salpetén, Lake
Lake Yaxhá. See Yaxhá, Lake and center
Lamanai, 95, 176
Largo Red-on-cream: Largo Variety, 55, 72–74 (fig. 33)
Line sinkers. See Net sinkers; Notched sherds (pellets)
Lombriz Orange Polychrome type, 57
Loom weights. See Notched sherds (pellets)
Lupe Dichrome type, 123

Macanché, Lake, 6, 8 (pl. I)
  CPHEP operations, 9, 10 (fig. 2)
  "mainland center", 2, 9, 44, 45–46 (figs. 24, 25), 72, 82, 89, 145, 157, 159, 163, 173
Macanché Island
  Bullard excavations, 2, 7, 12, 15 (fig. 4), 17–27 (figs. 6–13; pls. IV–VI), 36 (fig. 21)
  CPHEP excavations, 3, 9, 27–35 (figs. 14–20; pl. VII), 36 (fig. 21)
  occupation summary, 33–44 (fig. 22)

Macanché Red-on-paste(cream): Macanché Variety, 92 *(table 4)*, 96 *(table 6)*, 103 *(table 10)*, 131, 132 *(fig. 45)*, 133–35, 149, 161, 163
Majolica, 49, 238
Manos/metates, 27, 43, 221–26 *(figs. 75, 76; pls. XXI–XXIII; table 16)*
Maskall Unslipped type, 173
Matillas ceramic group, 169
Mayapán, 2, 123, 138, 149, 150, 163, 176, 179, 185, 187, 203
Mayapán Red ware, 138, 145, 154
Mayapán Unslipped ware, 176
Miniatures, 201–2 *(fig. 67)*
Miseria Appliquéd type, 178
Molcajetes, 100, 237. *See also* Grater bowl
Mold, 203, 204 *(fig. 69)*, 238
Montículo Unslipped ware, 93 *(table 4)*, 94 *(table 5)*, 103 *(table 10)*, 173. *See also* La Justa Composite; Pozo ceramic group
More Force Unslipped type, 176
Mul Polychrome
  Manax Variety, 92 *(table 4)*, 94 *(table 5)*, 96 *(table 6)*, 146–49 *(fig. 50; pl. X)*, 164
  Mul Variety, 147
Mumul Composite: Mumul Variety, 93 *(table 4)*, 96 *(table 6)*, 192–95 *(fig. 65)*
Muralla de Leon, 9, 10 *(fig. 2)*

Naco, 100, 133, 135, 137, 149, 150, 163, 179, 207
  lithics, 213
Naranjal Red-on-cream type, 74, 86
Navula Unslipped type, 179
Negroman-Tipú, 49, 67, 122, 123, 130, 145, 159, 163, 167, 179, 181, 187, 197, 204, 208, 237, 239
Net sinkers, 43, 100, 237. *See also* Notched sherds (pellets)
Neutron activation analysis, 5, 109
New Town complex/phase/sphere, 72, 77, 84, 95, 102, 167
Nohpek Unslipped type, 102, 173
Nolasco Bichrome type, 135, 150, 163
Notched sherds (pellets), 40, 99, 204, 206–8 *(pl. XVI; fig. 71; table 14)*, 237, 238

Obsidian, 21, 27, 39, 43, 102, 210, 219–20, 238, 239

hydration dates, 37, 39, 40 *(table 2)*, 42, 43, 50, 95, 101, 103
Ochre, 231

Pachychilus, 43, 230
Paixban Buff Polychrome type, 58
Palmar ceramic group, 85–87
  Palmar Orange Polychrome type, 58
Panabá Unslipped type, 176
Pantano Impressed type, 63, 68 *(fig. 32)*, 70–71
Papacal Incised type, 138
Pasión (river) region, 56, 57, 58, 61, 69, 70, 82, 85, 138, 170, 235
Pastelaria Composite type, 179
Pastel Polychrome: Pastel Variety, 92 *(table 4)*, 96 *(table 6)*, 103 *(table 10)*, 116, 160–61
Patojo ceramic group, 93 *(table 4)*, 96 *(table 6)*, 184–95
  Patojo Modeled: Patojo Variety, 93 *(table 4)*, 96 *(table 6)*, 179, 184–92 *(pls. XIII–XIV; figs. 61–64)*
Paxcamán ceramic group, 4, 5, 40, 42, 43, 44, 47, 49, 56, 58, 59, 90–99 *(tables 4–6, 8, 9)*, 101–17 *(tables 10, 12; fig. 39)*, 122–23, 141, 145, 149, 155, 157, 159, 163, 164, 167, 172, 176, 179, 184, 198, 204, 209, 235, 236, 237, 238. *See also* individual types
  dichrome slips, 122, 123. *See also* Zaczuuz ceramic group
  paste variations, 105–12. *See also* Snail inclusions (in paste); individual type descriptions
  relation to Tinaja ceramic group, 59, 63, 64, 71, 72
  slip variations, 115–16, 123, 128–29, 130
Paxcamán Red type, 94 *(table 5)*, 96 *(table 6)*, 103 *(table 10)*, 140, 141, 160
  Paxcamán Variety, 118–22 *(figs. 40, 41)*, 134
Payaso ceramic group, 76–77, 85
  Payaso Orange-brown: Payaso Variety, 39, 40, 58, 59, 76–77, 80, 91
Pedregal Modeled type, 187
Pele Polychrome type, 130
Pencuyut Incised type, 154

Pestles
  clay, 203–4, 205 *(fig. 70)*
  stone, 226
Petén-Itzá, Lake, 2, 6, 9, 47, 90, 101, 102, 104,
    105, 106, 107, 110, 112, 116, 122, 123,
    129, 130, 133, 134, 135, 138, 145, 151,
    159, 163, 167, 170, 173, 178, 179, 181,
    187, 239. *See also* Punta Nimá; Tayasal
Peto Cream ware, 130, 145, 149, 153, 154
Picté Red-on-paste(cream): Picté Variety, 92
    (table 4), 94 *(table 5)*, 96 *(table 6)*, 134,
    148 *(fig. 50)*, 149–50, 163
Picú Incised type, 151, 153, 164
  Picú Variety, 92 *(table 4)*, 94 *(table 5)*, 96
    (table 6), 101, 134–37 *(fig. 46)*
  Thub Variety, 56, 92 *(table 4)*, 96 *(table 6)*,
    103 *(table 10)*, 136 *(fig. 46)*, 137–38
Pixtún Trickle-on-gray type, 168
Plumbate ware, 61, 95, 238
Poite Incised type, 94 *(table 5)*, 96 *(table 6)*,
    169–70
Polvero Black type, 89
Polychromes, Late Classic, 47, 57, 58, 74,
    85–89 *(figs. 37, 38)*. *See also* individual
    type names
Pomacea, 27, 43, 230
Posas Polychrome type, 133
Pozo ceramic group, 40, 42, 43, 47, 49, 91, 93
    (table 4), 94 *(table 5)*, 96 *(table 6)*, 99
    (table 9), 102, 103 *(table 10)*, 170–79
  Pozo Unslipped type, 80, 93 *(table 4)*, 94
    (table 5), 96 *(table 6)*, 100, 101, 103
    (table 10), 170–76 *(figs. 56, 57)*, 178, 201
Projectile points, 210, 212–15, 237 *(fig. 72,
    pl. XIX)*
  obsidian, 219, 220
  sidenotched (arrow), 212 *(pl. XVIII)*, 213,
    215, 219, 237, 238
Proyecto Lacustre. *See* Macanché Island,
    CPHEP excavations; Macanché, Lake,
    CPHEP operations
Pulpería Red: Pulpería Variety, 166 *(fig.
    55)*, 170
Punta Nimá, 3, 47, 58, 65, 67, 70, 71, 72,
    74, 77, 80, 81, 86, 87, 89, 100, 101, 122,
    123, 134, 135, 145, 157, 159, 163, 165,
    167, 170, 173, 177, 178, 181, 183, 184,
    185, 187, 192, 193, 195, 203

Puuc Slate ware, 145, 154
Puxteal Modeled type, 178

Quexil, Lake, 6, 145, 153, 167, 203, 238

Radiocarbon dates, 34, 40 *(table 2)*, 41
Reptile motifs, 101, 102, 116, 125 *(fig. 43)*,
    126 *(fig. 44)*, 128, 129, 130, 135, 231, 238
Rio Juan Unslipped type, 173, 176
Romero complex/phase, 37 *(table 1)*, 39, 40,
    46, 56, 57, 58, 59, 60 *(table 3)*, 82, 90,
    91, 113, 235, 236
  definition, 39, 59–60
  pottery type descriptions, 63–89
  sphere identification, 56–58

Sabloff, Jeremy A., 79, 82, 85
Sacalum Black-on-slate, 154
Sacá Polychrome: Sacá Variety, 92 *(table 4)*,
    94 *(table 5)*, 115, 116, 122, 130–33 *(fig.
    45)*, 134
Sahcabá Modeled-carved type, 64
Salcajá, 130
Salpetén, Lake, 6, 12, 44, 50, 76, 101, 102,
    103, 105, 106, 110, 145, 153, 167, 181,
    203, 238
San Joaquin Buff ware, 123, 130, 134, 145,
    150, 153, 154, 157
San José, Petén, 110, 112, 181, 239
Santa Rita, 122
Saxché ceramic group, 85–87
  Saxché Orange Polychrome, 58
Sayán Red-on-cream, 74
Seibal, 64, 67, 69, 70, 71, 72, 74, 76, 79, 82,
    84, 85, 130, 173, 178, 179, 187
  lithics, 215
Sierra Red type, 89
Slateware, 61, 94 *(table 5)*, 107, 113, 138,
    145, 150, 154, 157, 167–68. *See also*
    individual type and ware names
Snail inclusions (in paste), 4, 47, 58, 61,
    104, 105–7, 112, 117, 123, 171, 202,
    203. *See also* individual types in the
    Paxcamán and Trapeche ceramic groups
  in censers, 184, 188 *(fig. 61)*, 192
Spanish Lookout complex, 72
Spindle whorls, 39, 43, 208, 228–29 *(fig.
    77)*, 230

Striation, 57, 82, 176. *See also* Encanto
    Striated type
Style, decorative
    continuities, Classic to Postclassic, 101,
        116, 129
    regional dichotomization, 165, 238
Subín Red type, 37, 39, 56, 58, 63, 67–69
    (fig. 32), 70, 85, 99, 204
Sula valley, 100

Taak ceramic group, 84
Tachís ceramic group, 100, 101, 170
Taman paste variant, 64
Tancah, 74
Tanché ceramic group, 95, 108
Tases complex/phase, 145, 149, 165
Tayasal, 47, 49, 60, 61, 83, 84, 94, 95, 99,
    101, 102, 107, 108, 112, 129, 130, 133,
    134, 135, 138, 145, 146, 149, 150, 151,
    154, 159, 167, 168, 170, 173, 178, 179,
    181, 239. *See also* Petén Itzá, Lake
Tecoh Red-on-buff, 134, 150, 163
Tekit Incised, 154
Tepeu 1 and 2, 33
Thin Slate ware, 145
Thompson, J. Eric, 79
Thul Appliqué, 176, 179
Ticul Thin Slate, 72, 168
Tikal, 55, 57, 58, 60, 65, 67, 70, 82, 104,
    110, 129, 133, 170, 178, 187, 236
    emblem glyph, 44, 46, 57
Tinaja ceramic group, 55, 56, 57, 61, 63–71,
    72, 85
    Tinaja Red type, 37, 39, 55, 56, 58, 59, 63,
        64–76 *(fig. 31)*
Tinaja paste variant, 64
Tipú. *See* Negroman-Tipú
Topoxté ceramic group, 41, 42, 43, 47, 49, 64,
    74, 90, 91, 92 *(table 4)*, 94 *(table 5)*, 95,
    96 *(table 6)*, 97 *(table 8)*, 98, 99 *(table 9)*,
    101, 102, 103 *(table 10)*, 108–9 *(table
    11)*, 114, 115, 116, 123, 130, 133, 150,
    153, 157–65, 204, 239
    Topoxté Red: Topoxté Variety, 4, 92 *(table
        4)*, 94 *(table 5)*, 96 *(table 6)*, 103 *(table
        10)*, 157–59 *(fig. 54)*, 209
Topoxté Island(s), 12, 46, 61, 90, 95, 101,
    122, 134, 145, 153, 159, 161, 163, 165,
        167, 171, 173, 176, 177, 178, 181, 185,
        208, 209, 236, 237, 238
    lithics, 213
    spindle whorls, 228
Trace element composition (of pottery and
    clays), 108–12 *(tables 11, 12; fig. 39)*
Traino Brown type, 77
Trapeche ceramic group, 4, 5, 39, 40, 42,
    43, 56, 58, 74, 91, 92–93 *(table 4)*, 94
    (table 5), 95, 96 *(table 6)*, 97 *(table 8)*,
    98, 99 *(table 9)*, 101, 102, 103 *(table 10)*,
    104–17 *(table 12; fig. 39)*, 133, 134,
    137, 159, 163, 164, 176, 184, 198, 204,
    235, 236, 238
    double slipping, 115, 116, 140. *See also*
        individual type descriptions
    paste variations, 105–12, 139. *See also*
        Snail inclusions (in paste); individual
        type descriptions
    relation to Harina group, 59, 63, 64, 71,
        72, 145
Trapeche Pink type, 72, 160
    Tramite Variety, 92 *(table 4)*, 94 *(table 5)*,
        96 *(table 6)*, 103 *(table 10)*, 139–45
        (figs. 47–49)
    Halal variety, 108, 139
Trapiche Incised: Decorated Interior
    Variety, 168
Tres Naciones ceramic group, 94 *(table 5)*,
    96 *(table 6)*
Trickle Slate ware, 94, 168
    Trickle-on-gray, 94 *(table 5)*, 166 *(fig. 55)*,
        167–68
Tulum, 187

Uapake Unslipped ware, 93 *(table 4)*, 96
    (table 6), 103 *(table 10)*, 178, 179.
    See also Chilo ceramic group; Gotas
    Composite: Gotas Variety
    ware characteristics, 179–80
Uaxactún, 67, 69, 70, 76, 83, 85, 170, 179

Vagando Polychrome type, 133
Villahermosa Incised type, 169
Vitzil Orange-red ware, 93 *(table 4)*, 94 *(table
    5)*, 96 *(table 6)*. *See also* Augustine
    ceramic group
Volador Dull-Slipped ware, 92 *(table 4)*, 94

(table 5), 96 *(table 6)*, 103 *(table 10)*. *See also* Paxcamán ceramic group; Paxcamán Red; Trapeche ceramic group ware characteristics, 117

Volcanic ash temper, 56, 57. *See also* Ash (tempered) paste

White Creek Incised type, 138

Xcanchakan Black-on-cream type, 149, 154
Xcocom complex, 56, 72, 74, 154, 168, 179
Xuluc Incised type, 164
    Ain Variety, 92 *(table 4)*, 94 *(table 5)*, 96 *(table 6)*, 101, 130, 135, 137, 150–53 *(figs. 51, 52)*, 165
    Tan Variety, 154

Tzalam Variety, 92 *(table 4)*, 94 *(table 5)*, 96 *(table 6)*, 152 *(fig. 52)*, 153–54

Yacmán Striated type, 176
Yaha Creek Cream type, 72, 145
Yalain, 9, 12
Yaxhá, Lake and center, 6, 61, 63, 64, 65, 67, 70, 79, 83, 95, 103, 106, 108–9 *(table 11)*, 110, 114, 161, 165, 167, 173, 236
Yokat Striated type, 82

Zacatel Cream Polychrome type, 58, 74
Zacpetén, 9, 46, 50, 181, 203
Zaczuuz ceramic group, 123, 145
Zanahoria Scored type, 154